Revolutions of the End of Time

Revolutions of the End of Time

Apocalypse, Revolution and Reaction in the Persianate World

By

Saïd Amir Arjomand

BRILL

LEIDEN | BOSTON

Originally published in hardback in 2022.

Cover illustration: Equestrian battle in front of a city gate. Rashid ad-Din, *Jami' al-tavarikh*, From the Diez Albums, 1300–1325 MS. DIEZ A. Folio 70, Staatsbibliothek Berlin.

The Library of Congress has cataloged the hardcover edition as follows:

Names: Arjomand, Saïd Amir, author.
Title: Revolutions of the end of time : apocalypse, revolution and reaction in the Persianate world / Saïd Amir Arjomand.
Description: Leiden ; Boston : Brill, 2023. | Includes bibliographical references and index.
Identifiers: LCCN 2022050207 (print) | LCCN 2022050208 (ebook) | ISBN 9789004517134 (hardback) | ISBN 9789004517158 (ebook)
Subjects: LCSH: Revolutions—Iran—History. | Islam and politics—Iran—History. | Shi'ah—Iran—History. | Iran—History—640–
Classification: LCC HM876 .A754 2023 (print) | LCC HM876 (ebook) | DDC 303.6/40955—dc23/eng/20221103
LC record available at https://lccn.loc.gov/2022050207
LC ebook record available at https://lccn.loc.gov/2022050208

Typeface for the Latin, Greek, and Cyrillic scripts: "Brill". See and download: brill.com/brill-typeface.

ISBN 978-90-04-73346-6 (paperback, 2025)
ISBN 978-90-04-51713-4 (hardback)
ISBN 978-90-04-51715-8 (e-book)

Copyright 2023 by Saïd Amir Arjomand. Published by Koninklijke Brill NV, Leiden, The Netherlands.
Koninklijke Brill NV incorporates the imprints Brill, Brill Nijhoff, Brill Hotei, Brill Schöningh, Brill Fink, Brill mentis, Vandenhoeck & Ruprecht, Böhlau, V&R unipress and Wageningen Academic.
Koninklijke Brill NV reserves the right to protect this publication against unauthorized use. Requests for re-use and/or translations must be addressed to Koninklijke Brill NV via brill.com or copyright.com.

This book is printed on acid-free paper and produced in a sustainable manner

Contents

Preface IX
Abbreviations XI

1   Introduction 1
    1   The Motivation of Revolution: Millennial and Modern Myths 1
    2   Consequences of Apocalyptic Messianism and Structural Models of Revolution 4
    3   Revolution and Counter-Revolution as Consequences of Apocalyptic Mahdism 8
    4   The Entangled Historical Sociology of the Persianate World and the Persianate Conception of Revolution 10

2   Shi'ism, Sufism, and the Symbolism of Kingship in the Formation of Persianate Islam 26
    1   The Revival of the Persian Language and the Emergence of Persianate Islam 27
    2   The Disestablishment and Refiguration of Islam in the Persianate World in the Age of Confessional Ambiguity 34
    3   The Estate System of the Turko-Mongolian Empires and the Subversive Symbolic Repertoire of the Persian Subject Estate 42

3   Sufism and Shi'ite Millennialism in the Il-Khanid and Timurid Empires 47
    1   Sufism and Frontier Millennialism in Turko-Mongolian Anatolia 48
    2   The Horufi Urban Movement and Its Struggle against Turko-Mongolian Domination 53
    3   Apocalypticism and the Occult Sciences in the Uprising of Kadi Bedreddin during the Ottoman Interregnum 61
    4   The Shi'itized Sufi Mahdism of Sayyed Mohammad Nurbakhsh 66

4   Royal Reactions to Apocalyptic Messianism and the Reinforced Legitimation of Autocracy 72
    1   Royal Counter-Messianism in the Timurid Empire 72
    2   The Ottoman Containment of Sufi Millennialism 79
    3   Orthodox Reform and the Counter-Messianic Caliphate of God under the Āq Qoyunlu 82

5 The Causes and Process of Shah Esmāʿil's Mahdist Revolution 86
1. Sufism, the Safavid Order, and Its Turn to Militant Mahdism 87
2. Revolutionary Mobilization in a Khaldunian Revolution 95
3. The Opportunity Structure and Process of the Safavid Revolution 98
4. The Failure to Export the Revolution to the Ottoman Empire 102
5. The Containment of Millennialism and the Routinization of Mahdistic Charisma into Kingship 106

6 Sunni Reactions to the Safavid Mahdist Revolution and the Ottoman Imperial Counter-Revolution 110
1. The Transplantation of the Counter-Millennial Sovereignty to the Mughal Empire in India 111
2. The Sunni Counter-Revolution in the Uzbek Empire in Central Asia 112
3. The Ottoman Counter-Messianism and Its Sunni Counter-Revolution 116

7 The Mahdi of Light and His Millenarian Revolution in Tribal Afghanistan 127
1. Sufi Messianism in Northwestern India as a Prelude to the Rawshani Revolution 127
2. A Khaldunian Revolution on the Periphery of Timurid India and Its Failure 133
3. The Mahdist Movement of Shaykh Bāyazid Ansāri in Comparative Perspective 136

8 The Fall of the Safavid Empire as a Revolution in World History 139
1. A Proto-Modern Persianate Revolution without a Mahdi 140
2. The Collapse of the Center in the Safavid Empire and Its Causes 145
3. The Fragmentation of the Safavid Empire and Revolutionary Multiple Sovereignty (1722–1732) 148
4. From Revolutionary Violence to Wars of Conquest: Nāder's Imperial Autocracy (1732–1747) 158
5. The End of a Long Revolution: from the Safavid Empire to the Nation-State of Iran 162

9   The Persistence of Apocalyptic Mahdism and the Coming of the
    Modern Myth of Revolution   167
    1   The Other Revolutions of 1848: the Babi Uprisings in Iran
        in Comparison to the Taiping Revolution in China   168
    2   Millennial Beliefs and Iran's Constitutional Revolution
        (1906–1911)   178

10 The Millennial Motivation and Significance of the Islamic Revolution
    of 1979 in Iran   183
    1   The Modern Myth of Revolution and Its Unexpected
        Protagonists   184
    2   Khomeini's Apocalyptic Theosophy and Post-modern
        Apocalypticism in the Islamic Revolution of 1979   186
    3   The Significance of the Islamic Revolution in Iran   196

    Excursus: A Sunni Apocalypse at Last: the Islamic State of Iraq
    and Syria   201

    References   209
    Index   227

Preface

This book ends my engagement with revolution, an engagement that began in the first year of my academic career as an Assistant Professor at the State University of New York at Stony Brook when in early January 1979 I interviewed Ayatollah Ruhollah Khomeini, who was about to return to Iran. The interview appeared in the Long Island newspaper, *Newsday*, in February of that year, days after Imam Khomeini's Islamic Revolution toppled the Shah and put an end to 2,500 years of monarchy in Iran. The Islamic Revolution in Iran was the subject of two of my books, and the present study, which addresses revolution in the Persianate world, ends with an excursus on the minor apocalypse provoked by that revolution readers know as the Islamic State of Iraq and Syria or by its Arabic acronym as DAESH. In the meanwhile, my engagement continued for many years and has included a comparative study of revolution, the results of which were published recently.

Revolutions of the End of Time: Apocalypse, Revolution, and Reaction in the Persianate World covers the Shi'ite and Sufi millennial myths of the advent of the Mahdi at the End of Time and the gradual and partial transition to the modern myth of revolution as the redemption of mankind from oppression and tyranny. The main subject of this book is the old but persistent apocalyptic myth as the motive for revolutionary action in the Persianate world, a myth that has been effective since the eighth/fourteenth century. This myth remains an important factor in twentieth-century revolutions, though, as I examine in the last three chapters, it has gradually and partially been replaced by the modern myth of revolution. The first draft of the manuscript was completed in our restored house in the historic center of Kashan in Fall 2019, and the revisions were made in Goa, India, during the initial lockdown imposed by the government of India on 19 March 2020, to slow the spread of Covid 19. There can be no doubt that the Iranian government's insistence on going ahead with the celebration of the forty-first anniversary of the Islamic Revolution on 11 February 2020 decisively contributed to the early spread of the pandemic in Iran. That a book on apocalypse and revolution was completed in self-quarantine during a pandemic requires no further comment.

The disappointment with the first wave of the Marxist-inspired myth of revolution found expression in the 1950s in *The God that Failed* (1949), and *The Illusion of the Epoch: Marxism-Leninism as a Philosophical Creed* (1955), and yet the principle of hope found a compelling statement in the same decade and persisted to the 1989 collapse of Communism in 1989.[1] As hope cannot be eradicated from human history, apocalyptic messianism and its secular forms will survive all calamity, indeed thrive on it. This book therefore ends, appropriately, with the minor political apocalypse in neighboring Iraq and Syria inspired by the paradoxically modern Islamic Revolution in Iran. The final touches were put to the manuscript around Nawruz 1400 which inaugurated the new century of the Persian calendar—so far the bleakest in living memory.

Kashan, August 2022

1 Crossman 1949; Acton 1955; Bloch 1954, 1955, 1959.

Abbreviations

'Abdi Beg	'Abdi Beg Shirāzi, *Takmelat al-akhbār*, ed. 'A.-H. Navā'i, Tehran, 1369 Sh./1990
BSOAS	*Bulletin of the School of Oriental and African Studies, London*
CSSH	*Comparative Studies in Society and History*
EI^2	*Encyclopaedia of Islam*, second ed., 11 vols., Leiden: E.J. Brill, 1954–2002
EIr	*Encyclopaedia Iranica*
IJMES	*International Journal of Middle East Studies*
JAOS	*Journal of the American Oriental Society*
JNES	*Journal of Near Eastern Studies*
JPS	*Journal of Persianate Studies*
JRAS	*Journal of the Royal Asiatic Society*
JSAI	*Jerusalem Studies in Arabic and Islam*
Mokāfāt	*Mokāfāt-nāma*, in R. Ja'fariyān, ed. *Safaviyya dar 'arsa-ye din, farhang va siyāsat*, Qomm: Pajhuheh kada-ye Hawza va Dāneshgāh, 3 vols., 1379/2001, vol. 3, pp. 1231–1295
SI	*Studia Islamica*
SIr	*Studia Iranica*
Torka	Sā'en al-Dīn Torka Esfahāni, *Chahārdah resāla-ye fārsi-ye Sā'en al-Din 'Ali b. Mohammad Turka Esfahānī*, 'A. Musavi-Behbahāni and E. Dibāji, eds., Tehran: Ferdawsi, 1351/1973
Zobda	Mohammad Hasan Mostawfi, *Zobdat al-tavārikh*, B. Gudarzi, ed., Tehran: Bonyād-e Mawqufāt-e Mahmud Afshār, 1375/1996

CHAPTER 1

Introduction

Although the passing nod to millennialism as a precursor of modern revolution is not uncommon in sociology of revolution,[1] the visceral antipathy of modern analysts of revolution to religion has hampered serious examination of the religious motivation of revolutionary social action. The most such analysts can bring themselves to do is begrudgingly refer to religion as an "ideology" while assimilating the evidently religious dimension of a modern revolution to a non-religious ideological "ism," such as Khomeinism and much more widely "Islamism."[2] I have devoted a recent book entirely to the examination of the religious motivation of ancient and medieval revolutions as Messianism in general and Mahdism in its Islamic variant;[3] millennial motivation continues to play a major part in the early modern and even modern revolutions covered in this study. The terms 'religion' and 'revolution' are too broad, we must sharpen our focus on the aspects of religion that are revolutionary, and the dimensions of revolution that are religious or quasi-religious.

Accordingly, I identify apocalyptic messianism as the element of religion with the highest revolutionary potential, and the myth of revolution as the religious dimension of modern revolutions. I examine the modern myth of revolution as a secular variant of the earlier religious source of motivation to revolution, namely Messianism and its Islamic variant which I call Mahdism. The myth of revolution that first emerged in nineteenth-century Europe is analyzed here as the functional equivalent of apocalyptic Mahdism that accounted for the major revolutions and counter-revolutions in the Persianate world in the early modern period. In the twentieth century Mahdism persists as an important factor in motivating revolutionary social action, though it is ceding its primacy to the modern myth of revolution.

1   The Motivation of Revolution: Millennial and Modern Myths

The messianic figure of the Mahdi, the rightly-guided leader at the End of Time is particularly prominent in Shi'ite Islam, where it fully retains the original

---

1 See Lawson 2019: 11–12 for the latest example.
2 Abrahamian 1993.
3 Arjomand 2022.

apocalyptic messianism of the Qāʾim (lit., "the riser"). The term *qāʾim* (riser/ redresser) is rich in connotations and abundant meanings, for example, it appears as the riser by the sword (*al-qāʾim biʾl-sayf*), as the redresser of truth (*al-qāʾim biʾl-ḥaqq*) and the [rights of] the House of Mohammad (*qāʾim āl Mohammad*). The term *qāʾim* was used in Shiʿi circles from the second/eighth century to refer to a figure from the family of the Prophet; it was believed that this person would rise up against the illegitimate regime and restore justice.[4] The idea of the Mahdi entered Islamic history proper in the last quarter of the first/seventh century with the uprising in Kufa of Mokhtār, an anti-apocalyptic form as Mohammad redivivus, a descendant of Mohammad with the same name and same father's name as the Prophet. In a tradition attributed to the Prophet's disciple, ʿAbdallāh b. Masʿūd. This trope of historical repetition, degeneration and regeneration, was amalgamated with the Shiʿite apocalyptic Qāʾim into the composite figure of the Qāʾim-Mahdi representing the apocalyptic messianic leader of the End of Time. The Qāʾim-Mahdi myth acted as a powerful stimulus to apocalyptic messianism and revolutionary social action in medieval Islamicate civilization.[5]

In the nineteenth century Europe saw the birth not only of the modern myth of revolution but also a class of revolutionaries as the social bearers of that myth. With the French Revolution, "revolution was revolutionized in 1789 when the notion of revolution as fact gave way to the conception of revolution as an ongoing act … There were no 'revolutionaries' before revolution was revolutionized."[6] Karl Marx, a young revolutionary during the European revolution of 1848, shaped the myth born of the great French Revolution into an elaborate and highly influential theory of revolution. Marx's famous verdict on religion as the opiate of the masses should be assessed with the hindsight that the system he was constructing was, in fact, a gigantic secular religion. Revolution was a central myth of this new secular religion. While dismissing the old religion to propagate his new one, Marx adopted and amplified the modern myth of revolution as the moment of redemption in history. Revolution became in Marxism what the millennial myth and the messianic idea had been in the Judeo-Christian religions and in Islam.[7] Marx's two Asian contemporaries, Sayyed ʿAli Mohammad the Bab, the messianic leader of the Babi uprising in Iran (1848–1850) and Hong Xiuquan (1850–1864), who lead the Taiping revolution (1850–1864) in China, as we see, fully enacted the old

---

4 Madelung 1978.
5 Arjomand 2022.
6 Baker 2013: 189, 210–213.
7 Arjomand 2019: epilogue.

religious millennial myth in their respective failed revolutions. This conjunction should inspire a more dispassionate view of both religion and revolution than Marx's, and in fact reveals a more varied and complicated relationship between the two types of myth—one religious, the other secular—capable of motivating revolutions. In this study, both the revolutionary potential of apocalyptic religion and the religious dimension of the modern myth of revolution are in fact conspicuous.

However, we owe the most perceptive analysis of the birth of the modern myth of revolution out of the great French Revolution of 1789 not to Marx but to his older contemporary, Alexis de Tocqueville (d. 1859), who was himself a major participant in the European revolution of 1848. It is fascinating to see that the political religion thus born was characterized by Tocqueville as a new Islam that terrified contemporary observers by its missionary fervor. The great French Revolution had indeed "developed into a species of religion ... This strange religion has, like Islam, overrun the whole world with its apostles, militants and martyrs."[8]

The myth of revolution, given a sociological inflection by Marx during the European revolutions of 1848, was propagated in the rest of the world by Marxism-Leninism in the twentieth century. The Marxist-Leninist variant of the myth long served as an ersatz theory of revolution.[9] In the twentieth century, however, the inadequacy of the Marxist idea of revolution as a theory became apparent to the more perceptive observers of Communism and Fascism. In 1929, Karl Mannheim compared the spiritualization of politics (*Vergeistigung der Politik*) in twentieth-century revolutionary movements to the chiliasm of the Peasant Wars and Anabaptists in early modern Germany. He emphasized the qualitative difference between the sacred, *kairotic* time of chiliasm, when the here and now is pervaded by eternity, with the secular, routine conception of time in modern post-Enlightenment, non-revolutionary politics.[10] In the following decades, Eric Voegelin coined the somewhat unfortunate term, "modern Gnosticism," to refer to the so-called spiritualization of politics in Europe between the two world wars. Voegelin (1952) later developed the more suggestive idea of "political religions" with reference to twentieth-century revolutionary Communism and Fascism, very much in line with Tocqueville's characterization of the French Revolution. Manuel Sarkisyanz (1955) similarly showed how the Bolsheviks harnessed Orthodox Christian themes in Russia and Islamic and Buddhist millennial beliefs in Asia to Marxist

---

8   Tocqueville 1955: 13.
9   Arjomand 2019: introduction.
10 Mannheim 1978: 184–196.

scientific socialism. Among these pioneering studies, Norman Cohn's (1957) study of Christian revolutionary messianism and its bearing on twentieth-century "political religions" had the greatest immediate impact.

In the Islamicate civilization, the myth of the Mahdi, forged as Mohammad redivivus for the End of Time as the earthly prelude to the day of judgment, served as an inexhaustible resource in medieval and early modern times for those living in routinized chronological and secular times. The pressure of daily grievances could, however, build up and eventually suspend this routinization and stimulate a reversion to liminality in the form of an outbreak of redemptive millennial action. The messianic leadership of the Mahdi is charismatic and generates intense commitment to social action while the here and now is made into *kairotic* time. The apocalyptic view of politics is thus particularly appropriate for the moment of revolutionary liminality. At this point, a great opening and freedom occurs, with no boundaries set to political will, and everything social is transformable by politics. The charisma of the Mahdi as a messianic leader, however, must be routinized to create post-revolutionary stability. Sooner or later, life returns to normal and revolutionaries live in routinized chronological and secular time with a sacred memory of the liminal break—a condition I define as "realized messianism."[11]

2 Consequences of Apocalyptic Messianism and Structural Models of Revolution

In this study I use Max Weber's conception of social action and its motivation in my analysis of the motivations of millennial and revolutionary militance as social action.[12] The subjective motivation of the historical agents of millennial uprisings and revolutions can be considered a cause of their social action whose consequences will depend on the social and political structures that frame it. The narrative of a revolution proper as an event must begin with the moment of revolutionary liminality, a great opening that enables the freedom of action created by the disintegration of the political structure. Liminality refers to the removal of structural constraints on human agency. It can, to varying degrees, be accompanied by a collective "sentiment of empowerment, which occurs in certain moments, transforms the group into a charismatic community, transforms, ultimately, social structure into agency."[13] As soon as millennial action is

---

11   Arjomand 2022.
12   Weber 1978: 4–26.
13   Tiryakian 1995: 274.

launched, however, the structure of social power begins to impinge on it. After the liminal break social action in a structured political environment steers messianic beliefs and political conditions become interdependent and mutually determinant. My analysis of this post-liminal structuration of social action draws on the distinction between religiously-conditioned (primarily) political action and the politically-conditioned (primarily) religious action, as noted in my first study of the mutual articulation of religion and political action.[14] The transformation of the Mahdi's charisma into an authority structure with the consolidation of revolution is a major instance of its political conditioning. This political conditioning, as we shall see, is particularly relevant to the dynamics of revolution and reaction or counter-revolution. We also see how the political pressures from below caused by the mushrooming of Sufi dervish orders can politically condition religious action motivated by world-rejecting apocalypticism in the direction of revolutionary action aimed at transforming this world. The Turko-Mongolian rulers and their officials had to reckon with this same pressure in their policies. The governmental response could be repression or preemptive accommodation; hence the religious conditioning of counter-revolution or reaction by apocalyptic messianism.

To put this motivational analysis in its macrosociological context, I use two structural models of revolution to explain the objective structural causes and consequences of revolutions in the Persianate world, and a model I call the Persianate conception of revolution to explain the subjective motivation of their historical agents. In my earlier study of revolution, I presented two basic ideal structural types of revolution—one integrative, the other centralizing—linking its causes and consequences. My model of integrative revolution has three subsidiary ideal types, only one of which is systematically applied in this study. The first, Constitutive Revolution, was applied to the rise of Islam which remains constitutive for the subsequent epicycle of Islamicate revolutions, including Mahdist revolutions in the Persianate world. The second subtype, Aristotelian-Paretan Revolution, is the model for revolutions of counter-elites excluded from power in narrowly based political regimes. For this study, I incorporated the major insight of the second model into the role of dispossessed counter-elite to my modified Tocquevillian (centralizing) ideal type. The third subtype of integrative revolution and the one applied in this study is the Khaldunian Integrative Revolution, which is a model of revolution based on nomadic tribal confederations from the periphery of empires.[15]

---

14   Arjomand 1984: 18–21.
15   Arjomand 2019.

'Abd al-Raḥmān Ibn Khaldūn (d. 1406) formulated a theory of the cycles of rise, decline, and disintegration of dynastic states that is well known, though its conscious derivation from Greek thought is not. In fact, he explicitly discussed Aristotle's rhetoric and political science as the two branches of knowledge closest to his new positive science of history.[16] As a good, empirically-minded Aristotelian Ibn Khaldūn explains cyclical change in terms of the structural properties of historical Muslim polities, which are grounded in a dual social organization. The social structure he portrays consists of urban centers of civilization and tribal peripheries. Its political order rests on two distinct elements: ruling authority (*mulk*) and the instrument for gaining it, group solidarity (*'asabiyya*). According to Ibn Khaldūn both these elements are generated in tribal societies but are separated as a result of the complexity of civilization. Ruling authority is transferred to urban centers, while group solidarity is sustained and reproduced only in the tribal periphery. A cyclical rise and fall motion of tribally-originated dynastic states is generated by the interaction between the centers of civilization, where group solidarity is weak, and the tribal societies of the periphery, where strong group solidarity is constantly reproduced. It is important to note that Ibn Khaldūn's term, which I translate as "dynastic state," is *dawla*, the term for revolution in the sense of "turn in power" that first gained currency in reference to the Abbasid revolution and later came to mean the state (whose turn in power was divinely ordained, a claim made by all states).

In short, Ibn Khaldūn offered the endemic translocation of ruling authority and group solidarity between the periphery and the center in a dual social structure as a structural precondition of dynastic change. He also paved the way for a theoretical move from dynastic change to revolution by considering the superimposition of new religiously (or by modern extension, ideologically) based solidarity on existing, tribal group solidarity (*'asabiyya*). A religious cause and movement, therefore, needs group solidarity if it is to succeed: "Religious mission cannot materialize without group solidarity. This is so because any mass [political] undertaking by necessity requires group solidarity ..."[17] The prophets and religious reformers who fail are precisely those who do *not* recognize the significance of group solidarity. Those who succeed, are the ones who do. Khaldunian Integrative Revolution begins in the periphery with a militarized solidarity group that is united by a religious cause. The key factor in explaining the failure of the regime and the success of insurgents is differential

---

16 Ibn Khaldūn 1992: 1:39–42; Ibn Khaldûn 1958 (trans. Rosenthal), 1:77–83; Dale 2006: 435–438.
17 Ibn Khaldūn 1992: 1:168–171.

solidarity. The urban base of the regime lacks social cohesion while the already strong group solidarity of the insurgents is strengthened by a unifying religious cause.

The second ideal type of revolution I call Tocquevillean. This model of centralization of power as both the cause and the consequence of revolution is named after Alexis de Tocqueville who offered a compelling explanation of the French Revolution as a consequence of the growth of the state under absolutism. The paradoxical result of the French Revolution Tocqueville highlights was the further centralization of power in the state. The Tocquevillian focus on the concentration of power and its dysfunctional results highlights the importance of the breakdown of centralized power, the state, as a cause of revolution.

The Tocquevillian ideal type of revolution is the one most familiar to sociologists and political scientists. In this modern type of revolution, a centralized state is already in place. However, the Tocquevillian model should be modified with respect to the causes as well as the consequences of revolution. With regard to the causes, a systematic treatment of the revolutionary role of the groups that are dispossessed by the growing state is of great importance. The considerable revolutionary role of *declining* classes, and of cohesive social groups with strong solidarity that are dispossessed by centralizing states or threatened by socioeconomic change, is generally neglected. My own analysis of the impact of the state formation on Iranian society as a cause of the Islamic revolution of 1979 focused on the role of the adversely affected and dispossessed elites and social groups, most notably the clerical estate.[18]

We also need to explain the teleology of revolutions and direction of their consequences in structural terms. The two structural ideal types are particularly useful in explaining those consequences of revolutions traceable to their causes. In the short run, the consequences of revolution depend on the outcome of the revolutionary power struggle and the victory of one of the partners in the revolutionary coalition over the others. In the long run, however, the consequences of revolution depend on what I call its constitutional politics. The teleology of revolution consists in those long-term consequences that depend on the institutionalization of the value-ideas that set the revolution in motion and are completed during its process.[19]

---

18   Arjomand 1988.
19   Arjomand 2019: ch. 1.

3   Revolution and Counter-Revolution as Consequences of Apocalyptic Mahdism

In what follows I consider the common sense understanding of the word 'revolution,' which I defined more rigorously in terms of the significance of its consequences in world history.[20] This focus on the consequences of revolution has important implications, most notably that it raises the issue of reaction or counter-revolution as a consequence of revolution itself, and this therefore requires conjoint consideration. In a recent study of revolution, George Lawson asserts "Revolutions and the avoidance of revolutions, whether through autocratic modernization … or counter-revolution, are not occasional punctuation marks, but the very grammar of modern world history."[21] We can certainly go further back in history and find the interweaving of revolution and counter-revolution in Antiquity and the Middle Ages;[22] presently we examine the intimate connection between revolution and reaction in the form of the taming of apocalyptic Mahdism through counter-revolutionary appropriation in the premodern and early modern Persianate world.

The interaction between revolution and reaction in cases of apocalyptic messianism is not the same as that in modern revolutions and requires a different analytical approach. Successful modern counter-revolutions selectively appropriate acceptable features of the revolutionary program to preempt their recurrence while suppressing the unacceptable ones through the use of force. The reaction of the dynastic states of the early-modern Persianate world similarly contain the millennial impulse through a variety of beliefs that postpone the End of Time indefinitely and preferably to the other world, which suppressed radical apocalyptic movements and their outbreaks in the here and now. I call the ideational process of preemptive appropriation "containment"—in the double sense of temporary suppression and inevitable retention. The second process, the suppression of messianic outbreaks, is a matter of establishing the historical record. The superimposition of a rationalizing layer on the original millennial beliefs contains them in the sense of preserving them and placing them in quarantine. In "The Consolation of Theology" (1996), I analyzed the formative phase of this process by the fifth-/eleventh-century architects of the Imami doctrine of the Great Occultation (*al-ghayba al-kubrā*) of the Hidden

---

20   Arjomand 2019; Arjomand 2022.
21   Lawson 2019: 7. Lawson bases this assertion on Martin Wight's rediscovered 1946 study, *Power Politics*, that highlights the inevitable connection between revolution and counter-revolutionary states from early modern times.
22   See Arjomand 2019; Arjomand 2022: ch. 3.

Imam, an occultation that was purported to last until the End of Time. In the subsequent centuries the result was a pendulum's oscillation between millennialism and law:

> The next three centuries were a period of enormous growth of Imami Shi'ite law in which chiliasm remained firmly contained. Only in the latter part of the fourteenth and throughout the fifteenth centuries ... would the chiliastic Qa'im-Mahdi of the [apocalyptic] traditions burst through the rationalized integument of the theology of divine Grace [*lutf*] and push aside the nomocratic order for millennial activism under the leadership of Mahdistic incarnations of divine charisma.[23]

The treatment of apocalyptic messianism as revolution further requires the assimilation of routinization through the institutionalization of messianic charisma to the long-term consequences of revolution. The transformation of the Mahdistic authority structure with the consolidation of revolution is a consequence of realized messianism that can be built into our analytical framework by making a distinction between two overlapping stages in the process of revolution: the revolutionary power struggle among the contenders in the competition engendered by political mobilization, and the constitutional politics of post-revolutionary political and social reconstruction. The routinization of revolutionary charismatic leadership of the claimants to Mahdihood belongs to the second stage—that is, to the constitutional politics in the struggle for the reconstruction of political order. The present study, furthermore, introduces the concept of counter-revolution to explain the preemptive reaction of dynastic states to revolutionary ideas as long-term consequences of the revolution. In fact, these long-term institutional consequences of revolution are not achieved by the revolutionaries themselves, as is often the case with so-called failed revolutions, but appear as a result of the counter-revolution that ends the revolutionary power struggle and aims at preempting and forestalling its return.

In the three major cases of Islamicate revolutions in the medieval period, the transformation of the Mahdist authority took the form of the assumption of the millennial titles as part of the process of routinization of the charisma of the messianic revolutionary leader for the legitimation of patrimonial monarchy.[24] Likewise, the dynamics of revolution and reaction, often expressed

---

23 Arjomand 2016a: 120.
24 In the case of the Abbasid revolution in the mid-second/eighth century, the transformation of charismatic authority under realized messianism meant the appropriation of

in the context of modern revolutions as "hijacking" the revolution, explains an important feature of apocalyptic Mahdism in the Persianate world. In several notable cases surveyed in chapter 3, apocalyptic Mahdist uprisings among the Persian subject estate in cities of the Persianate world were met with preemptive attempts by Turko-Mongolian rulers or princes of the ruling estate to claim Mahdihood and thereby forestall revolution by counter-revolution. The most spectacular interplay of revolution and reaction took place in early tenth/sixteenth century. As we see in chapter 5, the dynamic interaction between the Mahdist revolution of Shah Esmāʿil the Safavid (r. 1501–1524) and the Ottoman counter-revolution of Soltān Suleymān the Lawgiver/Magnificent (r. 1520–1566) offers an entangled history of the Mahdist revolution of Shah Esmāʿil that gave rise to the Safavid Empire in Iran (1501–1722) and the early Muslim empires. The establishment of millennial sovereignty in the Ottoman and Mughal patrimonial bureaucratic empires and the counter-millennial Sunni orthodox in the Uzbek nomadic empire are analyzed here as counter-revolutions provoked by the Safavid Mahdist revolution throughout the Persianate world.[25]

4 The Entangled Historical Sociology of the Persianate World and the Persianate Conception of Revolution

Like the contemporary reformation in Christian Europe, and like the European revolutions of 1848, and the failed Arab revolutions of 2011,[26] Mahdist millennialism and its preemption or containment in the Persianate world requires an entangled and unified analytical framework. The formation of the Persianate world from the revival of Persian as a literary language in the fourth/tenth century through the Mongol invasion and formation of the Turko-Mongolian nomadic empire in the seventh/thirteenth and eighth/fourteenth centuries (covered in chapter 2) endowed it with the cultural and historical unity that made it a world region or civilizational zone. The histories of revolution and

---

the apocalyptic titles of Qāʾim, Mansur, Mahdi, and Hādi by successive Abbasid caliphs. During the Fatimid revolution in North Africa in the first half of the fourth/tenth century, the messianic titles of Mahdi, Qāʾim, and Mansur were similarly appropriated by the Fatimid caliphs. The routinization of the charisma of the Mahdi, Ibn Tumart, into the charisma of the lineage of the Almohad caliphs in the sixth-/twelfth-century Maghreb and Andalusia occurred without any appropriation of messianic titles, as these were already claimed by the rival Mahdis suppressed by ʿAbd al-Muʾmin who founded his own new patrimonial dynasty. (Arjomand 2022).

25 Moin 2012; Fleischer 2018.
26 For a comparison of the 1848 and 1911 revolutions in a single civilizational zone, see Arjomand 2015.

reaction in the Persianate world are connected and should be analyzed in a single framework as an entangled history within that world. Central to this analytical framework for entangled historical sociology is a shared conception of revolution as derived from the Persianate political culture of the region, which we can call the Persianate conception of revolution.

The Persianate world after the Mongol invasion as the arena of Mahdist revolutionary movements already had a well-developed conception of revolution that differed considerably from the modern myth and conception of revolution; this Mahdist type of revolution is independent of the Mahdist myth, though it adopted some of its terms. To understand the meaning and motivation of revolutionary social action to our historical actors themselves, we must first understand what "revolution," as it is now called, meant to them.

Unlike the modern Arabic term for revolution, *thawra*, which literally means rising and whose medieval incidence is not very significant, the modern Turkish and Persian term for "revolution," *enqelāb*, was current in the medieval period and corresponds more exactly to the Latin term. *Fitna*, the term used for the upheavals also called the first, second, and third civil wars of early Islam, primarily denotes sedition and corruption, while *enqelāb* mainly refers to fundamental change, and is used in medieval texts alongside another term that quickly changed its meaning in the aftermath of the Abbasid revolution, namely *dawla* (this refers to a "turn" in power interpreted as the rotating of domination or empire of one nation after another).

I argue that the term *enqelāb* is in fact synonymous with *dawla*, and its usage in Arabic texts stretches as far back, and that it was used before New Persian was written in the Arabic script. The transfer of sovereignty (*translatio imperii*) and the rise and fall of empires and nations as expressed in the idea of *dawla*, was a common theme in Antiquity; it was rooted in the Book of Daniel and transmitted through the Qur'ān, as examined elsewhere.[27] This second Islamicate conception of revolutionary change, as represented by the term *dawla*, is far more intriguing and dynamic because it is unstable. In the course of history, it acquired the antithetical sense akin to that of certain primal words in which, as Freud noted, the concept is "the twin of its opposite."[28] *Dawla* thus came to mean the established power of the "dynastic state," while retaining the opposite sense of the impermanence of power and its revolutionary reversibility. Implicit in this meaning of the term is the possibility, indeed likelihood, of revolutionary reversal in the divinely appointed turn in power.[29]

---

27   Arjomand 2022: ch. 9.
28   Freud 1957: 187.
29   Arjomand 2010.

In the Qur'ān, God speaks of different nations taking turns in rule: "Such days We turn out in turn ([*nudāwilhā*, from *d-w-l*, the root of the concept of *dawla* (turn in rule/domination)] among peoples! ... so that God may know the believers and blot out the infidels" (Q. 3:140). We find the same idea in another verse: "To every nation a term; when their term comes, they shall not put it back by a single hour nor put it forward" (Q. 7:34).

The antithetical transformation of the apocalyptic transfer of sovereignty can be fully expected under realized messianism such as triumphant Islam. The idea of the everlasting kingship of God most high thus becomes central in the Qur'ān:[30] "His is the kingdom" (*mulk*) (Q. 64:1). Therefore, He grants it to and withdraws it from the sons of Adam as He wishes: "Say: 'O God, possessor of kingship, You grant kingship (*mulk*) to whom You will, and You seize kingship from whom You will. This is God's bounty. He grants it to whom He wills!'" (Q. 3:26). In this Qur'ānic verse, quoted more than any other in the so-called advice literature or mirrors for princes, the apocalypse is transposed into the principle of legitimacy of kingship, and yet the possibility of re-transposing this principle of the legitimacy of patrimonial monarchy into apocalyptic messianism seems ineradicable.

We can go further and say that the original Danielic apocalyptic transfer of sovereignty as the succession of five world empires could undergo the same antithetical transposition. In fact, its teleology was altered in the *Zafarnāma* (Book of victory or Epic of kings) by the last architect of the Il-Khanid political theology, Hamdallāh Mostawfi (d. 1340), to make Chinggis Khan and his descendants the rulers of the last world empire, following those of the Persians and the Arabs.[31] Similarly, the early Sufi practitioner of the science of divination (*jafr*), Yazicizāda Ahmed Bijān (d. after 1465) asserted as an ex post facto prophecy, that the God-given turn in power (*dawlat*) travels from dynasty to dynasty; it resided in Iran, then Khorasan (an echo of Abu Muslim's Hashemite revolution), and then Cairo; it will next move to Rum, where the signs of the hour (*alā'em al-sā'a*) will manifest themselves.[32]

The idea of a divinely ordained transfer of sovereignty finds eloquent expression in early Persian literature. To the historian and secretary of the Ghaznavid court, Abu'l-Fazl Bayhaqi, the transfer of sovereignty meant that "the Arabs' turn in power (*dawlat*)—may it last forever—came and invalidated

---

30 "Verily God's is the kingship of the heavens and the Earth" (Q. 3:189, 5:20, 7:157, 24:42, 42:48, 45:26, 48:14).
31 Arjomand 2016c: 9.
32 Şahin 2010: 347.

the tradition (*rosum*) of the Persians (*'ajam*)."³³ Bayhaqi sought to peg the science of history on political ethics, and accordingly elaborated a normative theory of revolution (which is at the same time an ethic of accountability) on the basis of the notion of a divinely ordained transfer of royal power. Immediately following the above-mentioned citation of Q. 3:26, Bayhaqi adds: "Thus one must know that when God's decree removes the robe of kingship (*molk*) from one group and places it upon another, there is divine wisdom and general interest (*maslahat-e 'āmm*) for people on this earth."³⁴ As Meisami correctly interprets this passage, "If divine providence is instrumental in the transfer of rule, the retention of rule depends upon human agency, and specifically upon the virtue, and political skill, of the just ruler."³⁵

One of the most poignant expressions of revolution as the termination of a divinely ordained turn in power comes from the pen of the chief secretary of the last Khʷārazmshāh, Jalāl al-Din Mohammad. While fleeing from the inexorable advance of the Mongol armies in the company of the monarch in the 1220s, Shehāb al-Din Mohammad Nasavi records Jalāl al-Din's attempt to send a vanguard of four thousand horsemen and give control of the government to "a queer who was neither a man nor a woman."³⁶ He then reflects that these measures proved futile as the term of the turn in power (*dawlat*) had expired and the turn of kingship and monarchy had come to an end; the crier of calamity read the verse [2:134] "This nation just annihilated," and the announcer of the death of revolution (*enqelāb*) raised the call, "This turn in power has just reversed" (*hadhihi dawla qad tawallat*).

Historians also often narrowed it by pairing *enqelāb* with *fatrat* (weakness; power vacuum). With even greater precision, some historians pair *enqelāb* with *dawlat*, now in the sense of the state, in the expression *enqelāb-e dawlat* (revolution in the state [turn in power]). Ibn Bibi thus tells us of "the cause of the revolution in the state and the annihilation of the House of Seljuq."³⁷

---

33 Bayhaqi 1997: 2:1017.
34 Bayhaqi 1997: 2:1017.
35 Meisami 1999: 84–85. Bayhaqi's superior, the great vizier of the Ghaznavid *soltān* Mas'ud (1030–1040), [A]Bu Nasr-e Moshkān, states what is, in substance, the same, while he admonishes the ruler (in vain, as it turns out): "The world's affairs depend on kings and on the Law.... When God removed His favour from a king so that he can be beaten by such people [Seljuq nomads] it is a sign that God is angry with him. Let the king reflect on how he stands with that heavenly Lord." Cited in Meisami 1999: 101.
36 This was a certain Tarkhān, who, according to the editor was a maternal relative of Jalāl al-Din. (Nasavi 1964: 37)
37 Ibn Bibi 1971: 501. Interestingly, the cause was the friction between the Rum Seljuq *soltān* Rokn al-Din, "the Soltān of Islam," and his spiritual mentor, Mawlānā Jalāl al-Din Rumi.

The idea of a divinely-ordained transfer of sovereignty was easily absorbed into what I call the normative conception of revolution as the fall of a dynasty—i.e., the end of its divinely-ordained turn in power, an end caused by injustice and inequity. Probably the first expression of this idea in Persian, with regard to a deliberately revolutionary purpose, is recorded in Arabic because it precedes the revival of Persian as a literary language written in the Arabic script.[38] The ethico-theistic notion of the transfer of sovereignty in the Book of Daniel was thus transmitted to Islamic Iran unaltered. In what we call a normative conception, the turn in power is ordained by God and is terminated when injustice and corruption in government becomes widespread. This concept is explicated in the *Siyāsat-nāma* of the great Seljuq vizier, Khʷāja Nezām al-Molk (d. 1088), arguably the most influential work on Persianate statecraft. We know Nezām al-Molk added the second part of this work, beginning with chapter 40, in the short period before his dismissal by Malekshāh and his assassination by the Ismaʿilis. This chapter offers an explication of imminent revolution. According to Nezām al-Molk,

> At any time, some celestial accident may overtake the kingdom through the evil eye and the state [empire/turn in power, *dawlat*] is either transferred from one house to another or thrown into disorder.... Noble and learned men will be dispossessed, and any wretch will not hesitate to assume the title of king and vizier ... Turks and Persians (*tāzik*) alike will call themselves the learned and the Imams, the king's women will command, and the divine law (*shariʿat*) is weakened, the subjects become unruly (*bifarmān*) and the military become oppressive.... Later when through celestial good fortune, the evil times (*nohusat*) pass, God most high will bring forth a just and wise king from royal stock, and give him empire/turn in power (*dawlat*) to vanquish his enemies ... in order to restore all the proper forms and rules (*āʾin*) of kingship....[39]

In Nezām al-Molk's conception, ruling with justice primarily consists of maintaining the social order according to the classes of subjects. Notably, his conception of social injustice as the cause of revolution is inflected by his resentment of the women of the royal household—his perception is that of a disgruntled grandee dismissed as the result of intrigue by the queen. Perhaps

---

    The *soltān* ignored Mawlānā's advice and went to Āqsarā where he was murdered by his amirs.
38   Arjomand 2012.
39   Nezām al-Molk Tūsi 1978: 189f.

even more interesting is that the time of the appearance of injustice and corruption in the government is determined by heavenly conjunctions, as is the passing and transfer of power from one royal house to another. In other words, Nezām al-Molk's normative conception takes political astrology for granted.

A major transfer or turn in power (*dawlat*) was thus a revolution willed by God in response to the failure of the ruler and the dynasty. A century and a half later, the famous *qasīda* by Saʿdi (d. 1292) of Shiraz laments the contemporary overthrow of the Abbasid caliphate in 1258, which it describes as the "extinction of the sovereignty (*zavāl-e molk*) of Mostaʿsem the Commander of the Faithful."[40] It contains the following verse describing it as an unimaginable revolutionary turn in world events:

زنهار از دور گیتی و انقلاب روزگار   در خیال کس نیامد که وآنچنان گردد چنین

> Beware of the vicissitudes of the world and of the revolution of the days
> Who could imagine such topsy-turvy reversal![41]

Here Saʿdī uses the term exactly as it was used in a poem he may have known from an eyewitness; it relates to the civil war between the sons of the caliph Hārun al-Rashid, al-Amin, and al-Maʾmun (r. 811–813)—events described as *enqelāb al-zamān* (revolution of the days).[42]

In a book on ethics in Persian verse, Khʷāju (d. 1349) of Kerman has a chapter on the "revolution of affairs and earthly disturbance of times" (*enqelāb-e ʿomur o ezterāb-e dohūr*). In it, Khʷāju begins with a general description of the notion:

چرخ همانست که نوشین روان بازگرفت از لب نوشیروان
جام جم از دست شد و جم نماند ملک دگرگون شد و خاتم نماند
....
خسرو پرویز که پرواز کرد خسروی ملک عدم ساز کرد[43]

---

40 Browne 1902: 3:29.
41 The entire lament is translated into English by Browne (1902: 3:29–30). I have not, however, followed Browne's fluent and ornate translation in the interest of conceptual precision.
42 Al-Tabarī 1879–1901: 3:805.
43 Khʷāju 2008: 24–43, vv. 668–669, 677.

The wheel is the one which took the sweet beverage from Anushirvān's lips.
Jamshid's chalice[44] fell from his hand, and he perished....
The high flying Khosrow Parviz set forth to rule over the realm of non-being.

More poignant is the way Khʷāju applies this notion of revolution to the collapse of the rule of his patron, Qotb al-Din Mohammad Nikruz (d. 1340) over Kerman. For "the turn of time (*dawr-e zamān*) read [the latter's] decree of dismissal,"

چرخ بداختر ز ارادت بگشت و اخترش از برج سعادت بگشت
من متفکر که از این انقلاب بخت من این لحظه چه بیند بخواب[45]

The inauspicious wheel passed from favor, and his star from the sign of felicity.
I was preoccupied thinking how my lot in this revolution was being cast at this moment.

Khʷāju's younger contemporary and the other great poet of Shiraz, Hāfez (d. 1389), refers to revolutionary turns in world events without the shock and surprise of immediacy of his predecessors, and with much greater philosophical detachment:

ز انقلاب زمانه عجب مدار که چرخ ازین فسانه هزاران هزار دارد یاد
....
که آگه است که کاووس و کی کجا رفتند که واقف است که چون رفت تخت جم برباد[46]

Do not be surprised at the revolution of the time; the wheel
Remembers a thousand thousand such stories.
Who knows wither vanished [kings] Kāvus and Kay [Khosrow]?
Who is sure how the throne of Jamshid vanished with the wind?

The idiomatic expression *enqelāb-e zamāna* used by Hāfez in this verse is synonymous with Saʻdi's equally idiomatic *enqelāb-e ruzegār*, corresponding

---

44 Jamshid was the legendary king and founder of the first dynasty in ancient Iran; it was said that he could see the entire world in his chalice.
45 Khʷāju Kermāni 2008: 45, vv. 716–717, 720.
46 Hāfez 1980: 1:210, vv. 3, 5.

exactly to the *enqelāb al-zamān* of the Abbasid poet. In all these cases, as also with Khʷāju's *zamān* and *dohūr* (the plural of *dahr*, for time), it would not be too fanciful to see a secularized shadow of Zurvān, the old Iranian divinity of time, the one most venerable, the demiurge of earthly revolutions.

A second and very different conception of revolution can also be found in Persianate literature in the form of a deterministic theory of revolution in earthly kingdoms as a natural phenomenon. The idea has Indian origins, it was developed in late Sasanian Iran, and then absorbed into the astronomical theories of Māshāʾallāh and Abu Mashʿar Balkhi in the early Abbasid period. It was the central concept of the theory of the astral determination of major turns of dynasties, nations, and religions in power—what I call political astrology. Muslim political astrology as the theory of the astral determination of revolutions in world history thus provided a conception of gradations of revolution, the highest grade of which was surely meant to be a major change in the social and political order, which is just what we mean by Great Revolution and social revolution today. Furthermore, modern revolution constitutes an act of foundation legitimating the regime it installs. Likewise, according to political astrology, the conjunction of stars that causes the revolution legitimates the new turn in power of the dynasty (*dawlat*). As we see, the key term, *sāheb-qerān* (Lord of the Auspicious Conjunction) for the founder of the dynasty performed just this function.

The Islamicized political astrology that became a theory of revolution by the Ismaʿilis in the fourth/tenth century also served to enhance the legitimacy of the founders of new dynasties. The late Ghaznavid poet, Masʿud Saʿd Salmān (d. 1121) called Soltān Mahmud, the founder of the dynasty, *sāheb-qerān* (Lord of the Auspicious Conjunction) on account of his conquest of India and asserted that his dynastic state (*dawlat*) would have no bounds in time and space.[47] Other poets extended the compliment to several Seljuq rulers, and to the founder of the Delhi Sultanate, Qotb al-Din Aybek.[48] Qelich Arslān (d. 1192), the founder of the Seljuqs of Rum in the recently conquered Anatolian frontier of Islam, was similarly called *sāheb-qerān*. Baybars, who stopped the Mongol advance at Ayn Jālut in Syria in 1260 and subsequently founded the Mamluk state, similarly inscribed his title "the Alexander [world-conqueror] of the Age and the Lord of Auspicious Conjunction"[49] in the three monuments he built after his victory.

---

47 Masʿud Saʿd Salmān 1960: 4, 36.
48 Markiewicz 2019: 167–168.
49 Flemming 1987: 45.

As complete "revolutions in religion and state"—Ibn Abi Ṭāher Tayfur's characterization of the Abbasid revolution—were rare,[50] one would expect local histories to discuss lower levels of revolution. In fact, we find valuable accounts in local histories of the Seljuq Empire, accounts that cover two perhaps unusually tempestuous periods of political instability in the city of Kerman and were written by bureaucrats who served successive rulers of the local kingdom. I first consider two interesting works by Afzal al-Din Ahmed b. Hāmed Kermāni, which cover the history of Kerman down to the first decade of the seventh/thirteenth century. Typically referring to Qurʾān 3:25: "You give the kingdom to whom You will, and seize the kingdom from whom You will" in his writing on statecraft, Afzal al-Din Kermāni is fully aware of the precariousness of kingly rule as a temporary turn in power. To this effect, he cites a verse by Bohtori: "And the world has turns in power (*dowal*) which shift among mankind,"[51] followed by the Qurʾānic verse 3:140: "Such days We deal out in turn among men." Similarly in his history, entitled *Tārīkh-e Afzal yā Badāyeʿ al-zamān fi vaqāyeʿ-e Kermān*, Afzal considers various political tribulations and seditions (*fetna* in the singular) in his native city of Kerman, as "Revolution of states and changes of kings (*enqelāb-e dowal o tabdil-e moluk*)"; he refers to one particular instance of civil war between two rulers of Kerman, Malek Arslān and Bahrāmshāh as "the revolution of Kerman" (*enqelāb-e Kermān*).[52]

Afzal offers two kinds of explanations for these political vicissitudes, one ethical and normative, focusing on human agency, and the other astrological, showing the underlying cosmic forces that determine events. These complementary theoretical perspectives are elaborated in the course of Afzal al-Din's explanation of the ongoing political revolutions that followed the defeat of Torkānshāh by the invading Ghuzz tribesmen from Khorasan in the fall of 1179 and his subsequent murder by a servant. The main normative cause is the tyranny of rulers: "You are the shadow of falsehood, not the shadow of truth (*haqq* = God)." This tyranny is a deviation from the principles of statecraft and the norms of political ethics: excessive punishment, the appointment of incompetent Turks and *atabeg*s, and the exploitation of the subjects in violation of the Prophet's maxim: "You are all shepherds, and all of you are responsible for your flock." Finally, there is the neglect of the clerical estate (*ʿolamāʾ*) in violation of the old maxim of statecraft (attributed to Ardashir), "religion and kingship are twin-born," and "religion is the foundation, and kingship the guardian." With this misrule, men of understanding could see that "the pulse of

---

50   Arjomand 2012: 7.
51   Afzal 1977: 73.
52   Afzal 1947: 53.

the kingdom had lapsed, and the star of this state had fallen ... as every state/turn in power has an end."⁵³

At this point, Afzal al-Din supplemented his moral theory of revolution with the traditional political astrology of the rise and decline of dynasties and nations. As he stated, the falling star of every state as a turn in power is not just a metaphor. On the contrary, it refers to the more fateful astral determination of human events. Both periods of peace and prosperity and the onset of the contemporary revolutionary upheaval were astrologically determined, and Afzal al-Din gives the horoscope for each.⁵⁴ Afzal al-Din's contemporary in western Iran, Abu'l-Sharaf Jorbāzaqāni of Golpāyagān, conjoins the astral and normative theories to explain the revolutionary period of chaos and tyranny of the Seljuq *atabeg*s and *mamlūk*s after the death of the last important Seljuq *soltān*, Togrel III, in 590. Noting that the astrologers had predicted the end of the world in 1186, the year of the death of *atabeg* Jahān Pahlavān and of the inauspicious great conjunction of all seven planets in Libra, Jorbāzaqāni argued for a figurative, political interpretation of this great conjunction, predicting that during its twenty years, "seen in our own lifetime," the name of the Seljuqs would be erased from the pages of history. This is the age when the justice of the rulers disappeared and "tyranny dominates their natures." It is interesting to note that Jorbāzqāni seems to give at least some temporary priority to the normative over the astral theory by allowing the appearance of just rulers to delay the process of political collapse. He self-servingly attributes the rare incidence of just rule in the age to his own patron, the *mamlūk* Jamāl al-Din Ay Aba, and the latter's sons who were said to enjoy God's protection "from afflictions and from the tempest of this bloodthirsty Conjunction and this treacherous age."⁵⁵

Writing a few decades after Afzal al-Din Kermāni, Menhāj-e Serāj Juzjāni, statesman and historian of the Delhi Sultanate, twice refers to the contemporary deposition of the only female ruler of the Delhi Sultanate, Soltān Raziya (r. 1236–1240), as a "revolution in the kingdom" (*enqelāb-e molk*).⁵⁶ This expression corresponds exactly to the Latin *revolution regni*, which does not appear until much later, while the earliest European political applications of the term in Italian, *revoluzione*, date from the mid-eighth/fourteenth century—that is, a century later.

---

53   Afzal 1977: 70–73.
54   Afzal 1977: 64–65.
55   Jorbāzqāni as cited in Meisami 2004: 88–92.
56   Menhāj 1984: 1:464, 474.

The edicts of the Mongol Empire bore the signature "by the power of eternal heaven" (*möngke tngri-yin küčün-dür*).⁵⁷ The Mongols' belief in Heaven and Earth as two principal deities governing the universe, and the legitimacy of world conquest by the power of the eternal heaven shows remarkable continuity with those of the old Turk empire of the seventh century CE. Heaven gave power to a supreme leader (*qān, qā'ān*; Turkish, *khāgān*), and with Heaven and Earth increasing his power, he conquered the universe and ruled it by Heaven's command/law (*yarliq*). His military victories of the world conqueror were the sign of his Good Fortune (*suu*; Turkish *qut*). All this is confirmed by the famous letter to the Pope by Qā'ān Ögödei (r. 1229–1241) that was composed in Mongolian and sent in a Persian translation. In it, the Pope is told: "The command of Heaven, Chinggis Qān and the Qā'ān [Ögödei], both of them, sent it [i.e., the command of Heaven] to cause to be heard ... If you act contrary to it, ... Heaven will know!"⁵⁸

The Mongol political doctrine of universal empire had an immediate impact in the Muslim world; it reinforced the impact of political astrology in the Persianate world that remained under Turko-Mongolian domination in the following centuries. The historian Jovayni, who served in the Mongol administration of Iran, found the Persianate notion of Lord of the Auspicious Conjunction as a suitable equivalent to the Heavenly Mandate of his imperial master, Qā'ān Möngke (r. 1251–1259), and the idea even penetrated into the popular legend of Amir Hamza who was called "Lord of Auspicious Conjunctions and world-conqueror (*giti-setān*).⁵⁹ The Mongolian political doctrine was Islamicized after the conversion of the Il-Khanid Ghāzān Khan in 1295 and in the early decades of the eighth/fourteenth century. The great Il-Khanid vizier, Rashid al-Din called the next Il-Khan a peerless *sāheb-qerān* (Lord of the Auspicious Conjunction), and further equated the Mongolian power of Eternal Heaven with prophecy.⁶⁰ Other historians and poets, too, in their eulogies of the Muslim Il-Khans, found an equivalent for the world-conquering universal monarch by coupling the Lord of the Auspicious Conjunction with the Mahdi.⁶¹ In the last decade of the eighth/fourteenth century, 'Aziz b. Ardashir Astarābādi Baghdādi (d. ca. 1399), on the basis of a detailed analysis of the conjunction of Saturn and Jupiter in his patron's horoscope, considered the local ruler of Sivas in Anatolia "a just Solṭān and a perfect Lord of Conjunction" (*solṭān-e 'ādel o ṣāḥeb-qerān-e kāmel*).⁶² The Timurids of Iran and India (the

---

57 See Baumann 2013.
58 Cited in Rachewiltz 2007: 119; translation slightly modified.
59 Chann 2009: 95–97.
60 Rashid al-Din 1994: 1:4–6.
61 Brack 2018: 1157–1160.
62 Cited in Melvin-Koushki 2019.

Mughal emperors), for instance, persisted in calling the next world conqueror after Chinggis Khan and the founder of their dynasty, Timur (Tamerlane), the *sāheb-qerān* (Lord of the Conjunction) to legitimate their divinely sanctioned turn in power, following Timur's posthumous elevation to that rank (discussed in chapter 3).

In the introduction to his universal history, *Jāme' al-tavārikh*, Rashid al-Din Fazlallāh celebrated the restoration of peace and order under his royal Il-Khanid patrons, Ghāzān Khan and Üljeitü (Mohammad Khodā-banda), after decades of anarchy following the Mongol invasion. Describing the latter's coronation in July 1304 as the "final goal of the appearance of the Chinggis-Khanid turn in power (*dawlat*) and the promised elimination of the power vacuums (*fatrat*, pl. *fotur*) of the Muslim nation," Rashid al-Din expands on the new ruler's "advent in the sphere of sovereignty/turn in power (*dawlat*)" as a Lord of the Auspicious Conjunction and the most just of the Il-Khans, in whose reign of justice no sword will be drawn. This introductory discourse also contains a very revealing statement on the negative normative valence of the Persianate concept of revolution. In the Mongol period, he tells us, it became especially evident to everyone "how much disturbance and disorder (*bulghāq*) occurs in every revolution (*enqelāb*), and how much blood is shed as a result of the fire of dissension (*fetna*) ignited by the sword." Revolution is complete disorder, for which Rashid al-Din uses the ancient Turkic word, *bulghāq*, which is attested in several second-/eighth-century Orkhon inscriptions.[63]

An illustration of this meaning of revolution as a fateful reversal of the turn in power can be found in Rashid al-Din's account of Arghun Khan's victory over Tegüder (Ahmad) in Rābī' II 683/July 1284. The rebellious prince, Arghun, had been arrested and placed in the custody of Tegüder's general, Elināq. One night, when the latter was drunk "and oblivious to the revolution of the days (*enqelāb-e ruzegār*)," Arghun was released by a group of his conspiring generals who soon put him on the throne; he was greeted by their leader with this proclamation of the good news:

بگفتا که دولت ترا یار شد   سر بخت دشمن نگونسار شد

He said "the sovereignty/turn in power has become your companion
The enemy's fortune (*bakht*) has been beheaded."[64]

---

63 Rashid al-Din 1994: 1:2–6, 4:2327.
64 Rashid al-Din 1994: 2:1142–1143. *Bakht* is a key concept in the Zurvanist astrological fatalism.

In sharp contrast to this negative characterization of revolutionary action as sedition, Rashid al-Din in effect appropriates the above-mentioned Isma'ili idea of the astral determination of earthly revolutions as a transfer of sovereignty and elevates the status of Persianate kingship by sacralizing it. In an interesting unpublished treatise, he elaborates on the assimilation of Islamicate kingship and prophecy to the Mongolian Heavenly Mandate of the world conqueror. He redefines the Lordship of the Auspicious Conjunction endowed with good fortune (*suu*) as the highest rank of kingship, one in possession of the House of Chinggis Khan. In Q. 4:59: "Obey God, and obey the Messenger and those in authority among you," Rashid al-Din argues, "He gave the absolute kings (*motlaq pādshāhān*) a relation to the prophets and even to Himself."[65] The implication of this assimilation of Mongolian and Islamic notions of divinely sanctioned sovereignty for the appropriated Persianate conception of astrally determined revolution is most interesting; it offers a parallel to the paradoxical transformation of the notion of *dawlat* as a divinely ordained turn in power and changes the meaning of the term after the Abbasid revolution.

Moving from the Il-Khanid to the Timurid Empire, Tāj al-Din Hasan b. Shehāb Yazdi was another historian of Kerman who lived in the latter part of the Timurid period, or mid ninth/fifteenth century. Tāj al-Din Yazdi uses the term *enqelāb* in a matter-of-fact manner. Writing about yet another Timurid prince approaching the gates of the city in September 1453, he reports that the people of Kerman began spreading false rumors as they "were snake-bitten as they ... had suffered three or four revolutions (*enqelāb*) in seven months."[66] Even more interesting is his use of the term *dawlat* in the original sense of turn in power. In the confrontation between the Timurid Abu Bakr b. Mirānshāh and the Jalayerid Soltān Ovays, as the latter's "army was dominant and his turn in power (*dawlat*) greater, Abu Bakr could not resist." Furthermore, as "Abu Bakr was at the end of his turn in power (*dawlat*), ... his fortune (*bakht*) had expired, and he was defeated":

به دولت توان برد کاری ز پیش
چو دولت نماند شود نوش نیش[67]

By the turn in power, all deeds are done
When the turn in power ends, mead turns to venom.

---

65   Cited in Brack 2018: 1162.
66   Yazdi 1987: 172.
67   Yazdi 1987: 34.

Perhaps more amusing is Tāj al-Din Yazdi's explanation of the fall of the Timurid prince, Mohammad Soltān b. Bāysonghor, to whom his *Jāmeʿ al-tavārikh* was originally dedicated. In January 1452, Mohammad Soltān was defeated and killed by his brother, Zahir al-Din Bābor, ancestor of the founder of the Mughal Empire. Yazdi then rededicated his book to prince Bābor. Mohammad Soltān's dismissal of Tāj al-Din Yazdi's immediate patrons in the government of Kerman, that is, the sons of Amir Ghenā-Shirin, "who were the pillars of his state (*dawlat*) and sovereignty," meant that "he, with his own hands, sullied his turn in power (*dawlat*) and there remained no endurance or stability in that state (*dawlat*) and sovereignty"[68] With this in part self-servingly moral explanation, Tāj al-Din Hasan Yazdi then turned to the divine sanction provided for the turn in power by the Qurʾān, and began his eulogy of his new royal patron, Bābor, with the citation of verse 3:25, "The decree of 'Thou givest the kingdom' was enforced in the world!"[69]

We noted the complementarity of the normative political and astral theories with regard to the appearance of just rulers under auspicious signs to delay the process of political collapse. It is in accordance with this theory that Edris Bedlisi, whom we meet in chapter 5, saw the collapse of the Āq Qoyunlu (Bāyandor) Turko-Mongolian empire signaled by the death of its last effective ruler, Soltān Yaʿqub in 1490: "Gradually the misfortune of the state appeared in his own bodily illness and the discordant condition of the state appeared to him. Several illnesses of his temperament were prolonged ... [by] the weakness of his spiritual strength." Yaʿqub's death was accordingly seen as a "storm of strife and tumult throughout the lands," which Bedlisi's father attributed to "meteorites of misfortune in the Bāyandor domains."[70]

When discussing what I have elsewhere analyzed as the failure to export the Safavid revolution to the Ottoman domains during the serious crisis of succession to Soltān Bāyezid II in 1511–1512,[71] The Safavid historian, Hasan Rumlu, tells us that when Shah Esmāʿil "heard the news of the revolution (*enqelāb*) in the realm of Rum, he sent Nur-ʿAli Khalifa Rumlu to that country to gather the sincere Sufis ... and close to three or four thousand horsemen with their nomadic households joined him."[72] Here I would say the term *enqelāb* is used in the same sense as the Europeans used the term revolution before the French Revolution, for instance, in a German dictionary in 1728 it

---

68 Yazdi 1987: 60. In this sentence, *dawlat* is used twice, in two different senses.
69 Yazdi 1987: 66.
70 As cited in Markiewicz 2019: 40, 60.
71 Arjomand 2005: 61.
72 Rumlu 1931: 134.

appears as "Revolution, the upheaval…, *revolutio regni*, the change or overturning of a kingdom or of a land, if such suffers any special alteration in government or police."⁷³ The same term is used in Father J.T. Krusinski's *The History of the Late Revolutions of Persia* in 1740, with reference to the fall of the Safavid Empire. It is in this sense that, as late as 1788, Edward Gibbon calls the decline and fall of the Roman Empire, the rise of Islam, and the Turkish conquest of Constantinople revolutions.⁷⁴

The Hashemite revolution in Khorasan that established the Abbasid Caliphate in 750 and the Mongol overthrow of the Abbasids 508 years later were indeed revolutions in the Muslim empire that comprised Iran but extended far beyond it. The overthrow of the Safavid dynasty by the Afghans in 1722, after they had ruled Iran for 225 years was indeed a *revolutio regni* and was seen as such. The modern concept of revolution began to appear in Iran in the latter part of the nineteenth century after it was popularized by the Young Ottomans with reference to the French and other modern revolutions. It is very interesting to note that the term and the concept in the modern sense was then used with reference to the rise of the Safavids in an unpublished manuscript commissioned by the Minister of Publications, Mohammad Hasan Khān Eʿtemād al-Saltana, for Nāser al-Din Shah (r. 1848–1896), who was preoccupied with modern revolutionaries and anarchists. The author of *Enqelāb al-eslām bayn al-khāss wa'l-ʿāmm* (Revolution in Islam between the particular and the general), written in 1889 or 1890, carefully considers major Safavid and Ottoman primary sources on "the events of the time of the revolution"—that is, during the reign of Shah Esmāʿil—in order to demonstrate that there could be a revolution in religion, or in his words, that God could "produce and make manifest such a revolution in this perishable abode (i.e., the earthly realm) as to astonish this wisest of political scientists and the most learned of the materialist men of science."⁷⁵

It was only with the Iranian revolution of 1906 (known as the Constitutional Revolution) that the conceptual shift was completed, and the modern concept of revolution shaped the self-understandings of its historical actors. But the term *enqelāb* was selected for modern revolution for good reasons; its

---

73   Cited in Koselleck 1985: 43–46.
74   Gibbon 1932: 1:1, 2:521.
75   Motarjem: preface, folios *alef* and *jim*. Pārsādust (2002: 857) identifies the author of this manuscript, Tehran, National Library MS no. 1634, as Mohammad Motarjem ("the translator"), known as Espināqchi Pāshazāda. *Enqelāb al-eslām* is in fact a scholarly and historically reliable account of the Safavid revolution, which I have drawn on for my own analysis.

old connotations did not disappear overnight and in May 1906, for instance, Mohammad Qazvini used the idiomatic plural, *enqelābāt-e ayyām* (revolutions of the days).[76]

---

[76] Motarjem: p. *dāl*. The old usage also persisted further into the twentieth century. In 1935, the equally learned Mohammad-Taqi Malek al-Shoʻara Bahār (Motarjem: p. *tayn*) typically coupled the plural term with the destructive *fatrat* (lit., power vacuum) in the plural and spoke of the vicissitudes of power in Sistan as its "revolutions" (*enqelābāt-e Sistān*).

CHAPTER 2

Shi'ism, Sufism, and the Symbolism of Kingship in the Formation of Persianate Islam

Having outlined the conceptual framework of our study, we now set the arena for the appearance of apocalyptic messianism in the eighth/fourteenth and ninth/fifteenth centuries, and locate the Persianate world for the reader and highlight its distinctive features. Here the Persianate world denotes a region as a civilizational zone. Already in the late fourth/tenth century, the Persianate civilizational zone was called Irān-shahr (the land of Iran). According to Abu Mansur Tūsi, who wrote the earliest known *Epic of Kings* in New Persian, Irān-shahr "extends from the Oxus River to the Nile."[1] Abu Rayhān Biruni (d. 1050), used the ancient notion of circles from Ptolemy's *Geography* to locate Irān-shahr as the central circular region of the world:

> For political reasons ... the inhabited world was divided into seven circular parts, with six circles which encircle a seventh [central] circle ... The reason for this division is that the great kings were natives of Iranshahr ... This partition has nothing to do with natural climatic conditions, nor with astronomical phenomena. It is made according to kingdoms [i.e., polities] which differ [because of] different features of their peoples and different codes of morality and customs.[2]

Biruni thus goes beyond geographical determinism and adds culture as a factor that delimits the Persianate world. Arnold Toynbee, using civilization instead of culture, defines the distinctiveness of the society and civilization in the world region from the Sea of Marmara to the Gulf of Bengal in the mid-tenth/sixteenth century, and called it "Iranic."[3] Last but not least, Marshall Hodgson

---

1 Cited in Mottahedeh 2012: 156.
2 Mottahedeh 2012: 156–157.
3 Toynbee 1935: 514–515: "In the Iranian world,.... the New Persian language ... gained a currency as a lingua franca; and at its widest, about the turn of the sixteenth and seventeenth centuries ..., its range extended ... from the Ottoman *pashalyq* of Buda to the Muslim 'successor-states' which had been carved, after the victory of the Deccanese Muslim princes at Talikota in AD 1565.... For this vast cultural empire the New Persian language was indebted to the arms of Turkish-speaking empire-builders, reared in the Iranian tradition and therefore captivated by the spell of the New Persian literature, whose military and political destiny it had been to

called the cultural tradition and ecumenical unity that grew on the basis of the Persian language, "Persianate," and further contrasted the continued vitality of the "Persianate zone" with the early flourishing of the "Arabic zone" of the Islamicate civilization, going so far as to divide the Arabic zone historically "into an earlier 'caliphal' and later 'Persianate' phase."[4]

1   The Revival of the Persian Language and the Emergence of Persianate Islam

New Persian was first written in the Arabic script at the end of the third/ninth century. It was quickly transformed into the *lingua franca* of monarchies and empires and became the second *lingua franca* of Islam during its expansion into eastern Muslim lands.[5] It thus created a vast civilizational area that I call the Persianate world.[6] The developmental path for the growth, consolidation, and expansion of this Persianate world was set by the rise of local monarchies in the Iranian zone of the caliphal body politic, most notably the Samanids (r. 204–395/819–1005) who switched their official language from Arabic to Persian, thus inaugurating what the Indologist Sheldon Pollock called the 'vernacular millennium,' and at the same time, creating the first Persianate polity. The culture of the Persianate zone of Islamicate civilization was made distinctive by two major components: Persianate Islam and Persian kingship.

The major revolution under the banner of Islam—the Abbasid revolution (though its participants called it the Hashemite revolution)—occurred in the mid-second/eighth century, before the revival of Persian as a written language. One of its leaders, however, had already given expression to the

---

provide one universal state for Orthodox Christendom in the shape of the Ottoman Empire and another for the Hindu World in the shape of the Timurid Mughal Raj. These two universal states of Iranian construction on Orthodox Christian and on Hindu ground were duly annexed, in accordance with their builders' own cultural affinities, to the original domain of the New Persian language in the homelands of the Iranian Civilization on the Iranian plateau and in the Basin of the Oxus and the Jaxartes; and in the heyday of the Mughal, Safawi, and Ottoman regimes New Persian was being patronized as the language of literate humanizers by the ruling element over the whole of this huge realm, while it was also being employed as the official language of administration in those two-thirds of its realm that lay within the Safawi and the Mughal frontiers."

4   Hodgson 1974: 2:293–294; Arjomand 2015.
5   Fragner 1999.
6   It has rightly been claimed that "no other language has ever maintained such a monopoly of the medium of writing over so large a territory for so long a period." (Spooner and Hanaway 2012: 3)

Persian conception of revolution in a speech later recorded in Arabic.[7] We have also alluded to the massive uprising of the followers of Abu Moslem, another Khorasanian revolutionary leader. This uprising followed his murder in the power struggle that paradoxically ended with the integration and Islamicization of greater Khorasan into the Abbasid Empire.[8] In the following centuries, instead of replicating the metropolitan Islam of the Abbasid Caliphate, however, Islamicization developed a Persianate variant of Islam, one whose distinctive hallmark was Sufism.

The Shi'a, or partisans of 'Ali who claimed a link to the Hashemite revolution which, to use a current term anachronistically, was "hijacked" by the Abbasids, played an important role in the progressive conversion of the people of Khorasan and Transoxiana to Islam. They certainly saw the Hashemite revolution and its leader, Abu Moslem, in an apocalyptic light. The messianic Qā'im was later identified with its Sunni counterpart, the Mahdi, as the rightly-guided leader of the End of Time,[9] and, along with the Persianate idea of revolution, was a key motivating belief of the Hashemite movement in Khorasan.

In the third/ninth and early fourth/tenth centuries, we witness remarkable proselytization and growth of the Imami branch of Shi'ism in Nishapur, followed in the last quarter of the third/ninth century by a serious crisis of the Shi'ite Imamate (the divinely-inspired leadership). In the fourth/tenth century the Imami or Twelver Shi'a chose the path of quietism and sectarian growth over millennial uprising. Millennialism was contained through the elaboration of a doctrine of occultation that merged the Qā'im-Mahdi myth with a belief in the existence of a Hidden Imam, the twelfth holy Imam, who was said to have gone into concealment in 874, from there he performed all the essential functions of the Imamate while in indefinite occultation; it was believed that he would reappear as the Mahdi at the End of Time and not before.

The crisis of the Imamate splintered Shi'ism, giving birth to Isma'ili Shi'ism which showed an impressively fast growth throughout Khorasan in the early fourth/tenth century. The Isma'ili Shi'a were fully active in Khorasan and in contrast to the Imami Shi'a, chose a path of apocalyptic uprising. The initial

---

7   That is, before Persian could be written. See introduction.
8   Arjomand 2019: ch. 8.
9   The idea of the Mahdi entered Islamic history proper in the last quarter of the first/seventh century through the uprising of Mokhtār in Kufa, in an anti-apocalyptic form as Mohammad redivivus, a descendant with the same name and same father's name as the Prophet. In a tradition attributed to the Prophet's disciple, 'Abdallāh b. Mas'ud. This trope of historical repetition, degeneration and regeneration was amalgamated with the Shi'ite apocalyptic Qā'im into the composite figure of the Qā'im-Mahdi representing the apocalyptic messianic leader of the End of Time. (Arjomand 2022: ch. 3)

success of Ismaʿili Shiʿism in the early fourth/tenth century involved the conversion of a Samanid king and important members of the ruling elite, but did not result in an Mahdist revolution in Khorasan. Revolutionary Mahdism had its heydays elsewhere—in the Fatimid and Almohad revolutions in North Africa from the fourth/tenth century onward.[10] The growth of Sufism in Khorasan made the region inhospitable for apocalyptic Mahdism in this period. Ismaʿili revolution was nevertheless exported to the Iranian cities of the Seljuq Empire by the rival Fatimids from Egypt, and by the beginning of the sixth/twelfth century its agents established a foothold in the mountain fortresses in northern Iran and eastern Khorasan. A branch of Ismaʿili Shiʿism gained control of the clandestine eastern organization operation in the Seljuq Empire under a redoubtable leader, Hasan Sabbāh (d. 1124) who broke from the Fatimids and propounded a "new mission" (daʿwat-e jadid) in contradistinction to the old Fatimid mission.[11]

Meanwhile, a new and increasingly dominant trend emerged in the remarkably pluralistic Khorasanian religious scene: Sufism. The emergence of Persianate Islam can be traced to the appearance in the second/eighth and third/ninth centuries of two prototypical Sufi masters, Ebrāhim-e Adham of Balkh (d. 788) and Bāyazid of Bastām (d. 874), both of whom predate the revival of written Persian, though the development of Persianate Islam needed the Persian language and its conceptual structure.[12] The fifth/eleventh century is thus a period in which Sufism emerged as a distinct form of Islam in the Persianate world.

We know almost nothing about the life of Ebrāhim-e Adham,[13] except that he was, like the Buddha, a world-renouncing prince and scion of the dynasty of local kings of Balkh, where the Nawbahār Temple continued to be a major center of Buddhism into the Islamic era. He renounced worldly power for the realm of the spirit and thus instituted world renunciation (tark-e donyā) in Islam. We are somewhat better informed about Bāyazid Bastāmi who was considered the first in the chain of transmitters of this "leaven of the royals" (khamirat al-khosravāniyyin), by which expression he meant the Mazdaean-Manichaean heritage, alternately called the "royal wisdom" (hekmat-e khosrovāni). The transmission of Persian wisdom is indirectly confirmed by an autobiographical remark by Bāyazid that it took him five years of strenuous effort to break the "Magian girdle" around his waist! Shehāb al-Din Yahyā Sohravardi (d. 1191)

---

10 Arjomand 2022: chs. 7–8.
11 Hodgson 1955.
12 Fragner 1999.
13 Ebrāhim, son of Adham.

further specifies the channel of transmission as entirely Khorasanian: The leaven of the royals was passed on by Bāyazid and a certain "bright *fatā*"[14] through the late fourth-/tenth- and early fifth-/eleventh-century Sufi masters, the Butcher of Āmol and Abu'l-Hasan Kharaqāni.[15]

The early Sufi masters of Khorasan in the third/ninth century were strongly associated with the guilds or civic associations of craftsmen in the cities of Khorasan; these were commonly called *fotowwat* (youth organizations), but were also variously identified with *'ayyāri* or *fotowwat/javānmardi* (bravery/chivalry). At the same time, Sufism was acquiring its own specific designation. *Darvish* as a synonym for the Arabic *faqīr* was the Middle Persian or Pahlavi word for "poor"; it became the very designation of Sufi wayfarers as *darāvish/foqarā'* (in the plural). The differentiation between the Sufi religious elite and the *fotowwat* was gradual and not without resistance. Nevertheless, the professionalization of Sufi masters called shaykhs or *pir*s (elders) was well advanced by the fifth/eleventh century.

With the exposition of mystical concepts in the elegant Persian prose of Khʷāja 'Abdallāh Ansāri (d. 1089) in Herat in the mid-fifth/eleventh century and the treatise on Sufism by his contemporary, Hojviri of Ghazna in 1077,[16] Persian replaced Arabic as the primary medium for the expression of Sufism. Ansāri's followers, Rashid al-Din Maybodi (d. after 1126), Ahmed Ghazāli (d. 1126), and 'Abd al-Karim Sam'āni (d. 1167) continued to write in Persian in the sixth/twelfth century, as did 'Ayn al-Qozāt Hamadāni (d. 1131) and Hakim Sanā'i of Ghazna (d. 525/1131).[17] Sufism was thus incorporated into Persianate Islam, and in fact became its new distinctive feature. World renunciation was a major value idea taken from Ebrāhim-e Adham, who had been inspired by Buddhism. World rejection and the glorification of poverty went hand in hand in the development of Sufi identity. Ansari used *faqr* and *darvishi* interchangeably for poverty as a critical stage of spiritual progression on the path. World rejection was, however, tempered with an emphasis on divine love, which could, in the long run, be interpreted differently.[18]

From the beginning New Persian was forged as the complementary *lingua franca* of Islam, and became, as Hodgson emphasized, the main vehicle for the spread of Islam as a world religion and of the Islamicate civilization in the

---

14 So far unidentified.
15 Arjomand 2020: 14.
16 He is known as Hazrat-e Dātā Ganjbakhsh, and his shrine is Lahore's foremost sacred site of pilgrimage.
17 Ahmed Ghazāli's older brother, the famous Abu Hāmed Mohammad (d. 505/1111) also joined the trend after his spiritual illumination.
18 Chittick 2013.

eastern lands of the caliphate. Sufi literary works in Persian presented a non-legalistic mystical variant of Islam. The Sufi-tinged Persianate Islam traveled to India and was received as the central, universalistic tradition of Islam, not as a form of "local knowledge"; this contributed to the creation of an ecumenical civilizational zone we call the Persianate world.

The emergence and spread of the Persian language did not happen in a political vacuum—its developmental pattern was critically shaped by the rise of local monarchy within the caliphal body politic and these local monarchies revived the idea of ancient Persian kingship. A new type of Islamicate political regime was created in fourth-/tenth-century Khorasan and Transoxania by the Samanids, who traced their descent to Bahram Chubin, the Parthian who rebelled against the Sasanian Khosrow II. It grafted the idea of Iranian monarchy onto an entirely novel form of political organization, consisting of patrimonial government with a *mamlūk* army of royal slaves. Military slavery in the form of soldiers and generals who were owned (*mamlūk*) by the patrimonial rulers emerged in Transoxania at the end of the third/ninth century. In the Samanid kingdom, the Ghurid rulers of present-day Afghanistan, who in the latter part of the sixth/twelfth century belonged to the Iranian House of Shansab, adopted what I consider a prototypical "Persianate polity." This Persianate polity then traveled to India via the institution of royal military slavery. The childless Ghurid *soltān*, Moʿezz al-Din, who conquered India at the end of the sixth/twelfth century, treated the military slaves as the sons of the king, and left his conquered subcontinent to his slave generals who perfected their distinctive political regime into the Delhi Sultanate. Within two centuries the Persianate polity in India spread beyond the *mamlūk* Delhi Sultanate into the Deccan, and with it, the close association of rulers and Sufi saints spread, along with the ancient Persian idea of monarchy as kingship based on justice.[19] Therefore, along with Sufi Persianate Islam, the Persianate kingship and polity can be considered the second main source of the enormous growth and spread of Persianate culture and society.

Although Persianate Islam combined the norms of Sufi mysticism and kingship, it was heterogeneous and conflicts were possible. The great poet and mystic, Majdud b. Ādam, known as Hakim Sanāʾi (d. 525/1131), was also a contemporary of the Ghazālis. Toward the end of his life, Sanāʾi put together a compendium of his verse most commonly known as *Hadiqat al-Haqiqa wa shariʿat al-tariqa*. Bahrāmshāh, the local king to whom it was dedicated, was hyperbolically praised as the Mahdi of the age and the Jesus of the present. Nevertheless, a subtler political hint appears as an incidental verse:

---

19   Arjomand 2009.

> None of the friends on the path of love has attained
> The kingdom (*molk*) of the spirit without the extinction of the kingdom of appearance (*surat*)

This sets the stage in which to contrast the nullity of the earthly ruler to the omnipotence of God:

> O ruler (*soltān*) whose ruler is anger and desire,
> You have no title before the ruler of the rulers [i.e., God]!

Sanā'i's other poetry is marked by biting sarcasm. He calls the dominant social classes "dogs covered with human skin" (*ādam-kimokht*) and the "dog-natured in human form" (*ādam-suratān-e sag-sefat*) and hopes for deliverance from their misrule by the Mahdi.[20]

Meanwhile the Nezāri branch of the Isma'ili Shi'a had reappeared in Iran. The Nezāris believed their Imam was in occultation and would return as the Qā'im-Mahdi; their leader Hasan Sabbāh believed in a hidden Imam and presented himself as his visible proof (*hujja*) at the head of the mission. Hasan seized the fortress of Alamut in 1090 and proceeded to create an Isma'ili state consisting of fortresses in the mountains of northern and northeastern Iran. Crucial to Sabbāh's mission was his proselytizing among settled Persians recruited in the cities of northern and central Iran. Hasan Sabbāh took the unprecedented step of replacing Arabic with Persian as the language of the Ismā'ili mission. Forty years after his death, on 17 Ramadān 559/8 August 1164, the ruler of the Nezāri Isma'ili fortresses, Hasan II b. Mohammad b. Bozorg-Omid, proclaimed the Resurrection as the deputy (*khalifa*) and Proof of the Imam, the Qā'im of the Resurrection (*qiyāma*).[21] The resurrection meant that the era (*dawr*) of the law and external reality had come to an end and the era of inner reality had begun. All believers could know God and the cosmic mysteries through the Imam, and God would constantly be in their hearts. Hasan II was fatally stabbed in January 1166, but his son Mohammad II confirmed the continuation of the resurrection, which lasted to 1210, for a total of 46 years. The mission was now "the call to [or, preaching of] resurrection" (*da'wat-e qiyāmat*), and the Nizāris considered themselves "the saved community of the Qā'imites (*qā'imiyun*)." Mohammad II added the Sufi level of truth (*haqiqa*) to the Isma'ili levels of external and inner reality and identified it with the Resurrection. This paved the way for the transformation of the Nezāri Isma'ili

---

20   See Arjomand 2020 for all the citations.
21   He later hinted that he himself was the Imam and the Qā'im of the resurrection.

state into a Sufi order after the conquest of its mountain fortresses by the Mongol Hülegü in 1256.[22]

By completing the cycle of divine revelation, the so-called Great Resurrection is the apocalyptic appropriation of the world through the universal integration of salvific knowledge into the daily lives of the people of truth. With this ultimate kenosis of the apocalyptic into Sufi mystical pantheism, the "realized apocalypticism" of Isma'ilism took the form of the mystical life of a Sufi order in what purported to be post-history.

By this time, popular Sufism was spreading from the cities of Khorasan to the rest of Iran, expressed in a language understandable by its ordinary adherents. Persianate Sufism was thereby created and made distinct from trends in popular culture and folk religion with which it had been mingled earlier. The development of Sufism, recorded in Persian texts from the fifth/eleventh and sixth/twelfth centuries and surveyed here shows how Persianate Sufism developed with three distinctive components: the Sufi theory of the stations of spiritual wayfaring (*soluk*) as a journey to God, the shift of focus from world renunciation to divine love, and the transfiguration of the symbolism and imagery of ancient Iranian kingship. These three components of Khorasanian Sufism find their consummate expression in the great work of Farid al-Din 'Attār (d. most probably 1230) written at the beginning of the seventh/thirteenth century on the eve of Mongol invasion. 'Attār was the last authority in a line of Khorasanian Sufi virtuosi that came to an end with the destruction of Nishapur and other major cities of Khorasan and Transoxiana by Chinggis Khan. Persianate Sufism, expressed by 'Attār in an accessible Persian poetic form that greatly shaped its normative pattern, subsequently spread throughout the Persianate world from the Caucasus and Anatolia to northern India.

The Persianate world became more sharply differentiated from Islamicate civilization as a consequence[23] of the Mongol integrative revolution in the seventh/thirteenth century. Whether or not we accept the thesis of a 'Eurasian seventh-/thirteenth-century renaissance' as an axial turning point in world history, there can be no doubt that the Mongol Empire established by Chinggis Khan (d. 1227) unified Eurasia as never before or since. Therefore, we can speak of the Mongol revolution because of the unmatched significance of its consequences in world history.[24] After a generation or two the Mongol Empire was divided de facto into three parts, and developed along different paths under the influence of the varying cultures of its main regions. After

---

22   See Arjomand 2022: ch. 7 citations and further details.
23   Arjomand 2019: ch. 10.
24   Arjomand 2004; Arjomand 2019: ch. 10.

the death of Chinggis Khan's grandson, the great Qā'ān Möngke, in 1259, two cultural ecumene quickly developed under the latter's brothers, Qubilai and Hülegü, one Uighur-Chinese, the other Persianate. One-third of the empire, the Ulus Jochi (i.e., the tribes and country assigned to Chinggis Khan's eldest son, Jochi), which later became known as the Golden Horde, and where the nomadic empire lasted the longest, had minimal cultural interaction with the settled population. The longevity of the Golden Horde's nomadic empire can plausibly be attributed to its ability to subject Russia to "tributary rule ... from the borderlands of pastoral territory [around the Caspian], while itself remaining within steppe country."[25] By contrast, in China and Iran, by the eighth/fourteenth century new compound nomadic-settled societies under the Yuan and Il-Khanid dynasties generated two distinct political cultures.

The ancient Persian idea of kingship over a territory was alien to the Mongol steppe tradition. It was introduced to the Il-Khanids, the Mongol rulers of Iran, by their Persian bureaucrats. This was the consequence of the division of Chinggis Khan's Empire of the Great Mongols (Yeke Mongghol Ulus) between his grandsons, Qubilai and Hülegü. It consisted in the transformation of the Ulus Hülegü, constituted by Möngke in the mid-1250s, into the independent Il-Khanid imperial kingdom of Irān-zamin (the Land of Iran). The Persian administrators of the Il-Khanids promoted the ancient Iranian idea of kingship with the approval of Hülegü (d. 1265) and his descendants, the Il-Khanid rulers of Iran, who were eager to enhance their autonomy. These Persian bureaucrats easily persuaded their Mongol overlords of the Persian idea of kingship over a territorial empire, or to be precise, the Kingship of the Land of Iran (*pādshāhi-ye Irān-zamin*). The rise of the "national state" in Iran took place under the Il-Khanids and was thus a long-term consequence of the Mongol revolution.[26]

2   The Disestablishment and Refiguration of Islam in the Persianate World in the Age of Confessional Ambiguity

The Mongol conquest of Iran resulted in the disestablishment of Islam; this was generalized to the rest of the Persianate world with the overthrow of the

---

25 Anderson 1974: 227.
26 For the idea of the Mongol revolution and its consequences, see Arjomand 2016b: 41–46. Walter Hinz (1936) and others following him wrongly place it at the beginning of the Safavid era.

Abbasid Caliphate in 1258, the revolution[27] bemoaned by the poet Saʿdi of Shiraz:

> The Sky can by right rain blood
> Upon the fall of the sovereignty of the Commander of the Faithful al-Moʿtasem.[28]

Strictly speaking, the disestablishment of Islam meant the Islam of the clerical elite, the *ʿolamā'* (the learned). This shift opened the way for Sufi shaykhs and the spread of Persianate Sufism, on one side, and on the other, of Shiʿite devotion to the House of the Prophet, meaning the descendants of ʿAli. The adaptation of Islam to the collapse of Islamic political and religious authority manifested itself in a new pattern of religious authority, one born from the synergy between Sufism and Shiʿism in the eighth/fourteenth century, a period that was aptly characterized as the age of confessional ambiguity.[29]

Two important trends of the era of confessional ambiguity have roots in the preceding century. Just as with the Shiʿitization trends from below among seventh-/thirteenth-century dervish groups, the origins of the Sufi penetration of grassroots urban civic associations go back to the reforms from above during the long reign of the late Abbasid caliph al-Nāser li-Din Allāh (r. 1190–1225). Al-Nāser tried to blend these two traditions to strengthen the caliphate against the challenges first of the expanding nomadic empire of the Turkic Khʷarzmshāhs and then of the Mongol onslaught. There were two important aspects to what al-Nāser called "the rightly-guided mission" (*al-daʿwa al-hādiya*): one legal, the other sociological. On the legal front, he sought to strengthen autocracy by bringing the Sunni theory of the caliphate closer to the Shiʿite doctrine of the imamate. At the sociological level, his goal was to wed the Sufi orders and the *fotowwat* associations of young men and artisans of the city-quarters, who idealized ʿAli. His counselor and spiritual master, Shaykh Abu Hafs ʿOmar Sohravardi (d. 1234) played a critical role in the formulation of this ideology.[30]

Al-Nāser's efforts to save the caliphate came to naught with the Mongol overthrow of his descendants, and a new pattern that blended the grassroots of mass Sufi movements gradually emerged. This new pattern of authority greatly

---

27 See the general introduction.
28 Cited in Browne 1902: 2:29, trans. modified:
آسمان را حق بود گر خون ببارد بر زمین   در زوال ملک مستعصم امیر المومنین
29 Pfeiffer 2014.
30 Arjomand 2004: 222–231.

intensified the millenarian and mystical elements latent in Sunni Islam. The rise of popular Sufism, and with it the religious and political prominence of the Sufi shaykhs, was concomitant with the disestablishment of the orthodoxy of the clerical elite (the 'olamā').[31]

The destruction of Khorasan by the invading Mongols dislocated Persianate Sufism, which took refuge in the Seljuq kingdoms of Rum that had not been invaded. Najm al-Din Rāzi, known as the Dāya (tutor) (d. 1256), followed the call of the eponymous shaykh of the Kobraviyya order, Shaykh Najm al-Din Kobrā (d. 1221), to preserve and propagate Islam in the face of extinction by the Mongol invasion. Indeed this threat to the survival of Islam was stimulus for the spiritual mission; Najm al-Din Kobrā wished to recruit a "king of Islam" at the time of its prophesied estrangement. His fear was that the name and trace of Islam that still survived will would also vanish, as a result of ill-omened and useless disputes, then no sign of religion would remain, and it would withdraw behind the veil of dignity as in the prophetic hadith: "Islam began as a stranger, and again shall become a stranger as it began."[32]

The kingdom of the Seljuqs of Rum in Anatolia was the best and only suitable location for Rāzi's project, as the shrunken realm of the Abbasid caliphate was engaged in a different policy of self-preservation. Rāzi fled the Mongols from city to city from Khorasan to Anatolia, where Sohravardi introduced him to the Seljuq *soltān* of Rum, 'Alā' al-Din Kayqobād. There Rāzi offered Sohravardi his magisterial treatise, *Mersād al-'ebād men al-mabda' ela'l-ma'ād* (The path of God's bondsmen from origin to return).[33]

Rāzi's personal calamity was naturally taken as confirmation of the necessity of world renunciation:

> Your abode, dear unheeding friend, is the grave
>   Why raise a high *ivān* as home is the grave? ...

---

31 Mir-Kasimov 2014.
32 Rāzi 1973a: 18; Rāzi 1982 (trans. Algar): 41.
33 Rāzi evidently did not receive the royal favors he expected from the Seljuq suzerain as we find him, three years later, at the court of the local ruler of Erzincan, Dāvud Bahrāmshāh, to whom he dedicated an expanded version of the mirror for princes section of the *Mersād al-'ebād*. It was appropriately renamed *Marmuzāt-e asadi dar mazmurāt-e Dāvudi* (after his new royal patron and presented as a commentary to sayings of the latter's namesake, the prophet/king David). Although the mirror for princes, *Marmuzāt-e asadi dar mazmurāt-e Dāvudi*, has survived in a single manuscript, compared to the numerous manuscripts and translations of *Mersād al-'ebād*, its sharper focus makes it reflective of the relationship Rāzi envisioned between Sufism and kingship.

Inner-worldly mysticism is by no means inconsistent with world renunciation. On the contrary, Rāzi enjoined his readers to leave the "city of egotism (anāniyyat)" to be insulated (mojarrad) from the cloak of humanness.

> The [true] possessor of the turn in power (sāheb-e dawlat) is he who has witnessed and examined the way of the transient world and the impermanent turn in power.... And endeavors to learn the way to drink the unsavory chalice of death and thus attain salvation from the abode of tribulation [i.e., this world].[34]

The function of the Sufi king of Islam is defined within the framework of the education of mankind, where

> the soil of the human frame was prepared in such a way that when the seed of spirituality was sown in it by the husbandry of divine inhalation, and nurtured with the sunlight of God's grace and watered with His law, there should grow from it the fruits of nearness and knowledge in [unimaginably] abundant measure.

Different classes of society perform their specialized functions to assure the cultivation of the seed of spirituality and knowledge, and each class needs the others to perform its functions: "Finally, a just and politic king (pādshāh) is needed to maintain equilibrium among the people, to repel evil and prevent the oppression of the weak from the strong, and to preserve and protect the subjects ..."[35]

Rāzi's mirror for the wayfaring of kings opens with Qur'ān 38:26 on God's appointment of David as His deputy to rule among men with justice and with the hadith attributed to the Prophet: "The king is the shadow of God upon earth, in whom the oppressed take refuge." Together these are taken to establish that "monarchy (saltanat) is the deputyship (khelāfat) and viceregency of God Almighty,"[36] and is followed by the conventional hyperbolic legitimation of kingship. The foremost divinely established principles of kingship are stated as follows: "First, [God] said, 'O, David, We made you a deputy (khalifa),' indicating that the king must regard his kingship as God's gift and consider his kingdom the result of His beneficence: 'You give kingship to whom You wish'"

---

[34] Rāzi 1973b: 84–85.
[35] Rāzi 1973a: 111–112.
[36] This hadith was mentioned earlier, and is further cited and commented on to prove that "kingship is the deputyship of Truth (haqq)" on Rāzi 1982 (trans. Algar): 429.

(Q 3:26).[37] The second principle introduces a Sufi note on the impermanence of temporal power, alongside Rāzi's repeated reminders to the sovereign of the impermanence and nullity of earthly power:

> Second, there is a reminder to the king contained in the indication that God gave him kingship. He—i.e., the king—will know that God took it from another to give it to him, and that one day it will be taken from him to be given to another—"You take kingship from whom You wish."[38] He will therefore strive to attain true and abiding kingship by means of this *borrowed and transient kingship*, and not deprive himself of fair reputation among men and reward in the hereafter.[39]

Najm al-Dīn Rāzi's transplantation of Persianate Islam from Khorasan to the furthermost western frontier of Islam in Asia for its preservation is of world historical significance because he was able to successfully combine the two distinctive elements of Persianate Islam: Sufism and Persianate kingship. Kingship was accordingly Islamicized through the application of the Sufi theory of salvation of the soul. Rāzi entitled his chapter on the tradition or manner of kings "spiritual wayfaring" (*soluk*), where the Sufi king's wayfaring sets an example for the spirifual progression of all the other classes in society. This produced a distinctively Sufi conception of kingship and society. The novelty

---

[37] Rāzi 1982 (trans. Algar): 397, slightly modified. These two are the most frequently cited Qurʾānic verses for establishing the legitimation of kingship in Sufi and non-Sufi texts alike. The so-called "authority verse" (*uluʾl-amr*) Q. 59:4, appears more rarely.

[38] This half of Q. 3:26 is usually left out in mirrors for princes.

[39] Rāzi 1982 (trans. Algar): 397, emphasis mine. In an earlier passage (123), we read:
> This world's turn in power (*dawlat*) is indeed pleasant,
> But do not give it your heart—it kills all its lovers....
> This world and its turn in power is like a mirage—
> It entices you, then gives you no water.
> Many a king and vizier the Wheel has made,
> Given them kingship and treasure, a crown and a throne....
> Thus they became as rich as Nimrod
> And each was the pharaoh of his age.
> They sucked the blood of the poor (*darvishakān*)
> And drew out the brains of the wretched....
> Suddenly the hurricane of wrath began blowing
> And pulled them from the throne onto the bier.
> It delivered their bodies to festering clay ...
> Go seek the kingdom of eternity as in the eye of reason,
> To the kingdom of eternity, Solomon's kingdom is but wind.

Also see Rāzi 1982 (trans. Algar): 456–457; Rāzi 1973b: 71.

of Rāzi's approach, which was the first to reflect the substantial impact of world renunciation on the conception of kingship, thus consisted in treating kings as real Sufi disciples.[40] In doing so, he set a trend that culminated in the theories of millennial sovereignty in the first quarter of the tenth/sixteenth century.

In the preface to the *Mersād* Najm al-Din Rāzi affirmed that the Mongol invasion was an unprecedented catastrophe, unlike any recorded in history but foretold by the Prophet as one of the calamities at the End of Time. Rāzi added a final chapter on these calamities to the *Marmuzāt*.[41] Apocalyptic expectation of a world savior from among the *awliyā' Allāh* (friends of God), as the great Sufi shaykhs were called, also entered Persianate Sufism in this period. However, clarification of this was left to Rāzi's disciple and next shaykh of the Kobravi Sufi order, Sa'd al-Din Hammuya (d. 1252). But he showed no interest in finding a king of Islam and making him into a Sufi wayfarer. Sa'd al-Din returned to Khorasan later in life and instead, based on a numerological letterist interpretation of Qur'ānic verses, put his hope in the advent of a gnostic messiah. In *al-Mesbāh fi'l-tasavvuf* (The lantern in Sufism), he expected the appearance of the *khātam al-awliyā'* (Seal of the friends of God) as the Mahdi and the *sāheb-zamān* (Lord of time), whom he identified with the Hidden Imam of the Twelver Shi'a.[42]

Hammuya's younger contemporary Mawlānā Jalāl al-Din Rumi (d. 1273), who was an émigré and the established son of a prominent refugee in the Seljuq realm from Balkh, developed different political ideas from the Sufi doctrine. He was so convinced of the superiority of spiritual over temporal power that, in his major surviving prose work, he used the prophetic hadith, "the worst of the learned is he who visits the princes (singular, *amir*), and the best of the princes is he who visits the learned."[43] In order to appropriate the attributes of sovereignty for the Sufi virtuosi, who are identified with the learned in the hadith and compared with the light-giving sun to be venerated by visiting princes, he proceeded to chide the *amir* [Mo'in al-Din] Parvāna for selling Islam to the Tartars. The Persianate reconstruction and transformation of Sufism in Khorasan in the fifth/eleventh and sixth/twelfth centuries, as noted, involved a shift in conceptual priorities from initial world renunciation (*tark-e donyā*) and asceticism (*zohd*) to the love of God and inner-worldly mysticism. Mawlānā Jalāl al-Din Rumi called himself the heir to the Sufi love mysticism of 'Attār, for whom mysticism of divine love was strongly inflected toward

---

40 Landolt 1973: 5.
41 Rāzi 1973a: 16–17; Rāzi 1973b: ch. 10.
42 Hammuya 1983: 34–34, 99–100.
43 Mawlavi 1990: 1.

a pantheistic affirmation of the world. Rumi's contemporaries in Anatolia followed the similarly world-affirming Shaykh Muhyi al-Din Ibn al-'Arabi (d. 638/1240), the latter's Persian stepson, Sadr al-Din Qonavi (d. 1274) and the great ecstatic mystic and poet, Fakhr al-Din 'Erāqi (d. 1289), who is buried near Ibn al-'Arabi in Damascus. The fact that the seventh/thirteenth and early decades of the eighth/fourteenth century were marked by a striking absence of millennial revolution can in no small part be attributed to this trend in innerworldly Sufi love mysticism that substantially decreased interest in revolution.

Anatolia was not the only refuge of Sufism from the Mongol invasion. Fars in central-southern Iran was also spared depredation by accepting Mongol suzerainty. There, the great master of Persian prose and verse and practicing Sufi, namely, Shaykh Mosleh al-Din Sa'di of Shiraz (d. 1292), chose the older method of advising the ruler, that is, without seeking to transform him and without yearning for him to be a messianic savior. Sa'di's inner-worldly mysticism was also world-embracing; he highlighted ethical paradoxes, and his very first parable on the manner of kings controversially proposed that an expedient lie is better than a seditious truth. In the preamble to the *Bustān*, written in 1257, Sa'di is surprisingly sparing in his praise of the deceased ruler of Fars, Abu Bakr b. Sa'd, and his young successor, Sa'd b. Abu Bakr, who is called *shāh-e darvish-dust* (the dervish-loving king), and is enjoined "To pray like beggars with heart burning at night / While ruling as a king in the daytime."[44] The first chapter of the book is on the ethics of governance; its title, "On justice, management, and reason," combines the Persian principle of justice (*'adl*) with the idea of management (*tadbir*) from Greek (Aristotelian) practical philosophy, and reason (*ra'y*) from Indian statecraft.[45] It begins with the purported testament of Khosraw I, Anushirvan the Just:

> Go and keep watch on the needy poor (*darvish*)
> For the king holds his crown because of the subjects (*ra'iyyat*).
> The subjects are like the roots, and the ruler the tree
> The tree, my son, stands firm owing to its roots.[46]

In the following fateful year, 1258, when the Mongols overthrew the Abbasid caliphate in Baghdad, Sa'di wrote the *Golestān*, the most influential mirror for princes in Persian literature. Sa'di's first chapter addresses the tradition (normative) manners of kings (*sirat-e pādshāhān*), as wielders of earthly

---

44   Sa'di 1984: 8 v. 191, 9 v. 205.
45   On the synthesis of these three traditions, see Arjomand 2004.
46   Sa'di 1984: 11 vv. 222–223.

power,[47] followed by a chapter on the ethics (*akhlāq*) of the religious elite who wield spiritual power and are, significantly, called dervishes (*darvishān*). This ordering is quite remarkable because it shows that after the Mongol invasion the Sufi virtuosi as dervishes, replaced the jurists (not to mention the proponents of philosophy as perennial wisdom) as the religious elite in Persianate societies.[48]

Although in the preface dedicating *Golestān* to his royal patron Abu Bakr Saʿd b. Zangi, the *atabeg* ruler of Fars, Saʿdi grants the usual accolades legitimizing kingship (as the shadow of God on earth), this is more a matter of form than substance. Justice is conventionally given as the main principle by which to legitimize kingship, but most of Saʿdi's stories on the manners of kings concern tyranny (*zolm*) or the absence of justice rather than justice itself. And it is interesting to note that the most populist or democratic of the *Golestān*'s parables comes from the mouth of a solitary world renouncer (*darvishi mojarrad*), who boldly asserts: "know that the kings are for the guarding of the subjects (*raʿiyyat*), not the subjects for obedience to kings":

> The king (*pādshah*) is the guardian of the poor (*darvish*)
> Even if its prosperity is through his charisma of God-given power (*farr-e dawlat*).
> The flock is not for the shepherd
> But the shepherd for its service ...
> The difference between kingship and servitude is removed
> When the writ of [divine] judgment is issued.
> If the grave of the dead is opened,
> It shows neither the rich nor the poor.

Saʿdi proceeds to admonish the prince just as pithily: "Help the needy, while you have your turn in power (*dawlat*) / As this turn in power and kingdom turns from hand to hand." Well over a third of the parables in the chapter on the dervishes as the spiritual elite concern the relation between kings and ascetic world renouncers; in one of them, a pious man sees the other world in a dream: "This king is in paradise because of his devotion to dervishes, and this ascetic is in hell because of his closeness to kings." One could not ask for a better illustration of the superiority of spiritual authority over earthly power.[49]

---

47   See Arjomand 2004.
48   Nevertheless a jurist (*faqih*) and even more rarely a proponent of perennial wisdom (*hakim*), are occasionally mentioned in the parables of *Golestān*.
49   Saʿdi 1966: 61–62, 84–85.

When the Il-Khanid ruler of Iran, Ghāzān Khan, converted to Islam and assumed the title of *pādshāh-e eslām* (King of Islam), his Sufi mentor, 'Alā' al-Dawla Semnāni, conducted the conversion ritual. One of his first acts to establish his Islamic credentials was to donate a substantial house to the descendants of 'Ali (*dār al-siyāda*).[50] Ghāzān Khan's brother and successor, Üljeitü (1303–1316) went further and converted to Shi'ism, striking coins in the names of the twelve Imams. But he also did not neglect to have his Sunni vizier declare him the renewer (*mojadded*), that is said to appear in each century. Thus, as the century of confessional ambiguity began, Sufism, Shi'ism, and Sunni orthodoxy—the most prominent of the confessional identities, were all appropriated by the Il-Khanids, the new kings of Islam, as a Persianate dynasty.

Anatolia was the one region in which the caliph al-Nāser's reforms of the *fotowwa* organization had considerable long-term effect. One of the terms mentioned by Shaykh 'Omar Sohravardi for the members of the *fotowwa* (alongside comrade) is *akhi* (brother), which already had currency among the Sufis and gained currency in Iran and Anatolia. The presence of Akhis (from *akhi*s, lit., "brothers") in Anatolia was widespread, and they built convents (*khāneqāh*s) for warfare (*ghazā*), were deeply penetrated by Shi'itized Sufism, and some fought with wooden swords. Sohravardi's prohibition of carrying arms gave way in the frontier conditions of Anatolia.[51] Accordingly, the leadership of the confraternity could be divided between the shaykh who initiated its men into Sufism by investing them with a cloak, and the Akhis, who initiated them to *'ayyāri*[52] by tying a belt. The Akhis took part in the Ottoman conquest of Bursa in the eighth/fourteenth century, but Soltān Mehmed the Conqueror then began to limit their activities, confiscated some of their endowments, and seized many of their *khānaqāh*s.[53]

3   The Estate System of the Turko-Mongolian Empires and the Subversive Symbolic Repertoire of the Persian Subject Estate

The challenge to royal authority by the dervishes and the urban confraternities was evident in the ceremonial crowns (singular, *tāj*) they wore and their

---

50   Pfeiffer 2014.
51   The *Fotowwat-nāma* of Najm al-Din Zarkub (d. 1313) accordingly divides the confraternities into three types: those whose initiation is verbal (*qawli*), or by drinking (*shorbi*) salt water, or by the sword (*sayfi*).
52   For a discussion of the terms *'ayyār* and *'ayyāri* in connection with the Akhi confraternities, see Arjomand 2020.
53   Arjomand 2004; Yildirim 2015.

leaders' assumption of the title *shāh* and *amir*. The reaction provoked by the upward mobility of the Sufi masters into the ranks of the spiritual elite of the post-Mongol Turko-Mongolian world was the tremendous growth of Shi'itized Sufism of antinomian dervish groups, or God's unruly friends, as Karamustafa calls them. The Qalandars, Haydaris, Malamatis, and Abdāl of Rum, turned Sufi world renunciation into a rejection of society, or "renunciation of society through outrageous social deviance,"[54] and the detachment of the solitary ascetic into the deviant individualism of the spiritual master as the *müfred* (detached individual virtuoso).[55] Above all, they professed their ecstatic love of 'Ali as *shah-e mardān* (king of men). Sa'di's second stratum of the realm, the Sufi elite, became the target of the socio-political criticism of these antinomian Sufis by the ninth/fifteenth century. Kaygusuz Abdal called them deceitful and hypocritical Sufis and "idolaters of haughtiness."[56]

The carnivalesque travesty by Persian/Tajik urban groups of the notions and images of Iranian kingship turned into an idiom of popular protest against the sultanate of the Turko-Mongolian nomadic empires. With the Seljuq and the Il-Khanids, who flourished from the fifth/eleventh to eighth/fourteenth centuries, the *soltān*s who assumed the title of *shāhanshāh* were Turks, or Turanians—Iran's archenemies in the *Epic of Kings*. So the *fotowwa* confraternities became Persian underground kingdoms of the real or metaphorical prince (*shāhzāda*) cum leader of the Sufi Path (*tariqat*) and chivalry (*fotowwat/ javānmardi*), like our Shāh-e Shojā' of Kerman, or the more famous illiterate, fifth-/eleventh-century butcher and Sufi of Āmol, Abu'l-'Abbās Ahmed b. Mohammad al-Qassāb, nicknamed the Javānmard-e Qassāb.[57]

In this chapter, I have tried to show the blending of the two distinctive features of Persianate Islam in the formative period. In addition to the professional ethics just surveyed, this picture must be completed by turning to the popular epic stories of the underworld of the *'ayyāran* and the *fotowwat* associations. We have mentioned the close association between the early Sufi masters and the guilds. Popular stories that were committed to writing between the sixth/twelfth and eighth/fourteenth centuries contain much earlier material that was orally transmitted. The most important work in this genre is the voluminous *Samak-e 'Ayyār*. Samak is the head of the confraternity of *javānmārdān*, and consists of him and his brethren (*barādarān*), with whom he has made a sworn

---

54   Karamustafa 2014: 332.
55   Karamustafa 1994: 13, 76; Yildirim 2013: 69; Bashir 2014.
56   Karamustafa 2014: 336.
57   Hojviri 2004: 246–247, *773.

contract (*'ahd-e javānmārdān*). Oaths are taken to *yazdān-e dādār kerdgār* (the just God of creation) in ceremonies where cups called *qadah-e javānmārdān* are used to make a toast "To happiness (*shādi*)." Samak's liege is Khorshid Shah, the Sun King, whose marriage to Mah Pari, the fairy moon, causes cosmic celebration. Khorshid Shah's vizier is called Mehrān, one of the seven families of the Sassanian elite who were in fact Parthians. Samak's confraternity, I submit, is the model for the *darvish* and Akhi confraternities that ruled in the so-called "republics" of the Sarbedars in Khorasan and Ankara in the eighth/fourteenth century.[58] To understand the symbolic travesty of the urban *fotowwat* confraternities and their concurrent and subsequent messianic resistance and rebellion of the Persian/Tajik subjects against the Turko-Mongolian ruling estate after the Mongol conquest of Iran, we should remember that the ruling and the subject estates were socially segregated and did not intermarry, making them (technically speaking) castes, and that the Turko-Mongolian ruling estate was subject to the Yasa, or Law of Chinggis Khan, which was applied by a special administrative court (*divān-e yārghu*) until 1408, when the Timurid Shāhrokh abolished it, at least in theory.[59]

The royal symbols and appellations in what I call these "underground kingdoms"[60] were not sufficiently strong motives for revolutionary action, rather they required reinforcement from the apocalyptic Shi'ite messianism that became readily available in the age of confessional ambiguity. The combination of Sufi symbols and Shi'i messianism provided sufficient motivation for the urban population to take revolutionary action against nomadic Turko-Mongolian domination.

The Turko-Mongolian domination of the subject Persian/Tajik class continued unabated through the ninth/fifteenth century. The world conqueror Timur (d. 1405) conquered Iran and India in the 1380s and 1390s and defeated Yıldırım Bāyezid I in the Battle of Ankara in 1402. By 1370, Timur had become the khan of the Ulus Chaghatay, the tribal polity of Chinggis Khan's second son. In the decade prior to his ascent, he changed the tribal leaders from allies to subjects and transformed the Ulus from a tribal coalition to an army of conquest.[61] The Turko-Mongolian empires had an endemic instability because the rules of nomadic patrimonialism for the division of conquered lands and peoples, which inevitably resulted in wars of succession, remained in place.

---

58 See chapter 3.
59 By 1426, according to Kadi Sā'en al-Din, the *yārghu* type of judiciary inquiry was only made in secret. (Binbaş 2013: 414)
60 See Arjomand forthcoming.
61 Manz 1989: 57–85.

Joseph Fletcher calls this contentious succession struggle *tanistry*, making an analogy with Celtic practices.⁶² After the conquests and establishment of his empire, however, Timur's tribal armies gradually lost some of their importance to locally recruited troops under the command of his sons and companions (*nökers*), while Timur made a descendant of Chinggis Khan a *pādshāh-e eslām* (a nominal puppet king) until the latter died in 1402. With his death in 1405, Timur's empire disintegrated, in accordance with the nomadic patrimonial succession rules for the division of the conqueror's empire among his sons. The disintegration of Timur's empire into a growing number of Timurid principalities ruled by his sons and grandsons allowed the remarkable rebound of the Ottomans and their westward conquest of Byzantium and the rise of rival Turko-Mongolian nomadic empires of the Qara Qoyunlu and Āq Qoyunlu in western Iran, Iraq, and eastern Anatolia. In all of these nomadic empires, however, Persian remained the official court language and the Persianate ideal of kingship prevailed. The political culture of the polycentric Timurid empire was deeply tinged by Sufism as the dominant Persianate form of Islam spread throughout the Persianate world with the free movement of its bearers, namely the bureaucratic estate of *divān monshi* (chancery secretaries), from one court to another.

We examine this migration across the kingdoms and empires with regard to the Sunni exiles of the Safavid revolution to the Ottoman and Uzbek empires; what made it possible was the cultural unity of the Persianate world before and after that revolution. Soltān Mehmed II relied on Persian secretaries to build the Ottoman empire after the conquest of Constantinople, and his son, Bāyezid II continued the trend while also inviting Sufi masters from Iran. One of the most important of his court officials, Mu'ayyedzāda 'Abd al-Rahmān Efendi, was educated in Shiraz, and became the patron of Iranian *monshi* émigrés in Bāyezid's court; these *monshi* included his schoolmate, Hakim Shāh Mohammad Qazvini who promoted their reputation in his *Majāles al-Nafā'es* (Assemblies of the precious). The migration of the bureaucratic class continued under Selim I and Suleymān the Lawgiver (1520–1566),⁶³ and as we see in the chapters that follow, these émigré chancery scribes brought the late Timurid Persianate political culture with them. After the Ottoman-Safavid rift in the late tenth/sixteenth and eleventh/seventeenth centuries, the strengthening of the political and intellectual ties between the Safavids and the kingdoms of the Deccan and the Mughal empire went hand in hand; the migration trend of Iranian secretaries and poets then turned eastward, and India became

---

62 Fletcher 1979–80.
63 Markiewicz 2019: 67–91, 187, 236.

the primary destination of the poets and scribes who left Iran after the chaos following the collapse of the Safavid empire in 1722.

The formation of Persianate Islam surveyed in this chapter is remarkable for the absence of apocalyptic messianism, which was the hallmark of the Abbasid and Fatimid revolutions in the preceding centuries.[64] This cannot be accidental. Neither the rise of Persianate monarchy that paradoxically culminated in the Turko-Mongolian Il-Khans, nor the development of the inner-worldly Persianate Sufism in Khorasan that translocated to Anatolia were conducive as motivators of revolutionary social action. The Imami Shi'a who played a minor role in Iran's conversion to Islam had sublimated their messianic impulse with the doctrine of the Great Occultation of the Mahdi as the Hidden Imam, and were known for their political pragmatism. In this sense, the transformation of post-great resurrection revolutionary Isma'ili Shi'ism into inner-worldly Sufi mysticism in the early decades of the seventh/thirteenth century is significant for setting a trend that was inhospitable to revolution for another century. As we shall see, the conditions of the Persianate world under Turko-Mongolian domination changed in the following centuries, making it highly receptive to apocalyptic Shi'ite millennialism and its Mahdist myth.

---

64 Arjomand 2022.

CHAPTER 3

Sufism and Shiʿite Millennialism in the Il-Khanid and Timurid Empires

As Sufism was exported from Khorasan westward with Sufis escaping the invading Mongols, it entered a region of the Persianate world with very different political conditions from its native land of Seljuq and Khʷarazmshadid Khorasan. In the domains of the Seljuqs of Rum and its vassal principalities, it was "politically-conditioned" differently, or to be more precise, it was politicized and militarized. Popular Sufism was not the only export from Khorasan to Anatolia; it came alongside a tradition of expansionist frontier militarism that was already suitably acclimatized for Anatolia.

Already in the sixth/twelfth century and before the Seljuqs, we find rulers of principalities, such as the Dāneshmands, along the Byzantine frontier (*uj*). They were engaged in raids (*ghazā*) against the infidels on the frontiers of Islam, as reported in the *Dāneshmand-nāma*, and were referred to in popular legends of heroes/raiders such as Sayyed Battāl. Eastern Khorasan and Transoxiana was an earlier site of frontier *ghazā*, from where Islam expanded into Central Asia and northern India. The Seljuqs of Rum had loosely organized the frontier areas, appointing a "frontier commander" (*amir-e uj*) for each region. Immigrant scholars from Samarqand and Khorasan brought ethico-legal literature on *ghazā* dating back to the fourth/tenth century from the eastern to the western frontier of Persianate Islam. Anatolian raiders recruited wandering dervish groups as well as Turkman tribesmen, leading to the emergence of *ghazā* lore blended with popular Sufism. Meanwhile, the tremendous expansion of popular Sufism in the Turko-Mongolian era changed the social function of Sufi orders, resulting in the political prominence of Sufi shaykhs as leaders of popular movements among the subject, sedentary population.

The disintegration of the Il-Khanid empire in 1335 offered unprecedented political opportunities to shaykhs, who became the virtually uncontested spiritual elite of the Muslim community. The highly changeable and decentralized Turko-Mongolian nomadic successor polities induced some, though not all, of the leading shaykhs to compete with antinomian dervishes by drawing on Shiʿite beliefs in the coming of the Mahdi, the veneration of ʿAli and his descendants, and in esoteric and cabalistic wisdom; this gave popular Sufi movements a distinctly millennial inflection. Millennialism is a well-known expression of popular opposition to alien rule. Under these political conditions, this worldly political orientation transformed their world-rejecting outlook and gave popular Sufi movements a novel and distinctly millennial inflection. Thus, in the ninth/fifteenth century, we have a larger number of Sufi movements that are emphatically millennial, though their militancy may have been episodic and the relative weight of Sufi and Shiʿite influences may have varied in their mix.

1   Sufism and Frontier Millennialism in Turko-Mongolian Anatolia

Meanwhile, the intensive Islamicization of Anatolia resulted in the spread and consolidation of two fundamental elements of Persianate Islam: the spread of Sufism from below and the imposition of Persianate monarchy, statecraft, and political ethics from above. Persianate Sufism came to Anatolia as Transoxiana and Khorasan were overrun by the Mongols, and the Seljuqs of Rum gave refuge to Sufi masters, such as Najm al-Din Rāzi, and the antinomian Qalandar and Haydari dervishes in great numbers. The Turkman tribesmen who had settled in Anatolia since the ouster of the Byzantines by the Seljuqs in the 1070s were now joined by an influx of Turkman cousins. Around 1239–1242, while Mawlānā Jalāl al-Din Rumi was settling in Konya, the antinomian dervish, Bābā Eshāq, called Bābā Rasul Allāh by his followers who wore red caps, led a massive rebellion of Turkman tribesmen who had been displaced from Khʷarazm. The Turkmen followers of Bābā Rasul, the Bābāʾis, wore red caps (the prototype of the headgear of the Kizilbash/Qezelbash [red head]), black robes, and sandals. After the suppression of the Bābāʾi rebellion, in 1243 the Seljuq sultanate of Rum became a Mongol vassal state. To the Khʷarazmi Turks who had fled Chinggis Khan in the 1220s were joined by the nomadic Turkmen crowded out by the Il-Khanid occupation of the pastures in Azerbaijan.

After its invasion by the Mamluk Malek al-Zāher Baybars and the widespread retaliatory massacre ordered by the Il-Khan Abāqā in 1277, Anatolia was annexed and incorporated into the Il-Khanate. As the Seljuq vassal state collapsed after the execution (*yārghu*) of Moʿin al-Din Parvāna for complicity with Baybars, a number of rebellions took place in Anatolia, the most serious of which was that of the Turkmen of Qarāmān and Mantasha who captured the Seljuq capital Konya under the leadership of a dervish who pretended to be a Seljuq prince. The dervish proclaimed, "O, disciples, I am the Soltān of Rum!" (*keh man soltān-e Rumam ay moridān!*), and sent out a *fathnāma* (victory letter) claiming to be the avenger of the blood of Hosayn against the Yazids of the time.[1] He occupied the government building, appointed the

---

[1] For this and all other source citations in this section, see Arjomand 2016.

Qarāmān Mohammad Beg as his vizier, replaced Persian with Turkish as the official language of the state, and ascended the Seljuq throne upon the surrender of the citadel in May 1278. The royal drums were sounded five times and he availed himself of 'Alā' al-Din Key-Qobād's parasol (*chatr*) and other royal insignia.

The pretender was called, most probably by his detractors, the "beggar sultan" (*soltān-e jemri* [or *jomri*]).[2] The Mongol army first quelled a different Turkman rebellion in nearby Āqsarāy by sacking the city, and was proceeding to do likewise in Konya. The vizier Sāheb Fakhr al-Din persuaded the commanding Mongol prince to spare the capital, pledging that he and the Seljuq Sultan would retake it themselves. A recently published anonymous chronicle shows that the Konya patricians then repelled the Turkmen under the leadership of Akhi Ahmed Shah, who dominated the city's politics until his death in 1294. The tumult horrified Mawlānā's son and successor, Soltān Valad, a leading patrician of Konya with close ties not only with the Akhis of his own city but also with the chief Akhi of Sivas, Akhi Mohammad Divāna. The army gathered by the Seljuq Sultan and vizier then confronted the *soltān-e jemri* (the "beggar sultan"), killed "the entirety of his followers" (*jam'-e morid*), captured and flayed him, and paraded his stuffed skin on a donkey in the cities of Anatolia. According to Āqsarā'i, the Jemri rebellion (as it was known) was sustained by a coalition of Turkman tribes from the frontier province (*velāyat-e uj*), whose base was in the western frontier province, and whose undoing in 1278 was the work of the Germiyān (Kermani or Kurdish) tribesmen. In spite of the suppression of this rebellion, disorder and banditry persisted after Jemri's defeat.

The consolidation of Persianate monarchy in Anatolia was, paradoxically, the work of the Mongol Il-Khanids. After the Turkman tribal rebellion of Jemri, the beggar *soltān*, Arghun who became the Il-Khanid in 1284, sent his son, Geykhātu, to Anatolia for training in governance. The prince arrived in 1285 and remained in Anatolia, where he was formally appointed governor in 1290, shortly before ascending the Il-Khanid throne. Meanwhile, the Persianization of administrations in the Seljuq dominions continued on par with that of the Il-Khanid empire, as shown especially by the large number of Persian immigrants serving as *qādis* in core cities. The Qarāmān, Germiyān and other frontier Turkmen were not subdued, however, and rebelled again in 1292, forcing Geykhātu to return to Anatolia, now as the Il-Khan. After quelling their rebellion, Geykhātu sought to alter the Il-Khanid administration of Anatolia by

---

2 *Jemri* (also vocalized as *jomri* and *jamri*) is, interestingly, a Transoxanian word for beggar. Its more general use in Persian is always in the plural, *ajāmer*, meaning riff-raff. (Dehkhodā 1959–74, 5:7854)

appointing (on the Chinese model) two officials for each post. This measure proved centrifugal and disintegrative, however, producing misgovernment and the debasement of coinage.³

The rebellions of acculturated sons of Mongol generals (with Persian given names) who sought greater autonomy also made trouble for the Il-Khanids. Nevertheless, the frontier areas were somewhat more integrated into the empire through increasing penetration by its Persianate administration.⁴ Amir Chobān, the Il-Khanid general who had been sent to quell the Turkmen unrest in 1314, became the empire's de facto ruler as regent to Soltān Abu Saʿid (r. 1316–1335) who ascended the throne at the age of ten. Amir Chobān's descendants remained Il-Khanid governors of the region and made Kastameno their capital. Amir Chobān's son Timurtāsh, who rebelled against the Il-Khan in 1321, was defeated by his father and punished, then rebelled yet again in 1323. Along the lines of the conception of ancient Persian kingship of his officials, he claimed to be the *Khosrow-e ʿādel* (just emperor), and also called himself the *shah-e eslām* (king of Islam), following the first two Muslim Il-Khanid rulers. Above all, he sought to appropriate the Sufi millennial expectancy by claiming to be the Mahdi.⁵

We dwell on the nature of his claim to Mahdihood and the social base of his rebellion, as examined recently by Jonathan Brack. As Brack shows in his careful scrutiny of the available historical evidence, the social support for the Timurtāsh rebellion came from the Persianate notables of the cities of Tuqāt, Niğde and Kayseri; it was led by those who had retained their positions from the time of the Seljuqs of Rum, and headed by a kadi from Kayseri who was perhaps the chief kadi of Anatolia, Mawlānā Najm al-Din Tashi. The historian-bureaucrat Āqsarāʾi was another typical urban notable who supported the Timurid prince; he advised Timurtāsh on his anti-Turkman policies and urged him to strengthen the Anatolian cities and repel the "filth" of the nomadic Turkmen. Indeed he considered Timurtāsh's measures "among the signs of the manifestation of the Mahdi!" The best account of Timurtāsh's self proclamation as the Mahdi, however, comes from a purported eyewitness to his entry at the head of his army into Konya in 1323. According to this witness, the young

---

3   Darling 2004; Arjomand 2016c: 6–7.
4   We have manuals for secretaries written in Persian at the end of the seventh/thirteenth century, recopied in early eighth/fourteenth century by their successors, the Jāndārlu, who surrendered their principality with its Persianate administration to the first Ottomans. (Darling 2004: 137)
5   Darling 2004: 136; Brack 2019: 614.

Chobānid prince proclaimed his mission (*da'wa*): "I am the *sāheb-qerān* (Lord of the Auspicious Conjunction); indeed I am the Mahdi of the End of Time!"[6]

Timurtāsh was defeated and executed; thus, this first attempt at the preemption of Mahdihood is not historically significant, but it foreshadows similar preemptive attempts by Timurid and Ottoman princes in the ninth/fifteenth century. For now we must note the sharp contrast between the Persianate urban elite social base of Timurtāsh's rebellion and the nomadic Turkman base of the dervish-led Bābā'i rebellion in 1240.

Meanwhile, the Persianate model of kingship was undergoing consequential change under the paradoxical impact of Sufi world renunciation. As we have seen in chapter 2, Najm al-Din Rāzi, who had moved from Khorasan to Anatolia, was the first to reflect the substantial impact of world-renunciation on the conception of kingship, an influence that involved treating kings as real Sufi disciples. Rāzi accordingly entitled his chapter on the manner of kings, "*soluk*" (spiritual wayfaring); likewise he addressed his work to all classes in society for which the king's wayfaring provides the model. This produces a distinctively Sufi conception of kingship and society. According to this conception of Sufi society, the various classes perform their specialized functions to assure the cultivation of the seed of spirituality and knowledge; each class needs the others to perform its functions: "Finally, a just and politic king (*pādshāh*) is needed to maintain equilibrium among the people and to repel evil and prevent the oppression of the weak from the strong and to preserve and protect the subjects …"[7]

Rāzi's mirror for the wayfaring of kings also introduced a Sufi element in relation to the impermanence of temporal power. The dismissal of earthly kingship implied by world-renunciation is echoed a century and a half later by the Sufi man of letters, Ahmedi, in his *Eskandarnāma*, which was completed in 1390 to celebrate the spirit of *ghazā*. In a later section appended on the history of the early Ottomans, we read that

> The world is no place to be valued   Its faithlessness is no hidden thing.
> All those who have been caliph   Have died by one another's swords!
> … The Sultanate is transitory   Taking pride in it is the work of Satan.[8]

---

6 Brack 2019: 614–618, 621 n. 52, 624.
7 Rāzi 1973a: 112.
8 Cited in Sawyer 1996: 146.

We have mentioned the challenge to royal authority by the dervishes and the urban confraternities who called their leaders *shāh* and *soltān*. The nemesis of the upward mobility of Sufi masters into the ranks of the spiritual elite of the post-Mongol Turko-Mongolian world was the tremendous growth of antinomian dervish groups, or God's unruly friends,[9] who professed their ecstatic love of 'Ali as the "king of men" (*shāh-e mardān*). Antinomian Sufism was thus increasingly Shi'itized.

After 1336, as the Il-Khanid empire disintegrated, the Akhi associations established a de facto "Akhi republic" under the Akhi Mu'azzam Sharaf al-Din (d. 1350); this lasted until 1361 when they handed Ankara over to Murād I, the first contemporarily attested Ottoman *ghāzi*. Murād's father, Orkhān, had built a *khāneqāh* for dervishes in Bursa in 1324 (the first year of his reign), and used the services of his Persian scribes who had drawn up its deed of endowment to set up schools and dervish *khāneqāh*s elsewhere in his realm.[10] The Akhis continued to enjoy the early Ottomans' favor: one Akhi named Ya'qub built a mosque in Ankara in 1391, while Hājji Bayrām Vali (d. 1430) established his own Sufi order, and the Akhi Bābās, who were descendants of Hājji Bektāsh's friend and patron of the tanners, Akhi Evrān, acted as representatives of all guilds under the Ottomans.

Better documented than the above-mentioned Ankara "Akhi republic" is the history of the so-called "Sarbedār republic" (1338–1381) which emerged in Sabzavar in eastern Khorasan in the aftermath of the disintegration of the Il-Khanid empire. The Akhi *fotowwat* artisans of Sabzavar participated in government with patricians and local amirs, and briefly became actual rulers between 1346 and 1362. The local amirs twice coopted the shaykhs of a local Shi'ite dervish order to be partners in the government. This order was founded by Shaykh Hasan Juri, which had been recruiting a militia in Khorasan for the advent of the Mahdi. But ultimately the amirs murdered the shaykhs and reverted to autocratic rule, once after three years in 1343, and the second time after a year in 1363. Another dervish leader gained control of Sabzavar for two years between 1377 and 1379, but he could not rule without the help of a young mercenary amir from the neighboring region of Māzandarān, and was finally defeated by the ousted autocrat, Amir Mo'ayyad.[11]

---

9   See chapter 2.
10 Darling 2004: 141.
11 There was also the much less known case of Akhijuq (Little Akhi), who ruled for a year (1358–1359) in Tabriz. (Arjomand 2004: 244)

2 The Horufi Urban Movement and Its Struggle against Turko-Mongolian Domination

Millennialism is a well-known expression of popular opposition to oppressive alien rule. The built-in instability of Turko-Mongolian nomadic polities offered Sufi shaykhs great political opportunities for oppositional mobilization and induced many of them to draw on Shi'ite, esoteric, and cabbalistic wisdom. Such political opportunities were frequent in the Timurid Empire during prolonged crises of succession and with the rise of the rival Qara Qoyunlu nomadic empire in the west. This-worldly political reorientation transformed their world-rejecting outlook, giving popular Sufism a distinctly millennial inflection. Thus we have a large number of Sufi movements coming under the sway of Shi'ite millenarianism, beginning with the Juriyya order that became a coalition partner with the notables and *fotowwat* leaders of the city of Sabzavar as part of the Sarbedār movement in Khorasan, as I have examined elsewhere.[12] In this chapter we examine other outbreaks of millennialism: the Horufi movement, founded by Sayyed Fazlallāh of Astarabad (d. 1394) in Timurid Iran; the rebellion of Kadi Bedreddin (i.e., Kadioğlu = son of the Kadi) of Samawna in Ottoman Rumelia (d. 1416); and lastly the Sufi/Shi'ite Mahdism of Sayyed Mohammad Nurbakhsh in the second quarter of the eighth/fourteenth century. I analyze the political conditioning of these movements as key to the switch from inner-worldly Sufi mysticism to this-worldly millenarian militance.

The Horufi movement was one of the most important Sufi millennial movements to emerge in this milieu of confessional ambiguity after the disintegration of the Il-Khanid Empire. Its leader, Fazlallāh Astarābādi, was the son of the kadi of Astarabad who informally inherited his deceased father's office but renounced the world before he was twenty and joined the Qalandars, wandering from Mecca to Kh^warazm. At the beginning of his peregrinations he spent a formative period in revolutionary Sabzavar, the capital of the Sarbedār republic, whose nominal head from 1347 to 1353 was the Sufi Shaykh Hasan Juri, the founder of a local dervish order. Fazlallāh joined the order and became Shaykh Hasan's disciple around or after 1358 but before the Juriyya dervishes, led first by a certain Darvish 'Aziz (d. 1362–1363),[13] came back to power. We are told of a steed caparisoned at the gates of the city, ready for the coming Mahdi. Around this time, Fazlallāh was accompanied by a fellow exile, Amir 'Ali Dāmghāni

---

12   Arjomand 1984: 69–71.
13   The Juriyya came back to power for the third and last time under the darvish Rokn-al-Din (d. 1380–1381).

(son of the Sarbedār Pahlavān Hasan) while Soltān Ovays (r. 1356–1374) was at the Jalayerid court in Tabriz.[14]

Around 1361–1362, Fazlallāh was in Isfahan, where, by interpreting the mystical apocalyptic dream of Sayyed ʿAli (later called ʿAli al-Aʿlā, d. 1419), he recruited the young notable into his Sufi order (*tariqat*). ʿAli al-Aʿlā then became his most important disciple and future successor. In 1374, Fazlallāh applied the science of letters he had developed along with his dream interpretation to the interpretation of the Qurʾān and the "mysteries of the foundation of the sharia," and considered it revelation. Thus he developed his esoteric cosmogony into the "divine (*elāhi*) science" of the Horufis.[15] In the same year, after three days of ecstasy, Fazlallāh heard a voice referring to him as "*sāheb al-zamān* (Lord of time), the *soltān* of all prophets, one who was able to attain faith by clear revelation (*kashf o ʿeyān*), not by imitation and learning as others do."[16] He retired into seclusion in Isfahan, apparently reluctant to make his revelation public. It was only in 1376, in response to pressure from his followers, that he made public his proclamations, and beginning with the *Jāvdān-nāma* (Book of eternity), he formed the Horufi sect. Many of the numerous followers he had gained during his extensive peregrinations became his missionaries and spread widely throughout the Persianate world.

The core of Fazlallāh's teachings was his exegesis of the Qurʾān, which he did by giving numerical values to the letters of the alphabet (*horuf*). This method was widely practiced and known as the science of letters (*ʿilm al-horuf*); on account of this his followers were called the Horufiyya. Fazlallāh was accordingly called *sāheb-e taʾwil* (master of exegesis). He was also a master of dream interpretation; his dreams were an integral basis of his teaching, as were the dreams of some of his disciples. One disciple dreamt of him as the *sāheb-qerān* (Lord of the Auspicious Conjunction). The Horufi doctrine accorded him an even higher status and clearly implied his divinity.[17] According to that doctrine, however, all humanity could partake in divinity through gnosis, or more precisely, the knowledge of the esoteric meaning of words. As Zarrinkub aptly observed, Fazlallāh Astarābādi claimed to inaugurate a new and final age in the history of humanity, the age of divinity (*oluhiyyat*) that completed the revelations of the preceding ages of prophecy (*nobovvat*) and sainthood (*velāyat*).[18]

---

14   Āzhang 1990: 11–12; Bashir 2005: 12–14.
15   Arslan, 2022.
16   Cited in Arjomand 1984: 72.
17   Bashir 2005: 31, 81.
18   Zarrinkub 1983: 57.

Fazlallāh saw his new religion as destined for universality and sent his closest disciples as missionaries to various regions of the Persianate world. ʿAli al-Aʿlāʾ was charged with the westward mission in Syria and Anatolia. He traveled to Syria in person a decade or so after his master's death, taking the latter's books and some of his own, then proceeded to Anatolia and Rumelia. In Syria, he recruited the foremost Horufi poet, ʿEmād al-Din Nesimi (d. 1417), to take over the Syrian mission.

The conversion of a ruler is no small boon to a missionary religion; we have seen Fazlallāh in Tabriz at the court of the Soltān Ovays whom he sought to convert. When Ovays died and Tabriz was overrun (probably in 1376) by a temporary ally of the Sarbedārs, the Mozaffarid Shah Shojāʿ, Fazlallāh dedicated a book to him and tried to win him over. Last but not least, he tried to convert Timur. He then turned to Timur's son, Mirānshāh (Amirānshāh, d. 1408) who appears to have shown some interest in his mission, but ultimately changed his mind and ordered the Horufi leader's execution. Fazlallāh's successor, ʿAli al-Aʿlāʾ, seems to have had better luck with the heterodox Qara Qoyunlu ruler of Iraq, Qara Yusof (r. 1405–1420) who ousted the Jalayerids. ʿAli al-Aʿlāʾ was delighted when Qara Yusof fought and defeated Mirānshāh who fell in battle in 1408.[19]

Fazlallāh's dreams presciently oscillated between apocalyptic triumph and cataclysmic martyrdom. According to a Horufi text that is difficult to date, it was probably in the last years of Fazlallāh's life (in 1390 or 1391) that, after his dream premonition of his being killed, a dying dervish in a hermit's cave announced to him the advent of the revelation of divine glory (*zohur-e kebriyāʾi*). The seven eyewitnesses led by ʿAli al-Aʿlāʾ seemed to have agreed that this pronouncement meant they should prepare for the second coming of Fazlallāh as Jesus.[20] Be that as it may, his foreboding dream was realized in 1394 when Timur ordered Mirānshāh (who in turn ordered his vassal, Shervānshāh) to execute him. On the eve of his execution, he inserted himself into the Shiʿite theodicy of suffering by calling himself the Hosayn of his age: "The Hosayn of the age am I, and each worthless foe a Shimr and a Yazid. / My life is a day of mourning, and Shervān is my Karbala."[21] He then bid farewell to his disciples and told them he had no worries concerning religion (*din*); they should record and spread his teaching as "this is a new ordinance (*āʾin*)."[22]

---

19 Arslan 2022.
20 I follow Arslan in this dating against the earlier one that has been more generally accepted.
21 Cited in Arjomand 1984: 73.
22 Cited in Āzhang 1990: 25.

The new religion Fazlallāh declared was believed to surpass Islam as the truly universal religion of Adam. Its new book, the *Jāvdān-nāma* (Book of eternity), written in the Astarabadi dialect of Persian, was to supersede the Qur'ān, the main source of his gnostic exegesis, and the Torah, the New Testament (according to John, and the apocalypse of John) on which he also commented. The new religion was indeed the religion of Adam, the initiator of the major cycle of prophecy to whom God had "taught all the names" in pre-eternity (Q. 2:31) and whose body was the locus of the manifestation of divine word. In this prophetic cycle, an epicycle of "motherly" (*ommiyun*) prophets began with Jesus who, in his second coming was believed to be the Mahdi, and ended with Mohammad who completed the "descent" (*tanzil*) of the revealed word and began its "return to origin/interpretation (*ta'wil*)"; this was to be completed by Fazlallāh (lit., "bounty of God"). This Persianate gnostic reading of salvation history was numerological/letteristic in the sense that Mohammad's revelation was expressed in the 28 letters of the Arabic alphabet; it was completed by Fazlallāh with the 32 letters of the Persian alphabet as a numerical analogue to "the thirty-two perfect, pre-eternal and post-eternal words."[23] This final realization of the world meant the "return to the origin (*ta'wil*)" and the recovery of the religion of Adam:

> When the Black Stone [of the Ka'ba], [representing] the original nature of Adam and Eve, is opened by the divine line of balance, the science of 32 "words" without beginning and without end will be manifest, as well as the secret of "Am I not your Lord?" [Q. 7:172] [At this moment,] you will be able to see that all the members of your body are brought [into existence by the Word of divine command] *Be* (Q. 36:82)![24]

Fazlallāh's letterist, gnostic conception of Mahdihood in no way implies this-worldly militancy. It is compatible with the late Isma'ili idea of living with full knowledge in a post-resurrection world with no need for the law, as it was indeed interpreted by some of the Horufis after Fazlallāh's death. The Mahdi, according to the *Jāvdān-nāma*, is a form of Adam, standing for all human beings, and is numerologically identified with 'Ali as the "point under the letter *b*[*ā*], and equally with Jesus as the word of God" in Q. 3:35 and Q. 3:45: "The Mahdi will be the Word of God. [And 'Ali said] 'I am the point under the *bā*.' It is known that the 28 words and the 32 words are, in their essence, one Word."[25]

---

23 Cited in Algar 2004. See also Mir-Kasimov 2008.
24 Mir-Kasimov 2015: 380, text 439b [in the Persian text].
25 Mir-Kasimov 2015: 369, text 319b [in the Persian text].

The execution of the Horufi prophet and messiah was, however, a horrendous shock to Fazlallāh's devoted followers and as such was bound to provoke apocalyptic messianism in response. It is possible that after his failure to convert Mirānshāh, who was initially responsive, Fazlallāh contemplated advancing his mission by violent means; the probability of this speculation is strengthened by references in the Horufi texts that show clear political ambition, notably, they sought to make Fazlallāh the *sāheb-e devlet* (Lord of the turn-in-power) and make 'Ali al-A'lā' *khalifat Allāh* (God's deputy). We know for a fact that his violent death activated messianic hope based on the Mahdistic tenet, seconded by the Shi'ite theodicy of suffering and martyrdom. There may well be anachronistic aspects to the report of 'Ali al-A'lā''s declaration of Fazlallāh's imminent return as the second coming of Jesus and of the interpretation of the cave hermit's prediction as a signal of the onset of militant millennialism. 'Ali al-A'lā' relaxed the obligation to fast so as not to affect the ability of Horufis to carry weapons, such as swords and maces, and his brother died fighting Mirānshāh's army with the Qara Qoyunlu. He narrates the battles against Mirānshāh in *Qiyāmāt-nāma* (Book of rising/resurrection).

Under 'Ali al-A'lā''s leadership, Fazlallāh's shrine became a site of pilgrimage for the Horufis and the site of Fazlallāh's re-manifestation; they visited it and made circumambulations modeled on the hajj. Mirānshāh became the Dajjāl (anti-Christ) of a messianic Horufi apocalypse, while the second coming of Fazlallāh, according to the Shi'ite idea of "return" (*raj'a*) spread. The Horufi tract, *Mahram-nāma*, written three decades after the martyrdom of Fazlallāh in the year 828/1424–1425 speaks of the supremacy of the Hidden Imam, the Mahdi, and the *sāheb al-sayf* (Lord of the sword) who will appear to deliver the Horufis from tyranny and persecution.[26]

In the meantime, there was certainly tyranny and persecution. Persecutions occurred not only because of the apprehensiveness of those in power about the possible political designs of the movement, but also because the Muslim clerics, the *'olamā'*, as guardians of Islamic orthodoxy whose power was on the increase through the first half of the ninth/fifteenth century considered it a heresy, while Shāhrokh saw Horufism as a political threat. At least one injunction (*fatwā*) was issued for the execution of Fazlallāh, and a conference of *'olamā'* was probably held in which he was condemned to death.

Horufi messianic militancy went underground with the closing of political opportunities from 1421 on, when Shāhrokh's supremacy went unchallenged. On 14 February 1427, the clandestine Horufi millenarians struck as the year 830/1426–7 was calculated by 'Alī al-A'lā' as the date when Fazlallāh

---

26   Arjomand 1984: 73.

would return as the Mahdi, or more probably as Jesus.[27] Ahmad Lor, variously described as a Horufi or a follower of Fazlallāh, stabbed Shāhrokh in the congregational mosque of Herat. Shāhrokh was wounded and survived but the assailant was killed on the spot by Shāhrokh's attendants. Shāhrokh investigated and discovered the identity of the assailant and the Horufi conspiracy. According to our least biased contemporary source, Khʷāja Azod al-Din (Fazlallāh's grandson and the son of his other disciple, Majd al-Din Astarabādi) and six other Horufis, along with others who were mistaken for Horufis, were executed. Kadi Sāʾen al-Din Torka (d. 1432) who had served Shāhrokh's nephew, Eskandar Mirzā, in Shiraz, was imprisoned in a fortress and his papers were impounded.[28] Among the Horufi conspirators who were pardoned was the Baghdadi calligrapher, Maʿruf-e Khattāt, who had also served as the librarian of his fellow Horufi, Prince Eskandar Mirzā, who had vied with Shāhrokh during the crisis of succession.[29] Amir Nurallāh (ʿAli al-Aʿlā''s son, Fazlallāh's grandson through his daughter), and Sayyed Ghiyās al-Din Mohammad (ʿAlī al-Aʿlā''s nephew and the author of *Estevā-nāma*)[30] were investigated later and were eventually released because the Timurid prince, Olugh Beg, who was called *al-sultān al-faylasuf* (philosopher king) by the (ex-)Horufi Qāzizāda-ye Rumi,[31] found the Horufi doctrine of intellectual interest, and refused to carry out his father Shāhrokh's order. Instead he dispatched the detained Horufi leaders from Samarqand to other Timurid governors who eventually set them free.

It may well be that the date set for the messianic second coming was known to the Timurid government, as its investigation of the prominent Horufis began before the attempted assassination.[32] The most prominent among those investigated in the year preceding the expected second coming of Fazlallāh was the above-mentioned Sāʾen al-Din Torka, scion of a family of *qādis* from Isfahan who was being investigated for the second time in five years. Sāʾen al-Din may have known Fazlallāh in his youth, as he kept company with a close friend and fellow Horufi, Sharaf al-Din Yazdi[33] in Cairo, where they became disciples of the Sufi shaykh Sayyed Hosayn Akhlāti (d. 1397), whose blend of Sufism, letterism, and occult sciences became known as the science of the saints (*ʿelm al-awliyāʾ*). Sāʾen al-Din and Sharaf al-Din Yazdi also joined Akhlāti's circle of disciples who called themselves the Brethren of Purity (*ekhwān al-safāʾ*) after

---

27 Bashir 2005: 90–97; Binbaş 2013: 411.
28 Torka 1972: 205–206; Binbaş 2013: 402, 408–409.
29 See chapter 4.
30 Āzhang 1990: 45.
31 Şen 2017: 602. On him, see chapter 4 below.
32 Binbaş 2013: 412.
33 Torka and Yazdi are discussed extensively in chapter 4.

the third/ninth century Ismaʿili revolutionary encyclopedists, and remained active in Cairo after Akhlāti's death. Around 1400–1405, the Brethren of Purity appear to have highlighted, as the motto of their gnostic occult group, the Qurʾānic verse, Q. 57:3, "He is the first and the last, the appearance and the inner reality (*al-zāher waʾl-bāten*)."[34] To the great chagrin of his other protégé, Ibn Khaldūn, the Mamluk Sultan Barquq (r. 1382–1399) invited Akhlāti to his court from the Horufi stronghold of Azerbaijan. Akhlāki had made his own claim to Mahdihood, presumably according to his spiritual interpretation of the *axis mundi* of the age (*qotb-e zamān*). The circle of his followers in Cairo included Kadi Bedreddin of Samawna in whose rebellion against the Ottomans (considered presently), the Anatolian Horufis participated.[35]

Clandestine messianic Horufi activism continued after Ahmad Lor's failed assassination attempt against Shāhrokh. Five years later, in 1432, there was a Horufi uprising in Isfahan under the leadership of a certain Hajji Sorkha (the red hajji). It was suppressed and the Timurid governor of Isfahan ordered Hajji Sorkha to be skinned alive.[36] A decade later, at the instigation of a local cleric, Mawlānā Mohammad, and on the basis of an injunction begrudgingly issued by Mawlānā Najm al-Din Oskuʾi, the somewhat reluctant Jahānshāh Qara Qoyunlu (r. 1438–1467), who was then Shāhrokh's vassal, was prevailed upon to order a massacre in which some 500 Horufis perished. The victims included a certain Mawlānā Yusof who represented the Horufi community in Tabriz, the founder's revered daughter Kalimat al-ʿOlyāʾ (lit., [God's] highest word, also known as Qorrat al-ʿAyn, lit., delight of the eye), and Sayyed Amir Eshāq (another disciple of Fazlallāh and the author of *Mahram-nāma*).[37] The rebellion must have been planned and postponed, as one of the charges against Nurallāh in 1427 was that he had armed the Horufis in Tabriz in collaboration with Jahānshāh's predecessor, Eskandar (r. 1420–1433). Mashkur correctly treats this incident as an uprising; the Tabrizi cleric Mawlānā Mohammad must have had knowledge of clandestine Horufi activities and their planned uprising must have been something of an open secret.[38]

A few years after his trial and release, Ghiyās al-Din Mohammad wrote a highly critical letter to other Horufis; this shows their internal divisions. He is critical of messianic radicalism, implying that his own views were not messianic and more moderate politically and yet his views represented the true

---

34 Melvin-Koushki 2018: 358; Melvin-Koushki 2019.
35 Kastritsis 2012: 237; Binbaş 2016: 3–15, 104–140; Gardiner 2017: 18.
36 Āzhang 1990: 87–88.
37 Āzhang 1990: 37, 96–102.
38 Mashkur 1969.

meaning of Fazlallāh's teaching. Ghiyās al-Din Mohammad may have served in the Anatolian mission under his uncle, ʿAli al-Aʿlāʾ, after the latter returned to take up residence near the shrine of Fazlallāh in 1408. In *Estevā-nāma*, Ghiyās al-Din shared the view he attributes to the Horufis of Anatolia, a view that is remarkably similar to the gnostic ideas of the post-resurrection Ismaʿilis:

> Paradise consists in knowledge and hell in ignorance. As we become knowers/gnostics (*ʿāref*) of the 32 words and our existence, everything is paradise for us. There is no daily prayer, no fasting, and no ritual ablutions, as all these are obligations and there is no obligation (*taklif*) in paradise. Nothing is forbidden and all is permissible (*halāl*).[39]

The split among the Horufiyya in this period, as indicated by Ghiyās al-Din's letter and other evidence, is particularly important for explaining why some of them became turncoats willing to be co-opted by the Timurid rulers, as we see in the next chapter.

The last and most important issue to examine is the social and ethnic background of the Horufis. It is critically important for our thesis that messianism in this period was the ideational basis for the resistance and rebellion of the Persian/Tajik subjects against the Turko-Mongolian ruling estate. On this issue, our sources offer unusually clear evidence. They allow us to form a fairly clear picture of the social position and ethnic identity of the millenarian rebels and their leaders. Horufism was a literate urban movement and gained a widespread following above all among artisans and intellectuals in the cities of Aberbaijan, Anatolia, Iran, and Syria. Its leaders consisted of Persianate/non-Turkish urban elite. Fazlallāh and his disciples and followers that we have mentioned so far bore titles of Sayyed and/or Amir and/or Khʷāja, which shows that they were Persianate urban notables. Additional evidence for the elite Persian background of the leadership stratum of the Horufis is clear from the list of ten of Fazallāh's *khalifa*s that appears in a Horufi manuscript by a certain Ishkurt Dede. This manuscript includes four Sayyed Amirs or Khʷājas (showing that they were urban notables), and six Mawlānās or Shaykhs, indicating that they belonged to the learned elite. Ishkurt Dede claims that Fazlallāh had four hundred Sayyed followers.[40] His other known disciples and Horufi authors had similar backgrounds, though some of the latter group are identified as dervishes (which is compatible with these family backgrounds). As for the Horufi rebels, Ahmad Lor was a craftsman who made Sufi caps (*tāqiya*),

---

39 Cited in Āzhang 1990: 119.
40 See Arslan 2022.

as Fazlallāh himself reportedly did during his peregrinations after he resigned his position as a *qādi* in Astarabad; and Hajji Sorkha must have been a well to do craftsman or trader. The adepts who urged Fazlallāh to make his mission public in Isfahan were literate urbanites, and included two clerics.[41] Not a single adept is identified as a member of the Turko-Mongolian ruling estate, with the exception of the Timurid prince, Eskandar Mirzā, whose motives for joining the Horufiyya are explained in chapter 4. In short, the Horufi movement exemplifies the millennial revolt of the Persian urban subjects against the Turko-Mongolian overlords.

3 Apocalypticism and the Occult Sciences in the Uprising of Kadi Bedreddin during the Ottoman Interregnum

Fazlallāh Astarābādi's martyrdom has been alternatively placed at the beginning of Shāhrokh's reign (1405–1447) and during the prolonged succession crisis that did not end with his complete victory in 1421 or 1422.[42] This date makes sense if we take Timur's death in 1405 as the opening of political opportunities for the Horufi movement, a circumstance that was a result of the internecine succession struggle. Be that as it may, the political crisis and strife in the Ottoman Empire in the first two decades of the ninth/fifteenth century offered even greater political opportunities for a messianic uprising, and these opportunities were taken up by Kadi Bedreddin and his followers in their extensive millennial uprising again the Ottoman Sultan Mehmed I (r. 1413–1421).

According to the Chinggisid idea of universal empire, there was no room for two leaders. While Timur claimed Chinggis Khan's heritage of world conquest in the east, Ottoman power was rising fast under the "Thunderbolt" (*yıldırım*) Bāyezid I (r. 1389–1403); the clash of these two empires resulted in the defeat and capture of Bāyezid in the battle of Ankara in 1402. Timur became his suzerain and overlord of the Ottoman princes when Bāyezid died shortly afterwards. But Timur also established other local Anatolian dynasties as his vassals. Thus Ottoman rule was severely shaken and civil strife broke out between the seven sons of Bāyezid and the Ottoman princes (singular, *čelebi* [high-born]) and lasted until 1413, when Mehmed I ascended the throne and restored the integrity of the Ottoman Empire. Nevertheless, in the first three years of his reign his

---

41   Āzhang 1990: 5, 9, 14, 41–44.
42   Manz 2007: 24–35.

successor Murād II (r. 1421–1444, 1446–1451) was confronted with the rebellions of two Ottoman princes both named Mustafā, his uncle and his brother.[43]

One of the ideal types of revolution, which I call the Aristotelian-Paretan, highlights the role of leaders of dispossessed aristocracies as revolutionary counter-elites.[44] A few of the Anatolian leaders who challenged the Il-Khanids in the early eighth/fourteenth century belonged to the dispossessed Seljuq elite, and the rebel Timurtāsh, as we have seen, was backed by the offspring of the Seljuq urban notables. The major rebel of the early ninth/fifteenth century, Shaykh Bedreddin (Badr al-Din) Mahmud, was likewise related to the Seljuqs of Rum; his father was a kadi and a veteran (*ghāzi*) of the conquest of Edirne and his grandfather was a Seljuq vizier.[45] He attended school in Edirne and then went to Konya where he studied with a Horufi scholar, Fayzallāh, who is said to have studied with the Horufi prophet, Fazlallāh. His fellow student was Kadizāda Musā Čelebi, who emigrated to Samarqand upon Fayzallāh's death in 1410 or 1411 and became known as the Qāzizāda-ye Rumi; he had a brilliant career as an astronomer in the service of the Timurid Olugh Beg. Bedreddin did not remain as long in Konya, in the 1390s he left his native land to study in the Mamluk capital, Cairo.

In Cairo, Bedreddin became a disciple of the Sufi pantheist, Shaykh Hosayn Akhlāti, and was initiated into the Horufi movement in Akhlāti's *khāneqāh* at the Mamluk court. There, while seeking higher learning and spiritual guidance he met the above-mentioned Iranian Horufis. Among Akhlāti's disciples were several Horufis from Iran and the Antiochene ʿAbd al-Rahmān Bestāmi (d. 1454) who was reformulating the Horufi doctrine as part of the occult sciences. Bedreddin drew close to Shaykh Hosayn and his initiation to Sufism culminated in an overwhelming mystical experience that resulted in what we might today call a nervous breakdown. After days of seclusion with Shaykh Akhlāti, he was able to make sense of it. While in a trance, Bedreddin understood that the soul of the Prophet and that of his Shaykh were united, and the latter assured him that he, Bedreddin, also partook in this mystical union and, although externally he was his deputy (*khalifa*), in inner reality he was the deputy of God.[46] This event must have been shortly before Akhlāti's death in 1397, as Bedreddin led his circle in Cairo until he returned home in 1403, after the defeat and death of Bāyezid I during the ensuing strife over his succession among four of his sons.

---

43   Şahin 2010: 329; Kastritsis 2012.
44   Arjomand 2019: ch. 1.
45   Kastritsis 2012: 223.
46   Binbaş 2016: 128.

During the civil strife caused by the eleven-year succession struggle after Bāyezid's death, Bedreddin returned to Anatolia and traveled widely in most if not all major Anatolian cities, recruiting followers as a Sufi master. Bedreddin had been a student of Bestāmi, who was a member of the *Ekhwān al-safā'* (Brethren of Purity), and may have persuaded the latter to return to Anatolia with him in 1404 or 1405.[47] In a tract he composed there in or around 1408, Bestāmi showed a definite apocalyptic bent. He blended the *jafr* (divination) of the Shi'ite Imams, 'Ali and Ja'far al-Sādeq, with the generic *malāhem* (tribulations of the End of Time) and predictions of the invasion of Gog and Magog and the second coming of Jesus, in the company of the Mahdi, on the basis of the traditions that Muslims would take "grand Constantinople and the greater Rome (*rumiyya*)."[48] In fact, Bestāmi himself tells us that he read his short apocalyptic tract to Bedreddin. This tract bears a significant title, *The Cry of the Owl* (*sayhat al-bum*) *on the Events of Rum*, as is refers to an important sign of the apocalyptic Hour in the Qur'ān (Q. 11:76, 94; Q. 15:73, 83 and elsewhere) and accordingly makes Constantinople the site of the imminent apocalypse. Bedreddin thus received the teachings about apocalyptic messianism from Bestāmi and confirmed it in a commentary on Q. 20:105–106 as referring to

> The appearance of an essence (*dhāt*) and the spread of unity (*tawhid*) at the End of Time. Thus command (*hokm*) will belong to the single essence who has no crookedness ... Master of that Time will be the propagator of the absolute unity, and he will call people to it![49]

All this undoubtedly influenced Shaykh Bedreddin, and may have encouraged him to undertake his messianic uprising a few years later after the collapse of Musā Čelebi's rule.

---

47   Bestāmi's autobiographical remark on a visit to Chis traces the same itinerary as Bedreddin's (Kastritsis 2012: 228), including the latter's visit to Izmir and Chios where Christian priests, according to Bedreddin's grandson and hagiographer, confirmed his messianic claim as "the Second Jesus (*Masih-e thāni*)." (Binbaş 2016: 125)
48   Gril 2005: 189.
49   Gölpınarlı, as cited in Binbaş 2016: 129, translation modified. Binbaş's contentions that Bedreddin's refutation of physical resurrection was contradictory to his alleged messianism is unconvincing. In the passage he cites, Bedreddin also refutes the then current belief that the Mahdi would "bring an end to sainthood (*velāya*)." (Binbaş 2016: 130) It seems to me that Bereddin considered Mahdihood and sainthood as essentially identical. But in any case, such "refutations" as well as Bedreddin's practical legal writings point to the two-track mind of the letterist-occultist intellectuals that could serve revolution and reaction alternately.

Kadi Bedreddin's tumultuous career in the last five years of his life demonstrated that serving revolution and reaction were not mutually exclusive; on the contrary, for the intellectual elite of the Persianate world in the ninth/fifteenth century, these were alternative paths for advancement. Bedreddin took the opportunity to court the local anti-Ottoman Turkman rulers of Qarāmān, Germiyan, and Cüneyd. He was also welcomed by a thousand Turkmen who asked him to build a *khāneqāh* in Aleppo for them. Bedreddin eventually joined the faction of Bāyezid's son, Prince Musā, who appointed him the *qādi 'asker* of Rumeli in late 1410 or 1411, doubtless because of Bedreddin's growing reputation and his success in recruiting followers. Bedreddin resumed his earlier studies of Islamic jurisprudence and wrote an important manual of Hanafi law when he took up his appointment as the highest-ranking judge in Edirne. Prince Musā or Musā Čelebi (r. February 1411–July 1413) appears to have claimed the Mahdihood and was supported by the frontier raiders (*ghāzi*) against the established local leaders and Christian vassals who sided with Musā's brother Mehmed I and helped the latter win the war of succession. At this point, Bedreddin appeared poised to combine his knowledge of the apocalyptic and occult sciences with jurisprudence for the benefit of the counter-messianic Ottoman autocracy under Musā Čelebi, but destiny had another design. Musā was defeated and executed by his brother, Mehmed I, and Bedreddin was dismissed, humiliated, and banished to Iznik in 1413. Having lost his high office, he reverted to his earlier identity as Kadioğlu/Ibn Qazi of Samawna.[50]

As a demonstration of the alternative uses of millennial symbols by revolution and counter-revolution alike, we may note that 'Abd al-Wāse' Çelebi, the court poet of Mehmed I (1413–1421), repeatedly called him the Mahdi: in fact it was not Prince Musā but Sultan Mehmed who was the Mahdi; this implied that the courtiers of both Ottoman princes drew on the same repertoire of apocalyptic ideas as the revolutionary Mahdists.[51]

In considering the social basis of Bedreddin's uprising, we should not neglect the disgruntled local Tartar and Turkman begs who were partially dispossessed by the Ottoman *siphāhi* horsemen who had received land grants as part of the Ottoman *timār* system, which was well-developed by the time of Mehmed I. In addition, we must bear in mind the presence of the odd anti-Ottoman Seljuq descendants, such as the Bektashi Hajji Ilbegi, whose memory was all but erased by Ottoman historians, and supporters of the rebel Sufi Ottoman prince

---

50　Kastritsis 2012: 224–226, 230–231; Binbaş 2016: 131–132.
51　Kastritsis 2012: 237.

called the false Mustafā.⁵² As for the mass support for the rebellion, the Safavid connection should be highlighted as there is a tendency to minimize it,⁵³ and because it explains the choice of Anatolia for revolutionary mobilization by the Safavid Jonayd half a century later. Bedreddin reportedly traveled and took part in a learned discussion in Tabriz and visited the Safavid shrine in Ardabil. The Safavid order (*tariqa*) already had a flourishing branch in Tekke-eli and Hamid-eli, and we know that many of Bedreddin's followers joined it because they constituted over one-third of those in the marauding band of the Safavid Shaykh Jonayd who were killed by the governor of Aleppo in mid-ninth/ fifteenth century.⁵⁴

The Horufi support must also not be excluded. The importance of the Horufi connection to Cairo should be interpreted cautiously, given that the Cairene science of letters (*'ilm al-horuf*) was derived from the Andalusian Ibn al-'Arabi (d. 638/1240), the Maghrebi al-Buni (d. after 1225), and Abu 'Abdallāh al-Kumi (fl. 1407) and not from the Persian Sa'd al-Din Hammuya. In fact, the Horufi presence was established in Anatolia when Fazlallāh himself put 'Alī al-A'lā' in charge of the Anatolian mission and, as we have seen, 'Ali took the Horufi scripture to Rumelia, on the other side of the Black Sea. Bedreddin met Horufis, including his old master, Fayzallāh and fellow student, Kadizāda Musā, among other Sufis and dervishes during his nearly decade-long peregrinations in Anatolia.⁵⁵

Bedreddin's rebellion may well have been staged in the wrong location— that is, in Rumelia rather than in Anatolia or even further east where thousands of followers had been recruited. Among those recruited were Turkish dervishes whom the army, led by Mehmed I's twelve-year-old son Murād and his grand vizier, slaughtered on the way to Rumelia. A Frankish ship forced Shaykh Bedreddin to land on the opposite side of the Black Sea in Wallachia in 1416, and Bedreddin chose to stage his own rebellion in Dobrudja. In Wallachia, Bedreddin had support from displaced Turkman chiefs and disgruntled locals who took the oath of allegiance (*bay'a*) to him.⁵⁶ We can also assume that the old dispossessed Seljuq aristocrats like himself, and even officerholders and *ghāzi* raiders of Musā (who were destituted more recently by Mehmet I, like Bedreddin) took the oath. According to an eyewitness report, Shaykh Bedreddin thus proclaimed his uprising: "From now on government

---

52 Inalcik 1991; Kastritsis 2012: 224, 238.
53 For instance, Ocak 1989; Fleischer 2018: 57.
54 Babinger 1921: 82–83; Sohrweide 1965: 119–123; Zarrinkub 1983: 2:70–72.
55 Kastritsis 2012: 228; Gardiner 2017: 17–21; Fleischer 2018: 48–51.
56 Kastritsis 2012: 231, 234–236.

(*beglik*) and the throne is given to me. I am called *malek mahdi* (Mahdi the King) and will unfurl the banner and rise!"⁵⁷

Meanwhile, Bedreddin's agents and his followers in Rumelia who called him *dede sultān* had already started their rebellion. His missionaries in Chios and in Aydın, Bürkülje Mustafā and Turluk (lit., "naked dervish") Hu Kemāl, recruited many "poor Sufis" (*badbakht sufilar*), and began their uprising late in 1415, when Bedreddin was in Iznik. They lived in voluntary poverty, went around barefoot, and reportedly preached communal property. The first to rise up near Izmir was Bürkülje Mustafā, a "simple-minded Turkish peasant" who, according to the Byzantine historian Doukas, "sought to win the friendship of the Christians," and "taught the Turks that they must own no property and decreed that, except for women, everything must be shared in common."⁵⁸ Mustafās rebellion was separately and violently put down. As his dervish followers were beheaded in front of him, before he was crucified, they simply said "Come (*eriş*) Dede Sultan!"⁵⁹

Bedreddin's own uprising was also ruthlessly suppressed, and Mehmed I executed him based on a *fatwā* (injunction) solicited from a Persian émigré and jurist who declared that his blood could be shed lawfully and his goods confiscated.⁶⁰ In 1417, a year or so after Bedreddin's rebellion, Fazlallāh's close disciple, 'Emād al-Din Nesimi, was martyred in Aleppo, reportedly by being flayed alive.⁶¹ The date suggests his connection to Bedreddin's rebellion. The Horufi uprisings in 1444 in Edirne, roughly coinciding with the Tabriz massacre of the Horufis in the Qara Qoyunlu realm, most likely included the survivors of Shaykh Bedreddin's rebellion. By that time, however, the opportunity structure for these uprisings against Ottoman rule was much less favorable—in fact they were easily suppressed.

4   The Shi'itized Sufi Mahdism of Sayyed Mohammad Nurbakhsh

In 1423, with the close of the political opportunities of the earlier decades of Shāhrokh's rule, a rebellion arose in Central Asia. There the shaykh of the Kobravi Sufi order, Khʷāja Eshāq b. Ārāmshāh Khottalāni (who was over ninety at the time) called a young sayyed (*sayyed-zāda*) the Mahdi and some

---

57   Cited in Babinger 1921: 29.
58   Cited in Fleet 2010: 2:323.
59   Cited in Kastristis 2012: 233.
60   Babinger 1921: 30.
61   Csirkés 2015: 156.

said that he was the Hidden Imam. Kh^wāja Eshāq belonged to a noble family of Khottalān, as indicated by his title and father's name.[62] His father opposed Timur and the affair must have be seen by Shāhrokh as a local political uprising. Shāhrokh probably sent a small force to quell the uprising which was backed by Kh^wāja Eshāq's two sons, who seemed to be disloyal local notables. The rebellion was easily suppressed; some eighty Sufis perished and Kh^wāja Eshāq and his two sons were executed. The life of the young sayyed was spared, however, on the grounds that his guilt was not as great "as his Shaykh told him you are the Mahdi and made him rise."[63]

The role of the young sayyed in his early thirties who was proclaimed the Mahdi is subject to scholarly debate, but his biography and Shi'ite background suggests that he had a more active role than that depicted in the above account. The young sayyed in question is Sayyed Mohammad Nurbakhsh (d. 1464) whose father had emigrated from the Shi'ite region of Qatif and Bahrain and settled in the Isma'ili Shi'ite region of Qohestān. He claimed descent from the Seventh Imam, Musā al-Kāzem, as do the vast majority of sayyeds in Iran. Sayyed Mohammad's mother was of Turkish origin. Nurbakhsh's early education must have been in Hilla in Iraq with a leading Twelver scholar, Ahmad b. Fahd al-Hilli (d. 1437).[64] Although later in life he formulated his own conception of Mahdihood in gnostic and cosmological terms, there seems little doubt that at this stage and in the following decade, Nurbakhsh subscribed to a pristine Shi'ite messianic concept of the Mahdi.

The uprising by or on behalf of Nurbakhsh split the Kobravi order; he moved from Khottalān to Iran, and was accepted there as Kh^wāja Eshāq's successor, assuming his epithet Nurbakhsh ("light-giver"). The Central Asian branch of Kobraviyya followed the manager of the Khottalān Kobravi *khāneqāh* who rejected Nurbakhsh's claim to Mahdihood.[65] In Iran, Nurbakhsh moved from city to city as a Sufi master and acquired a considerable following. Of the disciples whom he initiated during this long peregrination, thirteen were from his native city of Qā'in, seventeen from Kurdistan and Lorestan, thirty-five

---

62   Bashir 2001: 110 [24]. Duplicate pagination of the Arabic text is given in hard brackets.
63   Arjomand 1984: 75. A politically less logical but by no means implausible alternative explanation is that Shāhrokh had a severe stomach ache which his physician attributed to his intention to kill a sayyed, a descendant of the Prophet! (Nurbakhsh 1971: 38 n. 1; Bashir 2003: 62)
64   De Weese 1988; Bashir 2003: 42, 48–54. Ebn Fahd stipulated that "the greater [inner] Jihad necessitates that there be an Imam, a *vali* (friend of God) perfect in the stage of *vilāya* (sainthood)." (Cited in Arjomand 1984: 75)
65   De Weese 1988.

from Gilan, eight from Ray and Qazwin, and several individuals from other regions.⁶⁶

It appears that for a long time Nurbakhsh was reluctant to declare his Mahdihood publicly. His followers, on the other hand, were firmly convinced that he was the expected Imam and had visions of him. It is reasonable to assume that Nurbakhsh's primary preoccupation was to guide his followers spiritually. In his writings he explicitly emphasized the importance of world renunciation in the form of poverty (*faqr*), which he practiced, as their "perfect guide" (*morshed-d kāmel*).⁶⁷ Even so, there remained the inevitability of some "politically conditioned" pressure from below in the form of Persian urban resistance to Turko-Mongolian domination and the possibility of using the absolute Mahdistic authority in worldly political action. This was especially true in view of the thirst for militant action on the part of the as-yet-unenlightened followers that Nurbakhsh certainly had. They struck coins and delivered the Friday sermon in his name in Kurdistan. Needless to say, political powers were apprehensive of such a possibility and ready to respond harshly. Shāhrokh had Nurbakhsh arrested and sent to Herat, where he was made to mount the pulpit during a Friday congregation in 1436 and repudiate all "claim to caliphate."⁶⁸ According to one account, he said: "When we earlier called ourselves the promised Mahdi based upon certain methods of dream interpretation, we intended only that we can provide guidance (*hedāya*) on the path.... Guidance and support are from God ..."⁶⁹ This disavowal is quite ambiguous, and his subsequent action did little to clear up the ambiguity; in March 1437, Nurbakhsh was arrested and imprisoned again.⁷⁰

Some five years later, Nurbakhsh made it clear that his ambiguous disclaimer did not relate to his spiritual authority. In a letter to Shāhrokh, written around 1442, Nurbakhsh arrogantly stated that it was evident to the wise that he and only he was "the Lord of the Age," and "the Imam of the Age and the expected Mahdi."⁷¹ Nurbakhsh then urged the monarch to repent for having imprisoned him three times as "the end of monarchy and the turn of the House of Mohammad has come, and [he should] do so before the approaching End

---

66 Bashir 2003: 69.
67 Nurbakhsh 1971: 151.
68 Arjomand 1984: 75.
69 Arjomand 1984: 75.
70 Bashir 2003: 59–60.
71 The printed version has "Deputy" before "Lord of the Age and "Imam"; this insertion only occurs in one of the three manuscripts used! (Nurbakhsh 1971: 75 n. 9, 76 n. 1) The insertion follows an orthodox Shi'ite formula that the editor accepted to avoid the implication of heresy.

of Time so as not to [be] ashamed in front of the Prophet in the Hereafter."[72] After Shāhrokh's death in 1447, Nurbakhsh settled in the village of Suleqān for the remaining two decades of his life.

In comparison to Fazlallāh's type of Sufism that belonged, in Zarrinkub's above-mentioned terminology, to the age or type of Sufism of divinity (*oluhiyyat*), Nurbakhsh's conception is more typical of the age of Sufi sainthood (*velāyat*). He followed his Kobravi predecessor Saʿd al-Din Hammuya's view that sainthood was the continuation of prophethood after the Seal of the Prophets, Mohammad,[73] and went further to posit that there would be 290,000 saints in the Mohammadan *umma* before the End of Time. Among these were the "perfect friends of God" (*kāmelān-e awliyāʾ*). Of the latter he considered himself the most perfect; he signed his letters and essays, "by the sanctity of the most perfect of His friends among the poles and the solitaries" (*be-hormat-e kemal-e awliyāʾ men al-aqtāb vaʾl-afrād*)![74]

Finally, in the *Resālat al-Hodā* (Essay on guidance) written after 1455, when he was over sixty, Nurbakhsh explained the nature of his claim to Mahdihood more systematically. He affirmed that the Mahdi was a descendant of Mohammad and of ʿAli and will rule this world by the final *translatio imerii* as predicted by "my ancestor, the Adam of the Saints (*Ādam al-awliyāʾ*) ʿAli ... [who] said 'to every people is a turn in power (*dawla*), and our turn in power/empire is at the End of Time.'"[75] The advent of Nurbakhsh as the Mahdi was dependent not on militant messianic action but on astrological determinism. He affirmed "Philosophers and astrologers" among the "heavenly proofs" (*al-dalālat al-samāviyya*) of his divine mission, and said these "have determined that my lifetime is eighty-eight solar years ... Thus, if God pleases, I will acquire temporal rule when I am eighty solar years of age."[76] But why and how did Nurbakhsh publicize his predetermined advent when he did? As to why, he insisted that he did so reluctantly and without the slightest worldly ambition; it is certainly true that the treatise does not discuss jihad, armed rebellion, or military conquest. He claimed to be rebelling as the incumbent duty of a Friend of God to guide his followers:

---

72   Nurbakhsh 1971: 75–77.
73   See chapter 2.
74   Nurbakhsh 1971: 77, 98, 124–125, 131. According to the Sufi doctrine of the period, the pole (*qotb*) of the universe was the perfect saint, and the solitary (*fard*) was the individual saint who had attained mystical union with God.
75   Bashir 2001: 106 [20].
76   Bashir 2001: 113–114 [27–28].

> It is incumbent on me to write what comes to my mind from the saying of my predecessors and discoveries of my contemporaries regarding the signs, characteristics, qualities and distinctions of this poor man [i.e., himself] so that whoever does not know me should know me and thereby be rescued from ignorance, as in the Prophet's saying: "whoever dies without knowing the Imam of his age, dies the death of Ignorance";[77] and so that [salvific] knowledge of those who already know me should increase. I therefore open with what my ancestor, the Master of the Messengers [of God] said: "Even if a single day is left in the world, God will lengthen it until a man from my offspring rises up (*yakhruj*); his name will be my name and his *kunya* my *kunya* and he will fill the earth with equity and justice as it is now filled with tyranny and oppression!"[78]

How Nurbakhsh publicized his Mahdihood so that his followers would be saved is less interesting from a theoretical point of view. He puts forward "rational" (*'aqli*), "traditional" (*naqli*), and most interestingly, proofs through "revelation" (*kashf*) by other friends of God who were his predecessors as shaykhs of the Kobravi order. The traditional proofs, the most important of which I have cited, are the sayings of Mohammad and 'Ali, introduced by the possessive pronoun, "my," which highlight Nurbakhsh's status as their descendant—a sayyed. In addition he adopts the Shi'ite principle of 'Alid legitimism of the Imam and extends this to himself as the "promised Imam" whose recognition is the prerequisite for salvation. The revelatory proofs include numerous visions, including Nurbakhsh's own. Among the "rational proofs," he states that he has guided more students over the past forty years than anyone else and that apocalyptic events foreshadowing the advent of the Mahdi took place in his lifetime. The ultimate proof of Mahdihood is his own mystical experience. According to Nurbakhsh, the Mahdi is like a light and is not incarnate. The Mahdi was seized and infused in him as a celestial spirit coexistent with the terrestrial body of Sayyed Mohammad Nurbakhsh. Through what he calls manifestation (*boruz, barazāt*) of one soul in another, the body of Nurbakhsh thus became the receptacle of the soul of Mohammad, Jesus, 'Ali, and the other eleven Imams, as well as that of some of the Friends of God.[79]

In its developed version, the Mahdism of Nurbakhsh replaces apocalyptic messianism by an inner-worldly eschatology of the soul; he equates Mahdihood with the Shi'ite Imamate and the "perfect sainthood" of the Sufis.

---

77 Death in ignorance dispelled by the coming of Islam refers to being deprived of salvation.
78 Bashir 2001: 105 [19].
79 Bashir 2001: 96–97.

There is, however, no discussion of the End of Time, the signs of the Hour or the violent messianism of the Mahdi. In the midst of his followers clamoring for millennial action, which more than once tempted him to seek worldly power, this was a serious effort to depoliticize Mahdistic authority and wed it to the authority of the Sufi saints who perceived (Platonic) ideas as images reflected in the mirrors of their souls. Thus, in his later years he claimed to know the realm of spirit through his heavenly journeys to guide his followers along the path of spiritual perfection. His son and successor, Shāh Qāsem, continued this Sufi tradition of spiritual guidance, and chided whoever reminded him of his father's claim to Mahdihood.[80]

Concerning Sufi practice or wayfaring as a path to spiritual enlightenment, having a perfect guide was absolutely necessary for salvation because salvation through initiation with an imperfect person leads the novices astray. In this context, he gave currency to (or may well have coined) a term for the perfect guide (*morshed-e kāmel*).[81] The perfect saint who could, through gnosis, leave the rank of servitude (*'obudiyyat*) to God and attain that of Lordship (*robubiyyat*)[82] could also attain the sovereignty of poverty (*saltanat-e faqr*) which is the combination of all perfections."[83] In short, Nurbakhsh's final conception of Mahdihood substitutes spiritual sovereignty for temporal sovereignty and worldly domination. Nevertheless, over the course of the ninth/fifteenth century the ideas of the absolute authority of the Sufi saint partaking of divinity and his designation as the Perfect Guide were appropriated by the messianic leaders of the Safavid order, and the Safavid revolution, as we shall see, created a new pattern of autocracy in the Persianate world.

What clearly emerges from the popular trends and movements in the Persianate world in the seventh/thirteenth and eighth/fourteenth centuries covered in this chapter is the Janus face of the gradually Shi'itized apocalyptic Sufi mysticism facing the spiritual and the political spheres both simultaneously and alternately. The same Janus face made it possible to tap its potential either for revolutionary action under the conditions of political fragmentation and instability or for pre-emptive state reaction. The possibility of counter-revolutionary containment of politically radical millennialism in the ninth/fifteenth century, hinted at in this chapter, is fully explored in chapter 4.

---

80   Nurbakhsh 1971: 118–123; Arjomand 1984: 76.
81   Nurbakhsh 1971: 115, 124.
82   Nurbakhsh 1971: 127.
83   Nurbakhsh 1971: 108.

CHAPTER 4

Royal Reactions to Apocalyptic Messianism and the Reinforced Legitimation of Autocracy

The religious conditions of the Timurid Empire and neighboring kingdoms, especially the growing numbers of dervishes and Sufi orders, gave the masters of Sufi orders great power and influence over urban and rural populations. The rulers and their patrimonial officials had to reckon with this power as Sufi orders were becoming, in effect, states within or across states. This religious conditioning of imperial and princely governmental policies especially affected the measures state officials took to deal with the millennial propensities of their subjects. Foremost among these were measures aimed at neutralizing the appeal of Mahdism by preemptively appropriating apocalyptic and messianic symbolism for kingship and the dynastic state, that is, by using millennial beliefs and symbols to the ruler's benefit.

1   Royal Counter-Messianism in the Timurid Empire

Around the time Bedreddin was preparing for his uprising, we find an intriguing example of a preemptive royal reaction. In a brief episode in the early ninth/fifteenth century this reaction proved to be a forerunner of the millennial inflection of sovereignty. Mirzā Eskandar b. ʿOmar Shaykh (the grandson of Timur and a patron of arts and learning) who ruled Fars from 1409 to 1414 during the succession strife among the Timurid princes, was an initiate into Fazlallāh Astarābādi's Horufi millennial movement. He also welcomed other initiates to his court; these included Sharaf al-Din Yazdi (d. 1454) and Sāʾen al-Din Torka (d. 1432), who were returning from the Cairene center of the *Ekhwān al-safāʾ* (Brethren of Purity). In addition, he appointed the Horufi Khattāt Baghdādi as his librarian. This was roughly the same time Sharaf al-Din Yazdi and Shaykh Bedreddin (Torka's colleague in the *Ekhwān al-safāʾ*) returned from Cairo and met the Ottoman prince, Musā (d. 4013), who appointed Bedreddin the army judge (*qādi ʿasker*) of Rumelia. Having found a prince who could be molded into a gnostic philosopher king (the way his Cairene master Akhlāti had worked with the Mamluk Soltān Barquq), Sharaf al-Din Yazdi lost interest in the revolutionary, messianic interpretation of their occult letterist science. He advanced steadily in the prince's service, became a vizier of the Fars province, and developed a royalist interpretation of the occult sciences and letterism (Horufism). His friend, Sā'en al-Din Torka, who called Sharaf al-Din Yazdi his "brother in God,"[1] was less able to detach himself from his past and remain aloof from the pressure for apocalyptic messianism from below.

Mirzā Eskandar sought knowledge far and wide and gathered many intellectuals around him. Like the Qāzizāda-ye Rumi of the *Ekhwān al-safā'* (Brethren of Purity) who was enticed by Olugh Beg (Eskandar Mirzā's cousin) to his court in Samarqand, the astronomer Ghiyās al-Din Jamshid Kāshi (d. 1429) was invited to Eskandar Mirzā's court in Shiraz. The theologian Mir Sayyed Sharif Jorjāni (d. 1414), an authority on theosophy (*hekmat-e elāhi*) whom Timur had deported to Samarqand, agreed to return to Shiraz. Last but not least, Eskandar Mirzā maintained excellent relations with the Sufi master, Shāh Ne'matollāh Vali (d. 1431); in exchange for a land grant for his *khāneqāh*, Vali dedicated an essay to him, in which he called him "the manifestation of divine bounties and the source and origin of limitless perfections."[2] Eskandar Mirzā sought to amalgamate the Horufi teachings and the Sufi theory on his own, to detach the so-called "science of [divine] unity" (*'elm-e tawhid*) from militant messianism, and use them both alongside the latest trends in gnostic cosmography and occult sciences. His goal was to forge a new concept of monarchy that would enhance autocracy and reduce the influence of messianic Sufi revolutionaries. Sā'en al-Din Torka served him well as a teacher and wrote two treatises on the new science of letters (*'elm-e horuf*) at his court; one was written in 1411 and the second and the more systematic treatise was dedicated in 1414, the last year of Prince Eskandar Mirzā's short reign.[3]

Jāme'-e solṭāni, a work on astronomy informed by the new science of letters, revealed divine secrets and astrology and was the science most useful for statecraft. In this work, Eskandar Mirzā was presented as the shadow of God on earth; it put forward his claim to be "the robe of the apparent and spiritual caliphate" and claimed that God vouchsafed His favor on the prince, "making his appearance both the manifestation of the minutiae of expediencies of monarchy and kingship, and [making] his reality the manifestation of minutiae of divine knowledge and sciences."[4] Indeed, Mirzā Eskandar claimed to be the Mahdi of the End of Time who unified the apparent and the spiritual monarchy.[5]

---

1 Melvin-Koushki 2012: 317 n. 5.
2 Cited in Aubin 1959a: 79.
3 Binbaş 2016: 89–95.
4 Yazdi 1987: 209.
5 Binbaş 2014; Markiewicz 2019: 162.

Mirzā Eskandar did not have time to propagate his theory of spiritual and temporal kingship—his uncle Shāhrokh defeated and executed him in 1414. Paradoxically, the full indirect elevation of kingship through Sufi world renunciation and the abasement of the world of appearance as compared to the inner, spiritual world of reality took place under Shāhrokh's son, Ebrāhim-Soltān (r. 817–837/1414–1434), who ruled Fars for his father after the defeat and execution of his cousin Mirzā Eskandar. For decades Ebrāhim-Soltān retained Sharaf al-Din Yazdi as his vizier. In the preface to a didactic work on the four rites of Sunni Islam written for his sovereign prince, Sharaf al-Din Yazdi expounds on the theory of the two divinely-ordained powers—the guidance of prophets and the policy (*siyāsat*) of kings—with an equation of kingship and the caliphate typical of post-Mongol Islamic royalism. Yet he continued to emphasize the king's power to punish as the essential tool for the maintenance of order in the world.[6]

In *Zafarnāma* (Book of victory), his famous biography of Timur that was commissioned by Eskandar Mirzā and completed in 1429, Timur is posthumously elevated to the astrally foreordained *sāheb-qerān* (Lord of the Auspicious Conjunction).[7] In a preface written in 1424, Timur, known for his false modesty in refusing the title of king and instead bestowing the title of king on a puppet Chinggisid and calling himself *gürgen* (son-in-law), was said by Sharaf al-Din Yazdi to have "ascended, with God's help, to the throne of caliphate and kingship" and was posthumously called *sāheb-qerān-e akhar al-zamān* (the Lord of the Auspicious Conjunction of the End of Time)."[8] More generally, Sharaf al-Din Yazdi offered a new formulation of the early medieval theory of the two powers of prophets and kings, with a Sufi element in the isomorphism of the human microcosm and the divine macrocosm. Elaborating on the third-/ninth- to fourth-/tenth-century division of God's elect into prophets and kings,[9] he states that the caliphate of God (*khelāfat-e elāhi*) is invested in two classes of persons. Accordingly, "world order" (*nezām-e 'ālam*) depends on "monarchy which consists in a formal/apparent (*suri*) caliphate," but he states this only in order to claim for the divinely ordained ruler both "the apparent (*suri*) and spiritual (*ma'navi*) caliphate and dual royal and religious princehood (*riyāsatayn-e molki o melli*)."[10]

---

6 Yazdi 1987: 7–10.
7 Melvin-Koushki 2018: 357–358.
8 Yazdi 1987: 27–28.
9 Arjomand 2010: 234. In an unpublished Timurid manuscript brought to light by Moin (2012: 50–53), the identity of prophets and kings is established through details of their horoscopes.
10 Yazdi 1987: 27, 29; Binbaş 2016: 284–284.

This full indirect and paradoxical elevation of kingship by way of Sufi world renunciation was thus the work of a mystic practitioner of the apocalyptic occult sciences who shaped a royalist ideology of gnostic autocracy for a Timurid prince who was adept at exploring the potential of popular Sufism to enhance the legitimacy of the monarchy. Eskandar Mirzā was not the only Timurid prince interested in preempting messianic symbolic resources; and the vizier Sharaf al-Din Yazdi was not the only member of the *Ekhwān al-safā'* (Brethren of Purity) seeking a gnostic philosopher king as an alternative to revolutionary messianism. As we shall see, the Safavid and Ottoman kings of the tenth/sixteenth century were also interested in preempting these resources.

Sharaf al-Din Yazdi held office in Fars, perhaps until 1435. In his revised *Zafarnāma*, in which Timur is compared to Alexander as the first world-conquering Lord of the Auspicious Conjunction, the elucidation of the latter title is even closer to the Mahdi myth in its use of apocalyptic vocabulary: Alexander's "manifestation (*zohur*) and uprising (*khoruj*) occurred in the cycle of the greater luminary [i.e., the sun], whereas the manifestation and uprising of the second Lord of the Auspicious Conjunction, Amir Timur ... occurred in the time of the lesser luminary, that is, the cycle of the moon."[11]

After losing the vizierate in 1435, Sharaf al-Din Yazdi did not stay away from politics for long; we find him in Isfahan in 1446 during the short rebellion of Prince Soltān-Mohammad b. Baysonghor, who was anticipating the death of the ailing Shāhrokh. In Isfahan, Sharaf al-Din Yazdi supported Soltān-Mohammad's bid for the imperial throne as a would-be autocrat of the occultist counter-revolution by unifying temporal and spiritual sovereignty under his guidance. However, Shāhrokh lived just long enough to march to Isfahan to quell the rebellion. He executed many of the notables who had invited his grandson to Isfahan, including a nephew of Sharaf al-Din Yazdi's close friend, Sā'en al-Din Torka; Sharaf al-Din Yazdi himself narrowly escaped the gallows.[12]

Sā'en al-Din Torka's career path differed widely from that of Sharaf al-Din Yazdi. He was appointed to the office of kadi of Isfahan which had been held by his family. In Isfahan, he must have had a following of enthusiastic Horufi students because he was interrogated by the anti-Horufi commissars of the Timurid government in 1422 and 1426. By the latter date he presumably held no illusions about the coming apocalypse his students yearned for or the chance of a successful revolutionary uprising, rather he was ready to counsel any of the Timurid princes who were patrons of art and learning. Given his great learning, philosophical sophistication, and literary talent, he could provide the

---

11   Cited in Moin 2012: 36, translation modified.
12   Manz 2007: 257; Binbaş 2016: 18–21.

princes with an interpretation of the occult sciences that would enhance the legitimacy of their rule. In fact, he chose Shāhrokh's heir apparent Baysonghor (d. 1433) as his patron and in 1426 he offered the prince a work in a new and fashionable allegorical literary genre: *Monāẓara-ye bazm o razm* (The debate on feasting and fighting).[13] Feasting and fighting are the two main functions of kings, according to the Persian theory of kingship, and Torka took them as symbols of ontological opposites that are eternally in conflict but must be reconciled according to a basic cognitive principle of the science of letters and the occult, namely *Coincidentia oppositorum* (*jamʿ-e azdād*, that is, union of opposites), best epitomized in Q. 57:3: "He is the first and the last, the appearance and the inner reality (*al-ẓāher wa'l-bāten*)." In Torka's allegory the agent of this reconciliation was the hypostasis of imperial-gnostic love, Emperor Love (*solṭān ʿeshq*) who was, according to the political astrology embedded in the occult sciences, the *ṣāheb-qerān* (the Lord of the Auspicious Conjunction).[14]

In the same year Torka wrote a flurry of publications to explain his creed and clear himself of all charges of sedition in relation to the Horufis. In January 1426, he chose one of the most apocalyptic verses of the Qur'ān, Q. 54:1: "The Hour is near, and the moon is split," as the subject of a gnostic neo-Pythagorean Horufi commentary. His exegetical commentary seems to have two aims: First to establish a hierarchy of seven cognitive methods, each associated with a religio-historical group, and place at the highest level of the hierarchy (presumably corresponding to the seventh, highest sphere of the heavens), a new supreme gnostic occult science. His second aim, I argue, was to identify the new comprehensive occult science as the one made manifest for the present age through its founder, Sayyed Hosayn Akhlāti,[15] whom he does not mention by name but refers to as "our master" (*sayyed-e mā*).[16] Torka was a leading practitioner of this new science of the occult. The gnostic elite he identified with was thus invested with the intellectual leadership of humankind in the new post-apocalyptic age.

For the immediate purpose of clearing himself of the charge of sedition through his association with the Sufi and Horufi millenarians, he separated these groups and practitioners of the lower cognitive/epistemic levels (5 and 6)

---

13 In 1428, Torka also dedicated a long essay to Baysonghor's son, Prince ʿAlāʾ al-Dawla, on the esoteric interpretation of the obligations according to the Hanbali rite subscribed to by the young prince. (Torka 1972: 119–165)
14 Melvin-Koushki 2019.
15 He is correctly identified by Melvin-Koushki 2012: 317.
16 Torka 1972: 116.

as the less advanced seekers of divine truth.[17] His immediate concern did not, however, prevent Torka from using the public platform to state his doctrinal conviction, albeit with subtlety and ambiguity. We find two short descriptions of the highest echelon of the knowers of the divine mysteries. The seventh level was:

> The rank of the men of might and vision (*uli l-aydi wa-l-abṣār*) (Q. 38:45), who are special servants of the Seal [of the prophets] and the heirs of his supreme perfection. The appearance of this type is peculiar to the present time, ruled by an auspicious conjunction ... But the same family of the Seal—the Amir ['Ali] and his glorious sons (peace be upon them)—possessed a transcript on *jafr* that remains with us and in which the method of derivation of meaning to full perfection is demonstrated.[18]

Alternatively, the seventh level, "The rank of the *men of might and vision* (Q 38:45) is peculiar to the present time, as made manifest by our master (peace of God be upon him and his noble ancestors)."[19] If we combine the two descriptions and read between the lines, we can see that the method of divination and discovery of divine mysteries was divulged to 'Ali and that our age was determined for the new apocalypse and in it our master recovered the method first divulged to 'Ali in the book on *jafr*. The comprehensive occult knowledge was latent in the *Jafr* but was actualized by Sā'en al-Din Torka and the *Ekhwān al-safā'* (Brethren of Purity). To understand more of his views, we need to examine other works in which Sā'en al-Din Torka was more explicit about the identity of the members of the seventh level, which consisted of "the members of the House of the Prophet and those who can riddle their cryptic utterances from among the perfected saints of Islam, and the sages of antiquity (*ḥukamā-yi qadīm*) and disciples of the prophets of God."[20] This makes Sā'en al-Din Torka and his gnostic circle equivalent to the ancient Greek sages and the perfect Sufi saints of his time.

Neither the *Monāẓara-ye bazm o razm* (Debate on feasting and fighting), nor the *Shaqq al-qamar* (Splitting of the moon) could have any immediate impact, and the pressure on Kadi Ṣā'en al-Din Torka must have continued because he wrote an elaborate petition to Shāhrokh. In May 1426, he wrote *Nafasat*

---

17 There is no linear notion of progress behind this advancement; on the contrary, the hierarchy of levels follows a circular time pattern.
18 Torka 1972: 111–112.
19 Torka 1972: 116.
20 Melvin-Koushki 2012: 318.

al-masdur (Tubercular's spittle), in which he defended the new gnostic science he was championing, likening it to astronomy and astrology.[21] But before he received a response or saw any result of his rapprochement with Baysonghor Mirzā, the assassination attempt on Shāhrokh occurred (in February 1426), and Sā'en al-Din Torka's situation became even more desperate. He then published at least four more essays, most notably a second *Nafasat al-masdur* (Tubercular's spittle), this time dedicated to Baysonghor, whose mediation he was counting on. In this second version, he does not simply dissociate himself from Sufism as a less advanced type of gnosis, but even attacks those charlatans who opened "shaykhhood shops" (*dokkān-e mashikhat*) to attract the masses, some of which preach the approach of the "manifestation of the seal of sainthood" (*zohur-e khatam al-velāya*) when the world will be taken over by dervishes, and others who say that the obligations of the sharia are no longer incumbent. Further valuable information is provided that indicates the cause of Torka's trouble; this is shown to be the apocalyptic messianism of his circle of students and followers. As this had been pointed out to him by the commissars in their investigations, Sā'en al-Din Torka took pains to argue that he had disputed the dervishes' contention that he was the manifestation of the seal of sainthood, and that he had tried to dissuade his radical students and bring them to their senses.[22]

In 1430 Sā'en al-Din Torka moved to Herat, where he awaited pardon or a more favorable response from the Timurid monarch or his heir apparent, but by the time he died in that city in 1432 he had still not received a reply. Meanwhile, Shāhrokh had won the struggle for succession to Timur and also brought the other Timurid princes under his suzerainty. His strategy for dealing with popular millennialism was the opposite of his nephew Eskandar Mirzā's; Shāhrokh opted for orthodoxy and chose the anti-millennial Sunni trope of being proclaimed the renovator (*mojadded*) of the century. From the beginning of his long reign, he accordingly derived the legitimacy of his sovereignty by championing Sunni orthodoxy. In 1411, Shāhrokh disestablished the Turko-Mongolian law, the Yāsā of Chinggis Khan, or more precisely, "the Yārghu and the customary Töre," and replaced them, according to Qāyeni (his Shaykh al-Islam), with the "law of the Shari'a" (*qānun-e shari'at*).[23] In 1420, the same Shaykh al-Islam, Qāyeni, wrote a book of advice entitled *Nasāyeh-e Shāhrokhi*, to the king of Islam who had taken such momentous step. The treatise was modeled on Najm al-Din Rāzi's pathbreaking Sufi treatise on kingship or sovereignty in which

---

21 Fleischer 2009: 232.
22 Torka 1972: 212, 214–215.
23 Qāyeni, fols. 2, 20, 128.

the "[spiritual] wayfaring" (*soluk*) of the king was presented as the way to save Islam from the Mongols.[24] In substance, however, it amounts to a program for an Islamic state regulated, at least in part, according to the letter of the Shari'a. As such, it can be considered the first systematic constitutional proposal for the Turko-Mongolian "King of Islam," as Shāhrokh was called, and was modeled distantly on the prophet-kings of the Old Testament, and more proximately on Mohammad and the "rightly-guided caliphs" whom Qāyeni expressly considered sovereign kings. The monarchy of the prophet-kings was indeed the prototype and most perfect form of sovereignty (*saltanat*) as its political ethic corresponds to the "ethics of God" (*akhlāq allāh*). Having cited the well-known tradition of the Prophet: "the ruler (*soltān*) is the shadow of God on earth in whom anyone who is wronged (*mazlum*) takes refuge," he inferred that the "wrong-doing/tyrannical king" (*pādshāh-e zālem*) is indeed "the shadow of Satan!"[25]

2 The Ottoman Containment of Sufi Millennialism

After Bedreddin's uprising the Ottoman soltāns showed themselves as eager to preempt apocalyptic messianism as the Timurid princes further east. Having suppressed Bedreddin's rebellion and reintegrated the Ottoman domains, Mehmed I (1413–1421) must have realized that the suppression of apocalyptic messianism could not last without a royalist ideology that appropriated its key feature. Mehmed I proved himself receptive to the Cairene *Ekhwān al-safā'* (Brethren of Purity) and other millennialists and welcomed them to his court in Bursa. Foremost among the co-opted brethren were Molla Fenari, whom he appointed Shaykh al-Islam. Mehmed I's son and successor, Murād II (1421–1444, 1446–1451), whose brilliant court in Bursa welcomed many Sufi masters, writers, and poets, did likewise. The above-mentioned 'Abd al-Rahmān Bestāmi who had left Anatolia after the suppression of the rebellion of his student, Shaykh Bedreddin, returned to Anatolia. In 1423 while he was in Karaman, he wrote a book on the science of letters, then, in 1426, he went to Bursa, where he wrote a more elaborate treatise on the same subject and lived the last decades of his life. Yazicizāda Ahmed Bijān (d. after 1465) was another millenialist and protégé of Murād II. With this team of advisors and courtiers, the Ottoman

---

24 Three centuries later, Rāzi's formula was adopted by the Sunni jurist Fazlollāh Ruzbehān Khonji to save orthodox Islam from the heretical Shi'ite Qezelbash; his work is preserved in a treatise entitled *Soluk al-moluk* (The wayfaring of kings), as considered in chapter 6.
25 Qāyeni, fols. 11v–12v, 20, 127v, 160, 261.

Sultans Mehmed I and Murād II launched a counter-revolutionary policy of publicizing the hitherto esoteric sciences of the occultist saints. It is reasonable to attribute this publicity to the Ottoman rulers' preemptive reaction to the pressure for apocalyptic messianism from below. Bestāmi states that he reluctantly released to the public the esoteric sciences reserved for the elite because of the decay of the age, but the fact that he did this at exactly the same time (1426) as Torka, who was in the opposite corner of the Persianate world, shows that the pressure to make esoteric science public came from below.[26]

Bestāmi, the erstwhile master of the rebel Shaykh Bedreddin, now vilified Fazlallāh and the Horufis as followers of Satan. Bestāmi denounced Bedreddin's revolutionary followers as antinomian rebels and heretics and dualist impostors. He further discarded the designation Horufiyya as false letterism and replaced it with the literal alternative, Harfiyya, and referred to himself and his colleagues as *sādāt al-harfiyya* (masters of the science of letters) whom he ranked alongside the *sādāt al-sufiya* (masters of Sufism) as practitioners of the "science of the saints."[27] Bestāmi lived in Bursa to a ripe old age under Mehmed II and saw the actual conquest of Constantinople in 1453; two years after that, he wrote a mirror for princes for Mehmed the Conqueror; this work highlights the cosmic significance of Qur'ānic prophet-kings such Solomon, and thereby puts prophets and kings on the same footing. It follows Najm al-Din Rāzi in treating the royal patron as a wayfaring (Sufi) king, as suggested by its title, *Nazm al-soluk fi mosammarāt al-moluk* (Ordering of conduct/wayfaring in the stories of kings). In it, he considers the conquest of Constantinople/Rome as the prelude to the apocalypse: "The last Hour will not commence until Constantinople and its cities have been conquered.... The divine secrets and radiant clues have been completed on a day in which the Judgement will begin and the trials will be imminent ... 1 Sha'bān 859 (16 July 1455)."[28]

By this time, Bestāmi had been popularized in the Turkish vernacular *Dorr-e maknun* (Hidden pearl) written by Yazicizāda Ahmed Bijān in the 1440s. Bijān went beyond Bestāmi's analysis of the early Muslim apocalyptic traditions on the fall of Constantinople and placed the whole Ottoman historical enterprise in apocalyptic perspective; world history was presented as ten periods of seven thousand years each (according to Byzantine tradition), thus its immediate apocalyptic significance (he predicted that the Last Hour

---

26 Fleischer 2001: 292–292; Fleischer 2018: 42–48; Gardiner 2017.
27 Fleischer 2009: 234–235; Gril 2005: 186, 191–192.
28 Cited in Fleischer 2009: 232.

would come in 1000/1590–1591) was exchanged for a sort of long term manifest destiny.[29] If all this, which was written before the conquest of Constantinople was cryptic and ambiguous, Bijān's last work, *Montehā* (written in 1453, its last recension appeared in 1465), the pre-apocalyptic age was interpreted to mean that Sultan Mehmed II the Conqueror was in fact the apocalyptic warrior who would fulfill the prophecy of the conquest of Rome. Mehmed II had learned of the significance of Constantinople (which included Muslim as well as Byzantine apocalyptic lore) from the Sufi advisors of his father, Murād II, and was understandably susceptible to them. He embarked on his conquest at the age of twenty-one, and in fact supplemented this lore with his understanding of Horufi apocalypticism. He commissioned a translation of the Book of Daniel from Syriac into Arabic "for the treasury of the *soltān* ... named for the prophet of the End of Time"; this work included a seventh-/thirteenth-century commentary by a certain Ebn ʿEzra (presumably an apocalyptic pen name) that identified the fourth empire of the Book of Daniel with the abode of Islam ruled by the King of Rum.[30] Mehmed also invoked the impending terrors of the "Blond People" (Banu al-Asfār) and Gog and Magog in the endowment deeds of the mosque complex for the conquered city, Constantinople.

Through Bestāmi and more directly, through the calendars Mehmed II used to guide his daily activities, Mehmed incorporated the political astrology of the original (Ismaʿili) Brethren of Purity into the Persianate conception of revolution outlined in chapter 1. The calendars accordingly made Soltān Mehmed the Conqueror the Lord of the Auspicious Conjunction. Bijān built on all these sources to single out Mehmed II as the leader of the Muslims in the final apocalyptic battles against the Blond People (Banu al-Asfār) in Ottoman lands. His preordained objective to capture Rome (Rumiye) was taken to mean all the lands of the Blond People. Bijān thus converted Bestāmi's apocalypse to "realized messianism" even as Mehmed II's conquests of Serbia, Wallachia, and finally Bosnia (1463) were underway. According to this realized messianism, the goal of the Ottoman Sultan was to prepare the empire of post-history for future generations.[31] As we see in chapter 5, realized messianism served as the imperial Ottoman ideology of westward conquests and eastern-oriented counter-revolution against the Safavids in the first half of the tenth/sixteenth century.[32]

---

29   Şahin 2010: 328, 338, 343.
30   Fleischer 2009: 233; Fleischer 2018: 49.
31   Fleischer 2009: 235; Şahin 2010: 348–349.
32   To end our discussion of the royal appropriation by Mahdism by the Timurids and Ottomans with a comparative note, we can point to the parallel preemptive appropriation of Joachimite millennialism in Western Christendom by Emperor Frederick II, Hohenstaufen, in the thirteenth and by the French monarchy in the fourteenth century. See Reeves 1976: 61–62, 67–71.

3 Orthodox Reform and the Counter-Messianic Caliphate of God under the Āq Qoyunlu

While the Timurid Eskandar Mirzā posed as the counter-Mahdi to decrease pressure on the Horufis, the Jalayerid rulers of Iraq were being ousted by a rival Turko-Mongolian clan, the Qara Qoyunlu. It is indicative of the confessional ambiguity during this transition in 1411 in Turkman-dominated Baghdad, where the Shiʿite notion of occultation of the Mahdi existed alongside popular Christian and Sunni beliefs, that when the last Jalaryerid ruler, Ahmad b. Soltān Ovays, was killed fighting the Qara Qoyunlu many inhabitants of Baghdad believed that he had not died and was alive and issuing orders in concealment (occultation), like the Shiʿite Hidden Imam/Mahdi![33] As we saw in chapter 3, the Qara Qoyunlu ruler, Qara Yusof (r. 1405–1420) and his son, Eskandar (r. 1420–1433) were well-disposed toward the Horufis and their esoteric millennialism. The subsequent Qara Qoyunlu rulers, most notably Jahānshāh, who ruled first as a Timurid vassal from 1434 to 1447 and thereafter independently, remained receptive to heterodox apocalyptic ideas, some of which were displayed in Jahānshāh's poetry. Jahānshāh was defeated and killed in November 1467 by Uzun Hasan (r. 1457–1478), the founder of the Āq Qoyunlu (Bāyandor) dynasty.[34]

Uzun Hasan celebrated the establishment of his nomadic conquest as the Sunni renewer (*mojadded*) of the fourth/tenth century, just as the Timurid Shāhrokh was hailed as the renewer of the previous century. Uzun Hasan championed Sunni orthodoxy and the sharia, suppressed the anti-nomian Sufis, and issued codes of state law (*qānun-nāma*s). His chief ideologue, Mawlānā Jalāl al-Din Mohammad Davvāni (d. 1502), further claimed that his advent was predicted in the Qurʾān and hadith. Important families of Persian urban notables, the Kojojis of Azerbaijan, Sāvajis and Sāʿedis of central Iran, and the Daylamis of Gilan entered his service for state-building.[35]

Davvāni lived and taught in the city of Shiraz, the capital of Uzun Hasan's heir apparent Soltān-Khalil, whose court he frequented. In the preface of an extensive account of a military parade by the prince's army near Persepolis in 1476, Davvāni called Uzun Hasan "the one elected [by God] for the 900s" [i.e., the coming tenth century/sixteenth century]. Davvāni appropriated the title of the Shiʿite Mahdi and Hidden Imam for Soltān-Khalil and added an even more elevated Sunni title that became the standard appellation for the

---

33 Binbaş 2020: 214–219.
34 Minorsky 1954.
35 Woods 1977: 114–123.

secretaries of the Āq Qoyunlu chancery. Uzun Hasan was called the "Deputy of the Merciful [God] (*khalifat al-Rahmān*), the Lord of Time (*sāheb al-zamān*)."[36] Soltān-Khalil further commissioned a work known as *Akhlāq-e Jalāli* that was completed in 1478, the year in which Uzun Hasan died (on January 6) and Soltān-Khalil was hacked to pieces (on or about July 15) by the army of his mother, Seljuq-shāh Begum.[37]

Akhlāq-e Jalāli, a treatise on ethics that included political science (*siyāsat-e modon*) as its (highest) branch according to the tripartite Aristotelian division of ethics, proved the most influential book of the ninth/fifteenth century and the tenth/sixteenth century in Iran and the Ottoman Empire. In it, Uzun Hasan and Soltān-Khalil are called the "two Deputies of God" (*daw khalifa-ye khodā*) and the "two world-protecting suns, the one the center of the circle of caliphate, the other the means of the rein of sultanate!"[38] These titles are explained in a chapter of the treatise on "the governance of the kingdom and the manners of kings" in accordance with the Qur'ānic verse "O David! We have made you a deputy (*khalifa*) on earth" and the prophetic hadith, "the king is the shadow of God on earth." Governance is then divided into the excellent and the defective. The former is the Imamate, and whoever is endowed with it is "in truth the deputy of God (*khalifat Allāh*) and the shadow of God!"[39]

Though he found it useful for countering Sufi-Shi'ite millennial subversion for the benefit of the newly formed Āq Qoyunlu empire, Davvāni did not invent the "deputy of the Merciful God" for political-ideological purposes. On the contrary, the notion pertained to the conceptual context of gnostic Sufism of the period and was deeply rooted in the gnostic thought of Ibn al-'Arabi and had seventh-/thirteenth-century followers. In fact, as Dāvvāni sat among the civilian dignitaries of Soltān-Khalil's court viewing the military parade in 1476, Edris Bedlisi, the future *monshi* and political theorist we meet in the next chapters, was copying a Sufi treatise by his father, Hosām al-Din 'Ali, a disciple of the great Sufi master Nurbakhsh. In this Sufi treatise, the deputy of God was equated with the perfect man who had attained full spiritual perfection like the prophets of old.[40] Like Bedlisi, the Persian chancery scribes who

---

36   Minorsky 1939: 148.
37   Minorsky 1939: 144–145.
38   Davvāni 2014: 305. Uzun Hasan was once again given the title *hazrat-e sāheb-zamāni* (Lord of the age). The book ends with the evidently unheeded prayer to God to firmly place the two world-protecting kings "on the throne of the caliphate." (Davvāni 2014: 304, 306)
39   Davvāni 2014: 250–251.
40   Markiewicz 2019: 242, 254.

propagated the notion for the benefit of Āq Qoyunlu Turko-Mongolian rulers knew well the Sufi cosmogonic context in which it was embedded.

It took three more years for Soltān-Khalil's mother Seljuq-shāh to put her favorite younger son, Soltān Yaʻqub (1481–1490) on the Āq Qoyunlu throne in Tabriz and another half-dozen or so years for the Persian notables to resume Uzun Hasan's state-building project that was so rudely and repeatedly interrupted by the Turkman military commanders. In fact, signs of the ascendancy of the Persian bureaucratic elite did not appear until the later years of Yaʻqub's reign. In 1487, a staunch Sunni jurist, Fazlallāh Ruzbehān Khonji Esfahāni (d. 1521) dedicated a short work on Sufism to Soltān Yaʻqub and was commissioned to write a history of his reign as the true successor to Uzun Hasan and as a champion of orthodoxy. In 1489, Soltān Yaʻqub's vizier, the military judge and finance minister Qāzi ʻIsā Sāvaji, launched reforms aimed at both centralizing fiscal administration and enhancing the legitimacy of the dynastic state as orthodox and in conformity with the sharia. His team of reformist officials included Persian notable families and especially Sharaf al-Din Mahmud Daylami and his brother and son.[41] The fiscal reforms, however, alienated not only the Turkman military elite who held large land grants (*soyurghāl*) but also some of the Persian urban notables whose smaller land grants and religious endowments were also confiscated. The group that struck back immediately after Soltān Yaʻqub's unexpected death in 1490 belonged to the Turkman military estate. Qāzi ʻIsā Sāvaji was arrested and hanged and his top aides were tortured, killed, or dismissed.

Centralizing reforms were resumed for a few months by Uzun Hasan's grandson, Soltān Ahmed, who had been raised in Istanbul and was dispatched to Tabriz in 1497 by his maternal uncle, the Ottoman Soltān Bāyezid. Qāzi ʻIsā's surviving reformist officials doubtless participated in these Ottoman-style reforms, notable among these officials were Mahmud Daylami and his protégé Edris Bedlisi (d. 1520), who at some point edited Qāzi ʻIsā's poetry and was ordered to compose the victory proclamation to be sent to Soltān Bāyezid. Bedlisi later described these reforms as conforming to the sharia as well as the (state) laws of justice.[42] However, like the centralizing reforms of Qāzi ʻIsā, Soltān Ahmed's reforms were ended abruptly by rebellious commanders of Turkman clans who killed Ahmed and the Janissary contingent that had

---

41 Markiewicz 2019: 57–65, 81. On Khonji, see chapter 6.
42 Markiewicz 2019: 63–64, 242.

brought him back in December 1497.[43] After this came three or four years of chronic instability followed by the Safavid revolution, suggesting that in fragile political regimes characterized by endemic instability, reform can be the prelude to revolution.

Meanwhile, the chanceries in Tabriz and Shiraz functioned intermittently among feuding Āq Qoyunlu princes. Some of the leading *monshi*s were students of Davvāni and others were trained in the Timurid epistolary style; they propagated the idiom and vocabulary of sovereignty centered on the notion of monarchy as the caliphate of the Merciful God. As we shall see, quite a few did so by seeking employment in other kingdoms as the political conditions in Iran deteriorated.

---

43 Markiewicz 2019: 60 n. 133, 63. Parallel reforms in Herat under Solṭān Hosayn Bayqarā (initiated by ʿIsā's contemporary Timurid counterpart, Majd al-Din Khʷāfi) likewise ended in failure (Markiewicz 2019: 56).

CHAPTER 5

The Causes and Process of Shah Esmāʿil's Mahdist Revolution

The rise of the Safavids was clearly a revolution, according to our definition, because of the primacy of millenarian motives among the followers of Shah Esmāʿil. His followers saw him as a messianic leader, the "Grand Sophy" (a western corruption of Safavi) of Venetian traveling merchants. Esmāʿil was called a new prophet, even among Christians, who pinned their eschatological hopes on him; excitement about his advent was recorded in Istanbul.¹ The rise of the Safavids fits our structural Khaldunian model of revolution (as outlined in chapter 1), given the unification of nomadic tribes. It also displays a typical revolutionary process in its course, and above all can be justified as a revolution in terms of its consequences—notably the conversion of Iran to Shiʿite Islam and a significant change in its political order. I therefore follow Jean Aubin in considering the rise of Shah Esmāʿil a "Shiʿite revolution." We differ, however, in our periodization of the Safavid revolution. In his three monumental "Études Safavides," Aubin focused on the process of revolution by highlighting a turning point in 1508–1509 in the revolutionary power struggle; this turning point resulted in a shift away from extreme radicalism to regime consolidation in Iran. By contrast, my approach does not confine the revolutionary power struggle to Iran, but sees it in the Persianate world, as a continuation of the Mahdist rebellions that began with that of Shaykh Bedreddin in Rumelia and continued or were resumed in Anatolia during the crisis of succession to Bāyezid II that began in 1511.

Looking at the rise of Shah Esmāʿil the Safavid as a Shiʿite revolution from this viewpoint, we can see the transformative impact of Shiʿite political messianism on popular Sufism in millennial revolutionary movements in the second half of the ninth/fifteenth century, as exemplified in the cases of the Horufi movement and the Mahdism of Nurbakhsh (examined in chapter 3). These movements engaged in an intense worldly struggle against Turko-Mongolian domination in the absolute politics of the here and now by activating the syndrome of extremist (*gholoww*) Shiʿite beliefs around the core Mahdist myth.² The rise of the Safavid Sufi movement and its turn to Shiʿite Mahdism belongs

---

1 Fleischer 2018: 38–39, 54.
2 Tucker 2014.

to this period and type. Given the extensive mobilization and recruitment in Anatolia in the last quarter of the ninth/fifteenth century, it is very likely that Esmāʿil knew and was influenced by the latest model apocalyptic messianism circulating after the conquest of Constantinople with predictions of the appearance of the *sāheb-e zamān* (master of the age) in 900/1494–95 and of the devastation of the East (of Syria and Rum) as the Banu al-Asfar (Blond People) fought the Muslims.[3]

1 Sufism, the Safavid Order, and Its Turn to Militant Mahdism

The beginning of the Safavid millenarian movement can be dated to the mid-ninth/fifteenth century, when Shaykh Jonayd (a descendant of Shaykh Safi al-Din Ardabili (d. 1335), the eponymous founder of the Safavid Sufi order) began to mobilize his followers for warfare (*ghazā*) in the northwestern frontier of Iran. His son, Sadr al-Din Musā (d. 1392) claimed that his father was a sayyed (descendant of the Prophet), a claim that accorded with the late Il-Khanid trend and should not be taken as proof of their Shiʿism.[4] In fact, Shaykh Jaʿfar, the head of the Safavid order in Ardabil after 1447, was an orthodox Sunni. He disowned Jonayd, who was his nephew, and prevailed upon the Qara Qoyunlu ruler, Jahānshāh, to exile him from the city.[5]

Not being Shiʿite or millenarian did not mean that the Safavid shaykhs lacked political ambition. On the contrary, their political involvement and consequent radicalization had already begun under Safi al-Din's grandson, Khʷāja ʿAli (d. 1427), also called Soltān-ʿAli; he was also known even more revealingly, as Siāhpush (lit., one who dresses in black). Khʷāja/Soltān ʿAli welcomed some of Bedreddin's surviving followers after the suppression of his rebellion. In addition he returned from his pilgrimage to Mecca with what he claimed to be the banner of the Messenger of God and erected it in the *khāneqāh* in Ardabil. Furthermore, he named his son Soltān-Ebrāhim, and the latter became known, more revealingly, as the Shaykh-Shāh![6] The incorporation by the Safavid shaykhs of royal titles, *soltān* and *shāh*, into their proper names in the ninth/fifteenth century represented an appropriation of royal symbols (as surveyed in relation to the underground kingdoms of the urban *fotowwa*

---

3 Şahin 2010: 348, 353.
4 A decree of tax exemption for Shaykh Sadr al-Din Musā by the Jalayerid Soltān Ahmed in 1372 does not indicate that he was a sayyed. For additional evidence, see Arjomand forthcoming.
5 Aubin 1959b: 46–47; Pārsādust 2002: 133.
6 Zarrinkub 1983: 67–69.

confraternities) into a significantly higher level of contestation.[7] As contentious counter-claims thus became more open and evident, the metaphorical sovereignty of Sufi shaykhs became more plausible and closer to realization.

Mahdism, however, came later. After being exiled from Ardabil by his uncle, the young Shaykh Jonayd (d. 1460) became an adventurer in Anatolia, where he gathered a band of Sufi raiders (*ghozāt-e sufiyya*) that (as noted in chapter 3), including Turkman tribesmen and some of the survivors of the millenarian movement of Shaykh Bedreddin of Samawna and their offspring. Anatolia was a fertile region for the growth of unorthodox millenarian movements, as the population of Anatolia since the Bābā'i uprising in the seventh/thirteenth century was only superficially Islamicized. Various groups of antinomian dervishes—Akhis, Qalandars, and Abdāls—mushroomed in the region. The Horufiyya were particularly notable for the spread of millennialism among antinomian Sufis; Jonyad recruited among these Turkman tribesmen, and the survivors of the uprising and their offspring that doubtless included some of the Abdāl.[8] Thus, it is likely that Jonayd imbibed extremist (*gholoww*) Shi'ite beliefs in Anatolia.

Shortly before his death in a raid on Shervān in 1460, Jonayd married the sister of the Āq Qoyunlu ruler, Uzun Hasan, whose power was on the rise. Jonayd's son, born after his death, was named Haydar (d. 1488), and in the following years he replaced Ja'far as the head of Safavid order.[9] Jonayd's death resulted in a split among his millenarian followers, with one group accepting his son Haydar as his successor and another following a stone-carver (*hakkāk*) as their messiah.[10] Haydar's maternal uncle, Uzun Hasan, took Haydar under his protection, and later married him to his daughter, Martha. Once Uzun Hasan had conquered the area and made Tabriz his capital, he installed Haydar in Ardabil, first under the strict tutelage of Shaykh Ja'far in 1470, and a few years later as the head of the Safavid order in his own right. Haydar certainly had complete control of Ardabil after the death of Shaykh Ja'far, and began to recruit Anatolian adepts to the order in Anatolia through local representatives (*khalifa*s).[11] To the Ottoman authorities who tried to persuade them to go to Mecca and Medina instead of Ardabil, the Turkman adepts replied that they preferred to go on pilgrimage to the living rather than the dead.[12] Since the eighth/fourteenth century, various groups of nomads fighting on the frontier (*uj*) against the Byzantines had worn

---

7   See chapter 2.
8   Karakaya-Stump 2020: 147–178.
9   Morimoto 2010: 464.
10 Aubin 1988: 36; Shervāni 2001: 106.
11 Hinz 1936: 72–73. The stone-carver's followers presumably accepted Haydar at this point.
12 Sümer 1992: 17.

distinctive white and red caps. Haydar now devised a more colorful headgear for his followers; this was made of red cloth, with twelve plumes representing the twelve holy Imams of the Shi'a. It was called the Haydari crown (*tāj-e haydari*), on account of which they became known as red heads (*qezelbāsh*). In 1488, the impressive network of local agents (*khalifas*) was used very effectively to mobilize Haydar's followers for an attack on Shervān to avenge Shaykh Jonayd; however, Haydar was killed during the attack.[13]

Although there are similarities between the religion of the Qezelbāsh and Shi'ite extremism (*gholoww*), including the second/eighth-century Shi'ite millenarian sect of Kaysāniyya and their refusal to accept the death of their apocalyptic charismatic leader,[14] there are also considerable differences, notably the belief in the transmigration of souls. These differences have two sources, the central Asiatic heritage of the Turkmen and Sufism. In the preceding centuries, Sufism had become the dominant force in popular religion in Iran and Anatolia during the era of Turko-Mongolian domination; initially it dampened revolutionary activism, but in the ninth/fifteenth century it produced the Sufi millenarian or Mahdist movements (as surveyed in chapter 3). This new wave of political messianism built around the sacral idea of absolute and charismatic religio-political authority espoused by Jonayd, but rejected by his uncle Ja'far who upheld the separation of Sufi spiritual authority from political authority. Haydar opted for the new messianic mixture of spiritual and temporal power, or in the apt words of a contemporary historian, the "unification of dervishhood and kingship" (*jam'-e darvishi o shāhi*).[15] The immediate result of this mixture of "the material and the spiritual monarchy" (*saltanat-e suri o ma'navi*), was his death and the imprisonment of his young children.[16]

Haydar's sons and their mother, Martha (Halima Begum) who was the daughter of the Uzun Hasan and a devout Christian Greek princess, were imprisoned in a castle in Fars for a few years but then released in 1492 and received in Tabriz with robes of honor by their Āq Qoyunlu cousin, Rostam Beg (d. 1497), who counted them as allies in the prolonged power struggle for succession to Soltān Ya'qub. But the Safavids had their own project, and the network of local agents was again used to gather Anatolian followers for a planned uprising. Rostam Beg's officials suspected something and were planning to arrest his Safavid cousins when they escaped to Ardabil.[17] There, in

---

13   Hinz 1936: 83.
14   Arjomand 2022, ch. 3.
15   Khʷānd-Amir 1993: 4:426.
16   Mazzaoui 1972: 72 n. 2.
17   Woods 1976: 166–167.

900/1500–1501 they joined some 300 Qezelbāsh followers, and confronted an Āq Qoyunlu army said to number 5,000. The Āq Qoyunlu army confronted Haydar's oldest son and successor, Soltān-ʿAli, who is credited with remarkable prescience and reportedly took the Haydari crown off his head in the battlefield and put it on his brother Esmāʿil's head. He also appointed seven veterans seasoned in Āq Qoyunlu internecine warfare as his commanders. Except for one sedentary native of Tālesh in northern Iran, his commanders were leaders of the Qezelbāsh nomadic clans of Shāmlu, Qāramānlu, Ayqutoghlu, and Qājār. Soltān-ʿAli fell in battle, and the seven commanders in the inner circle of the movement took his two younger brothers, Ebrāhim and Esmāʿil, into hiding in Gilan, accompanied by some eighty surviving Sufis of the order.[18]

Soltān-ʿAli presumably assumed the leadership of the Qezelbāsh movement, and is referred to in the early Persian sources on the Safavid movement as Soltān-ʿAli Pādshāh. A year or two after his death, Rostam Beg was prepared to allow the return of his brother, Ebrāhim, to Ardabil to assume the spiritual guidance of the Safavid order, while Esmāʿil remained in Lāhijān. It is significant that Ebrāhim is reported to have "removed the twelve-pronged Haydari *tāj* [the Qezelbāsh headgear] …, and put on the Turkman cap in the fashion of the Āq Qoyunlu."[19] According to one account, Ebrāhim conveniently died in 1499 just before Esmāʿil set out.[20] In fact, however, Ebrāhim probably did not die but led an expedition for Esmāʿil to Trabzon. It seems likely that in 1508 he and another brother may have been spared by the intercession of several *amir*s, but were confined to Ardabil and forbidden to raise more than 200 horsemen each. He may finally have been executed, together with Esmāʿil's mother and other brothers, in 1513.[21]

The earliest Persian source on the Safavid movement, written around 1490, leaves little doubt about the heterodox, millenarian, and extremist attitude of the Qezelbāsh followers toward Jonayd and Haydar, Esmāʿil's grandfather and father: "They openly called Shaykh Jonayd God, and his son, the Son of God." They refused to accept Jonayd's death even when they saw his corpse and would kill anyone who said he was dead. As for the child Haydar, "his fathers' *khalifa*s came from every direction and foolishly announced the glad tidings of his divinity (*oluhiyyat*)."[22]

---

18   Pārsādust 2002: 220–222, 250; Yildirim 2008: 251–252.
19   Khwānd-Amir 1993: 4:442.
20   Morton 1996: 35, 38.
21   Uğur 1985: 148; Aubin 1988: 104–105.
22   Khonji Esfahāni 1992: 272–273; trans., 57:
      شیخ جنید را بمجاهره اله و ولدش را ابن الله گفتند.... خلفای پدر از هر سو رو بدو آوردند و دعوای الوهیت او را بشهادت سفاهت آشکار کردند.

As for Esmāʿil as the leader of the revolution, there can be no doubt about his intense charisma as an invincible warrior incarnating divinity. The manuscript known as *Ross Anonymous*, which was until recently taken to be the earliest account of his reign, depicts him holding the sword of the Lord of the Age, the Mahdi, when Twelver Shiʿism was declared to be the official religion of Iran.[23] The work has been shown to have been composed much later, but we know that rival popular epics such as *Abu Moslem Nāma* were suppressed and within two decades of his death storytellers instead declaimed the heroic exploits of Esmāʿil alongside the stories of the *Shāhnāma*. This much later romance of Esmāʿil must reflect earlier beliefs and sources.[24]

In any event, there is no shortage of other similar evidence, the most striking being Esmāʿil's poetry recorded under the pen-name Khatāʾi. There are three extant, albeit defective, collections (*Dīvān*) from his lifetime. Esmāʿil was greatly influenced by the Turkish poetry of the Horufi poet ʿEmād al-Din Nesimi, whose ecstatic mystical union with God served as his model.[25] In his poems, Nesimi expressed his eager anticipation of the appearance of the Mahdi. Some of these poems came to be misattributed the Khatāʾi and were included in the latter's *Dīvān*. In these, the expected "Imam Mahdi, the [divine] Guide (*al-hādi*)" and the "Soltān-Imam" is described as the "light of the eyes of all the prophets." Khatāʾi responded to this millennial expectation by claiming to be its fulfillment:

> The promised age of the Lord of Time (*sāheb-e zamān*) has come:
> The sublime court set up; the resurrection (*mahsher*) has come![26]

Esmāʿil's poems, presumably used in religious rituals among his militant followers, precisely expressed the nature of his form of divinity as the reincarnation of God, the prophets, and the Imams. Esmāʿil was the divine, pre-eternal truth, just as in its previous prophetic manifestations:

---

23 It appeared under the title *Jahāngoshā-ye Khāqān* by a certain Bizhan in the middle of the tenth/sixteenth century (Jaʿfariyan 2001: 1:23) and even as late as the 1680s. (*Jahāngoshā-ye Khāqān* 1985: 148–149; *ʿĀlam-ārā-ye Shāh Esmāʿil* 1970: 41–43, 60–61; Morton 1990). That picture was the frontispiece of *The Shadow of God and the Hidden Imam* (cf. *ʿĀlamārā-ye Shāh Esmāʿil* 1970: 41–43, 60–61).
24 Hamavi 1984: 141–144; Membré 1993: 52; Morton 1996: 44–45.
25 Csirkés 2015: 158, 186–187.
26 Csirkés 2015: 183, 185, trans. modified.

> O, holy warriors say: God,
>   God!
> Come and meet; prostrate
>   yourselves
>
> I was with Mansur on the gallows;
> I was with Moses on Sinai!
>
> I have the essence of 'Ali
>
> Holy warriors, I am the faith of
>   the king!
> Holy warriors, I am the faith of
>   the king!
>
> I was with Abraham in the fire
> Holy warriors, I am the faith of
>   the king!
>
> O holy warriors, I am the faith of
>   the king!²⁷

And again,

> Today I have come to the world as a Master
> Know truly that I am Haydar's son!
> The mystery of "I am the Truth" is hidden in this my heart
> I am the Absolute Truth, and the truth I am telling!²⁸

There is also contemporary historical evidence from Venetian reports to the Signoria. Reporting on Esmā'il's second recruitment campaign in Erzinjān (in Anatolia) in December 1501, Marino Sanudo called him a shaykh (Exeth)²⁹ and a new prophet who claims to be God and who, when dignitaries present themselves, puts his hand over their heads, while his forty *khalifa*s do the same with lesser people who join the movement. A letter from Constantinople

---

27 Gandjeï 1959: 22, poem 20.1, 4, 7. "The faith of the king" is a difficult construction. I take it to mean the divine, numinous essence of the king, or a variant of "God" and "Absolute Truth."

الله الله دينك غازيلر دين شاه منم
قارشو كلونك سجده قيلونك غازيلر دين شاه منم
منصور ايله دارده ابدبم خليل ايله نارده ايديم
موسى اياه طورده ايديم غازيلر دين شاه منم
مرتضى على ذاتلويم
غازيلر دين شاه منم

28 Gandjeï 1959: 125, poem 198.1, 3. Further, "I am the Truth" are the words the mystic Mansur al-Hallāj uttered on the gallows at the time of his execution.

بو كون كلدوم جهانه سرورم من
يقين بيلونك كه ابن حيدرم من
انا الحق سرى اوش كونكلومده كيزلو
كه حق مطلقم حق سويلرم من

29 His name is mentioned a year later (Sanudo 1979: 30) but not typically. The title Shah appears much later.

on 7 March 1502, mentions rumors that 500 Turks wanted to join "the new prophet of Persia" but were prevented from leaving the city.[30]

What is reported here is not the rise of a new king or dynasty but a millennial religious movement led by an intensely charismatic divine leader, who was referred to in the West as the "Sophy" and who inspired "the greatest terror in all of Turkey."[31] This is generally consistent with the use of the terms *zohur* (manifestation) and *khoruj* (uprising) in the Persian sources and, in particular, with 'Abdi Beg's statement that Esmā'il was received in Anatolia "as the Helpers (*ansār*) received the Prophet and carried him to Medina, dancing and singing."[32] According to an Ottoman source, the inscriptions on his banners were "There is no god but God, and Mohammad is the Messenger of God," and on the other, "Esmā'il is the Deputy (*khalifa*) of God."[33]

The exiled polemicist Shervāni wrote decades later, "This sect says, explicitly and with a sincere heart and belief, that the God before our time was the Shah called Esmā'il and [this divinity] has transmigrated and manifests itself in the form of our Shah called Tahmāsb, and he is our God, and the God of our time."[34]

It seems that the presentation of Esmā'il as the Mahdi, or the forerunner of the Mahdi, or the wielder of the Mahdi's sword in the above-mentioned romance of Shah Esmā'il, was a revised version of this core Qezelbāsh belief. He endorsed this modification when he assumed the title of Shah.[35] Thus, on the one hand he opted for empire-building and the consolidation of kingship, and on the other hand, he embraced the establishment of Twelver Shi'ism to ensure that his followers moderate their millennialism.

The revised version of Shah Esmā'il's claim to his non-Qezelbāsh Persian followers and subjects is well presented by 'Abdi Beg:

> As the ruler of the age and the lord of command is absent, it is right for a competent member of the exalted 'Alid Fatimid dynasty to execute the commandments of the Imam of the age among God's creatures.... [and

---

30   Sanudo 1979: 7.
31   Sanudo 1979: 23.
32   'Abdi Beg: 37:

به طریقی که انصار مدینه شریفه حضرت رسالت را به مدینه بردند، پای کوبان و سرودگویان

33   Cited in Yildirim 2008: 271.
34   Shervāni 2001: 97.

هذه الطائفه فقد صرحوا و قالوا عن صميم القلب و الاعتقاد ان الاله قبل زماننا هو الشاه المسمى باسماعيل قد انتقل و تجلى الى صورة شاهنا المسمى بطهماسب و هو الهنا و اله زماننا.

35   It is interesting to note Shervāni's explication of the meaning of the term *shāh* to the Qezelbāsh: to some it meant 'Alī [the *shāh-e mardān*], to others Esmā'il b. Haydar and his offspring, and to yet others, it was one of the names of God. (Shervāni 2001: 94)

such a man is] the Solomon of the End of Time, the Lord of the Auspicious Conjunction, the forerunner of the army of the Lord of the Age, Abu'l-Mozaffar Soltān Shāh Esmā'il....[36]

Note, however, that the Mahdist expectation that Esmā'il deflected from himself in the course of imperial consolidation lingered on after his death. The extreme adulation of Shah Esmā'il by the Qezelbāsh is very well documented. Michele Membré graphically describes the elaborate Qezelbāsh ceremonies in which, a decade and a half after Esmā'il's death, power was transferred to his son Tahmāsb, who also expected the imminent appearance of the Mahdi. A white horse was accordingly kept prepared for the Hidden Imam, but more strikingly, Tahmāsb also kept his favorite sister unmarried, so she could become the Mahdi's bride.[37] For his Persian subjects, Tahmāsb was called the Mahdi's deputy (nā'ib); his courtier and historian, 'Abdi Beg, confirmed that "the reign of the End of Time is reserved for His Majesty."[38]

The one contemporary Persian history of Esmā'il's reign is Khʷānd-Amir's *Habib al-siyar*.[39] Reflecting the viewpoint of an orthodox Sunni man of learning who compromised with the new regime to save his life and property, the narrative is extremely restrained with regard to the nature of Shah Esmā'il's

---

36 'Abdi Beg: 34–35:

چون سلطان زمان صاحب امر علیه الصلوات الله ... غائب است حق آنست که از سلسله علیه علویه فاطمیه، شخصی که قابلیت این امر داشته باشد، در میان بندگان خدای حکم امام زمان را جاری سازد ... [و این شخص] سلیمان آخر الزمان، پادشاه صاحبقران، مقدمه الجیش صاحب الزمان، ابوالمظفر سلطان شاه اسماعیل ...

37 Membré 1993: 18, 25–26, 41–42. This generated rumors that Tahmāsb had an incestuous relationship with his favorite sister, Soltānem. (Shervāni 2001: 96) Tahmāsb was very attached to this sister, whose death in 1562 resulted in his withdrawal from active life. (Morton's inroduction to Membré 1993: xxiv)

38 Ja'fariyan 2001: 2:496–499; 'Abdi Beg: 60:

سلطنت آخر الزمان به آن اعلی حضرت مخصوص است.

39 The *Fotuhāt-e Shāhi*, University of Tehran Central Library, Meshkāt Collection # 1103, assumed to be written by Ebrāhim Amini, is in fact identical with part 4 of *Habib al-siyar*, except for the headings and more defective transcription of Qur'ānic verses. It was copied, according to the colophon, on 2 Rajab 979. In fact, the author identifies it as the last part of *Habib al-siyar*, though the sentence is corrupt. (fol. 4a; cf. Khʷānd-Amir 1984: 4:409 for the correct sentence.) It is surprising that Ja'fariyān, who used it, did not realize that the text is the same as *Habib al-Siyar*, part 4. Aubin (1984) cites a different MS at the Irān-e Bāstān Museum Library, but at present there is no such library. Khʷānd-Amir tells us that Amini was working on a work commissioned by Shah Esmā'il in 927/1521 (Khʷānd-Amir 1984: 4:326). Whether Khʷānd-Amir copied the work in its entirety, or the copyist misidentifies the present manuscript, we seem to have one and not two contemporary accounts of the reign of Shah Esmā'il. In any event, Amini was a friend and contemporary of Khʷānd-Amir and can safely be assumed to have shared his attitude and extreme restraint.

authority. The account substitutes the alleged inspiration by the Twelve Imams through dreams and visions for what must in reality have been more exaggerated claims and uses clichés and euphemisms for the violent enforcement of Shi'ism. Other main chronicles date to a period two generations later—that is, the latter part of Shāh Tahmāsb's reign, when orthodox Twelver Shi'ism had been established and accounts of the excesses of the revolutionaries was already severely doctored. Nevertheless, the novelty of the Safavid mixture of religious and political authority presents a historical narrative of the origins of the royal dynasty from the Sufi order of Shaykh Safi al-Din Ardabili, and this narrative varies greatly from the traditional narrative of the secular origins of kingship. Noteworthy among the supernatural aspects of this narrative is a variation on the theme of the occultation of the Twelfth Imam taken from the hagiography of Shaykh Safi, *Safvat al-safā*.[40] According to this narrative, Mohammad Hāfez, an ancestor of Shaykh Safi who had disappeared at the age of seven, manifested himself seven years later, having been taught the Qur'ān and religious sciences by the jinn, with whom he had spent the intervening years.[41] Dreams were of course an important medium for authentication of divine charisma. In a dream highlighted in the romance of Shah Esmā'il, a certain Dede Mehmed had a vision of the Hidden Imam girding Esmā'il with his sword. In another dream (in the mid-tenth/sixteenth century), a follower was inspired to write a tract on the significance of the Haydari crown. Hamza, the putative ancestor of the Safavids and son of the seventh Imam, Musā b. 'Ali, explained that the placing of the headgear had become an initiation ceremony for the Qezelbāsh and then spread to some craft guilds. The Twelfth Imam in Occultation transformed the headgear from the esoteric to the exoteric material form that was placed on Shah Esmā'il's head. Thus, he invested him as his deputy (*nā'eb*), and by the same token, whoever wore it was joining the Mahdi's army and would witness his advent and triumph in this world.[42]

2   Revolutionary Mobilization in a Khaldunian Revolution

Esmā'il's uprising began slowly. In the summer of 1499, he left Lāhijān with seven Sufi veterans and 300 men, he tarried in Tālesh and then visited his

---

40   Other supernatural elements, such as the maternal descent of the Safavids through the daughter of Shaykh Zāhed, from a Kurdish shaykh and the daughter of the king of the jinn who had become his disciple, were left out. (Togan 1959: 351)
41   Kh^wānd-Amir 1984: 4:411.
42   Bashir 2014: 347.

ancestral city of Ardabil which was under the control of his brother, Ebrāhim, who was the head of the Safavid order. He does not seem to have found any support from his now Sunni brother, Ebrāhim, nor presumably from his mother. So he began a long march into the heartland of eastern Anatolia, in search of millenarian Qezelbāsh supporters; this ended in Erzinjān in the summer of 1500.[43] It is important to note that at this point Esmāʿil, very much like his grandfather Jonayd who ventured into Anatolia when Ardabil was controlled by his hostile uncle, was leaving Ardabil to his brother and venturing into Anatolia in the hope of mobilizing the radical wing of the Safavid movement.

The Safavid agents in Qarāmān had undoubtedly sent him word of a rebellion (under a certain Mustafā) of the tribal leaders (*beg*s) and disgruntled cavalrymen (*sipāhi*) who held land grants (*timār*) in the region. Since the defeat of the tribal principality of Qarāmān by Mehmed the Conqueror in 1475 and its annexation in 1483, the Turkman tribesmen were systematically dispossessed by the centralizing policies of the Ottoman Empire. In 906/1500, a new land register (*tahrir*) doubled the administrative and military obligation of those with land assignments (*timār*s), causing discontent among their holders, some of whom joined the rebellion of the dispossessed tribal leaders. The governor of Amasya, Soltān Ahmed, however, put down the rebellion with the help of those from neighboring regions.

Nevertheless, Esmāʿil's venture to Erzinjān paid off, and his radical supporters decided that their moment had come. Bands of Sufis and raiders "from the Sufis of Qarajadāgh" and from the clans of Rumlu, Ostājlu, Shāmlu, Tekelu, Zuʾl-Qadr, Afshār, and Varsaq from the heart of Anatolia (Rum), Syria, Egypt, and Diyarbekir (Diyār Bakr) began to gather. An Ottoman source puts their number at 7,000.[44] Leaflets summoning those expecting the manifestation of His Majesty, i.e., Esmāʿil, who would be the prelude to the manifestation of the Lord of the Age, were sent in all directions."[45]

The expection of Lord of the Age is generally confirmed by a letter from Ayas, written in September 1500, stating that "a new lord has risen, and the whole country is in tumult."[46] Esmāʿil used the Qezelbāsh troops to conquer Shervān and Tabriz. During the sack of Shervān, Esmāʿil ordered the Qezelbāsh troops not to take any booty because the enemies were Sunnis and therefore impure (*najes*); one general recorded that he was tempted to keep a beautiful

---

43   Pārsādust 2002: 254.
44   Yildirim 2008: 276, 323–330.
45   ʿAbdi Beg: 38.
46   Aubin 1988: 12, with Sanudo 1979: 3:1119.

precious stone but he eventually threw it into a river in obedience to his spiritual master.⁴⁷ Esmāʿil then proceeded to conquer Tabriz.

In 907/1501, Shah Esmāʿil abandoned Tabriz and moved to Erzinjān in eastern Anatolia to gather more Qezelbāsh followers for his army. By mid-December, 8,000 people had gathered around him.⁴⁸ His movements were strictly determined by the location of his supporters and not the opportunity to seize power. The adepts coming from Tekke-eli were organized into the Tekelu clan as a military unit, alongside the existing Qarāmānlu clan. ʿAbdi (or ʿĀbedin) Beg brought some 200 young men from Syria (Shām) to join the Shāmlu clan under the veteran Lala Beg, and Mohammad Beg brought roughly the same number of men from an obscure geographical region—this group was organized into the Ostājlu clan, another mainstay of the rising Safavid military power.⁴⁹ Nine of the twelve known commanders of the army were from the Qezelbāsh tribes of Anatolia; they gathered and absorbed the local clans of Kheneslu, Bāybortlu, and Qarajadāghlu⁵⁰ and numbered 7,000 or possibly 12,000 when they defeated the Āq Qoyunlu forces in August 1501.⁵¹

The extensive recruitment among nomadic Turkmen in Anatolia was a result of the success of Safavid deputies/missionaries (*khalifa*s) in providing a powerful idiom of protest to dispossessed Turkman tribesmen. This idiom of protest was drawn from the Shiʿite theodicy of suffering based on the martyrdom of Hosayn, the son of ʿAli and grandson of the Prophet, in Karbala. In their poems (sang in Turkish) their reciters (*ozan*s) in red headgear cursed the "evil Yazid" (*Yezid-e pelid*) at whose bidding Hosayn and his family were massacred in Karbala, and identified the Ottoman governors as oppressors (*zālim*).⁵² Furthermore, Hosayn's martyrdom was given a millennial inflection by being presented as his uprising (*khoruj*), and similarly, their youthful Shaykhoghlu Esmāʿil was called the Lord of the Uprising (*sahib-e khoruj*) and presented as a messianic avenger of the blood of Hosayn. As such, he was the one who would lead a world revolution against oppression (*zolm*) and avenge Hosayn's martyrdom all at once.⁵³

Between 1495 and 1501, the dissident millenarian leadership of the Safavid Sufi order under the young charismatic Shaykhoghlus, Haydar's sons Soltān ʿAli and Esmāʿil, created a militant Turkman nomadic confederation called the

---

47 Pārsādust 2002: 259.
48 Sanudo 1979: 3.
49 *Tārikh-e Qezelbāshān* 1982: 8, 27, 45, 49.
50 *Tārikh-e Qezelbāshān* 1982: 25–26, 40.
51 Sümer 1992: 28–30.
52 Yildirim 2008: 148–149 and 354 n. 1168.
53 Yildirim 2015.

Qezelbāsh. In 1495, its core expanded from Soltān ʿAli's Shāmlu, Qāramānlu, Ayqutoghlu, and Qājār clans to Esmāʿil's larger confederation of 8,000 millenarian warrior nomads that also included, by 1501, the Ostājlu, Tekelu, Kheneslu, Bāybortlu, and Qarajadāghlu. They thus unified the Turkman nomadic tribesmen of Anatolia and western Iran under the banner for a Mahdistic millennial revolution, just as Abu ʿAbdallāh al-Shiʿi and Mahdi Ibn Tumart did with the Berber nomadic tribesmen of northern and southern Maghreb in the fourth/tenth and sixth/twelfth centuries respectively.[54]

3   The Opportunity Structure and Process of the Safavid Revolution

Like the contemporary reformation in Christian Europe, and like the European revolutions of 1848 and the Arab revolutions of 2011, the millennial Shiʿite revolution crossed state boundaries. In this case, those of the consolidating Ottoman and the disintegrating Āq Qoyunlu empires. As the outcome of revolution depends on the opportunities for success offered by the structure of the polities in which they occur, revolutions over regions with numerous states are bound to have different outcomes. This was certainly the case with the Safavid revolution.

Let us survey the opportunity structure of these two imperial states and the likelihood for the success of the revolution. By 1500, the Āq Qoyunlu nomadic empire was disintegrating fast while the Ottoman Empire survived the succession crisis and civil war following the death of Mehmet the Conqueror in 1481, and it was resuming the earlier centralizing policies under Mehmet's son Bāyezid II (1481–1512). Sultan Bāyezid II was securely on the Ottoman throne, and in the same year the Qezelbāsh forces conquered Tabriz (i.e., 907) Bāyezid conquered the Greek coastal strongholds of Morea, Coro, Moton, and Lepanto, and issued a much enlarged and modified form of Mehmed II's law codes as the *kitāb-e qawānin-e ʿorfiyya-ye ʿothmāniyya*. In 1501–1502, Bāyezid took firm measures to prevent his Qezelbāsh subjects from joining their Sufi leader in Ardabil by ordering his Anatolian governors, including his sons Ahmed in Amasya and Qorqud who was sent to Antalya specifically to punish those emigrating. When these measures appeared ineffective, he obtained *fatwās* declaring the Qezelbāsh unbelievers, and sent inspectors to identify Qezelbāsh leaders and the rank and file were deported in substantial numbers to the newly conquered Morea.[55]

54   Arjomand 2022: chs. 7–8.
55   Yildirim 2008: 316–323.

By contrast, the political opportunity for revolution created by the fragmentation of authority and persistent dynastic feuds in Iran was great. In this respect, it was Iran and not the Ottoman Empire that was ripe for a revolutionary takeover. What remained of the great Timurid Empire in the East was undoubtedly moribund, despite valiant efforts by Soltān-Hosayn Bayqarā (d. 1506) and his astute and learned vizier, ʿAli Shir Navāʾi (d. 1501), who foresaw the empire's doom in 1496, in the treacherous murder of his patron's grandson, Prince Mohammad-Moʾmen. By 1500, Iran was in fact divided into some twelve independent regions, including the newly conquered Safavid Azerbaijan. Two of these regions were ruled by urban notables, the rest by three groups of feuding princes and *amir*s of the decaying Āq Qoyunlu regime, and in the East by Timurid princes.[56] As the Safavid historian Hasan Rumlu attested:

> In the realm of Iran in that year [907/1501] quite a few governors claimed independence and put up the banner of 'I and none Else!': the equal-of-Alexander Khāqān [Esmāʿil] in Azerbaijan, Soltān-Morād [Āq Qoyunlu] in most of [the Persian] Iraq, Morād Beg Bāyandor [another Āq Qoyunlu prince] in Yazd, the alderman (*raʾis*) Mohammad Karrahi in Abarquh, Hosyan Kiyā Chalāvi in Semnān, Khwār and Firuzkuh, Bārik Beg Parnāk ... in the Arab Iraq, Qāsem Beg [Āq-Qoyunlu] ... in Diyār Bakr, Kadi Mohammad in association with Mawlānā Masʿud Bidgoli in Kāshān, [the Timurid] Soltān-Hosayn Mirzā in Khorasan, Amir Dhuʾl-Nun in Qandahār, [the Timurid] Badiʿ al-Zamān Mirzā in Balkh, and Abuʾl-Fath Beg Bāyandor [yet another dissident from the Āq-Qoyunlu] in Kermān.[57]

Esmāʿil therefore decided on the conquest of the Iranian cities, followed by those of Arab Iraq.

The centralizing policies initiated by the founder of the Āq Qoyunlu empire, Uzun Hasan (d. 1478), and his son Soltān Yaʿqub (d. 1490), (as we saw in chapter 4) unraveled fast in the power struggle over the succession to Soltān Yaʿqub and in the ensuing civil wars. Within a decade after Yaʿqub's death, the empire was divided between Yaʿqub's son, Soltān-Morād, who ruled central Iran, and Alvand Mirzā, who ruled Azerbaijan and eastern Anatolia. Shah Esmāʿil first took the Qezelbāsh followers he had gathered in Erzinjān eastward to fight Alvand's vassal, Shervānshāh, and defeated him to avenge his father and grandfather, Haydar and Jonayd. At this point, in the spring of 1501, the first important defection from the crumbling Āq Qoyunlu empire took place. A

---

56   Lari 2014: 2:878; Pārsādust 2002: 235–238, 280.
57   Rumlu 1931: 1:6.

vizier, Amir Shams al-Din Zakariyā Tabrizi Kojaji, joined Esmāʿil's camp. He was appointed vizier and was appropriately called "the key to Azerbaijan."[58] As Esmāʿil proceeded to conquer central Iran and Iraq, further submissions and defections took place from the *ancien régime*, notably those of Mansur Beg Afshār in central Iran and in 1507 that of the Āq Qoyunlu governor of Diyarbekir, Amir Beg Mawsellu. He and other *amir*s of the Mawsellu clan were given important functions by Shah Esmāʿil. With the last defections, the important Turkman tribes of Afshar and Mawsellu, like the Qarāmānlu and the former Āq Qoyunlu confederates, had joined the Qezellbāsh confederacy. The Zuʾl-Qadr followed suit after Shah Esmāʿil's conquest of their principality and defeat of their leader, ʿAlāʾ al-Dawla, in 1507.[59]

In the spring of 907/1502,[60] Esmāʿil returned to Tabriz, where the Sunnis were said to account for a two-thirds majority (leaving the Shiʿa a minority of one-third of the population), to crown himself, and declare Shiʿism the state religion. The Turkish-speaking *ozan*s could not be employed to rouse the Persian subjects in the marketplace, so their task was taken by Persian-speaking reciters who "dissociated" (*tabarrā*) themselves from the Sunni caliphs by cursing them. "The *tabarrāʾi*s," we are told, "despite opposition, raised the uproar of *tabarrā* to high heaven."[61] Esmāʿil issued an order that "the *tabarrāʾi*s should denigrate and curse the three cursed [caliphs] in public places, and kill whoever does the contrary."[62] Rival popular preachers were suppressed and the mosques delivered to the Shiʿite agitprops, the *tabarrāʾi*s.

The destruction of popular Sunni shrines was high on the agenda of the agitprops. The tombs of Abu Hanifa and Abu Yusof in Baghdad were desecrated and destroyed after the conquest of Iraq.[63] Despite his politic restraint and caution, Khʷānd-Amir mentions the Safavid agitprops and *tabarrāʾi*s, and hints at their unorthodoxy in his account of the rebellion of the people of Herat against the Safavid apparatchiks, which was caused by their indignation at the murder of their respected Sunni judge by the Qezelbāsh governor.[64] The putative tomb of Abu Moslem Khorāsāni in Nishapur was similarly destroyed after the conquest of Khorasan and Herat in 1510, and the *tabarrāʾi*s overran

---

58 ʿAbdi Beg: 39; Hinz 1936: 101–102.
59 *Tārikh-e Qezelbāshān* 1982: 22; Woods 1976: 197–198, 207–209, 212; Sümer 1992: 33, 39–40.
60 The year 1502 is the correct date. Many sources give the date as 1501, as I did in the *Shadow of God*, and Pārsādust (2002: 273 n. 86, 277 and 282–283 n. 1) is inconsistent.
61 ʿAbdi Beg: 40; *ʿĀlam-ārā-ye Shāh Esmāʿil* 1970: 60–61.
62 Qomi 1980: 1:73.
در اسواق تبرائیان همچنان زبان به طعن و لعن ملاعین ثلاثه گشوده هر کس خلاف کند او را به قتل رسانند.
63 Arjomand 1984: 112–121.
64 Khʷānd-Amir 1984: 4:468, 532–533, 583–586.

the mosques and markets of Herat and Khorasanian cities, with the cursing of Abu Moslem added to that of the first three rightly-guided caliphs of the Sunnis. The historical memory of Abu Moslem as the messianic leader of the revolution of the Persian *mawali* (clients) in Khorasan could not be eradicated, however. Abu Moslem's popularity was such that his tomb was rebuilt and was then destroyed again in the early years of Tahmāsb's reign. The leading Shi'ite jurist, Shaykh 'Ali al-Karaki wrote a book against Abu Moslem and the non-Shi'ite storytellers and issued a *fatwā* permitting the cursing of Abu Moslem and declaring anyone trying to prevent it as corrupt.[65]

On the political front, many if not most Āq Qoyunlu *amir*s and independent local magnates were killed or cruelly executed. In 909–910/1504, for instance, the above-mentioned Mohammad Karrahi and Hosayn Kiyā were put in iron cages and tortured until they committed suicide, and their corpses were burned; another Āq Qoyunlu *amir* was captured with the latter, then roasted and eaten by the Qezelbāsh. During the phase of revolutionary conquests, the zeal of the Qezelbāsh was harnessed for a military conquest that did great violence to the civilian population—no attempt was made to win over the population or admit them to the Safavid order. On the contrary, the capture of the cities was accompanied by the destruction of the other Sufi orders, the desecration of the tombs of Sufi shaykhs, and the fierce suppression of Sunnism. The major exception was the Ne'matollāhi order, which declared itself Shi'ite and was co-opted by Shah Esmā'il in a close alliance that lasted a century.[66]

The suppression of the rival Sufi orders made good political sense as Shah Esmā'il suspected many of their leaders of harboring the same ambitions his father and grandfather had, that is, to unify the dervishes and kingship. In this respect, the suppression of the Isma'ilis, who after the destruction of their mountain fortresses by the Mongols in 1256 transformed themselves into a Sufi order called the Khʷāndiyya in central Iran, is instructive. They were organized by the notables (*sādāt*) of Khʷānd near Qazvin. By the beginning of the tenth/sixteenth century these notables had moved their center to Kashan, where their leader, Shah Tāher, was warned by a fellow notable from Isfahan, Shah Qāsem Esfahāni, that "the King of Kings of Iran, Shah Esmā'il, the Safavid, who had himself become the lord of the state through the opportunity of discipleship and spiritual mastership" was bent on the destruction of all Sufi orders of the realm, especially the Khʷāndiyya!"[67] The order appears to have been marked for destruction as the new King of Kings was aware of the deeds of

---

65 Hamavi 1984: 182–189; Arjomand 2019: ch. 9.
66 'Abdi Beg: 43; *'Ālam-ārā-ye Shāh Esmā'il* 1970: 138–139; Arjomand 1984: 116; Aubin 1988: 45.
67 Ma'sum Ali Shāh 1966: 3:136.

the Isma'ili revolutionaries and Shah Ṭāher claimed descent from the Fatimid Mahdi! They barely had enough time to flee in the midst of a severe winter (1513), and Shah Ṭāher departed for India where he established himself in the Deccan and became known as Shah Ṭāher Dakani.

4   The Failure to Export the Revolution to the Ottoman Empire

In contrast to the disintegrating Āq Qoyunlu empire that was ripe for conquest, the Ottoman Empire was united and stable in 1500. Esmā'il, however, tenaciously persisted with the westward export of his millennial revolution, and the prospects looked better after his conquest of Iraq in the summer of 1507. He tested their strength by invading Ottoman territory and camping in Sivas under the pretext of dealing with the Zu'l-Qadr tribal principality of Diyarbekir that was ruled by the hereditary chief, 'Alā' al-Dawla, who had given asylum to the Āq Qoyunlu Prince Morād, his son-in-law.

Sultan Bāyezid II diplomatically downplayed the violation of his territory by Shah Esmā'il, whom he called his son, but also moved Rumelian troops and 4,000 Janissaries to Anatolia, as he did not trust his Anatolia troops whose Sufi sympathies he knew well. Whether touched by Bāyezid's paternal affection or deterred by his troop movements, Esmā'il decided the time was not suitable for a revolutionary takeover and he decamped.

It was not until 1511 that the window of opportunity for a revolution in Ottoman Anatolia opened. Sultan Bāyezid II had been bedridden with severe gout since 1507, and he was losing control over the recently centralized state bureaucracy. His viziers had taken over the central administration and were using it to fill their pockets while they could. There were widespread allegations of bribery concerning the repossession and reallocation of *timār*s (land grants) as the military prebends to the *sipāhi* cavalrymen, with the grand vizier 'Ali Pasha and the *beylerbey* of Anatolia, Qaragöz Pasha, heading the list for grand peculation. Soltān Qorqud left Antalya for Egypt in 1509 for a year, leaving his governorship vacant. In his absence, Ottoman authority in the province declined seriously while the number of *sipāhi*s dispossessed of their posts (*dirlik*), which went to higher bidders, increased and their discontent mounted.[68]

According to the Persianate conception of revolution presented in chapter 1, the normative disorder caused by the tyranny of malfunctioning government is accompanied by disorder in nature and natural calamities that portend

---

68   Uğur 1985: 154–156; Inalcik 2000: 32.

divinely-ordained revolution. A severe earthquake in September 1509 forced Bāyezid to move to Edirne; however, it was struck by a second and then a third earthquake. The ailing Bāyezid read the portents and summoned his viziers and generals to tell them: "It is the lament of the oppressed, which is the result of your oppression and corruption that reached God and ignited His wrath. This disaster is nothing other than the result of your oppression!"[69]

The expected death of the bedridden Bāyezid started a struggle for succession among three of his sons, Ahmed, Selim, and Qorqud. The Anatolian Qezelbāsh responded to this opportunity. Their uprising, however, was no longer aligned with post-revolutionary imperial consolidation in Iran. After the conquest of Khorasan[70] and the shift in the center of gravity in the empire in 1510, Shah Esmā'il was no longer keen on the westward export of revolution into Ottoman Anatolia and Syria. The ending of the export of revolution by the new imperial sovereign of the East and the West doomed the millennial uprising of his Anatolian followers to failure.[71]

Shaykh Jonayd had established a Safavid mission in Tekke-eli region in Antalya some fifty years earlier, appointed Hasan Khalifa Tekelu in its charge.[72] Despite Soltān Bāyezid's forceful shift of the Qezelbāsh to Rumelia in 1502, the order survived. Furthermore, the Qezelbāsh began to proselytize among the *sipāhi*s dispossessed of their lands by Bāyezid's viziers, and forced Bāyezid's son, Prince Selim, who was a governor in eastern Anatolia, to compete in recruiting dispossessed *sipāhi*s for a holy raid against Georgia.[73] In the spring of 1511, rumors of Bāyezid's death prompted the sudden departure of the prince/governor, Soltān Qorqud from Anatolia, while Soltān Selim rose against his father whom he considered senile.[74]

In these promising circumstances, Bābā Shāhqoli (Şāhkulu), the son and successor of Jonayd's agent, Hasan Khalifa, who had lived with his father in a cave as a Sufi hermit, led a fierce uprising in Teke. The Turkmen are said to have sold their farms and cattle at a loss and joined the Qezelbāsh, donning their red headgear. At the end of March 1511, Shāhqoli's men captured the treasury of Soltān Qorqud, who had left his post in a hurry and neglected to take it with

---

69 Cited in Yildirim 2008: 353.
70 He was still there when the Anatolian uprising occurred.
71 See below in this chapter.
72 Sohrweide 1965: 133; Yildirim 2008: 365.
73 Uğur 1985: 149–150, paraphrasing Nişanci.
74 According to Uğur (1985: 162–165) this move was done with the approval of Bāyezid's other son, Soltān Ahmed. Yildirim (2008: ch. 12), by contrast, argues that Soltān Ahmed was the favorite of his father and the grand vizier, 'Ali Pasha, and had no reason to deal with Selim and eventually executed him in 1513.

him. The revolt broke out on ʿĀshura, the fateful day of Imam Hosayn's martyrdom, 9 April 1511, and quickly spread.⁷⁵

At this point, the few *sipāhi*s who had become Sufis forged a coalition between the Qezelbāsh rebels and their dispossessed colleagues who were distinguished from Turkmen by their higher well-born (*merdumzāde*) status. Given their discontent, many joined the rebels. The reason is well articulated by one such cavalryman:

> All of our wealth went to buy our *timār*s. In order to buy a *timār*, one needs camels, wealth. There are no *timār*s for the comrades [fellow *sipāhi*s]. Every propertied Turk, sons of merchants, kadis, and *waqf* trustees became *timār* holders. All the relatives of the *soltān*, his stewards, his tent builder, his soothsayers, and others became *timār*-holders. No *timār* is left for the comrades. Now let them see what sort of sedition comes from giving *timār*s to absentee lords and oppressing the *sipāhi* folks.

The reporter goes on to say: "The *sipāhi*s are at the forefront of every trouble, and from now on there is no hope of them acting like comrades."⁷⁶ The struggle for succession, combined with a corrupt and dysfunctional government created very favorable conditions for a revolutionary coalition. Even Prince Shehanshāh, yet another son of Bāyezid who had no chance for succession and was the governor of Qarāmān but died during the unrest, briefly joined the Qezelbāsh, as did Shehanshāh's son Soltān-Mohammad.⁷⁷

In mid-April 1511 some 20,000 rebels and their families entered Burdur, and a week later proceeded to Kütahya, where Shāhqoli captured the *beylerbeg*, Qaragöz Pasha, and after consulting with the allied *sipāhi*s of Tekke, executed him outside the city. On May 3, he defeated Qorqod's army, the last sizeable one in the region, and the prince fled to the fortress of Mansa. Bābā Shāhqoli made his victory proclamation: "We have now seized the province of Anatolia!"⁷⁸ Amasya was then overrun, and the rebels reached the countryside of Bursa. The rebellion was extremely violent, with massacres of urban populations, jurists, and Sufi shaykhs alike, the destruction of mosques and Sufi *khāneqāh*s, the beheading and impaling of a governor, and even the ritual roasting of three officials and several *bey*s. According to the kadi of Antalya, Bābā Shāhqoli at times claimed to be the Mahdi, and at other times, he claimed that Shah

---

75 Uğur 1985: 166; Sümer 1992: 36–37 n. 16, citing Kemalpāshāzāde; Yildirim 2008: 386.
76 Cited in Yildirim 2008: 383. I owe the English translation to Dr. Can Ersoy.
77 Lari 2014: 2:932–935; Sümer 1992: 43; Uğur 1985: 165; Yildirim 2008: 379–384.
78 Yildirim 2008: 391.

Esmāʿil had died and his divine charisma passed to himself. One of his followers who was captured and brought before the same kadi still considered him God and a new prophet and was executed for apostasy.[79]

The rebellion then unraveled as Bāyezid was finally told about it; he forced Soltān Ahmed and ʿAli Pasha to lead reinforced Ottoman troops against the rebels. Although his army remained intact, the grand vizier, ʿAli Pasha, was killed in the early days of July 1511, just as the rebellion was spent and its leader Shāhqoli disappeared. A group of some three or five hundred Qezelbāsh rebels fled to Iran, attacking a commercial caravan from Tabriz on the way. Most chronicles place this event after the suppression of the rebellion of Bābā Shāhqoli, but, according to the intriguing account of Edris Bedlisi, Bābā Shāhqoli's "vizier" led the looting expedition into Azerbaijan in 1511 not after, but during the rebellion. Shah Esmāʿil, who was preoccupied with the consolidation of the newly acquired empire, refused to receive Bābā Shāhqoli's millenarian followers who fled to Iran.[80] When they finally realized their dream and reached the realm of their charismatic Sufi master, Shah Esmāʿil, they met with a rude awakening.

The Safavid attempt to export its millennial revolution to the Ottoman Empire ended definitively with Shah Esmāʿil's defeat by the Ottoman army in 1514. Esmāʿil's messianic charisma as a warrior made invincible by divine grace was shattered in 1514 by Selim, the new Ottoman *Sultan* who provoked him into fighting (with a sense of millenarian intoxication) the battle of Chaldiran, and finally suppressed the Safavid movement in the Ottoman Empire. Esmāʿil's defeat produced broad disaffection among his Qezelbāsh troops as well as with his Anatolian adepts. He wore black as a sign of mourning, and had cities draped with banners bearing the inscription "punishment" (*al-qesās*). Esmāʿil never again led his men in battle, and changed his style of ruling into that of a mere Persian king. Most notably, he desisted from religious persecution and forceful conversion to Shiʿism, and issued a decree ordering his provincial governors "not to inconvenience anyone, from now on, by [forcing him to] abandon his religion or convert, and to treat all subjects equally in matters of taxation and religious courts."[81]

79 Sohrweide 1965: 146–158; Uğur 1985: 164–196; Aubin 1988: 90; Yildirim 2008: 384–404.
80 Uğur 1985: 181–183; Aubin 1988: 90–91.
81 Cited in Pārsādust 2002: 497.

5 The Containment of Millennialism and the Routinization of Mahdistic Charisma into Kingship

The conception of the process of revolution determines our periodization of its stages. In his first Safavid study (1959), Aubin presented a general view of the incorporation of the Persian notables into Esmāʿil's Turkman empire of conquest over the course of its consolidation throughout his reign. In the second study, he considered the 1508–1509 turning point as "the victory of the Persians over the Turkmen, and also a revenge of the Ostājlu over the Shāmlu faction" among the Qezelbāsh.[82] The ousting of the small cluster of Qezelbāsh leaders who had raised Esmāʿil in his early exile in Lāhijān and were accordingly known as the "Sufis of Lāhijān" was seen as the critical turning point in the transition from the revolutionary phase to one of consolidation, not just because of tribal and factional infighting but mainly because the old guard was replaced by Persian notables at the expense of all the Qezelbāsh factions. I take a contrasting position and view Esmāʿil's suppression of Qezelbāsh extremism as part of his commitment to the export of millenarian revolution—or, to be more precise, the liquidation, in 1512, of his own most extreme and millenarian followers who had fled after the suppression of Bābā Shāhqoli's rebellion—as the decisive point in the revolutionary power struggle, the point that signaled the end of revolution and the beginning of consolidation.[83]

My periodization of the Safavid revolution against Aubin's dating rests on the logic of the revolutionary process. The "Sufis of Lāhijān" were not expelled from the movement in 1508, rather they were put in charge of the export of revolution to Khorasan in 1510. What is more, it is evident from Aubin's own earlier study that the incorporation of the administrative and judiciary cadre of the Āq Qoyunlu *ancien régime* was more gradual, and in fact began in the spring of 1501 with the defection of the above-mentioned Amir Zakariyā Khojaji, followed in 1503–1504 by another colleague and former Āq Qoyunlu vizier, Mahmud Khan, who belonged to the Daylami/Qazvini family; the Sāvaji family of clerical notables probably entered the Safavid service around that time.[84] Similarly, Qāzi Mohammad Kāshi, who was in control of Kāshān with another local notable, submitted to Shah Esmāʿil and became a Safavid official. Meanwhile, Shah Esmāʿil established the offices of the new Safavid state; the highest military and administrative offices were filled by Sufi veterans—Bayrām

---

82 Aubin 1984: 9. In the final study, Aubin (1988: 63) describes the same transition as that from "the reign of the tutors to that of the favorites." See also Aubin 1988: 85, 124–126 for further discussion.
83 Arjomand 1984: 110.
84 Aubin 1959b: 65.

Beg as the *amir-e divan* and 'Abdi Beg as the *tovaji-bāshi*,[85] and the highest religious office, that of *sadr*, was filled by his tutor Mawlānā Shams al-Din Lāhiji, who was also a member of his inner circle. In 1508, Shah Esmā'il conquered Baghdad and massacred the Pornāk clan that had ruled it for the old dynasty. He appointed the veteran Sufi of Lāhijan, Khādem Beg Khalifa, as its new governor. More significantly, he also appointed Lāhiji to the new office of chief deputy (*khalifat al-kholafā'*) of the Safavid order with the specific mission of exporting the revolution to Anatolia through his subordinate *khalifas*.[86]

Furthermore, Shaykh Najm al-Din Zargar Rashti, whose appointment as Shah Esmā'il's *vakil* in 1508 I take to be part of this turning point, may or may not support Aubin's argument. He was a jeweler (*zargar*) from the city of Rasht who had joined in the nearby Lāhijan very early. Although a Persian, he belonged to the core sectarian cell around Shah Esmā'il in Lāhijan and for sociological reasons should be classified as one of the "Sufis of Lāhijan," alongside the five leading members named by Aubin.[87] Therefore, I argue that the post-revolutionary transition began two years later, with the accession of Esmā'il's protégé, Yār Ahmad Khuzāni, who came from a family of notables of Isfahan; he was called the second star (*najm*) as he occupied the office of *vakil*. This signaled the geopolitical shift toward Khorasan which, according to my argument, was decisive for initiating the phase of consolidation of revolution in one country. Yet this appointment was contingent and happened because of the death of the first star, Najm al-Din Zargar Rashti, who was the first Persian to command the Qezelbāsh in the battle of Ghojdovān (1512) where he was, however, captured and killed.

From my perspective, the victory of the Ostājlu over the Shāmlu faction among the Qezelbāsh tribesmen in 1508–1509 is important but should be placed alongside the purge of the Qezelbāsh that had been carried out under the "Sufis of Lāhijan" in 1505 by one of its leading members, Dede Beg, the *qurchi-bāshi*.[88] We know very little about this extensive purge, but it is significant that 'Abdi Beg refers to this purged group as "hypocrites" (*monāfeqān*).[89] We must consider it part of the revolutionary power struggle, and ideologically based, that is, above clan rivalries. This power struggle between extremists and accommodationists ended with the suppression of the remnants of Bābā Shāhqoli's rebellion, who were seeking to radicalize the Safavid movement and rekindle its commitment to millennial world revolution.

---

85   Haneda 1987: 72–77.
86   Hinz 1936: 18; Pārsādust 2002: 281–282, 301–302.
87   Aubin 1984: 3.
88   Aubin 1984: 4.
89   'Abdi Beg: 44.

Meanwhile, a major shift of the center of gravity of the Safavid Empire of conquest occurred with the annexation of Khorasan and Herat and with Shah Esmāʿil's defeat of the Uzbek Mohammad Shaybāni Khan in the battle of Marv in December 1510. The victory was followed by the incorporation of a considerable number of Timurid officials and notables. The new conception of greater Iran as unifying the Āq Qoyunlu domains in the West and Timurid Khorasan and Herat in the East went hand in hand with a conception of imperial kingship, The decrees issued by Shah Esmāʿil's chancery accordingly emphasized the legitimacy of the Safavid lineage as an imperial dynasty. The same imperial conception of sovereignty is reflected in the description of Mirzā Shāh Hosayn Esfāhāni, Shah Esmāʿil's *vakil* ([plenipotentiary] deputy) from 1514 to 1523, as the "implementer of the command of the two easts and the two wests (*nāfez-e farmān-e mashreqayn va maghrebayn*)."[90]

I rest the case for my proposed periodization of the Safavid revolution with an explanation of the political theater staged by Shah Esmāʿil, in which he interrogated and cruelly executed his ardent Turkish followers, acts that have puzzled many historians. First, note that already in May 1511—that is, before the public trial in the fall of that year, and even before the collapse of Bābā Shāhqoli's rebellion in July—Shah Esmāʿil sent an ambassador to Sultan Bāyezid II, as one imperial sovereign to another, with the head of the Uzbek Shaybāni Khan whom he had killed in battle a year earlier. During the interrogation of the Anatolian refugees from Shāhqoli's rebellion, he never mentioned the Safavid millennial, revolutionary ideology but instead championed the Persianate raison d'état as an imperial monarch. Were they not subjects of "my father, Soltān Bāyezid" and under his protection!? If so, what right did they have to disobey him and rebel?[91] Judging them as a Shah and as the head of an imperial state rather than a millennial Sufi leader, Esmāʿil had the rebel leaders thrown into boiling cauldrons or otherwise executed. He confiscated the horses of the rest of the Turkman refugees, and gave some to the Qezelbāsh and left the rest of the Turkmen to beg in the streets with their wives and children.

Whichever of the two dates discussed above (Aubin's suggested 1508, or 1511) is taken as the inception of the phase of post-revolutionary consolidation, the implication is that by 1511 Esmāʿil was thinking of "Shiʿism in one country" as, centuries later, Stalin was to implement "socialism in one country." This transition from the radical to pragmatic phase of the Safavid revolution, however, made no difference to his sworn foes to the East and the West, the Uzbeks and Ottomans. They dealt Esmāʿil two decisive defeats in Ghojdovān

---

90 Cited in Aubin 1988: 114.
91 Yıldırım 2008: 406–408.

in November 1512, and in Chaldiran in May 1514. The revolution came to an end by necessity.

Administrative consolidation, on the one hand, and the conversion of the population to Shi'ism, to make Iran a single Shi'ite country, on the other, gained full force. These processes continued during the long reign of Shah Tahmāsb (r. 1524–1576) but was reversed after his death with the civil strife caused by Qezelbāsh tribal factionalism. It only became irreversible in the eleventh/seventeenth century after Shah 'Abbās I (r. 1587–1629) subdued the Qezelbāsh and imitated the Ottoman centralization policies. Hand in hand with the efforts to centralize military and administrative power, the Safavid chroniclers constantly repeated the formula that the rule of the Safavid dynasty would last until the coming of the Mahdi. This was a formula for the containment of Mahdism and its conversion to the post/counter-revolutionary principle of legitimacy of Safavid dynastic rule.

The concentration of power as the typical centralizing consequence of revolution was a long-term process after the Safavid revolution, a process that remained uncertain while the conversion of Iran, the heartland of the empire, was not yet complete, and was reversible as long as the Qezelbāsh-dominated polity remained tribal. The more immediate consequence of the Safavid revolution was the establishment of Shi'ite Islam, as this was the first crucial step in the conversion of the majority of Iran's population over the ensuing two centuries. Furthermore, in contrast to the short-term concentration of power, the lasting consequence of the Safavid revolution was the radical change in the conception of kingship. This change is evident in the narrative of the rise of the Safavids in Persian chronicles and other sources. In a decree issued in April 1511, Shah Esmā'il claims divine sanction for his kingship (*saltanat*) and caliphate (*kelāfat*) by citing the Qur'ān (Q. 2:118 and Q. 38:25), and referring to the Safavid house as the "dynasty of spiritual authority (*velāyat*) and Imamate." Popular Sufism, which was increasingly tinged with the Shi'ite expectation of the manifestation of the Mahdi in the mid-ninth/fifteenth century, infused a sacral element into the idea of kingship as temporal rule. The change in the conception of kingship made definitive by the Safavid revolution was as much the effect of Sufism as Shi'ism. The popular Sufi conception of a unified material and spiritual monarchy was institutionalized under Shah Esmā'il and reconciled with Twelver Shi'ism by his successors who claimed to be the lieutenants of the Hidden Imam.[92]

---

92 Navā'i 1969: 101–103. I argue that the new sacral idea of kingship was not fully consistent with the logic of Twelver Shi'ism, and collapsed with the Safavid Empire in 1722, allowing for the return of the traditional idea of monarchy as temporal rule. (Arjomand 1984)

CHAPTER 6

Sunni Reactions to the Safavid Mahdist Revolution and the Ottoman Imperial Counter-Revolution

The Safavid Mahdist revolution introduced a radical change in the conception of kingship. This was facilitated by the fact that popular Sufism, as we have seen, became increasingly tinged with the Shiʿite expectation that the Mahdi would manifest himself, an expectation prevalent since the mid-ninth/ fifteenth century. I have argued elsewhere that this trend ultimately produced the paradoxical sacralization (through world renunciation) of temporal rule. This was the combined effect of the Sufi and Shiʿite notions of *velāyat*, meaning sainthood to the Sufis and Imamate to the Shiʿa.[1] The culmination of this trend in popular Sufism came in 1501 with the empire established by the youthful *shaykh* of the Safavid order, Shah Esmāʿil. The fact of this paradoxical sacralization of the ruler, though not its precise nature, was evident to the Venetians who called Shah Esmāʿil the "Grand Sophy" and considered him a new prophet. This insertion of a sacral millennial element into the idea of kingship as temporal rule was in fact the project of Esmāʿil's father (and grandfather) who, as *shaykh*s of the Safavid Sufi order had sought, in the historian Khwānd-Amir's words, the "unification of dervishhood and kingship" (*jamʿ-e darvishi o shāhi*)—that is, the unification of temporal and spiritual monarchy.[2] The popular Sufi conception of a unified temporal and spiritual monarchy was fully institutionalized under Shah Esmāʿil. The Shiʿite conception of ʿAli as the *vali Allāh* was a key insertion into the Sufi notion of *velāyat* (friendship with God) and the juristic meaning of the term as 'authority'; the Safavids combined both senses. In a decree issued in 1511, Shah Esmāʿil claimed divine sanction for his sovereignty (*saltanat*) and caliphate (*khelāfat*) by citing the Qurʾān (Q. 2:118 and 38:25), and called the Safavid house the "dynasty of spiritual authority (*velāyat*) and Imamate."[3] The Safavid kings after him also retained the title of the Perfect Guide, first used by Nurbakhash, and remained the head of the Safavid Sufi order now exclusively reserved for Qezelbāsh tribal army.

---

1 See Arjomand 2022.
2 Khwānd-Amir 1984: 4:426 as cited in Arjomand 2005: 51.
3 Cited in Arjomand 2010: 264.

1 The Transplantation of the Counter-Millennial Sovereignty to the Mughal Empire in India

The rise of Shah Esmāʿil had significant repercussions throughout the Persianate world, and perhaps even beyond it. Venice paid keen attention to the rise of the Grand Sophy and maintained cordial relations with the Shah of the Safavid empire. The Timurid prince, Zahir al-Din Mohammad Bābor, who later established the Mughal Empire in India, was briefly (between 1510 and 1512) a vassal of Shah Esmāʿil and even professed Shiʿism before being defeated by the Uzbek ʿObayd Allāh Khan in Central Asia.[4] In India itself, the ruler of the kingdom of Bijāpur in the Deccan, Yusof ʿĀdelshāh (r. 1489–1510) established Shiʿism as the state religion in 1502, just as he heard of Shah Esmāʿil's similar proclamation in Tabriz; his successors are said to have employed some 300 Iranians to curse the first three caliphs.[5] The Ottoman case was far more complicated, as it was the culmination of the pre-emptive Mahdism that began in reaction to the 1416 rebellion of Shaykh Bedreddin, and was followed by the apocalyptic fervor that continued even after the conquest of Constantinople, and last but not least, by the new Mahdist revolution of Shah Esmāʿil the Safavid. It can be argued, however, that the Ottoman counter-revolution was the most successful and lasting; therefore, I discuss it in greater detail.

Khʷānd-Amir, the aging Timurid historian who made note of the new sovereignty emerging from the Safavid dervish heritage and saw his city change hands from the Timurids to the Uzbeks only to be annexed into Shah Esmāʿil's expanding empire, finally left Herat for Qandahar and India, where the displaced Bābor had reestablished a Timurid kingdom. Khʷānd-Amir's insight into the latest symbiosis of Sufism and kingship reached the court of the new ruler of India in 1528. As the chief chronicler of Bābor's son, who succeeded Bābor in 1530, Khʷānd-Amir committed his insights regarding the secret of the coming age to writing in *Qānun-e Homāyuni* and delivered it to Homāyun in 1534.[6] Khʷānd-Amir hailed his new royal patron as "the unifier of the real and the apparent sovereignty" (*jāmeʿ-e saltanat-e haqiqi va majāzi*).[7] Long after Khʷānd-Amir's death, the institutionalization of the Safavid-inspired model in India in the 1550s by Homāyun (after his long exile in Shah Tahmāsb's Iran) produced what Afzar Moin (2012) aptly calls millennial sovereignty in Mughal India. This was the beginning of the paradoxical sacralization of worldly kingship by

---

4 Roemer 1986: 126.
5 Cole 1989.
6 Quinn 2015.
7 Khʷānd-Amir 1993: 258.

way of Sufi world-renunciation that is, strictly speaking, counter-millennial. This movement that was originally intended to focus on Sufi ego annihilation and rejection of the world—a paradoxical sacralization—quickly spread throughout the Persianate ecumene.

Counter-millennial sovereignty was thus transplanted from Safavid Iran to Mughal India. The Safavid model of autocracy was evidently seen as the only remedy to nomadic patrimonialism and tanistry in Timurid Mughal India after Bābor. Bābor had divided his empire among his sons according to the rules of nomadic patrimonialism. This had disastrous consequences for Homāyun, who spent most of his reign humiliated in exile; he then replaced nomadic patrimonialism with millennial sovereignty, reflected in his own elaborate, cosmological design for ceremonies.[8] The typological affinity of Safavid and Mughal millennial kingship extended to the military political organization of the respective empires. Homāyun's son Akbar (1566–1609) adopted the Safavid model of the militant Qezelbāsh Sufi order, transformed it into an army led by the shah as the Perfect Guide (*morshed-e kāmel*), and created a devotional order of imperial discipleship (*moridi*). Various Muslims (orthodox and heterodox), Hindu nobles, and officials in his expanding empire were integrated into the imperial order under Akbar's supreme spiritual sovereignty. The institution of imperial discipleship was perfected by Akbar's son, Jahangir.[9]

2   The Sunni Counter-Revolution in the Uzbek Empire in Central Asia

Revolutions often generate counter-revolutions, and not necessarily in the same country. If Esmāʿil's Mahdist Shiʿite revolution spanned several Persianate imperial realms, we should expect a Sunni counter-revolution to do likewise. Revolutions typically produce a large number of exiles, and attempts to export revolutions alarm neighboring powers, resulting in their support for counter-revolutions and wars. The success of a millenarian Shiʿite revolution in Iran under the leadership of the child-god Esmāʿil drove many Iranian notables and Sunni jurists into exile. Unlike the Sasanian revolution under Ardashir and Shāpur I, whose counter-revolutionary exiles gathered in the Parthian kingdom of Armenia, and more like the Islamic revolution, whose exiles dispersed to the east and west,[10] the exiles of the Safavid revolution moved in three main directions: westward to the Ottoman Empire, north-eastward to Uzbek

---

8   Arjomand 2010: 269–270; Truschke 2016.
9   Moin 2012.
10 Arjomand 2019: ch. 6.

Transoxiana and south-eastward to India. Those who went to India[11] had little opportunity for counter-revolutionary political activism. The *ancien régime* exiles who fled to the Ottoman and Uzbek states found other opportunities. To the Ottoman and Uzbek rulers, the Qezelbāsh warriors seeking world domination were a dire and immediate threat. To stop the expansion of the Safavid Empire, these two rival powers made imperial counterclaims as upholders of Sunni orthodoxy with significant help from these exiles. The Ottoman and Uzbek states solicited help from jurists to defend Islamic orthodoxy against the rampant millennial heresy, and prominent jurists supplied both rulers with *fatwā*s (legal rulings) stating that shedding the blood of the Qezelbāsh was lawful, and indeed an incumbent duty.

It was difficult to gain acceptance for the Sunni counter-revolution in the nomadic Uzbek empire to the east, owing to Shah Esmāʿil's meteoric victory in the battle of Marv in 1510. Mawlānā Zayn al-Din Mahmud Vāsefi, a man of letters and Qurʾān reciter who had been trained as a preacher by the famous Molla Hosayn Vāez Kāshefi in Herat, begins his *Badāyeʿ al-waqāyeʿ* (Marvelous events) with an account of how he joined a caravan leaving Herat for Transoxiana at the last minute with two other Sunni notables fearing persecution. Approximately five hundred people left the city during the early spring of 1512. Among his companions was Shāh-Qāsem Nurbakhsh, the successor of one of our ninth-/fifteenth-century Mahdi and his entourage. On the way, the party, which included a group of musicians, singers, and poets, heard of the defeat of Mirzā Bābor by the Uzbek Khan, ʿObayd Allāh, and hastened to Samarqand to see the latter. When ʿObayd Allāh arrived in Samarqand to celebrate his victory, the welcoming oration was given by Khʷāja Mawlānā Esfahāni, a Persian émigré who was evidently already well settled in the city abandoned by the defeated Timurid Mirzā Bābor.[12]

Among the earlier Persian émigrés in Samarqand he met Mawlānā Hājji Tabrizi, the unfortunate Āq Qoyunlu Shaykh al-Islam of Tabriz who had fled from Shah Esmāʿil through Herat to Samarqand when it was still under Timurid rule under Bābor. He remained in the entourage of the Uzbek Khan and was eventually appointed by him to the highest religious office, that of *sadr*. Vāsefi calls the Uzbek Mohammad Shaybāni Khan the "Imam of the Age (*imām al-zamān*) and the Deputy of the Merciful God."[13]

---

11   Aubin 1988: 96.
12   Vāsefi 1970: 1:17–37.
13   Vāsefi 1970: 1:58–59, 288; 2:180. The appellation "Imam of the Age" was that of the expected Shiʿite Mahdi. ʿObayd Allāh, who was still a khan, had put his elder brother on the Uzbek throne, was hailed as a *ghāzi* (warrior against the Qezelbāsh heretics) (Vāsefi 1970: 1:173, 177, 180).

From our point of view, however, the foremost counter-revolutionary exile to move to Transoxiana was the Āq Qoyunlu patrician notable and court historian, Fazl Allāh Ruzbehān Khonji (d. 1521), recorded by Vāsefi as Khʷāja Mawlānā Esfahāni, as he was known in his new abode. Khonji had fled Kāshān after completing a refutation of Shiʿism and as the city fell to the Safavids in 1503. He went on to Herat, which was conquered by the Uzbek army of Mohammad Shaybāni Khan. By 1508 he had found his way into Shaybāni Khan's camp; he accompanied him on campaigns and completed the *Mehmān-nāma-ye Bokhārā* for him in 1509,[14] blazing the way for quite a few Sunni notables of Herat to join him when Herat was conquered by the Qezelbāsh army in 1510.

The *Mehmān-nāma-ye Bokhārā* is very interesting, not so much for the *fatwā*s it includes allowing jihad against the Qezelbāsh, but rather for showing Khonji's strategy of competitive appropriation and preemption of popular Shiʿite themes for counter-revolutionary mobilization. The most important popular notions and practices Khonji seeks to appropriate against the Qezelbāsh revolution are the belief in the Mahdi, which he modified to the expected Hāreth[15] and the renewer (*mojadded*) of the century (claimed by his Uzbek patron as against Esmāʿil's Mahdist incarnation), the love of the family of the Prophet, and pilgrimage to the shrine of Imam Rezā.[16] Above all, he uses the term that had been given currency by his colleagues in the Āq Qoyunlu chancery to match Shah Esmāʿil's millennial sovereignty by calling the Uzbek Khan the "deputy of the Merciful [God]" (*khalifat al-rahmān*).

Khonji continued to live as an *ancien régime* exile after his royal patron was killed by Shah Esmāʿil in the following year, and then sought a Sunni monarch to defeat Esmāʿil. By the end of 1512, the Uzbeks had regained power and defeated the Safavids in the battle of Ghojdovān and in 1514 Khonji wrote a remarkable work on Sunni sharia-based government for the next Uzbek khan, ʿObayd Allāh; he called it *Soluk al-moluk*. After hearing of the defeat of Shah

---

14   Khonji-Esfahāni 1976: 356; Khonji 1992, editor's introduction, 2–4.
15   Khonji-Esfahāni 1976: 95–99, 104–106. He cites a tradition reported in the *Sonan* of Abu Dāvud that predicts an *ex eventu* prophecy of the return of the Hāreth b. Sorayj, who had unfurled the messianic black banner in Transoxiana against the Umayyads some twelve years before Abu Moslem. (Arjomand 2019: ch. 8)
16   Khonji Esfahāni 1976: 339–346. In line with the confessional ambiguity of the age, Khonji adds a eulogy for Imam Rezā; in it he mentions the other eleven Imams (Khonji Esfahāni 1976: 336–338), and also mentions (344) another book he wrote in praise of the twelve Imams. The latter work is often cited as evidence of what Biancamaria Scarcia Amoretti calls syncretic Shiʿitized Sunnism, or what Rasul Jaʿfariyān refers to as "Twelver Sunnism." Without denying the existence of syncretic trends in Timurid Iran, I would take Khonji-Esfahāni's work as evidence of an attempt by opponents of the Safavid revolution at competitive appropriation of popular Shiʿite themes.

Esmāʿil by the Ottoman Solṭān Selim, Khonji urged Selim to follow the example of Alexander and annex Iran to Rum. He wrote this plea in a poem in Persian, to which he appended another poem in Chaghatay Turkish (written by a fellow Sunni doctor in exile) exhorting Selim to liberate Khorasan.[17] His counter-revolutionary appropriation of millennial sovereignty is expressed to Selim by hailing him as the Mahdi, Lord of the Age (sahib-e zamān) and the caliph of God and Mohammad.[18]

ʿObayd Allāh Khan (r. 1512–1540), who thought he owed his improbable victory over the much more numerous Qezelbāsh army in Ghojdovān to the prayer of Mir ʿArab, a disciple of the Naqshbandi Sufi master Khʷaja ʿObayd Allāh Ahrār, not only built a great madrasa named after him, but also many other madrasas, mosques, and shrines in his capital, Bukhara, known as the "Dome of Islam" (qobat al-eslām). He may have heeded the advice of the orthodox Khʷāja Mawlānā Esfahāni. A later historical enumeration of his monuments describes him as an observant or sharia-bound (motasharreʿ) king.[19]

The Uzbek counter-revolution, however, took an entirely different course from that outlined in Khonji Esfahāni's program for Islamic government or those suggested by other Persian exiles in Samarqand and Bukhara. The building of the Uzbek Empire began under Mohammad Shaybāni Khan (r. 1501–1512), who formed a confederate tribal army with fifty amirs serving as commanders of their own tribal contingents and expanded his domain from Samarquand, conquering Herat before he was killed on the battlefield by Shah Esmāʿil.[20] His nephew, ʿObayd Allāh Khan (d. 1540) revived the nomadic confederation centered on the Abu'l-Khayr/Shaybāni clan of the descendants of Chinggiss Khan's son Jochi, defeated the Safavid army in Ghojdovān, and continued the expansion of the Uzbek Empire. In the process, he acquired many additional appanages for distribution, when his cousin, the senior khan, died in 1533. He reorganized his nomadic empire on the basis of Chinggissid khanate principles, rather than on Khonji Esfanhāni's Islamic principles.

The rulers of the new nomadic empire were the Uzbeck khans who assumed the Chingissid title of bahādur (hero) khān, albeit augmented by the Perso-Islamicate titles of solṭān and pādshāh. Their nomadic empire was organized on Chinggissid principles even though they made the city of Bukhara (known as the "throne-place" (pāytakht)) their fixed capital and abode of sovereignty. Chinggisid nomadic principles also prevailed in their court ceremonies

---

17 Khonji Esfahāni 1992: editor's introduction, 3.
18 Cited in Yildirim 2008: 515.
19 Bukhārī 2014: 104.
20 McChesney 2009: 288.

and protocol, noticeably in the ordered placement of the *amir*s according to their Mongol ranks (*orunat*) around the throne.[21]

3 The Ottoman Counter-Messianism and Its Sunni Counter-Revolution

The Ottoman counter-revolution was immediate, and the Āq Qoyunlu *ancien régime* notables who fled the Qezelbāsh revolution westward, like Hosayn b. ʿAbd Allāh Shervāni appear to have been more numerous.[22] Notable among them was Shaykh Ebrāhim, the head of the Golshani Sufi order, who went into hiding after Shah Esmāʿil's conquest of Tabriz, and fled with the connivance of a high Qezelbāsh functionary. Edris Bedlisi, whom we met briefly in chapter 4, was another notable émigré who defected in 1502. Bedlisi was the son of a disciple of Sufi master Sayyed Mohammad Nurbaskhsh who had moved from his master's village of Suleqān to Tabriz, an important center of the Nurbakhshiyya. Bedlisi had joined the service of the Āq Qoyunlu state in Tabriz and risen to the position of the chief secretary of the chancery (*monshi al-mamālek*) in Soltān Yaʿqub's Hasht Behesht palace in Tabriz.[23] He was later advised by his father, who feared the political chaos of the disintegrating Āq Qoyunlu empire, to move to the court of the Ottoman Sultan Bāyezid II and to present the latter with a Qurʾān commentary he had written.[24] Bedlisi, who was then in his mid-forties, followed his father's advice and migrated to Edirne and then to Istanbul. He was introduced by a Persian-educated high official to the Ottoman court, where he presented a short mirror for princes to the *soltān* in 1503. At that time Sultan Bāyezid was unhappy with the existing Persian histories of the Ottoman dynasty and the way it was presented in the frame of world history, so he commissioned Bedlisi to write one. Bedlisi did so, producing the masterpiece which he named after the palace in Tabriz where he worked for many years, *Hasht behesht* (Eight Paradises).

After a bloody succession struggle and the death of Bāyezid in 1512, which he was fortunate to miss while on extended pilgrimage to Mecca, Bedlisi was invited by the new Sultan, Selim Khan, to return. Then, in 1514–1515, he played a major role in Selim's campaign in Azerbaijan and eastern Anatolia and

---

21 McChesney 2009: 284, 294.
22 Shervāni (2001: 92–93) mentions that a very large number of Sunni jurists were open opponents of the Qezelbāsh, and states that some of them were killed or burned by Qezelbāsh revolutionaries. He does not, however, say how many of them went into exile.
23 Genç 2019: 429.
24 Genç 2019: 432.

accompanied him in his campaign in Syria and Egypt in the following years. The migration of educated Iranians like Bedlisi began with the disintegration of the Āq Qoyunlu empire, which experienced intra-dynastic feuds after 1490; Tabriz frequently changed hands among the princes, including a grandson of Sultan Bāyezid who ruled it for a few months in 1497. It continued after the Ottoman victory over well into the mid-tenth/sixteenth century.[25]

Bedlisi was a key figure in the preemptive appropriation of millennial Sufism that was already afoot under Bāyezid II. Drawing on the Āq Qoyunlu reactive ideology of proposing the Sunni ruler as a counter-messianic deputy of the Merciful God, he wrote the influential *Qānun-e shāhanshāhi* and dedicated it to one of his sons, Prince Shehanshāh, on account of his possible succession but presumably also because of his name.[26] It drew heavily on the cosmogonic Sufi framework of the ethical theory of Jalāl al-Din Davvāni, with whom Bedlisi had studied in Shiraz in the early 1490s. In *Qānun-e shānshāhi* (Imperial law), imperial monarchy (*shāhanshāhi*) is synonymous withcaliphate (*khelāfat*) and the latter is conceived as the vicegerency of God. Following Davvāni, he declared that the ruler is the shadow of God and the deputy of God (*khalifa[t] Allāh*) and his rank is described as the caliphate of the Merciful [God] (*khelāfat-e Rahmāni*). Bedlisi also maintained, like the Timurid Sufi vizier Sharaf al-Din Yazdi, the distinction between apparent and real sovereignty and united them only in his royal patron: "when the formal caliphate and apparent sultanate (*khelāfat-e suri o soltanat-e zāheri*) is in accordance with the Prophetic Shari'a and the rules of spiritual (*ma'navi*) caliphate," its embodiment is indeed God's deputy. Bidlisi also allows for the role of Islamic orthodoxy. He says, given the perfection of Islam, there is no need to renew the divine law and the "kings (*pādshāhān*) of Islam" should assiduously implement Mohammad's sharia.[27]

The significance of this reference to the sharia should not be exaggerated. Bedlisi's real aim before being recruited to fight the Qezelbāsh/Safavid heresy in 1513 was not so much the preemptive containment of millennial radicalism as the importation of the most sophisticated and up-to-date political theory. He

---

25   One of the later westward exiles of the Safavid revolution was Mosleh al-Din Mohammad Lāri, who wrote a Persian history with the reflexive title of *Mer'āt al-advār* (Mirror of epochs); this was presented to the Ottoman rulers, beginning with Soltān Murad, the "Lord Holy Warrior (*ghazi khodāvandgār*), the "king of Islam" who led the "army (*lashkar*) of Islam" in conquest of the lands of the infidels. Selim I is also called the "king of Islam," and most interestingly, the reigning Selim II (1566–1574) is referred to as "Iran's Lord of the Auspicious Conjunction" (*sāheb qerān-e irān*), all by an exile who had evidently not given up hope that his new royal patrons would reconquer Iran for Sunni Islam. Lāri 2014: 2:912–960 at 2:940.
26   Markiewicz 2019: 79 n. 53.
27   Bedlisi 1974: 17, 22–23, 33, 36, 103 as cited in Arjomand 2016c: 14–15.

certainly knew about the Safavid combination of kingship and dervishhood,[28] and sought to enhance the temporal authority of his new sovereign, but did so by combining it with the model of spiritual authority in Sufi gnostic theory (*'erfān*) rather than the antinomian style of the dervishes. When he was introduced in court in 1503, he presented Sultan Bāyezid with *Mer'āt al-Jamāl* (Mirror of beauty), a short work that included a political allegory in imitation of the great Timurid thinker, 'Abd al-Rahmān Jāmi's *Salāmān and Absāl* and was conceived as the first of a four-part "constitution" (*dastur-nāma*) for the guidance of his Ottoman royal patron.[29] As advice to the imperial king, *Qānun-e shānshāhi* follows the same normative and rhetorical pattern as Davvāni's. While positing the virtues necessary to attain spiritual perfection as the ethic appropriate for the ideal ruler, the latter is rhetorically confused or conflated with the actual ruler served by the author. Thus, the typological discussion of corrupt (*fāseda*) polities and their tyrannical (*jā'er*) ruler notwithstanding, the enumeration of the virtues of the ideal ruler as the perfect gnostic and philosopher-king of the "virtuous body politic" (*madina-ye fāzela*) in the end (or rather the beginning, preface) serves the legitimation of the king of the actual body politic or the kingdom (*mamlakat*). The highest beneficence God confers upon mankind, Bedlisi thus affirmed, "is the bounty of the vicegerency of God, the Merciful (*khelāfat-e rahmāni*) and the gift of authority (*eqtedār*) to oversee the affairs of the people by way of divine commands and prohibitions."[30]

Bedlisi also set the Ottoman trend of using the prophet kings of the Old Testament as paradigmatic models for the combined temporal and spiritual sovereignty within the Timurid framework adumbrated by Sharaf al-Din Yazdi.[31] He also spelled out the implications of his distinction between apparent and spiritual caliphate: the caliphate of the Merciful or the divine (*rabbāni*) caliphate constitutes the link between the unseen spiritual world and the sublunary visible world, through which the divine attributes of spiritual perfection and Godly ethics (*akhlāq Allāh*) give order to the terrestrial body politic, the kingdom.[32]

---

28 Bedlisi 1974: 13–14 and other passages cited in Markiewicz 2019: 103, 269; Yilmaz 2018: 190, 207.

29 Markiewicz 2019: 164–165, 259; Yilmaz 2018: 44. It is interesting to note that Jāmi's political allegory was dedicated to Bedlisi's first royal patron, the Āq Qoyunlu Soltān Ya'qub.

30 Bedlisi 1974: 31.

31 Yilmaz 2018: 161, 173, 189, 196–199, 208, 216–217.

32 Bedlisi 1974: 26, 57–71, 74; Yilmaz 2018: 174, 188, 195–196, 206–207. The same combination of theory and rhetoric characterizes Bedlisi's historiography which combines the positive and the normative in idealizing the ruler (Markiewicz 2019: ch. 4).

After the overthrow of the Abbasid caliphate by the Mongols in 1258, the Muslim rulers of the Persianate world assumed the functions of the caliph, notably the appointment of judges, and added the appellation "Caliph" to the accolade of royal titles they assumed, creating a new type of political regime that can be characterized as Islamic royalism.[33] Bedlisi's redefinition of the caliphate as divine vicegerency represented the culmination of this process and set the constitutional paradigm for the Ottoman Empire in the tenth/sixteenth century. This paradigm was elaborated by the next generation of Ottoman *monshi*s in a number of treatises on political ethics and statecraft, the best known of which is Qinālizāda's *Akhlāq-e 'Alā'i*, an adaptation of Davvāni's trend-setting treatise.[34]

The Ottoman reaction to Shah Esmā'il's Mahdist revolution came after the death of Sultan Bāyezid II under his successor Selim I (1512–1520). The Ottoman counter-revolution proper consisted in the reconstruction of the Ottoman Empire by Sultan Selim and his son Sultan Suleymān Khan (1520–1566) as champions of Sunni orthodoxy and heirs to the Abbasid caliphate. The very succession of Prince Selim and his defeat of Bāyezid's favorite son, Ahmed, has been shown to have been an unintended consequence of the Qezelbāsh rebellion of 1511 in Anatolia.[35] During the succession struggle in anticipation of and after the death of Bāyezid II in 1511–1512, Shah Esmā'il supported Soltān Ahmed's son, Soltān Murād, on the losing side. After winning this struggle as the champion of the Janissaries in 1512, the new Sultan, Selim Khan the Grim (*yavuz*), deposed his allegedly incapacitated father and eliminated other Ottoman pretenders. When ascending the throne he also declared war against Shāh Esmā'il. He summoned a state council in Edirne and declared that, as the Shadow of God on Earth and the protector of Muslims, the jihad against heresy to put down the sedition and oppression (*zolm*) of Esmā'il was his incumbent duty (*farz-e 'ayn*) as no other Muslim had the power to do so. He then turned the table on the Qezelbāsh by putting their sedition and tyranny in apocalyptic terms and comparing it to the invasion of Gog and Magog and presenting himself as a second Alexander and their nemesis.[36]

Selim's military operations were conducted hand in hand with a propaganda campaign. In this campaign, Kemāl Pāshāzāda (Ibn Kamal, d. 1535), Bedlisi's nemesis and Bāyezid's foremost Turkish *monshi* who was commissioned, around 1510, with writing a rival Ottoman history in Turkish, also joined

---

33 Arjomand 2010.
34 Yilmaz 2018.
35 Yilmaz 2018: ch. 7.
36 Yilmaz 2018: 510–514.

Sultan Selim in Chaldiran. Unlike Bedlisi who spent most of his life in Iran, Kemāl Pāshāzāda had grown up in Amasya and maintained his connections in Anatolia. Like his contemporary Khonji in the east, Kemāl was a jurist and issued an injunction (*fatwā*) declaring the Qezelbāsh infidels, their territory a land of war (*dār al-harb*), and the waging of holy war (*jihād*) against them an individually incumbent duty (*farz al-'ayn*) of every Muslim. The *soltān*'s duty was to lead the jihad against the Qezelbāsh, and the massacre of the Qezelbāsh appears to have been justified as part of this duty.[37]

The pre-Chaldiran dating of this *fatwā* is speculative; likewise, there is only one other *fatwā* we can date with certainty. Most other known *fatwās* were issued later. The implication is clear. The injunctions were not as much for war mobilization before 1514 as for the consolidation of Islamic orthodoxy against Safavid Shi'ite heresy. It must have been after that time, or after his formal appointment by Sultan Suleymān, that Kemāl Pāshāzāda appears to have assigned the task of developing a more detailed refutation of the Safavid claims to his student, Abu'l-So'ud (that is, Mohammad b. Mohy al-Din 'Emādi). Abu'l-So'ud was also from the Kurdish region under Safavid domination, and his refutations indicate some familiarity with the activities of Shaykh 'Ali Karaki, the leading Shi'ite religious authority under Shah Esmā'il.[38] He goes further in enumerating the Qezelbāsh deviations from orthodoxy, and in refuting Shah Esmā'il's claim to descent from Imam 'Ali b. Abi Tāleb and the Safavid claim to being a Shi'ite sect. In one *fatwā*, Abu'l-So'ud considers fighting against the Qezelbāsh the most important duty of Muslims, comparable to the duty to fight the false prophet, Musaylama, under Abu Bakr and the Kharijites under 'Ali.[39]

After his epoch victory, Selim ordered the registration and selective imprisonment of the Anatolian Qezelbāsh and the execution of 40,000 followers of the Safavid Sufi order (in 1513) and proceeded to administer a decisive military defeat to Shah Esmā'il in the battle of Chaldiran in 1514.[40] Edris Bedlisi, who was a Kurd in origin and knew the Kurdish notable families, joined the *soltān* to recruit Kurdish notables, especially those who had recently been dispossessed

---

37   Inalcik 1962: 166–167; Eberhard 1970: 164–167.
38   In a compilation of these opinions, in 1581 he is referred to as Shaykh 'Abd al-'Ali al-Druzi. (Eherhard 1970: 223)
39   The Ottoman propaganda against the Safavids continued well into the reign of Shah Tahmāsb. It displaced the *'olamā'* from the lands conquered by the Safavids and appears to have played a leading role in it. We have two polemical tracts from a certain Nakhjavāni and the above-cited Shervāni, which was written in 1540. (Eberhard 1970: 53–56, 165–167) The propaganda campaign was revived under Murād III around 1580.
40   Sohrweide 1965: 161–164.

by Shah Esmāʿil, to join the Ottoman campaign. After Chaldiran, Bedlisi was charged with the pacification of the Turkmen tribes of the newly conquered eastern Anatolia. From September 1514 to May 1516, he was effectively Selim's proconsul and was authorized to integrate the region into the Ottoman imperial administration by setting up new directly administered districts (*sancak*s) and semi-autonomous fiefdoms under Kurdish lords. He also set up a network of Sunni madrasas throughout the region.[41] He accompanied Selim to Syria and Egypt in 1517 and began writing the *Selimshāh-nāma*, in which he presents his royal patron as the ideal ruler and universal caliph-*soltān*.[42]

Bedlisi, who had approached Shah Esmāʿil after being disappointed by Bāyezid II, changed sides again and joined Ibn Kemāl in labeling Bāyezid II an arch-heretic whose killing was required by sacred law. He consonantly shifted his rhetoric after being recruited by Sultan Selim. The caliphate of God formulaically included the implementation of the sharia, but now the ideal ruler for the new age held the "two world-illuminating candles" of jihad and sharia. Two years after Chaldiran, in 1516, Sultan Selim defeated the Mamluk Sultan in Syria and conquered Egypt, replacing the Mamluk Sultan as the "Protector of the Two Shrines" (Mecca and Medina).[43] Bedlisi continued to call Selim the deputy of God during and after his conquest of Syria and Egypt, but the phrase does not seem to have been used by his colleagues who issued victory proclamations and law codes for the conquered provinces.[44]

Selim I's son and successor, Sultan Suleymān Khan imitated Esmāʿil's claim to be the spiritual guide of the Qezelbāsh disciples and was proud to have been hailed the "Mahdi of the End of Time" by his admirers in Central Asia. He wavered between the appropriation of Shah Esmāʿil's specific Mahdistic claim and the more general claim to the unification of spiritual and worldly sovereignty. Bedlisi's paradigm prevailed but there was a perceptible change of mood. In *Kanz al-Jawāher*, Bedlisi's compatriot, Shah Qāsem Tabrizi, substitutes "religiosity" (*diyānat*) for one of the cardinal virtues for the new *soltān* (that is, Lord of the Auspicious Conjunction), according to Bedlisi. Tabrizi calls Suleymān the Imam of the Muslims and the Commander of the Faithful (*amir al-muʾmenin*), while other authors argued for the permissibility of calling the *soltān* the Imam and Deputy of the Messenger of God (*khalifa rasul Allāh*), and

---

41 Genç 2019: 437–444; Markiewicz 2019: 35, 117–131.
42 It was completed and published posthumously by one of his sons (Yildiz 2004; Genç 2019: 445).
43 In due course this was noted by Ottoman theorists who later even claimed that the mantle of the Prophet was taken from Cairo to Istanbul as proof that the caliphate had been transferred from the Abbasids to the Ottomans.
44 Markiewicz 2019: 270–274.

Tāshköprizāda in *Asrār al-khilāfa* (Secrets of the caliphate) shifts the emphasis altogether from the caliph to Imam.[45] Although Suleymān appointed Kemāl Pāshāzāda Shaykh al-Islam in 1526, it was not until after the first war against the Safavid Shah Tahmāsb that ended in 1535 and the fall and secret execution in 1536 of his powerful vizier, Ibrāhim Pāshā, that Suleymān opted to champion Sunni orthodoxy against the heretical ideology of the Safavid Qezelbāsh.[46]

In both the Ottoman and Safavid empires, the disintegrative nomadic patrimonialism of the Timurid and Turko-Mongolian successor states was countered by variants of Persianate imperial monarchy. As we have demonstrated by examining the work of Bedlisi and his followers, the Ottomans were tempted by this spiritual legitimation and enhancement of autocracy, and millennial sovereignty was not definitively ruled out until the middle of the tenth/sixteenth century. It was not until after the late 1530s that Suleymān definitively opted for a different approach, one that centered on the championship of Sunni orthodoxy and became the hallmark of the Ottoman counter-revolution. It was only in the following decade that he appointed Abu'l-So'ud (Ebu's-su'ud) al-'Emādi (d. 1574) as Shaykh al-Islam or Chief Mufti; he held the office of Shaykh al-Islam from 1545 until his death in 1574.

In 1547, Suleymān crowned his victories against the Hapsburgs in the West with a treaty that called Charles V the king of Spain and assumed the title of the Roman Caesar for himself. This was followed by the last two massive campaigns (in 1548–1549 and 1554–1555) in the east against Shah Tahmāsb, for which Abu'l-So'ud redoubled his propaganda campaign against the Safavid heretics. This time, the devout former grand vizier, Lutfi Pasha (d. 1564), joined the effort to redefine the sultanate by writing a treatise on the caliphate, one that undoubtedly benefited from the chief mufti's advice concerning Hanafi jurisprudence in relation the caliphate. To celebrate his universal rule as the Caesar of the Romans and caliph of the Muslims, Suleymān also began building his grand mosque complex for whose portal the chief mufti in Istanbul supplied the inscription, invoking the Qur'ān to prove that Suleymān was the protector of Islam and its sacred law against heresy, and further, "the Caliph, resplendent with divine glory.... Conqueror of the lands of the Orient and the Occident ... the Shadow of God over all peoples.... Promulgator of the Sultanic laws (*qawānin*), the Tenth Ottoman Khāqān, Sultan son of Sultan, Sultan Suleymān Khan ..."[47] Abu So'ud continued to use the non-Islamic titles of khāqān, *soltān*, and khan for his sovereign; these emphasize his function of

---

45 Markiewicz 2019: 283; Yilmaz 2018: 197–199.
46 Fleischer 1992: 163–167.
47 Necipoğlu 1985; Imber 1997: 74.

legislating state laws and highlight his world conquests, but avoid qualifying his caliphate except for capitalizing on its universality. Given the nature of his office as the chief mufti and head of judiciary, he could only define the caliphate ad hoc and implicitly in relation to the specific *fatwā* requests submitted to him. In the provincial law code of Buda he promulgated as military judge of Rumelia in 1541, he followed the example of his mentor Kemal Pāshazāda in Karaman and maintained the juristic expression "Caliph of the Messenger of the Lord of all Creatures" (*khalifa rasul rabb al-'ālamin*), and was likewise careful to eschew the phrase "Deputy of God." Nevertheless, he added that the *soltān* was the one "who makes smooth the path for the precepts of the manifest Shari'a and the Exalted Word of God!"[48]

The "Deputy of the *Messenger* of God [as compared to God Himself]" was the corrected definition of of the caliphate elaborated by jurists in the fifth/eleventh century. But the jurists' theory distinguished between the Abbasid caliph whose shaken authority it sought to shore up, and the *soltān*s who held power by might and military force and were legitimated by the former by formal decrees and robes of honor.[49] In sharp divergence from this bifurcation, Abu'l-So'ud combined the two offices of the sultanate, making the juristic definition of caliphate a support for the Ottoman dynastic legitimacy. His added formulation, furthermore, greatly strengthened the legal force of the reference, in the fifth-/eleventh-century juristic theories, to juristic competence (*ijtihād*) as a desirable quality of the caliph, making Suleymān entitled not only to temporal, "sultanic" legislation but also to the authoritative interpretation of the sharia—a provision Abu'l-So'ud used to buttress his own authority as the chief mufti to fill gaps in the provisions of the sharia.[50] This was, arguably, the most important consequence of Sultan Suleymān's claim to the caliphate, even though Abu'l-So'ud also used his own delegated authority as his chief mufti to bring Ottoman regulations in the areas jurists previously included among the functions of the caliph—namely, the congregational, Friday prayer, the implementation of *hodud* punishment for highway robbery, and the division of the spoils of war—closer to Hanafi jurisprudence.[51]

---

48   Imber 1997: 76, 104. The allusion is to Q. 9:40: "and the Word of God is the Exalted."
49   Arjomand 2010. The juristic theory was sidestepped at least once even before the overthrow of the Abbasid caliphate in the late sixth-/twelfth-century; Fakhr al-Din Rāzi, on behalf of the Khʷārazmshāh, proposed the earlier term, "God's caliph" (*khalifa-ye Khodā*), in lieu of the fifth-/eleventh-century jurists' Deputy of the Messenger of God. (Markiewicz 2019: 246)
50   Imber 1997: 95, 107–109.
51   Imber 1997: 79–94.

The counter-revolutionary intent of the new Ottoman redefinition of the caliphate in explicit contradiction to the Safavid Shi'ism and millennial sovereignty is evident in the treatise (*resāla*) translated into Turkish by Suleymān's grand vizier from 1539 to 1541. The treatise was written in August 1554 in Persian and Arabic with an interlinear translation, presumably in relation to the war propaganda for the *soltān*'s last campaign against the Safavid Iran. In it, the caliph is defined as Imam and identified with the *soltān*.

There was no need to reject the new mystical definition of the caliphate and books like Shervāni's *al-'Adliyya al-sulaymāniyya* (Solomonic justice), which fitted his sovereignty in the world of appearances under the cosmic sovereignty of the invisible saints; Shaykh al-Islam Kemal Pāshāzāda (Ebn Kamal) had no hesitation in associating the Ottoman dynasty with the invisible saints.[52] Nevertheless, the alternative juristic theory of the caliphate was bound to be brought to light after the policy change following the abrupt execution of Ibrāhim Pasha. As it amounted to the proclamation of the Sultan's new policy, it was another grand vizier Lutfi Pasha who published a treatise on the Imamate of the Ottoman Sultan, doubtless with the help of the Shaykh al-Islam, Abu'l-So'ud, who may have suggested its title, "Salvation of the community concerning knowledge of the Imam."[53]

It should go without saying that to Lutfi Pasha, as in the advice literature generally, the ruler was the Shadow of God over His creatures if he rules with justice. Lutfi Pasha dismissed the requirement that the caliph be a descendant of the Quraysh, as he can be the Imam and *soltān* who possesses domination through conquest and coercive force (the only two qualifications stipulated in the juristic theory Lutfi accepts) to maintain order and implement the commandments of God. The overwhelming emphasis is, however, on domination and subjugation. Sidestepping the mystical vocabulary of divine and human sovereignty, he plainly calls the *soltān* Imam and caliph: "What is meant by the Sultan is the Caliph," and again, "the Caliph is the Imam above whom there is no other Imam, and his is called the Sultan."[54] Lutfi Pasha emphasizes domination and the coercive power of subjugation from the Sunni juristic theory of the caliphate:

> If one possesses the mentioned conditions such as subjugation (*ghalaba*), domination (*qahr*), the upholding of religion by justice (*iqāmat al-din*

---

52 Yılmaz 2018: 202–203.
53 Gibb 1962: 288.
54 Cited in translation in Gibb 1962: 288–289.

bi'l-ʿadl), commanding the good and forbidding the wrong, and leading the people, then he becomes the *soltān* and deserves to be called *imām*, *khalifa*, and the one invested with authority (*wāli*).[55]

Undoubtedly, the grand vizier's primary intent was counter-revolutionary, as is clear from his explicit polemic against the Shiʿite theory of the Imamate and his repeated use of the title the "Imam of the Age" for his royal patron, Sultan Sulaymān b. Selim Khan b. Bāyezid Khan, who is said to be "the Imam of the Age without any doubt!"[56] This emphatic appropriation of the notion of the "Imam of the Age" for Suleymān as the Caliph-Soltān is striking. To the Imami Shiʿa, the Imam of the Age could only be the Hidden Imam-Mahdi; and Lutfi Pasha evidently knew this as he refuted their theory of the Imamate on the grounds that whoever considers anyone other than Suleymān as the Imam of the Age is a heretic (*zindiq*). Equally striking is Lutfi's appropriation of a favorite Shiʿite hadith to prove his contention: "Whoever dies without knowing his Imam, has died a death of paganism (*jāhiliyya*)!"[57] By contrast, the title "Commander of the Faithful," used by the Shiʿa exclusively for ʿAli, is avoided throughout the treatise. The most likely explanation for this surprising avoidance of the title of "Commander of the Faithful" is also his reactive, counter-revolutionary intent.[58]

In the long run, it was not so much Lutfi Pasha, the retired vizier, but Abu'l-Soʿud, the Shaykh al-Islam for three decades, who acted as the chief architect of Ottoman judiciary organization under Suleymān and his successor, Selim II. It was his achievement as the chief mufti that his royal patron was styled Suleymān the Lawgiver (*qānuni*).

In summary, the first wave that redefined the caliphate as the vicegerency of the Merciful God was imported by Iranian émigrés in the first quarter or so of the tenth/sixteenth century; it brought the generic aspect Sufi millennialism. The counter-messianism distinctive of the Ottoman Empire evolved slowly, as a consequence of Selim's counter-revolution; it gathered momentum some two decades after his death under his successor. Its full institutional translation can be seen in the construction of the imposing Ottoman judiciary system

---

55 Cited in Yilmaz 2018: 163; translation modified.
56 Yilmaz 2018: 292–293.
57 Yilmaz 2018: 287, 290.
58 Yilmaz 2018: 295. Given the later anachronistic transfer of sovereignty by the last puppet Abbasid caliph in Cairo to the Ottomans, it should also be noted that Lutfi Pasha explicitly refutes the Abbasid claim to the caliphate.

under Süleymān the Lawgiver. This was largely the work of his chief mufti, who provided this juristic redefinition of the caliphate. This institutional transformation is distinctive of the Ottoman reaction to radical Sufi millennialism, in contrast to the reaction of the Uzbek and Mughal empires. This reaction to the Safavid revolution, among other things, made the Ottoman counter-revolution the most significant of its long-term consequences in world history.

CHAPTER 7

The Mahdi of Light and His Millenarian Revolution in Tribal Afghanistan

We have met with the frontier raids (*ghazā*) against the infidels in the process of the Islamicization of Anatolia in chapter 3. Frontier raids continued under the Delhi Sultanate in India into the eighth/fourteenth century and in Central Asia (eastern Afghanistan) at least into the tenth/sixteenth century.[1] The Islamicization of many parts of Afghanistan was still superficial when its Timurid ruler, Zahir al-Din Mohammad Bābor, marched south from his capital, Kabul, to conquer India in 1526. Bābor died four years later in 1530 and divided his realm among his four sons. The kingdom of Kabul was given to his son Kāmrān Mirzā, who refused to help his brother Homāyun against the Afghan Sher Shah in 1540 and was eventually deposed and blinded by the latter in 1553.[2] The Timurid kingdom of Kabul was ruled by Homāyun's son, Mirzā Mohammad Hakim for the next three decades when the Mahdist movement we examine here developed. The political instability of this region on the periphery of a Timurid kingdom in the mid-tenth/sixteenth century created a favorable "opportunity structure" for revolution, to borrow a term from the sociology of social movements.

1 Sufi Messianism in Northwestern India as a Prelude to the Rawshani Revolution

As we saw in chapter 3, Anatolia, Mesopotamia, Iran, and greater Khorasan were awash with Sufi millennial movements throughout the ninth/fifteenth century. India, in the southeastern corner of the Persianate world, was bound to be affected. In fact, the Mahdist wave in popular Sufism reached the northwestern region of the Indian subcontinent before the end of the century. Sayyed Mohammad Jaunpuri (1443–1505) was already a venerable shaykh of the Chishti Sufi order in India when he began to turn world renunciation into a quest for world domination, just as his contemporaries Jonayd (d. 1460) and Haydar (d. 1488) had done with the Safavid Sufi order in northwestern Iran.

---

1 Arjomand 1984: 292 n. 70; Darling 2000.
2 Richards 1993: 9–12.

Sayyed Mohammad moved to Gujarat in the 1490s, where divine visitations (*didār*) encouraging him to take a worldly political direction became more frequent and urgent; this made him restless and the Sultan of Gujarat apprehensive. He was first exiled to Sind and then to the northwestern region of India in the early tenth/sixteenth century. There, he settled in Barli among the Pathan tribesmen, and in the last three years of his life he proclaimed his Mahdihood by divine order.[3]

Sayyed Mohammad took his divine visitations as a sign of the End of Time, the kairotic time of millennial action.[4] The apocalypse was expected to begin in the new abodes of migration called *da'ira*s, modeled on Sufi *khāneqāh*s, from which the final jihad was to be launched.[5] In a move that indicated his impatience with laborious proselytizing among Afghan tribesmen, as Jonayd and Haydar had done with the Turkman tribesmen of Azerbaijan and eastern Anatolia, Sayyed Mohammad also preached in favor of converting the rulers of the world. He wrote confidently to the Sultan of Gujarat who had exiled him:

> I declare upon the order of God Almighty that I am the Mahdi promised at the End of Time. It is obligatory for all the rulers, commanders, ... viziers ... and the people to verify and accept [my declaration].... It is incumbent upon the rulers of this time (*hākemān-e zamān*) to choose one of the two options [either accepting my Mahdihood or executing me]![6]

Sayyed Mohammad, the founder of the Mahdaviyya movement, thus set its direction toward millennial world domination for the disciples who continued his mission and expanded it under his five subsequent *khalifa*s (deputies). His second *khalifa*, Sayyed Khundmir (d. 1523), declared jihad on those who denied the Mahdihood of his master and who thereby became infidels, and prepared for their apocalyptic battle of Badr (*jang-e Badr-e vilāya*) against Soltān Muzaffar II of Gujarat (1511–1526); this battle ended in the defeat and martyrdom of the *khalifa*. The sultanate of Gujarat came to an end under Muzaffar II's successor, Bahādur Shah, whom the Mughal Homāyun failed to dislodge. Bahādur Shah was killed by his Portuguese allies, leaving Gujarat to be incorporated into the northern Indian domain of the Afghan Sher Khan

---

3   In a visitation, God told him: "You are the promised Mahdi; proclaim the manifestation of Mahdihood and do not be afraid of the people." (Cited in MacLean 2000: 240)
4   See the introduction.
5   Migration was accordingly considered incumbent duty (*wājib*) and placed above jihad.
6   Cited in MacLean 2000: 247.

(later Shah) who ousted Homāyun in 1540. The Mahdaviyya movement, meanwhile, not only survived but also expanded by converting Afghan tribal commanders in Gujarat and Rajastan as well as the military and the courtiers in the Deccan. Its heyday was the Afghan interregnum when the Mughal emperor Homāyun was ousted; it reached its peak during the reign of Sher Shah's successor, Islām Shah Sur (1545–1553). Islām Shah was, however, alarmed by the conversion of some of his important Afghan governors and their troops, and ordered the persecution of the Mahdavis. The movement thereafter became quietist, as its leaders were co-opted by the restored Mughal emperors after Homāyun's restoration in 1555.[7]

The Mahdaviyya spread their recruitment net widely and used every opportunity to expand the movement among the courtiers of Islām Shah and, by the mid-tenth/sixteenth century, throughout the kingdoms of the Deccan. We know nothing about what impact the movement may have had in the Afghan tribal hinterland where its founder spent the last years of his life. By comparison, the kindred Rawshani militant Mahdist movement we examine here limited their political horizons to opportunities to unify the Afghan tribes along the peripheries of the Kabul kingdom and did not proselytize in imperial Indian cities.

The Rawshanis rose in the Pakhtun tribal region, which was an inaccessible periphery of the Timurid kingdom of Kabul. This kingdom was recovered by Homāyun in 1553 after he returned from his long exile in Safavid Iran. Homāyun passed it on to his son, Mirzā Hakim (r. 1554–1585), while he proceeded to reconquer northern India. The Rawshanis continued their millennial militancy to the end of the tenth/sixteenth century—that is, after Mirzā Hakim's kingdom was absorbed into the Mughal Empire his half-brother Akbar was in the process of building.

Bāyazid Ansāri, the *pir-e rawshan* (enlightened shaykh) and *khatm-e wilāyat* (Seal of Sainthood), popularly known as Bāyazid-e Rawshanā'i (Bāyazid of light), was born in 1525 in Punjab to an Afghan family from Qandahar; the family claimed descent from Mohammad's companion, Ayyub al-Ansāri. They moved to Kaniguram in the mountainous heart of tribal Waziristan, an area inhabited by Pakhtun tribes. Bāyazid Ansāri traveled between Samarqand and Allahabad engaged in the horse trade, taking advantage of his travels to meet Yogis in India and Sufis in Central Asia. He also traveled to Khorasan, but more in search of spiritual enlightenment than for horse trading. This search brought him into contact with the latest trends in the world of Persianate Sufism. Among the Sufi ideas he imbibed there, the foremost of which was the

---

7 MacLean 2000.

doctrine of the "light of Mohammad" (nur-e mohammadi), which he adopted as his own. Accordingly, he was called the "Elder of Lightness" (pir-e rawshani).

The metaphor and the idea it signified had ancient roots in the Mazdaean dualism of light and darkness, most likely through the Manichaean doctrine of the salvation of the soul as a particle of light, a doctrine that was known in Khorasan in the Islamic era and resurfaced in Persianate Sufism toward the end of the fourth/tenth century and was fully developed in the Persian Sufi literature of the sixth/twelfth century.[8] Already in the fifth/eleventh century, Khʷāja ʿAbdallāh Ansāri called divine love the "endless light" (nur-e nāmotanāhi). In the sixth/twelfth century, Shaykh Ahmed Jāmi was evidently familiar with the Manichaean cosmological notion of light and its salvific link to the human world through prophets as divine messengers. The idea, however, could not be attributed to Māni as the Messenger of Light, rather it came from the Qurʾānic term *nur* ("light"). Jāmi therefore appropriates the idea of cosmological light as "Mohammad's Light (nur-e Mohammadi), as Mohammad is the final Messenger of God that Muslims must acknowledge. Prophecy was integrated into this doctrine and the salvific quality of light was accommodated by the claim that it—light—had created the 124,000 prophets preceding Mohammad. Ahmed Jāmi pegged his evidently novel formulation to an old principle in Sufi theory, namely poverty (*faqr*): Poverty is this light, and no other light can overpower it because it is the source of all light. A younger contemporary of Ahmed Jāmi, ʿAyn al-Qozāt Hamadāni (d. 1131), expounded on the theory of the pre-eternal Light of Mohammad in his *Tamhidāt*, a long commentary on the Light Verses of the Qurʾān. His theory of the light of Mohammad was influential in India through the commentary on his *Tamhidāt* by the Sufi master of the Chishti order, Sayyed Mohammad Gisu-darāz (d. 1422). We find a more accessible elaboration of the idea of divine light inhering in Mohammad in ʿAttār's poetry, which is also well integrated into the Sufi theory of divine love (*ʿeshq*) that is manifest in the soul. Mohammad was the recipient of the revelation sent down by God through the "light of the soul" (nur-e jān). This theory maintains that the spiritual, divine light replaced the person/ego of Mohammad during his heavenly journey (meʿrāj): "he came so near to God (*haqq*) that his soul (*jān*) became light," and Gabriel left him and then, "the divine light came and he went."[9]

---

8 Arjomand 2021.

9 درآمد نور ربانی و او رفت.

See Arjomand forthcoming for these and all other citations on the Mohammadan light.

By the ninth/fifteenth century, the idea of the light of Mohammad was widespread in the Persianate world. Sayyed Mohammad Nurbakhsh in Iran, as we saw in chapter 3, called himself Nurbakhsh (light-giver), with implicit reference to it.[10] Further afield in the Ottoman Empire, the Syrian ʿAbd al-Rahmān al-Bestāmi (d. 1454) likewise combined the idea of the pre-eternal light of Mohammad with the invisible hierarchy of the saints typical of Sufism in the age of sainthood (velāyat).[11] Significantly, their contemporary Mahdist Sayyed Mohammad b. Fallāh in Khuzestan also called himself the "Radiant" (Moshaʿshaʿ)![12]

Therefore, it is not surprising that in his spiritual search in Khorasan Shaykh Bāyazid, was impressed with Sufis who taught him the idea of the *nur-e Mohammadi*. He was especially influenced by members of the Khalwati order founded in western Iran by Dede ʿOmar Rawshani (d. 1487), a rival of the early Safavid shaykhs. Note that *nur* and *rawshani* are synonymous. The Khalwati chain of authority (*selsela*) goes back to his namesake and fellow wayfarer, Bāyazid Bastāmi (d. 874). It should be noted, however, that the doctrine of *nur-e Mohammadi* was widespread among Sufis in this period and was by no means confined to the Khalwāti order. Pir Jamāl Ardestani (d. 879/1474 or 1475), to give a notable example, wrote an entire versified treatise, *Misbāh al-arwāh* (The lantern of the souls), on the Light Verse (Q. 24:35) and related verses of the Qurʾān.[13] Bāyazid did not, however, join the Khalwati or any other Sufi order, perhaps because of his ambitious design to assume Dede ʿOmar's title himself. The Khalwati order flourished in the Ottoman Empire, though at least one branch went underground and merged with the radically millenarian Melamatis. Around the time of Bāyazid's spiritual explorations in Khorasan, the shaykhs of the Melamati Sufi order maintained a radically millennial interpretation of the distinction between apparent and true sovereignty (discussed in chapter 4); they held that true sovereignty belonged to their leader as the *qotb* (axis mundi), while Soltān Suleymān was just the apparent ruler. One of the Melamati leaders, Hamza Bāli Effendi (d. 1561), was, in fact, a Khalwati shaykh from Sophia and was considered both the *qotb* and the sovereign in the world of appearances for which, according to the record of his trial, he had already appointed viziers and other officials. The Melamati millennial uprisings were easily suppressed and preempted by the trial and execution of their

---

10   Nurbakhsh 1971: 110, 129.
11   Gardiner 2017: 13.
12   Arjomand 1984: 76–77.
13   Ardestāni 2001.

leaders and their avenue of success was blocked by the opportunity structure of Suleymān's centralized empire.¹⁴

Bāyazid Ansāri was also influenced by a later ecumenical Sufi trend that rejected imitation (*taqlid*) and consensus (*ejmāʿ*) in favor self-annihilation in the master (*fanāʾ fi'l-shaykh*)—positions he later endorsed. When he returned from Khorasan, furthermore, Bāyazid met Molla Suleymān, an Ismaʿili missionary in Kalinjar. By then the Ismaʿilis had become a Sufi order. Molla Suleymān taught Bāyazid the method of esoteric interpretation (*taʾwil*) of the Qurʾān and the distinctively post-Resurrection Ismaʿili understanding of the innerworldliness of resurrection, paradise, and hell.¹⁵ The influence of his Ismaʿili teacher is evident in Bāyazid's later proclamation of the redundancy of the daily prayer, and the irrelevancy of the qibla and ablutions for anyone who followed a master (*pir*) who had experienced union with God. Similarly, Bāyazid's institution of his mission (*daʿwat*) and his use of the term missionaries (singular, *dāʿi*) for his representatives also show the influence of Ismaʿilism.¹⁶

When he returned to Kaniguram, Bāyazid became a Sufi ascetic, following the Khalwati practice of living in a cave for seclusion (*khalwat*) and engaging in intense meditation (*zekr khafiy*) for some five years. He scandalized his father and uncle by allowing his wife and a male disciple into his cave, a practice that set the Rawshani precedent for the mixing of men and women in their sessions. Bāyazid became convinced of the corruption of the orthodox *ʿolamāʾ* and Sufi dervishes alike—a clear sign of the End of Time.¹⁷ Meanwhile, his spiritual progression continued until he reached, in eleven years, what he later conceptualized as the sixth station of unification (*waslat*) with God—that is, some time in the mid-1560s. God then instructed him to declare his Mahdihood; when he did so, he found himself in conflict with the authorities and was summoned to the local kadi court. He denied his claim to Mahdihood and asserted that he considered himself only a *hādi* (righteous guide)¹⁸ to his followers. His heterodox views then met with his father's violent antagonism, and he was forced to move to the mountains of Nangarhar around the Jalalabad River. This move was later called his *hejrat* (migration), to fit the model of the Prophet's life.

---

14   Ocak 1992; Yilmaz 2018: 201–202.
15   See chapter 1.
16   Malik 1993: 37–38, 48–50, 56.
17   Rizvi 1965–66: 74–75.
18   *Hādi* was a lower rank than Mahdi; etymologically it is from the same root (h-d-a).

2 A Khaldunian Revolution on the Periphery of Timurid India and Its Failure

In Nangarhar, Bāyazid found a following among the Mohmand, Ghorikhel, and Khalil tribesmen, who were as imperfectly Islamicized as the Masmuda of the Maghreb in the sixth/twelfth and the Qezelbāsh of western Iran and Anatolia in the ninth/fifteenth century. The chief of one of the branches of the Mohmand took Bāyazid under his protection. Bāyazid told them: "Come unto me, that I may bring you unto God; for the holy Qur'an directs you to seek after the divine union, and it is only through the intervention of a perfect Pir that this union can be accomplished."[19] From Nangarhar, Bāyazid moved to Hashtnagar to proselytize among the numerous Mohammadzai tribesmen.[20] One of his cousins who had a considerable following among Dawr tribesmen joined Bāyazid, who then sent a missionary to the Dawr tribes. This mission met with great success and secured Bāyazid, the *pir-e rawshan*, an invitation to Tirāh where many Pathan tribesmen welcomed him. Thus he spread his teaching among the Āfrids, the Orakzais, the Dawudzais, and the Tirāhis.[21] Bāyazid was hosted by a chief of the Khalil tribe whose conversion set an example for others. The Mohmands and the Āfrids became his ardent followers, and many of the Yusufzai tribesmen,[22] who were somewhat more integrated into the periphery of the Mughal Empire, were converted. However, another chief of the Khalil was alarmed by the success of the Rawshanis and reported Bāyazid to Mughal authorities, who summoned him to a kadi court in Kabul, Mirzā Hakim's capital, where he was forced to repeat the denial of his Mahdihood and claim only to be a *hādi*. This must have taught Bāyazid that he needed to consolidate his tribal support; he did this with a series of political marriages between the offspring of tribal chiefs and himself and his sons and future successors, 'Omar and Jalāl al-Din (the latter was contemptuously nicknamed Jalāla).[23] Like the Madhi Ibn Tumart who wrote in Berber in the sixth/twelfth century and Shah Esmā'il who wrote in the Turkish dialect of Turkman tribesmen at the beginning of the tenth/sixteenth century, Bāyazid was one of the first to write in the Pashtu of his Afghan tribal followers, though he also composed in Persian, Arabic, and Hindi for his actual and potential urban followers.[24]

---

19 Cited in Leyden 1812: 87.
20 Leyden 1812: 94–95.
21 Rizvi 1965–66: 76–81.
22 Their greater integration is indicated by the designation of their territory as an area that was responsible to pay the *galang* (a form of tax). (Malik 1993: 36)
23 Rizvi 1965–66: 81–84.
24 Leyden 1812: 82–90; Rizvi 1967–68: 69.

Feeling secure among the Afghan tribes of Waziristan on the periphery of the Mughal kingdom, Bāyazid unveiled his political project. Addressing what contemporary sociologists of religion call the dilemma of mixed motivation, he provided a strong material motive for militancy, in addition to a spiritual motive of obedience to the shaykh. He forbad begging but enjoined raids on caravans with the mystical justification that violence against the enemy—that is, all those who do not belong to the sect, is acceptable. He preached that all that exists is God and the material world is an illusion; as he wrote in two poems in Pashtu, "Come then, my friends ... lay hold of the sabre; the whole world is devoid of life, smite off the heads of the lifeless." Thus, "The inheritance of the wealth of the dead devolves upon the living. Their persons, wealth and wives are therefore yours by right!"[25] Bāyazid, who considered himself the *pir-e rawshan* and Mahdi, made two signets that were still used by his followers at the beginning of the nineteenth century. The first signet was used in his prophetic capacity, receiving praise on behalf of God: "Glory to Thee, the King, the Creator / Who hast distinguished the world of life from that of fire." The second signet reflected his role as a Sufi *pir* and the righteous *hādi*, it was engraved with: "The humble (*meskin*) Bāyazid, the guide (*hādi*) to those who err."[26]

The caravans the Rawshani tribesmen raided sought redress from the Mughal government and troops Mirzā Hakim sent troops to subdue the Mahdists. Bāyazid was forced to vacate Tirāh but later reoccupied it. Bāyazid's ruthless purge of some three hundred of his lukewarm followers who had opened the city to the Mughals came after he told them to come out unarmed and repent and after assuring them he would accept their repentance. Bāyazid then prepared to face the Mughal troops in battle near Hashtnagar. Many of his Mohammadzai followers deserted him because he had been defeated by the Mughal troops (with the help of the Hazāra tribe) and he was left to flee on foot. He perished on the way to Hashtnagar in 1573, after two and half years of millennial armed struggle.

After his death, his son 'Omar took over and declared that the Rawshani Mahdi was not dead: "Come on my friends, your Pir is not dead, but has resigned his place to his son, Shaykh 'Umar, and conferred on him and his followers the empire of the world!"[27] The Rawshani movement survived its founder and expanded under his successor who continued their raids and depredations, carrying the body of Bāyazid in a coffin. Although there were Rawshanis among the Yusufzai tribesmen, Shaykh 'Omar did not spare the Yusufzai from

---

25 As translated in Leyden 1812: 94.
26 Leyden 1812: 93.
27 Cited in Leyden 1812: 102.

his depredations. This turned out to be a fateful error in tribal policy, as the Yusufzai, the most powerful of the Afghan tribes of the region, reacted by joining the opposite camp.[28] Eventually, Shaykh 'Omar was killed in a violent confrontation with the Yusufzai, when an allied tribe of the latter threw the Mahdi's coffin into a river. This put a violent end to the leadership of Shaykh 'Omar in 1581. 'Omar's younger brother, Jalāl al-Dīn, was captured and kept prisoner by the Yusufzai. A few months later, as the Mughal emperor Akbar was returning from an expedition against his older brother Mirzā Mohammad Hakim[29] he stopped in Peshawar and asked the Yusufzai to hand over Jalāl al-Dīn, so Akbar could use him and the Yusufzai as a part of his tribal policy to annex his brother Mirzā Mohammad's kingdom. So Akbar took Jalāla al-Din with him and kept him for a year.

Mirzā Mohammad Hakim was deposed in 1580 and died in July 1585. Akbar appointed Man Singh, a Hindu Rajput, governor of Kabul. Meanwhile, Jalāl al-Dīn had returned to Tirāh in 1584 and taken active leadership of the Rawshanis. At this point, he was about twenty years old and managed to mobilize the tribes of Mohmand, Āfrid, and Khalil to resume their Mahdist militancy and lucrative depredations. In 1587, he made a surprise attack on Mughal troops with a tribal army consisting of 1,000 cavalry and 15,000 foot soldiers. Many of the tribesmen, however, deserted him and he was badly defeated. Some 2,000 Rawshanis were killed, but Jalāl al-Dīn himself found refuge with the Yusufzais, who had captured and imprisoned him after defeating his brother, Shaykh 'Omar. He persuaded them to join him and together they fortified Tirāh.[30] By the end of 1588 or the beginning of 1589, however, Tirāh again fell to Mughal forces. Jalāla al-Din spent the next three or four years moving from one tribe to the next, trying to unify the Afghan tribes and become their king. This alarmed the Mughal emperor, Akbar, who reinforced the Mughal occupying troops in Peshawar in late 1592 to suppress Jalāl al-Dīn's unrest and killed some 400 Rawshanis in the spring of 1593. Nevertheless, Jalāl al-Dīn remained an active rebel. Rawshani depredations resumed in 1596 and their strength continued to increase for the next few years. In 1601, Jalāl al-Dīn undertook a daring offensive and captured Ghaznin which was, however, retaken by the

---

28   Ahmed 1982: 48.
29   Mirzā Mohammad Hakim was invited to take over the Mughal Empire by rebellious Uzbek commanders in Bihar and Bengal in 1579; by way of indicating this, they had the Friday sermon read in his name. (Richards 1993: 40–41)
30   Ahmed 1982: 50–52. It was relatively common for rival border chiefs to hold relatives of other chiefs captive, or "official guests"; in fact they were held as hostages, but treated with respect and honor.

Hazāra tribesmen who were already on their way. The Hazāra defeated and killed Jalāl al-Din and hacked his body to pieces, sending his head to Akbar.[31]

Shaykh 'Omar's son, significantly named Ahad-dād (lit., "given by the One") succeeded his uncle as the leader of the Rawshanis, routed the Hazāra, and gained control of the Khaybar Pass, imposing *kharāj* (a form of tax) on the caravans passing through it; he then took the offensive by attacking Kabul. It was not until 1613 that he was decisively defeated. Some 15,000 Rawshanis were killed and the Mughals built a tower with 600 of their heads to remind the survivors of their victory.[32] Millenarian militancy subsided among the Rawshanis, and one by one the grandsons of their Mahdi were co-opted into the Mughal system. Jalāl al-Din's son, Ilāh-dād (lit., "given by God") was seduced with the title of Rashid Khan and a Mughal office (*mansab*) of high rank, and in the third decade of the eleventh/seventeenth century he persuaded the son and successor of his cousin Ahad-dād to do likewise. Rashid Khan then became the leader of the Rawshani movement until his death in 1648; as leader he oversaw the depoliticization of Rawshani Mahdism and its quietist redirection, thus replicating the post-millennial of the Mahdaviyya a century earlier.

3   The Mahdist Movement of Shaykh Bāyazid Ansāri in Comparative Perspective

A comparison of what sociologists call the "opportunity structure" reveals interesting factors that can account for the initial success and long-term failure of the Rawshani Mahdist revolution. We noted that the kindred Mahdist Mahdaviyya movement arose in the same peripheral region in northern India in a similar period of political instability, but its opportunity structure changed when the arena of proselytizing shifted to the imperial court of Islām Shah Sur. The open opportunity structure of the periphery of Mirzā Hakim's Timurid kingdom can account for the initial growth and success of the Rawshanis. This is suggested by our mention of the quick suppression of the Melamati millennialism in the Ottoman Empire at the peak of its consolidation under Suleymān the Lawgiver whose opportunity structure could be put at the opposite end of the spectrum.

By contrast, the Rawshanis under Bāyazid and Shaykh 'Omar faced the weak Timurid kingdom of Mirzā Mohammad Hakim and the enmity of the Mughal

---

31   Rizvi 1967–68: 72–80.
32   Ahmed 1982: 54.

CHAPTER 8

The Fall of the Safavid Empire as a Revolution in World History

The remarkable ecumenical unity of the Persianate world under the Il-Khanid and Timurid Turko-Mongolian empires survived the formation of the three early modern Muslim empires and continued through the Safavid-Ottoman wars into the eighteenth century. The collapse of the Safavid Empire in 1722, presented in this chapter as a proto-modern revolution, shattered the unity of the Persianate world and began a process of fragmentation that could not be repaired by Nāder Shah Afshār's export of revolutionary violence and his creation of an ephemeral tribal empire of conquest. This turbulent sequence of events was caused by the breakdown of the imperial state, in which neither Sufi nor Shi'ite Mahdism, nor Khaldunian tribal reformism played any motivating role. Nāder's Turko-Mongolian empire, the last and shortest-lived in world history, broke up violently upon his death in 1747. The crumbling and collapse of the imperial state fits the Tocquevillian type of modern revolution in terms of its causal pattern. As such, the fall of the Safavid Empire provides an outstanding case of "state-breakdown," as highlighted in the sociology of revolution.[1] This case also conforms to my definition of revolution in terms of the significance of its consequences in world history.

The collapse of the Safavid Empire was also seen as a revolution by contemporary European observers. During its slow decline in the 1720s, the word revolution was defined in a German dictionary as "the upheaval ..., *revolutio regni*, the change or overturning of a kingdom or of a land, if such suffers any special alteration in government or police."[2] An eyewitness account of the collapse by the missionary Father Krusinski was published in 1733 as *The History of the Late Revolutions of Persia*. These revolutions were not yet modern, and did not follow the Mahdist pattern. And yet the revolutionary convulsions of Persia were in remarkable accord with the Persianate conception of revolution. Last but not least, the Russian and Ottoman military interventions as both a cause and a consequence of the Persian revolutionary upheaval gave this collapse a significant international dimension, an element that became a

1 Skocpol 1979; Goldstone 1991.
2 See chapter 1.

prominent feature of modern revolutions.[3] Therefore, I examine it in terms of my Tocquevillian ideal type for modern revolutions, and modify it where necessary in the spirit of reducing the Eurocentricity of social theory, including the sociology of revolution.

It is easy to date the collapse of the Safavid Empire to the conquest of the city of Isfahan, its capital, by nomadic Afghan tribesmen in October 1722.[4] But the fall of the dynasty cannot be dated as precisely, as the dynasty nominally survived Nāder Shah's brief reign (1736–47) to the end of the eighteenth century and formally ended only with the coronation of Āqā Mohammad Khan Qājār in 1795. This periodization accords with our conceptual definition of revolution in terms of its significance in world history; this makes the rise of Nāder Shah very much a part of the process of revolution. His astounding conquests can then be explained as the export of revolution, taking the form of mass tribal mobilization and unification after the collapse of the non-tribal component of the Safavid army. This conceptual periodization comprises the meteoric rise and fall of Nāder Shah, but exclude the nominal sovereignty of the later Safavids in the Zand period (the third quarter of the eighteenth century). The fall of the Safavid Empire (1722–47) as an extended or composite event is thus treated as a revolution in world history in two closely interrelated acts.

1 A Proto-Modern Persianate Revolution without a Mahdi

Thanks to the recent publication of *Mokāfāt-nāma* (Book of punishment), we know that the Persianate theory of revolution proposed in chapter 1 can be applied, systematically and in detail, to the unexpected collapse of the Safavid Empire in 1722. We do not know the author of this book of verse, but we know that he was a high official in the Safavid state, that he carried out several missions for the last Safavid shah, Soltān-Hosayn, that he was imprisoned during the factional fighting among the remnants of the old regime during the period of Afghan rule (1722–29), and that he wrote his masterpiece in prison in southern Iran, most probably in 1726 or 1727. The author returned in January 1721 from a mission to Khorasan and recommended that Shah Soltān-Hosayn and his court move from Qazvin to Mashhad (which as we see presently, was overtaken); he must have witnessed the siege of Isfahan and its fall to the Afghans

---

3 Lawson 2019.
4 The depredations of the Afghan tribes from the eastern periphery of the Safavid empire in the previous five years appear to be its prelude.

in October 1722. The author was then embroiled in a factional fight between the remnants of Safavid forces in control of Fars and Kerman and was consequently imprisoned between 1725 and 1727. His long account of the decisive defeat of the Safavid army in the battle of Gelunābād in March 1722 preceding the siege of Isfahan strongly suggests that he was present on the battlefield.[5]

Unlike Condorcet (a prominent participant in the French Revolution later in the eighteenth century), who remained unflinchingly optimistic when writing his sketch of the progress of the human mind while in prison awaiting the guillotine, our author was completely overwhelmed by pessimism and, as the title of his book suggests, saw the fall of the Safavid state as unending divine punishment.[6] He analyzed his personal experience in considerable detail in order to craft the perfect synthesis of the two Persianate conceptions of revolution, the astrological and the normative, without contamination by the modern myth of revolution Condorcet helped to generate.

The *Mokāfāt-nāma*, however, was written before the Persian revolution ended and its account is therefore incomplete and mainly centered on the events in the capital, Isfahan. For another insider account, we look to the *Zobdat al-tavārikh*, completed in 1739 or 1740—that is, after the end of the revolution and the replacement of the Safavid dynasty by the Afshār dynasty. The invaluable account of Mohammad Mohsen Mostawfi, chief accountant of the treasury of the shrine of Imam Rezā in Mashhad, was also invaluable for covering the revolution in Mashhad, the capital of the province of Khorasan, which was subject to continuous depredations by Afghan tribesmen. This destruction and devastation were a prelude to the revolution. Mostawfi joined the service of the last Safavid shah, Soltān-Hosayn, in Isfahan, where he continued to serve in the bureaucracy after Soltān-Hosayn transferred his sovereignty to the Afghan Mahmud upon the conquest of Isfahan. Mostawfi is therefore a valuable source of statistics and information about Isfahan immediately after the conquest, but not on the later years of Afghan rule when he must have escaped Isfahan and returned to Mashhad. His account for the first year of revolution is supplemented by a detailed report from Rasht on the Caspian Sea, dated 22 September 1723, made by Petros Gilanentz who had organized a small band of Armenian fighters there. He received a few refugees there and included their eyewitness reports.

We first turn to *Mokāfāt-nāma*, as it applies to the Pesianate theory of revolution. The term *enqelāb* is used once in the sense of the revolution of the stars

---

5 *Mokāfāt*: vv. 1274–1402; Ja'fariyān 2001: 3: 1196–1197. References are to the verses of *Mokāfāt-nāma*, as numbered in the edition published by Ja'fariyān (2001: 3:1231–1295).
6 *Mokāfāt*: vv. 507, 769.

and six times as *revolutio regni* in Iran.[7] The word Iran is used at least thirteen times and Irān-zamin (the land of Iran) appears once.[8] The major difference between the author's conception of revolution and the traditional Persianate concept can be taken as indicative of early modernity: the arena of revolution is the nation-state of Iran, and there is no *translatio imperii* in sight or perhaps even conceivable. As a high official of the Safavid *ancient régime*, our author cannot bring himself to think God may have granted a turn in power to the Afghan "dogs," alternatively, "asses,"[9] as he refers to both Afghan rulers of Iran, Mahmud and Ashraf.[10] In contrast to the imperial frame of reference of the Persianate theory in Ibn Abi Tāher Tayfur and Sa'di and the provincial one in Khʷāju and Afzal al-Din Kermāni,[11] the focus of our author's analysis, Iran, is entirely novel. Iran is no longer conceived as the first Shi'ite empire of conquest, as it was in 1501, but as a territorial nation-state integrated under "the king of kings on the throne in the land of Iran" (*shāhanshah-e takht-e irān-zamin*).[12] It was the injustice and misrule in the core land of Iran that caused the rebellion of the tribes of the periphery—the Lezghis in the north and the "Kharijites" on the shores of the Persian Gulf, and finally the Afghans in the east, whose barbarous leader, Mahmud, God appointed as a "tyrannical avenger" and the instrument of His wrath and dire punishment.

The collapse of the Safavid state as a particular case of revolution is set within the general Persianate explanatory framework of its "heavenly and earthly causes." The inauspicious conjunction of Jupiter and Saturn (not countermanded by God's Shekina [*sakina*]!) produced "oppression, sedition and massacres" on earth: "Under its effects the world was ruined / revolution infected kingship and religion."[13]

Our author curses the heavenly wheel for afflicting this calamity on his country and for ruining him personally, but then reminds himself that its turn was required by divine justice to punish the injustices and inequities of late Safavid rule. The detailing of these is in line with the Persianate normative theory of revolution; he then offers a fascinating analysis of the weakness and fragility of the Safavid *ancient régime*.

---

7   *Mokāfāt*: vv. 181, 193, 448, 671, 760, 781, 1129.
8   *Mokāfāt*: vv. 286, 391, 406, 671, 925, 1026, 1052, 1057, 1077, 1134.
9   *Mokāfāt*: vv. 565–568.
10 In fairness, I should point out that he uses the same terms for the decadent Safavid elite.
11 See chapter 1.
12 *Mokāfāt*: v. 1134.
13 *Mokāfāt*: vv. 438–453.
    ز آثار آن گشت عالم خراب به ملک و بملت رسید انقلاب

In the normative Persianate theoretical tradition, the cause of revolution is the tyranny of the ruler. Our author does not exonerate the Safavid monarch from all responsibility for the present calamity, caused by divine punishment for misrule by Shah Soltān-Hosayn, but he spares him as much as possible by shifting the burden of blame onto the Safavid ruling elite. In doing so, he extends his analysis of the earthly causes of the revolution beyond the monarch to the *ancient régime* in its entirely.

Though not tyrannical, the last Safavid monarch was a cause of the revolution. His excessive piety,[14] pleasure-seeking,[15] and kindness to enemies the author finds incompatible with the required qualities of kingship. Above all, he lacked the ability to administer punishment to inspire the awe of majesty which is indispensable for kingship. Without sufficient punishment, about which he states, "punishment is the foundation of justice," injustice prevails in the realm, and this in turn invites divine justice and punishment. A much more important cause, however, was the "ruination of religion and the state" by the corrupt and decadent Safavid elite, whom our author consistently blames for the divine punishment of Iran.[16] He goes through every group in the court, especially the eunuchs, each group in the military, and those in the bureaucratic elite one by one, and subjects them to scathing criticism for their cowardice, corruption, and incompetence, and for trampling on the rule of law. Shah Soltān-Hosayn distributed the state revenue in an arbitrary fashion and contrary to the reason of state.[17] The political order was corrupt, unjust, and oppressive through and through; its moral order was gutted and caused the collapse of the social hierarchy that was consequently turned upside down.[18]

To the numerous examples of such ills given in the text of the *Mokāfāt*, we may add a couple of particularly striking illustrations from other historical sources on the last stable year of the old regime, 1720. Our sources are unanimous in stating that the court eunuchs were deciding about appointments and dismissals made by Shah Soltān-Hosayn, and in 1720, the Ottoman ambassador was astonished to find the chief white and black eunuchs seated respectively to the right and the left of the shah when he presented his credentials.[19] In the same year, Soltān-Hosayn gave the immense fortunes that had been

---

14 "As he disliked this world like ascetics / he put his efforts into ruining it!" (which is indispensable, *Mokāfāt*: v. 165)
15 "Neither saddened by injustice, nor gladdened by justice / His religion and justice dwelled in the pleasure garden [the palace of Farahābād]." (*Mokāfāt*: v. 266)
16 *Mokāfāt*: vv. 209, 247–267.
17 *Mokāfāt*: vv. 172–175, 289–324, 382–397, 419–437, 467–488.
18 *Mokāfāt*: vv. 204–210.
19 Matthee 2012: 202–203.

confiscated from the disgraced and blinded grand vizier, Fath-ʿAli Khan, and the latter's powerful nephew, Lotf-ʿAli Khan, to Esmāʿil Khan, one of his household slaves.[20]

The Shiʿite hierocracy was another pillar of the *ancient régime*; its members were found to be worldly and corrupt, and were fiercely criticized for trampling on the sharia, and for persecuting the true (Sufi) religious virtuosi.[21] Their dereliction is presented as the earthly cause of the revolution, as this turned the moral order of Iranian society upside down. Thus, we see that the notion of revolution as a turn in ruling power is extended to include reversals in the social hierarchy and moral order.

The *Mokāfāt-nāma* offers us extensive ad hominem attacks on individual military commanders, bureaucrats, and provincial governors, as well as the court physician and the last two prime ministers. This part of the book is of considerable historical interest in explaining the collapse of the Safavid state. But here the Persianate moral theory of revolution is ad hominin and does not give us a satisfactory explanation, though we can reconstruct one from Mostawfi's detailed account.

A lower-level functionary of the Safavid state composed a long lament while in exile in Najaf; it was written at the same time as *Mokāfāt-nāma* and displays a strikingly similar conception of the revolution in Iran. It even uses both words *enqelāb* and Iran several times. Revolution (*enqelāb*) is equated with power vacuums (*fotur*) in Irān-zamin, as a result of which "the country of Iran (*keshvar-e irān*) has been completely ruined." He mentions the depredations of the Lezghis and the Kharijites, and prays at length to Imam ʿAli to have pity on the suffering "people of Iran" (*mardom-e irān*)[22] under tyrannical Afghan rule.[23] The "Kharijites"[24] are the Arab tribesmen from Oman who ravaged the shores of the Persian Gulf and the Sea of Oman, alongside the Baluchis.[25] For now, we note that the moralistic accounts of our authors on the causes of unrest cannot be accepted as sociologically valid and should be explained in terms of the ongoing political struggles between the center and the periphery in Islamicate empires.

---

20   *Zobda*: 126.
21   *Mokāfāt*: vv. 236–240, 325–381.
22   Variant, *khalq-e ʿarsa-ye irān*; Jaʿfariyān 2001: 3:1299.
23   Jaʿfariyān 2001: 3:1299–1308.
24   Also mentioned here as earlier, in *Mokāfāt*: vv. 1132–1133.
25   Matthee 2012: 227–231.

2   The Collapse of the Center in the Safavid Empire and Its Causes

The collapse of the Safavid Empire can now be seen as a prototypically modern revolution in a patrimonial-bureaucratic empire. The last third of the eleventh/seventeenth century saw the unraveling of the impressive centralized bureaucracy and especially the military organization; this was accomplished by ʿAbbās I (r. 587–1629). This ended the nightmare of the Qezelbāsh tribal interregnum that took place during his adolescence. The Safavid standing army of musketeers led by Georgian and Armenian slaves on the Ottoman model proved ineffective and appears to have been dissolved gradually during the reigns of the last two Safavids, Soleymān (1666–94) and Soltān-Hosayn (1694–1722), or it may have been eliminated altogether under the latter. In the sources there are occasional references to the slave soldiers (*gholām*), but there is no evidence of them participating in military campaigns; only their commander, the Qollar-āqāsi, is mentioned as being among the corrupt and shortsighted courtiers and high officials involved in the infighting among the Safavid elite. The defense of the Safavid state outside the capital was left to the dispossessed Qezelbāsh tribal contingents. This is evident in the generic use of the word Qezelbāsh to denote the late Safavid armies and their confederates. The *Tadhkerat al-moluk*, the manual on the Safavid state written after its destruction for the Afghan conqueror of Isfahan, states that the Qezelbāsh troops received one-third of the state budget and their commander, the Qurchi-bāshi, ranked first among the four army commanders and bore the title *rokn al-saltana* (Pillar of Sovereignty).[26] Historically, it is ironic that the Qezelbāsh are the very tribal army Shah ʿAbbās I had worked to weaken and marginalize. The military weakening of the Safavid imperial state meant that it was increasingly dependent on Georgian troops that remained under the command of the former kings, and remained integrated in the Safavid Empire as a province with one of the former kings appointed as governor (*vāli*) on condition of formally converting to Islam. The last Safavid monarch sent the governors of Georgia and their Georgian troops, reinforced by Qezelbāsh horsemen, to govern the unruly region of Afghanistan. The Afghan rebels successfully exploited the resentment of their fellow tribesmen against the Georgian troops who were favored with preferential treatment by the governor.[27]

Reports of the French, Russian, and Dutch diplomats and agents are in full agreement about the deplorable state of the central government's military forces. The so-called military revolution bypassed Iran and the reforms of

---

26   Arjomand 1988: 17.
27   *Zobda*: 207 n. 117.

'Abbās I, who sought to tranform his state into a gunpowder empire, unraveled in the latter part of the eleventh/seventeenth century. The musketeers equipped with firearms were resented by the Qezelbāsh horsemen and were marginalized in the late Safavid armies; the artillery were in an even worse state.[28] The army also lacked infantry, which explains the dominance of the tribal cavalry and its interest in monopolizing military power. As a relatively small band of Ghelzai Afghans was able to conquer Isfahan and overthrow the Safavid Empire, it is not difficult to see that the "breakdown of the state" was due to the depletion of its military forces and their inability to handle the tribal resurgence as the major cause of the revolution.

The military weakness of the Safavid imperial state was closely related to the nepotism, factionalism, tax farming, and sale of offices that gutted its patrimonial administrative and fiscal structure and seriously undermined Safavid autocracy. In addition, the complete turnover of high officers, many of whom were members of the families of the grand viziers.[29] The council of state set up to advise the autocracy and make decisions became the scene of factional wrangling and infighting that paralyzed the central administrative machinery. This in turn led to endemic local tyranny and fiscal abuse throughout the empire. Above all, there was a serious crisis of legitimacy caused by the incongruence between the normative ideal and the actual reality of monarchical autocracy, as is evident from the details of *Mokāfāt-nāma*. This discrepancy implied the illegitimacy of the incumbent monarch, but not that of the Safavid dynasty, which, astonishingly, persisted throughout the eighteenth century. The incumbent autocrat, Soltān-Hosayn, failed to live up to the ideal of Safavid sovereignty embodied in Shah 'Abbās the Great. The Sufi pillar of Safavid sovereignty collapsed under growing pressure from the Shi'ite hierocracy, leading Soltān-Hosayn to close the Sufi "house of unity" (*tawhid-khāna*) of the Qezelbāsh. The shah was no longer the *morshed-e kamel* ("perfect guide") of the Qezelbāsh, he had become a puppet of the hierocracy called Mollā Hosayn![30]

The indubitable military weakness of the Safavid Empire meant that its sole effective component, the Qezelbāsh tribal army, could not keep in check the other tribes, even those close to the Iranian heartland, notably the Kurds, the Lors, and the Bakhtiyāris.[31] With regard to the tribes on the periphery of the empire, the Safavid failure was spectacular. These tribes included the

---

28   Matthee 1996: 408–410; Matthee 2012: 218.
29   There were two major instances of such complete turnovers—in 1715 and 1720 with the rise and fall of the grand vizier Fath-'Ali Khan Dāghestāni. (Matthee 2012: 209–210).
30   Matthee 2012: 202.
31   Lambton 1977; Matthee 2012: 222, 225, 236.

Leghzis in the northwest, the Arabs (especially those of Oman in the south), the Baluchis in the southeast, and above all the Afghans. The trouble on the Afghan eastern periphery of the empire began as early as 1706 with the rebellion of the Mir-Wais b. Shah 'Alam, the chief of the Hōtak clan of the Ghelzai tribe. In fact, Mir-Wais held the post of *kalātar* (headman). He rose against the Georgian governor of the province, Shahnavāz Khan (also known as Gorgin Khan), who was a former king of Georgia. All the Georgians, including Shahnavāz Khan, were massacred, and the Qezelbāsh troops captured, disarmed, and imprisoned them. In 1711, Shahnavāz Khan's nephew, Khosraw Khan, was appointed the governor of Georgia and the commander of an army of 12,000; this army was comprised of Qezelbāsh horsemen, Georgian soldiers, and the Shah's slaves (*gholām*, probably musketeers), who were expedited to Qandahar. That army and its commander were taken by surprise and destroyed and their equipment captured; Mir-Wais expanded his territory unopposed and held it until his death in 1715.[32] This aroused the envy and greed of the Ghelzai's rival tribe, the Abdālis, who besieged and captured Herat in 1716 under the leadership of Sa'dallāh Khan, who massacred the Safavid governor and "his followers consisting of three thousand men from the Qezelbāsh and the Heratis."[33] The Abdālis then invaded Khorasan and proceeded to capture Jām. Sa'dallāh then routed a special army recruited in Mashhad, and with his force of 6,000 laid siege to Mashhad and raided Nishapur and destroyed its fort before returning to Herat in 1717. Learning about the Abdāli incursion in 1717, an Uzbek tribal force of some 12,000 invaded Khorasan and laid siege to Mashhad but were repelled. The depredations of eastern Khorasan by Afghan tribesmen resumed after the collapse of Isfahan and continued from 1722 to 1744.[34]

At this point, approximately 1720, the seriousness of the situation in Khorasan registered in Isfahan, and the Shah was persuaded by his powerful aunt and the grand vizier to leave with his court to Isfahan in July in 1717 and settle in the old Safavid capital, Qazvin, for three full years before inching further toward Khorasan. The court arrived in Tehran on 2 November 1720. Meanwhile, Mahmud, Mir-Wais's son and successor as the chief of the Hōtak clan of the Ghelzai tribe, did what Safavid armies expedited to Herat had repeatedly failed to do; he captured Herat, killed Sa'dallāh, and expelled the Abdālis. Mahmud sent Sa'dallāh's head to Shah Soltān-Hosayn, who rewarded

---

32 Matthee 2012: 233–235.
33 *Zobda*: 118.
34 *Zobda*: 120–122, 208–209 n. 121.

him with the governorship of Qandahar.[35] Evidently, no new Mahdi or religious figure like Shaykh Bāyazid Rawshani[36] emerged to push the Ghelzai and Abdāli Afghan tribesmen to overcome their mutual animosity and refractory tendencies and unite along Khaldunian lines against the imperial Safavid state.

Be that as it may, many influential courtiers openly resisted moving on to the troubled region of Khorasan, and after a heated debate the council of state and the shah returned to Isfahan. The courtiers debated the issue in the presence of the shah in December 1720 in Tehran, expressing in ugly and abusive language their long suppressed animosities. On one side the last powerful Safavid grand vizier, Fath-'Ali Khan Dāghestān, led a faction, and on the other side, the *mollā-bashi* (royal chaplain) and the *hakim-bāshi* (king's physician), opposed him. The grand vizier lost the debate and fell victim to its venom and violence; he was dismissed and blinded after a few days and his immense wealth was confiscated. The Shah and his court then returned to the capital, arriving in Isfahan with much fanfare on 27 January 1721. The celebratory fanfare and royal drum (*naqāra*) notwithstanding, it could be argued that the breakdown of the Safavid imperial state, which was the prelude to the revolution, had already occurred in Tehran, and the collapse of the central edifice of Safavid autocracy in Isfahan, which was hollowed out after 225 years, was a foregone conclusion.

3   The Fragmentation of the Safavid Empire and Revolutionary Multiple Sovereignty (1722–1732)

After his victory over the Abdālis in Herat, Mahmud returned to Qandahar at the head of the Ghelzai tribesmen, then set out for Kerman with some 2,000 soldiers without waiting for the news of his appointment as the governor of Qandahar by the Shah. By that time, Arab predators from Oman had taken Bahrain and slaughtered some 6,000 Safavid troops. The expeditionary force sent against the Baluchis provoked rebellions on the way and was stuck in southern Iran, and therefore was unable to deal with the Baluchi unrest.[37] As the news of Mahmud's approach reached Kerman, however, panic broke out in the city. The governor and his Georgian soldiers fled and the 200 troops sent from Isfahan took to plundering the local and foreign merchants, and the additional troops Isfahan was planning to send never arrived. The great majority of the population fled the city, and the Zoroastrians among the remnants

---

35   *Zobda*: 120.
36   See chapter 6.
37   Matthee 2012: 229–231.

welcomed the Afghans as liberators from the bigotry of the Shi'ite hierocracy. The Afghans, however, did their own plundering before returning to Qandahar in the spring of 1720.[38]

In Qandahar, Mahmud was not placated by his appointment as the Safavid governor, as he coveted the Safavid crown. Once he had time to refresh his troops and recruit a few thousand more, he set out for the Safavid capital Isfahan. On 1 March 1722, the shah was informed that Mahmud and the Afghans were just eighty miles from Isfahan, so the shah put together a force of 18,000 with 24 cannons, and sent recruiters to collect 12,000 men from the surrounding villages to be quickly trained as musketeers. But there was no time for training as they had to be sent to meet the advancing Afghans in a day or two. The Shah asked the Armenians for 300 men to guard his palaces as no troops were left in the city.[39] By March 8, Mahmud and his 12,000 men, one-third of them well armed, reached the village of Gelunābād (some 20 kilometers from Isfahan) where the confrontation took place. The Georgian contingent fought well and lost 4,000 to 5,000 men, the Qezelbāsh troops sustained somewhat smaller loss of life because, for the most part, they fled back to the city or dispersed in the countryside and headed for other cities. Some 5,000 Kurds had been sent to help the Shah upon his urgent request, but they were met by an Afghan force; 1,500 of them were reportedly killed and the rest dispersed, leaving their equipment and provisions to the Afghans. The Safavid casualties were estimated to be ten times heavier than that of the Afghans.[40]

The Afghans occupied Jolfa (a suburb) and the outskirts of Isfahan and besieged it while the temporary walls and gates the Isfahanis had put up for defense turned the city into a concentration camp where famine raged for the next seven months; this led people to flee the city, and also resulted in cannibalism and a great reduction in the population. Indeed the loss of life was heavy. Mostawfi stated that the data collected by order of Mahmud reported 700,000 dead or missing, including 80,000 in one neighborhood alone. When presented with the dismal report Mahmud is reported to have thanked God for his success "to eliminate so many of the enemies of the four Companions [i.e., the rightly-guided caliphs of the Sunni reviled by the Shi'a]!" On 21 or 22 October 1722, the courtiers finally brought Shah Soltān-Hosayn to the pleasure palace of Farahābād, where he abdicated and affixed the diadem of sovereignty (*jigha*) on Mahmud's head. Three days later, seated on the Safavid throne in the Chehel-Sotun palace, Mahmud inaugurated his reign by

---

38   Matthee 2012: 238–239.
39   Gilanentz 1965: 35–37.
40   *Zobda*: 129; Gilanentz 1965: 53; Matthee 2012: 240.

announcing that he would retain the commanders of the Qezelbāh cavalry, the Qurchi-bāshi, and the commander of the royal slave corps, the Qollar-āqāsi; in addition, he appointed one Afghan and one Qezelbāsh commanding officer for each contingent. This reorganization of the state did not work, if it had been meant to, and in less than two months, Mahmud called the Qezelbāsh officers to march in a parade; he massacred all 715 of them and displayed their corpses in the center of Shah Square in Isfahan.[41]

Mahmud confiscated any gold, cash, or liquid assets he could find among the Armenians of Jolfa, the Banyan (Indian moneylenders) and foreign trading companies. He also sought to bring over one thousand Afghan families from Qandahar and settle them in Isfahan. Mahmud's Afghan state held Isfahan for the next nine years. Its armed forces consisted of 6,000 Afghans (as estimated in September 1723), 1,000 Zoroastrians who had thrown in their lot with them in 1720, and 110 other men. There were also 2,000 Safavid musketeers, among them 600 Armenians and 30 Georgians who had enrolled in the royal slave corps unwillingly and under duress. But Mahmud failed to use Isfahan as a base from which to conquer other parts of Iran, even the nearby regions of Hamadan and Kurdistan. This began a decade-long interregnum in which multiple leaders ruled the fragmented Safavid Empire.[42]

Shah Soltān-Hosayn's third son, Tahmāsb Mirzā, who was able to escape from the siege of Isfahan in June 1722 with a small retinue, headed toward the old capital, Qazvin. The council of state first persuaded the shah's oldest son, Soltān-Mohammad, to do this, but the prince reneged and took refuge in the harem. The second son was put forward by the shah himself and was willing, but was apparently unacceptable to the council. The task then fell upon the third son, Tahmāsb. On 9 November 1722, Mahmud sent out 3,000 or 6,000[43] Afghan troops and 2,000 Safavid troops under the command of Mahmud's vizier, Amānallāh, and Mahmud's nephew, Ashraf-Soltān, to deal with Tahmāsb Mirzā in Qazvin. Presumably in reaction to the news of the dispatch of this force, Tahmāsb chose November 24 to declare his sovereignty. On that day, Tahmāsb sat in the old Safavid government palace (*dawlat-khāna*) of Qazvin, appointed his grand viziers and other high state officials, and struck coins in his name. However, by December the hospitality of the people of Qazvin appears to have worn thin and they welcomed the Afghans to Qazvin. The Qezelbāsh troops accompanying the Afghan force fled, as did Tahmāsb and his court who proceeded to settle in Tabriz. When the Afghans imposed

---

41 *Zobda*: 131–135.
42 Gilenantz 1965: 92–104.
43 *Zobda*: 139–141; Gilanentz 1965: 69–71.

heavy fines on the population of the city and requisitioned 60 young women, the citizens of Qazvin changed their minds and rebelled under a *luti* (neighborhood strong man). The people of Qazvin were ruthlessly slaughtered by the Afghans, but only after they inflicted heavy casualties the Afghans and forced Ashraf-Soltān to leave with just one hundred men. With 600 men left to him, Amānallāh then left the city and encountered a much larger number of Safavid troops (as many as 6,000 according to one report) who fled as he confronted them, leaving their equipment behind. Amānallāh and his troops returned to Isfahan in January 1723.[44]

It is hardly surprising that, after the flight of the Safavid Tahmāsb and the departure of the Afghan Amānallāh, the traumatized inhabitants of Qazvin wrote to the commander of the Russian troops occupying northern Iran and asked for protection and declared their willingness to become subjects of the Russian czar. Armenians had rebelled in 1716 and killed their governor and although Safavid rule had been nominally restored, there was little effective central control there or in the rest of the northwestern periphery of the Safavid Empire. The Armenians in northern Iran were crossing the border to Russia, and few of them were left in Gilan and Mazandaran by 1723. Those on the northwestern shore of the Caspian Sea began to rebel against central control and turn toward Russia for protection against depredations by the Lezghis of Daghestān, who were compatriots of the grand vizier, Fath-'Ali Khan. Already in 1707, many inhabitants of Ganja favored Russian occupation as a way of switching loyalty to a sovereign who would protect them. The leaders of a rebellion in Shamakhi in 1716 likewise turned to the Russians. Peter the Great (r. 1682–1725) considered northwestern Iran ripe for occupation when he marched into Safavid territory in 1717, thus commencing the Russian expansionist policy toward the Persian Gulf. The (Sunni) Lezghis occupied Shamakhi in 1721 and put some 4,000 to 5,000 Shi'ites of the city to the sword. A number of Russian merchants were also killed, giving Russia the pretext for taking Darband in August 1722. The Safavid central government relied heavily on their Georgian vassals to deal with the Lezghis as it had no resources of its own even before its fall to the Afghans. After the fall, the government of Tahmāsb Mirzā was even more desperate. When the inhabitants of Talesh offered to fight the invading Russians on his behalf, Tahmāsb could not offer them military or material support; he could only grant a useless authorization to collect the taxes of Rasht themselves. Meanwhile, the collapse of the Safavid center

---

44   Gilanentz 1965: 77–79.

resulted in infighting among the two Georgian vassal kings, while a mismatched alliance between Armenian bands and local Iranian magnates misfired.[45]

The Ottomans were not prepared to let Russia benefit from the fragmentation of the Safavid Empire. In 1723, they took Yerevan in Armenia and Tbilisi in Georgia in an effort to compete against Russia; they also took a large part of western Iran, notably Kermanshah, Hamadan, and Marand, without any competition. The two foreign powers occupying northern and western Iran found it much easier to settle their differences in dividing the spoils than had the Ghelzai and Abdāli Afghan tribes in the eastern periphery of the Safavid Empire. They signed the Treaty of Constantinople in 1723, dividing northern and western Iran between them and giving the Ottomans the green light to occupy Tabriz in July 1725.[46]

Meanwhile the Afghans continued to hold Isfahan and Shiraz. Once Amānallāh and his troops were back in Isfahan at the end of January 1723, Mahmud massacred the middle ranks of the Qezelbāsh in the thousands, together with some 150 courtiers.[47] As Mahmud's failure to expand his rule beyond Isfahan became evident, he became morose and suffered increasing bouts of insanity that emboldened his cousin Ashraf to hatch a plot to kill him, using his few remaining Qezelbāsh officers. Ashraf killed Mahmud and then the Qezelbāsh conspirators on 26 April 1725.[48] The coup was supported by Amānallāh Khan, who was, nevertheless, put to death by Ashraf two days later, and his quickly-acquired property, gained from extortion, was confiscated. On the same day, Ashraf killed nineteen Iranian notables who had survived under Mahmud. In August and September of 1726, as the rumors of the advance of Prince Tahmāsb and news about the army sent by the Ottomans in November 1726 (purportedly to release Shah Soltān-Hosayn who had been kept alive by Mahmud), Ashraf massacred nearly 2,000 inhabitants of Isfahan, broke his oath, put Shah Soltān-Hosayn to death, and sent pieces of his body to the advancing Ottomans.

In contrast to his deranged cousin Mahmud, Ashraf saw himself as the consolidator of the Afghan revolution and crowned himself Ashraf Shah. During the incipient globalization of the Westphalian system of sovereign nation-states, he was the first coup leader in modern Iranian history to seek legitimacy through recognition by foreign powers. He wasted no time and sent an emissary to the Ottoman court in 1725, and, having defeated the invading Ottoman

---

45   Gilanentz 1965: 29, 131–140; Matthee 2012: 221–226.
46   Matthee 2012: 226–227.
47   Gilanentz 1965: 81–83.
48   Balland 1987: 794.

army in November 1726, he immediately sued for peace. In April 1726 the Ottoman Sultan sent an ambassador who was cordially received in Isfahan and was able to negotiate a treaty with Iran under its new Sunni leader. According to the terms of the treaty, consequently signed in January 1728, Ashraf ceded the Iranian territory already occupied by the Ottomans in exchange for the Sultan's recognition of him as the Shah of Iran. The signing of the treaty was followed by a rebellion in northwestern Iran occupied by Ottomans. The rebellion was led by a dervish named Qalandar Esmā'il, who had captured Tabriz and Ardabil and held them through the summer of 1728 with the support of an unspecified number of Iranians, Lezghis, and Georgians. His rebellion was nevertheless suppressed by the Ottomans who reoccupied Tabriz.[49]

Ashraf's policy in international relations was fully in line with his grand project of consolidation—namely the establishment of a new Hōtak dynasty, a previously impossible goal, given Mahmud's insanity. Immediately after seizing power in the coup of 26 April 1725, Ashraf persuaded a key Iranian collaborator, Mirzā Ahmad, who belonged to a distinguished family of Safavid civil servants and was serving as the mayor (*kalāntar*) of Isfahan, to recruit his father, Mirzā Rafi'ā Ansāri into the Afghan revolutionary regime. Ashraf appointed Mirzā Rafi'ā to the all-important position of *mostawfi al-mamālek* (minister of finance), and appointed his son-in-law the *vaqāye'-nevis* (court chronicler), then confirmed his (Mirzā Rafi'ā's) son as the *kalāntar* of the capital, Isfahan. Ashraf drew on Mirzā Rafi'ā's vast administrative experience as well as the state archive and commissioned him to write a manual of Safavid state organization, *Dastur al-moluk*, to guide the post-revolutionary rebuilding of a strong new dynastic state.[50] Ashraf was evidently following the Persianate theory of revolution as a divinely-ordained turn-in-power (*dawlat*) of a new dynasty—that is, his own.[51]

Ashraf also began building palaces and indulged in a royal lifestyle that included sumptuous entertainment and hunting. In pursuit of his state-building endeavor, there are indications that Ashraf sought to reconstitute his army and make it less dependent on Afghans. For instance, when he routed the army of a Safavid pretender in Fars in October 1727, Ashraf ordered his Afghan general to treat the defeated and captured soldiers kindly and give them provisions to return to their homes.[52]

---

49   Floor 1988: 1–4, 15–21.
50   The very early appointment of Mirzā Rafi'ā and his son and son-in-law was reported by the Dutch VOC (Floor 1988: 3). The early effort to write the *Dastur al-moluk* by Shah Soltān-Hosayn indicates that he was still alive at that point. (Marcinkowski 2005)
51   Floor 1988: 3; Marcinkowski 2005.
52   Floor 1988: 23, 48.

His adherence to the Persianate theory of revolution notwithstanding, Ashraf, the would-be consolidator of the Afghan revolution, failed to follow the precepts of the Khaldunian model of tribal coalition-building necessary to secure the revolution. Not only was he unsuccessful in bringing the Abdāli Afghans into the fold, but his murder of his cousin Mahmud even lost him Ghelzai support for the revolutionary change of dynasty. Of greater consequence was his failure to make a general and lasting alliance with the Baluchi tribes, despite the prominent role of Mohammad Khan Baluch, who served as his governor of Shiraz and plenipotentiary ambassador to the Ottoman Sultan.[53] This failure resulted in his inability to gain control of the Persian Gulf region whose trade could have provided considerable resources for state-building. Some 4,000 insubordinate Baluchi tribesmen who extirpated the rule of the Safavid Sayyed Ahmad in 1727–28 (considered below) also devastated the trading posts of the British and Dutch East India Companies in Gombroon and ended the role of that vital port as an international trade depot.[54] Some Baluchis then appear to have made a deal with a cousin of Ashraf in Qandahar who wanted to avenge Mahmud; they intercepted Ashraf during his final flight from Nāder Shah in the winter of 1730 and handed him over to Nāder's troops.[55]

During Ashraf's reign, the cause of the Safavid prince Tahmāsb continued to prosper. After two years of leading a government in exile from the capital, Nāder, a Turkman from the Qereqlu clan of the Afshār tribe that had resettled in Khorasan, called himself Tahmāsb-qoli (slave of Tahmāsb) and offered his service to the fugitive Safavid prince soon to be styled Shah Tahmāsb II (1727–1732). For a while, he was a bandit, then Nāder briefly joined Malek Mahmud and helped him extend his dominion into Khorasan before entering Tahmāsb II's service.[56] Nāder evidently judged the lingering Safavid legitimacy a greater asset than Malek Mahmud's mythical claims to the heritage of the ancient Persian kings, a claim that was not matched by any actual display of majesty when he haphazardly came to power in Mashhad. As we shall see, Nāder reconquered Mashhad for Tahmāsb Mirzā in November 1725, and this enabled Tahmāsb Mirzā to insert himself into the revolutionary politics of Yazd, Kerman, and the Persian Gulf region in 1726 and 1727. In 1729, he moved to Tehran with a view to proceeding southward to reconquer Isfahan. Seeking to forestall such a move, in August 1729 Ashraf preemptively led his army toward

---

53   Floor 1988: 22, 112.
54   Planhol 1988.
55   Balland 1987: 797.
56   Amanat 2017: 142.

Tehran but was defeated in a series of confrontations; he retreated to Isfahan in the last week of October, with the Safavid army under Nāder in hot pursuit.

Ashraf Shah gathered his remaining forces, packed up the treasury, and made hasty preparations to leave for Qandahar. Ashraf Shah's royal drum house (*naqāra-khāna*) in Isfahan went silent in the morning of 14 November 1729, indicating that there was no sovereign resident in the capital.[57] Two days later, Tahmāsb-qoli (Nāder) entered the city, which had been plundered in the meantime, and received the representatives of the British and the Dutch East India Companies. It took another month for Tahmāsb Mirzā to arrive in the sorrowful capital of the devastated Safavid Empire and begin to resuscitate it.

This brings us to Mashhad, the last important fragment of the Safavid Empire that was shattered by the fall of Isfahan. On 21 October 1722, in the havoc caused by news of the disasters in Isfahan and Herat, where the Abdāli Afghans had returned after Mahmud departed for Isfahan, two respected master craftsmen and traders, Mohammad-Amin Āqā and Mohammad-Taqi Āqā, together with the official in charge of the grain and food stores of the shrine of Imam Rezā, gathered the "riff-raff and the toughs" (*awbāsh o ajāmera*) of the city and looted the houses and property of the *sepahsālār* (commander-in chief),[58] Esmā'il Khan. The looted property was most likely the confiscated property of the blinded grand vizier Fath-'Ali Khan and his agents. Esmā'il Khan was replaced by the sub-governor, 'Ali-Qoli Khan Shāmlu, who had only recently been dismissed. Unrest continued, however, and the house of the vizier of Mashhad was looted and the vizier himself was killed. 'Ali-Qoli Khan appointed Mohammad-Amin Āqā and Mohammad-Taqi Āqā headmen (*kalāntars*) and "governed" the city according to their bidding until a fellow rebel, Hajj Mohammad (known as Bābā Qodrati, that is, 'the strongman'), an important *luti* of Mashhad, decided it was his turn. After the congregational prayer on 16 December 1722, at noon, Bābā Qodrati led the same "riff-raff and toughs" and killed 'Ali-Qoli Khan Shāmlu, Mohammad-Amin Āqā, and Mohammad-Taqi Āqā, and later the official in charge of the shrine stores as well. Bābā Qodrati took over the city of Mashhad and began making appointments, and declared Malek Hosayn Khan its governor. The latter, however, wrote to his brother, Malek Mahmud Sistāni (who claimed descent from ancient Persian kings), and invited him to Mashhad. Malek Mahmud

---

57 According to a VOC report, having the premonition that some Afghans may return to massacre the Dutch trading mission detained in a caravanserai, a VOC agent went to the drummers and got them to start beating the drums to make the nearby Afghans think the Safavid troops were already in the city. (Floor 1988: 33–34)
58 Like many other military and administrative titles, this was, by then, an empty sinecure.

arrived with an army of Arabs and tribesmen of Sistan, a cannon or two, and his royal drum house (*naqāra-khāna*), and held audiences in a suitable mansion on 14 March 1723. He appointed Bābā Qodrati governor of Sabzavar to get him out of the city. Bābā Qodrati was miffed and the makeshift condominium only lasted nine days. Malek Mahmud struck first. His few thousand troops, together with the city riff-raff, looted the house of Bābā Qodrati, who fled but was apprehended in a nearby village and handed over to Malek Mahmud, who killed him and his arrested aides on the spot. This ended the seven-month urban phase of the revolution in Mashhad. Malek Mahmud, who was in his late thirties, reinforced his retinue by recruiting men from the Arab tribes of Sistan; thus he came to boast an army of 3,000. He then had a throne and a crown, supposedly modeled on that of the ancient Kayanids whom he claimed as ancestors, made for him. Malek Mahmud ruled Mashhad for the next two and a half years, raiding Nishapur and other neighboring cities and expanding his rule in Khorasan and Sistan. It was not until the reassertion of Safavid power by Tahmāsb II, who sent two armed expeditions against him in 1725, that his rule in Mashhad was disturbed. He and his armed Arab retinue were pushed out of the city into its citadel, but then returned and looted some neighborhoods. On 22 November 1725, the citizens asserted themselves one last time and finally opened the gates of Mashhad to Tahmāsb-qoli, the Qurchi-bāshi and the Safavid army.[59]

After Tahmāsb's organized escape from Isfahan, two other Safavid princes fled Isfahan on their own initiative. One of them, Safi Mirzā, a younger son of Soltān-Hosayn, established himself in the tribal region of Kuh-Giluya in southwestern Iran for some two years; there he became known as "the donkey-riding prince" (*shāhzāda-ye khar-savār*). There is no evidence that Safi Mirzā paid allegiance to Tahmāsb after the abdication of Shah Soltān-Hosayn. During Ashraf's reign, from the summer of 1725 onward, Safi Mirzā tried to expand his rule further south to the Persian Gulf, but his army was eventually defeated and annihilated by the Afghan governor of Shiraz, Mohammad Khan Baluch, in October 1727.[60]

We hear of the defeat of Safi Mirzā's army from the Dutch in connection with Soltān-Mohammad (Soltān-Hosayn's firstborn), who had hidden in the harem when the decision to leave besieged Isfahan and form a Safavid government in exile was made. According to reports from the Dutch East India Company (VOC) in Gombroon, Soltān-Mohammad made it out of Isfahan in the last year of Mahmud's rule or during the coronation of Ashraf before the

---

59   *Zobda*: 175–183.
60   *Zobda*: 173–174; Floor 1988: 49, 112.

murder of his father, and took refuge in a shrine near Minab in the Persian Gulf region. There, in the spring of 1726, he was discovered by Jahāngir Khan, a local landlord and strongman who owned the village of Andarak,. Jahāngir Khan persuaded Soltān-Mohammad to reveal his identity and claim sovereignty, which the latter had refused to do while his father was alive. Nevertheless, Soltān-Mohammad agreed to form a Safavid government in exile in the summer of 1726; this was recognized by his younger brother, Safi Mirzā. After some hesitation, the mayor of Minab joined Jahāngir Khan and his son in supporting Soltān-Mohammad, and recruited six VOC mercenaries for his army, which consisted of 150 men by August 1726, when Soltān-Mohammad's Safavid government in exile (with 14 courtiers) moved to Sandarak, a village in the nearby mountains owned by another local landlord. Soltān-Mohammad's fortunes declined rapidly after the defeat of his younger brother's army and the reappearance in the Persian Gulf region of his cousin, Sayyed Ahmad Khan, who was then acting for the main Safavid claimant, Tahmāsb Mirzā. The last we hear from the Dutch concerning Soltān-Mohammad is a rumor in July 1728 that he had gathered a force to take Gombroon. It would seem that Soltān-Mohammad's character did not change much from the time he hid in the harem and later took sanctuary in the remote shrine near the Persian Gulf. The VOC reporter asserted that "This prince, rather than being the leader of his subjects, is their follower and subject!"[61]

The last contender for the Safavid throne was Sayyed Ahmad Khan, whose mother was a daughter of the preceding monarch, Shah Soleymān (r. 1666–94). He was in his late twenties, and unlike his above-mentioned two cousins, he was a fighter. Sayyed Ahmad had left Isfahan with Tahmāsb Mirzā in 1722 but later split from him and surfaced in Jahrom in 1725 with a forged decree of appointment from Tahmāsb Mirzā. Before long he began to rule on his own, in competition with his two royal cousins, Tahmāsb and Safi. From Jahrom he proceeded to a devastated Kerman, which by the end of the year, he took over. In January 1726 he crowned himself in Kerman and set up a full court with officers bearing titles of the collapsed Safavid state, just like the courts of Ashraf Shah and Tahmāsb. Sayyed Ahmad minted coins in his name and even extended his domain northward to Yazd and to Tabas in Khorasan; in the fall of 1726 he attempted to take Shiraz back from the Afghans, but failed and, with his army scattered, he returned to Kerman. By that time, Nāder had reconquered Mashhad for Tahmasb II, who then felt strong enough to order the governor of Yazd to arrest Sayyed Ahmed in Kerman. This was done in late March 1727, and Sayyed Ahmad was sent to Tahmāsb Mirzā who forgave his

---

61   Cited in Floor 1988: 117.

insubordinate cousin, and then sent him at the head of an expedition to Sistan. Sayyed Ahmad took Sistan and proceeded to govern Kerman on behalf of Tahmāsb Mirzā. In the last three months of 1727 he expanded his government to Gombroon (Bandar ʿAbbās) and Minab on the Persian Gulf until he was ousted by the Baluchi tribesmen. Sayyed Ahmad moved from place to place fighting the Afghans and was eventually killed by them in August 1728.[62]

We have covered the revolutionary turmoil outside the capital city, Isfahan, in the cities of Mashhad and Qazvin during this interregnum under Mahmud (October 1722–April 1725), while touching on the devastating vicissitudes of the revolutionary situation in the city of Kerman. The turmoil in Kerman, as noted, continued during the interregnum under Ashraf (April 1725–November 1729), when it briefly sustained its own sovereign, Sayyed Ahmad who minted coins as the Safavid Ahmad Shah. Sayyed Ahmad then returned as Tahmāsb's governor, only to be ousted by the Afghans and their Baluchi allies who punished the fleeing Kermanis and massacred the inhabitants of the nearby Rāvar early in 1728.

We end this section with a few words on events in the city of Yazd during the second interregnum. As mentioned, when Tahmāsb Mirzā's power grew after Nāder recovered Mashhad for him, he ordered the governor of Yazd to take Kerman and arrest the pretender Sayyed Ahmad. The latter hedged his bet and eventually sent his son to take Kerman for Tahmāsb. But Ashraf could not tolerate Yazd's allegiance to Tahmāsb, so he sent his general, Zebardast Khan, to use his own troops and mobilize allied Afghan and Baluchi tribesman in the area to subdue Yazd and Kerman and appoint a new governor for Yazd. This revolutionary situation caused by the clash of multiple sovereigns induced the citizens of Yazd to rise independently under the leadership of a military officer called a *min-bāshi* (lit., "commander of a thousand"). The Yazd rebellion lasted into November 1728, when it was brutally suppressed by Ashraf's troops and the *min-bāshi* and his sons were executed.[63]

4   From Revolutionary Violence to Wars of Conquest: Nāder's Imperial Autocracy (1732–1747)

Far more significant that the fall of the Safavid dynasty, which was a *revolutio regni* and *enqelāb* in the contemporary European and Persianate senses, its coda, the meteoric rise and sudden collapse of Tahmāsb-qoli, better known

---

62   Floor 1988: 35–43, 49–92; *Zobda*: 173.
63   Floor 1988: 49, 92–93.

to the world as Nāder Shah, constituted, by virtue of its long-term consequences, a revolution that accounts for its world-historical significance. More immediately, however, it was a revolution that consolidated and unified the nomadic tribes. In this revolution the consequence of mass mobilization was conquest—the form taken by the export of revolution. Nāder Shah showed no interest in the cities and their chaotic revolutionary politics and instead put his energy into creating yet another nomadic empire of the Turko-Mongolian type. After the conquest of Mashhad and Herat for Tahmāsb, he unified the Turkman, Qājār, and Kurdish tribes, as well as the rebellious Baluchi, Abdāli, and other Afghan tribes, and the Ghelzai Afghans who were added after the defeat of Ashraf in 1731. The Georgian troops under their princes and the tribes of western and northwestern Iran also joined his armed forces as he recovered much of the Iranian territory from Russia and the Ottoman empire.[64] Later, when he conquered Central Asia as Nāder Shah, he also integrated the Uzbeks into his army. This was a remarkable repeat of the pattern of integration of allied and defeated tribes for the purpose of conquest. This amounted to exporting revolutionary violence by channeling it into continuous warfare and conquest.[65] As a result, Nāder's army was predominantly tribal and Turko-Mongolian. As the Ottoman ambassador who witnessed his final year in 1746–47 put it, "because he had no need for Iranians in the army, he got rid of the Iranians in the army!"[66]

Nāder was, however, neither a tribal chief like Chinggis Khan nor a prophet or a mahdi like Shah Esmāʿil and Bāyazid Rawshani, and he did not create a tribal confederation on the Khaldunian pattern. Yet his religious policy for his heterogenous empire sought to approximate that pattern, and was especially attuned to the Sunni tribesmen who constituted the clear majority of his troops. He therefore forbade anti-Sunni Safavid practices, and when he invaded Iraq in 1743 he brought the Sunni clerics of Central Asia, Afghanistan, Iran, and Iraq into a council presided by his *mollā-bāshi* in the Shiʿite holy city of Najaf. The aim of the Najaf council was to promote the acceptance of Shiʿism as a fifth school, the Jaʿfari rite (*madhhab*)[67] of Islam, on the one hand, and to discontinue anti-Sunni Shiʿite practices, most notably the cursing of the Sunni rightly-guided caliphs, on the other.[68]

---

64   Amanat 2017: 142–146.
65   As such, it can be considered a parallel to what has been studied elsewhere, namely about the two important cases of the second Caliph ʿOmar in the mid-first/seventh century and of Chinggis Khan in the seventh/thirteenth (Arjomand 2019: chs. 7, 10).
66   Cited in Tucker 1994: 177.
67   As the school of law of the sixth Shiʿite Imam, Jaʿfar al-Sādiq (d. 765).
68   Tucker 1994.

As he rose to supreme command of his rapidly growing tribal army, in 1732 Nāder first deposed Tahmāsb II in favor of his eight-month-old son, ʿAbbās III, making himself the regent, and then, in 1736, decided to end the rule of the Safavid dynasty altogether. In the winter of 1736, he ordered Mirzā Mehdi Khan Astarābādi, the secretary of the royal chancery, to send summonses to the dignitaries of the state and the tribes to assemble on the plain of Moghān to elect him king. The one Safavid cleric who demurred, the *mollā-bāshi*, was strangled with a bow string. The other dignitaries put their signatures on long rolls prepared for the purpose, and granted sovereignty to Nāder Shah Afshār; Mirzā Mehdi, who collected them, was promoted to the rank of the *monshi al-mamālek* (chancellor of the realm).[69] In his acceptance speech, Nāder challenged Shiʿite Islam as the established religion of Iran and sought to reconcile the Jaʿfari rite as the fifth rite of Islam. As we shall see presently, this is best explained by the composition of Nāder's army of conquest, which was predominantly Sunni. The most remarkable feature of this unprecedented assembly, however, was that representatives of Iran "elected" a king. The coins Nāder Shah struck after his coronation thus bear the legend: "When the seal of state and religion has been displaced (an oblique reference to the termination of the Safavids' turn in power), God commanded Iran in the name of Nāder."[70]

Nāder also sped up military mobilization as the new king and in 1739 embarked on the conquest of India. He sacked Delhi and returned the most famous crown jewels of the Mughal emperor to Iran. Already in discussing the option of having himself elected king, Nāder reportedly reviewed the history of ancient kings of Iran in greater detail than the Turko-Mongolian world conquerors, namely Chinggis Khan and Timur (Tamerlane), had. On the surrender of Bukhara he was presented with the sword of Timur and the coat of arms of Chinggis Khan.[71] In the winter of 1740–41 he completed his imperial conquests in Central Asia by annexing "the entire domains of Khwarazm to territory of the imperial rule (*qalamrow-e shāhanshāhi*)."[72] In October 1740, Nāder confirmed Abu'l-Fayz Khan, a descendant of Chinggis Khan, as the ruler of Bukhara and as the king of Turkestan with the title of *shāh*. The title was being granted by the crown-giving (*tājbakhsh*) king of kings (*shāhanshāh*) of the new empire, the supreme Nāderi empire (*dawlat-e ʿelliya-ye nāderiyya*).[73]

---

69 Marvi 1995: 2:457.
70 Tucker 1994: 170.
71 Marvi 1995: 2:447–451, 794.
72 Astarābādi 2009: 526.
73 *Jahāngoshā*: 386–387.

On this occasion Nāder is reported to have remarked that "the sons and tribes of the realm of Iran [i.e., the core of the empire] are sufficient for us!"[74] Nāder marched on to conquer Khwarazm, and execute its Turkman ruler for treason, according to the Yasa of Chinggis Khan.[75] However, Nāder granted the population amnesty and appointed as ruler a (presumed) descendant of Chinggis Khan who had been raised in Herat and accompanied him in his campaign as the ruler of Khwarazm. In November-December 1740, the Jaghatai Mongolian and Uzbek tribal leaders and their subjects (*ra'iyyat*) were made to sign a covenant of loyalty to the "God-given Nāderi Empire/[turn-in-power]," and pledge not to buy and sell Iranian captives.[76]

Upon Nāder's return to the fortress in Khorasan, he reconstructed Kalāt as his new capital, and celebrated the completion of his empire-building by issuing decrees on the annexation of various fiscal districts of northern India and Central Asia into the supreme Nāderi Empire and the "realm of the shadow of God" (*mamlakat-e zellollāhi*). He further ordered that, henceforth, the title of *shāhanshāh* (king of kings) be used as his official title in all state correspondence and documents.[77]

Paranoia and insanity followed world conquest rather quickly; Nāder blinded his heirs and on the slightest suspicions he decimated the dignitaries who had helped him. The reign of terror he presided over in the last year of his life ended with his murder. To the chagrin of "the Iranians who had considered him the sign of divine mercy" in the words of his chancellor, he "destroyed the foundations of the state (*dawlat*) through the state!" The historian Astarābādi alternatively refers to the Iranians as the "people of Iran" (*ahāli-ye Irān*) or the inhabitants of the "flower-filled land of Iran" (*sarzamin-e golshan-e Irān*), the sedentary core of Nāder's ephemeral nomadic empire.[78]

From the time Tahmāsb-qoli (later Nāder Shah) liberated the territory of Iran from Russian and Ottoman occupation to the end of his reign, when he failed to gain recognition of Shi'ite Islam as the Ja'fari rite (*madhhab*) by the Ottoman soltān, he negotiated a series of international agreements and treatises with neighboring states that dealt with Iranian captives and residents abroad. In these negotiations, Nāder Shah acted as the representative not of the "God-given Nāderi Empire" (*Dawlat-e nādera-ye khodādād*) but rather as of

---

74 Marvi 1995: 2:797, 817.
75 *Jahāngoshā-ye Khāqān* 1985: 386–387, 393.
76 *Jahāngoshā-ye Khāqān* 1985: 395–396. *Dawlat-e nādera-ye khodādād* and *dawlat-e khodādād-e shāhanshāhi* are used alternately.
77 *Jahāngoshā-ye Khāqān* 1985: 398–400.
78 Astarābādi 2009: 640–642, 647–648.

the "sovereign state of Iran" (*dawlat-e ʿelliya-ye Irān*) and as the "people of Iran" (*ahāli-ye Irān*). The self-conception of Nāder's rule as a God-given empire of conquest was thus replaced by a novel one, the sovereign state of Iran and of the people of Iran.[79] This terminological shift reflects the incipient incorporation of Iran into the Westphalian world system of sovereign states.

After Nāder Shah's death in 1747, his grandson Shāhrokh held onto his fortress capital, Kalāt, and the surrounding region of Khorasan, but the rest of his nomadic empire of conquest disintegrated into three component realms, ruled by three local leaders who had been subordinate commanders in his army. Irakli (Hercules) II, the former vassal king of Georgia who served Nāder as one of his commanders, held onto his sedentary domain and ruled it as a fully independent sovereign until 1798. The Abdāli Ahmad Khan who had commanded the Afghan tribesmen under Nāder Shah, assumed the title of Ahmad Shah Dorrāni, and established a nomadic patrimonial polity in Afghanistan, which he used as a base from which to conquer Delhi in 1757. More consequentially from our viewpoint, Karim Khan, leader of the Zand clan of the Lor tribal confederation, gradually gained control of the rest of Iran and made Shiraz his capital. Karim Khan Zand (r. 1747–79) did not follow the other two heads of successor states by crowning himself, but instead maintained a certain ʿAbbās as a puppet Safavid king and detained him in a fortress where he learned to make knives, while Karim Khan assumed the modest title of *vakil al-raʿaya* (representative of the subjects).

The sudden death of Nāder Shah signaled the collapse of the last Turko-Mongolian nomadic empire of the Persianate world. His ephemeral Persianate empire disintegrated into three kingdoms destined to become the independent nation-states of Iran, Georgia, and Afghanistan. The Persianate ecumene was irreparably fragmented into these three kingdoms and a number of principalities in Central Asia, while the Mughal Empire in India, subdued and devastated by Nāder and after his death yet again by Ahmad Shah Dorrāni, gradually came under British domination.

5   The End of a Long Revolution: from the Safavid Empire to the Nation-State of Iran

With the rapid disintegration of Nāder's ephemeral nomadic patrimonial empire, the last Turko-Mongolian empire of conquest in world history disappeared, and the bumpy journey to the transformation of Iran into a modern

---

[79]   Astarābādi 2015: 395–395, 410–414, 430–431; Bayāt 2004: 79–81.

state began. It is significant that Karim Khan called himself the 'representative of the subjects' of the puppet Safavid king and not anything like the 'representative of the people' of Iran. The use of these terms, and likewise *dawlat-e Iran* (state of Iran), remains restricted to the diplomatic context in which Iran interacted with other sovereign states in terms of the Westphalian international order.[80] Nor was there any immediate conceptual change when the Zand relatives of Karim Khan were eliminated by the founder of a new dynasty stemming from the northern Turkman tribe of Qājār.

Nāder's meteoric rise and the collapse of his nomadic empire of conquest after only a decade did little to instill confidence in stable monarchy and sovereignty, and the relatively short spell of peace and stability in Shiraz under Karim Khan Zand from July 1765 to February 1779 ended abruptly with Karim Khan's death, and "the matter of sovereignty (*saltanat*)" was disrupted, then divided among infighting Zand relatives who competed to mobilize urban militias. These militias availed themselves of the muskets of the Safavid royal slaves and allied themselves with tribal factions of their own and other tribes. When the turbulent four years of Ja'far Khan Zand in Shiraz and Isfahan ended with his murder in January 1789, our chronicler recorded "a general revolution (*enqelāb*) in his armed retinue."[81]

Just before the rise of Nāder, the roaming Safavid prince, Tahmāsb II, had taken refuge with the Qājār tribe in Astarābād, and the Qājār leader Fath 'Ali Khan acted as his protector for a while. In the 1730s Nāder Shah had Fath 'Ali Khan Qājār killed, and a Qājār leader retaliated by participating in Nāder's murder in 1747. Karim Khan Zand then faced the successive, failed rebellions of his son, Mohammad Hasan Khan and his grandson, Hosayn-qoli, and kept the latter's brother, Āqā Mohammad Khan, who had been castrated by an Afsharid pretender, hostage in his capital, Shiraz. On the death of Karim Khan, Āqā Mohammad Khan fled to Astarbābād and gradually gained control of the surrounding regions in northern Iran. He finally eliminated Karim Khan's nephew, Lotf-'Ali Khan in 1794, and captured Shiraz, appointing the Zand official, Hajji Ebrāhim (d. 1801), his chief minister.

Indeed the matter of sovereignty was disturbed during the Zand-Qājār interregnum (1779–94). One of the Zand bureaucrats in Shiraz who entered the service of the new Qājār dynasty through Hajji Ehrāhim was commissioned to write the history of this turbulent period for his new monarch. His chronicle of the disturbances related to this interregnum in this period is poignant, given his evident sympathy for the old dynasty he had served. He dutifully recited

---

80   Arjomand 1988.
81   Shirāzi 1986: 34–44, 68, 82–87.

Q. 3:25: "He gives sovereignty (*mulk*) to whom He wills and empowers whom He wills, and He takes away sovereignty from whomever He wills, and debases whom He wills," but with an emphasis on the second part, making the post-Safavid eclipse of sovereignty the wrath of God. He gives a sympathetic account of the rule of Lotf-ʿAli Khan Zand, but ruminates that according to the will of God, the "eternal possessor of sovereignty" (*mālik al-mulk*), fortune favored the new 'shadow of God' and required the overthrow of the Zand dynasty.[82]

It is no wonder the legitimacy of the new dynasty remained shaky. Āqā Mohammad Khan (d. 1797) minted coins in the name of the Hidden Imam and obscure Safavid princes,[83] and yet again without the name of a sovereign.[84] He wore the sword of the founder of the Safavid Empire for his coronation, and he and his nephew and successor, Bābā Khan, ascended the throne as Fath ʿAli Shah (1797–1834) by concocting a syncretic and unconvincing basis for his legitimacy. That is, he advanced the unflattering claim that his father was the offspring of a concubine who was already pregnant when she was given by the Safavid Shah Soltān-Hosayn to Fath ʿAli Khan. This explains their adoption of the epithet Safavid-Qājār. More consequentially, he reaffirmed and consolidated his uncle's alliance with the *mojtahed*s (authoritative jurists) of the Shiʿite hierocracy that became fully independent of the rulers during the period of this 70-year post-Safavid interregnum. This alliance was the Qājār's remedy for their lack of legitimacy; it created a new dualistic structure of authority in nineteenth-century Iran, a structure in which the shah was the head of the state and a handful of *mojtahed*s constituted an independent Shiʿite hierocracy.

From an international viewpoint, the collapse of the centralized Safavid Empire and that of the Nāder's nomadic empire of conquest in the eighteenth century meant that Iran entered the nineteenth century with the traditional notions of sovereignty and the state badly shaken. When signing the treaty of Finkenstein with Napoleon against Russia in 1807, and much more forcefully in the humiliating treaties of Golestan (1812) and Turkamanchai (1828) with Russia after the Perso-Russian wars, Iran was incorporated into the Westphalian international order as a sovereign state and embarked on a program of defensive modernization that ended in failure, however. This failure can in no small measure be attributed to the disasters of the eighteenth century.

The long revolution initiated by the fall of the Safavids, contrary to the literal and premodern sense of revolution as a return to the status quo was not a

---

82 Shirāzi 1986: 29–30, 78.
83 Amanat 2017: 162.
84 Kondo forthcoming.

return of any reconstituted patrimonial bureaucratic empire but the complete destruction of the imperial pattern and the emergence of an entirely new entity in its heartland. The new patrimonial kingdom, slowly and in several reversible steps over a century or more, redefined itself as a modern nation-state. The slow pace of modernization was related to the character of the Qājār's patrimonial "state" consolidated by Fath 'Ali Shah, who divided the provinces and major cities among some of his over one hundred sons. It was described by an English traveler as "a race of royal drones, profligate and depraved, and the most noxious to their country."[85] Despite the judiciary reforms (discussed below), structurally it remained an unreconstructed patrimonial monarchy to the end of the nineteenth century. In the 1880s, three of Nāser al-Din Shah's (1848–1896) sons governed eleven of Iran's fourteen provinces.[86]

If we were to take the great French Revolution as the timeless model for all revolutions in the sense of an "anatomy of revolution,"[87] we could call the Afghan rule in Isfahan our revolution's "Reign of Terror," and Nāder Shah its Emperor Napoleon, "the child of the revolution." But we are far from that, as it would gravely exaggerate a partial analogy into a theoretical category. On the other hand, the theoretical models or ideal types used in this study, both the medieval Khaldunian and the modern Tocquevillian ideal type, capture important features of this revolution. It is reasonable to think of our case as falling halfway between the two types.

The Tocquevillian features of the collapse of Safavid central authority, namely "state breakdown" and its cause have already been highlighted in the preceding pages. The state focus of the Tocquevillian type also draws our attention to the emergence of a centralized polity stimulated by Iran's incorporation into the Westphalian international system of nation-states. To spell out the Khaldunian features of our case as a revolution in a polity with a dual tribal/urban social structure, we would note that its tribal component had by far the greater military weight. The leaders of our revolution were therefore tribesmen—that is, the Afghan Mahmud and Ashraf who brought about the change of dynasty according to the Khaldunian model, were Afghan tribesmen. Likewise, Nāder Shah was a Turkman tribesman who ended the revolution by concentrating power as an imperial autocracy in an unmistakably Khaldunian fashion, by creating a conquering army of tribal confederates.

---

85 Cited in Arjomand 1988: 25.
86 Ettehadieh Nezam-Mafi 1989: 54.
87 Edwards 1927; Brinton 1938.

The revolutionary period from 1722 to 1729 is treated by Safavid officials who expounded the Persianate theory of revolution as the foreign rule of the "Afghan dogs," while modern Iranian nationalist historians present it as foreign rule and an "Afghan invasion." These observers were as wrong as any Marxists who think of the Afghans as the "proletarians" of the revolution that destroyed the 225-year-old Safavid Empire. In fact, the Afghan nomadic tribes were just as much the subjects of the Safavid Empire as the sedentary subjects inhabiting the cities were, and furthermore, like the Turkman tribesmen such as Nāder Shah, they belonged, according to the Khaldunian model, to the element of the Safavid social structure in which group solidarity and the revolutionary potential resided.

CHAPTER 9

The Persistence of Apocalyptic Mahdism and the Coming of the Modern Myth of Revolution

Karl Marx's famous verdict on religion as the opiate of the masses should be assessed with the hindsight that the system he was constructing was, in fact, a secular religion. Revolution was one of the central myths of this new secular religion, the historic event that served as its model being the great French Revolution of 1789. While dismissing the old religion to propagate a new one, Marx adopted the modern myth of revolution as the moment of redemption in history. In Marxism, revolution became what the millennial myth and the messianic idea were in Judeo-Christian and Islamic religions. A more dispassionate and objective view of both religion and revolution indicates that there is a varied and complicated relationship between the two. In such a view, both the revolutionary potential of religion and the religious dimension of modern revolution are conspicuous. I have argued for the functional equivalence of the two in motivating revolutionary social action. In Iran's two revolutions in the twentieth century, which we examine here and in chapter 10, we find that the two myths mutually reinforce each other.

Apocalyptic messianism, as we have seen, had a tremendous revolutionary potential in the early modern Persianate world. It was fundamentally religious and therefore heteronomous as a political phenomenon. Only after the French Revolution secularized apocalypticism into the modern myth of revolution did the idea of revolution become an autonomous political phenomenon, conceived of as a redemptive act of popular will in the forward march of history.

A new religion was born of the passionate idealism of the French Revolution, according to Tocqueville. With the perspective of the communist and fascist revolutions of the twentieth century, this new religion can be typified as a political religion.[1] Unlike earlier political upheavals, according to Tocqueville the French Revolution aimed at the political, secular salvation of humanity. Furthermore, the French revolutionaries marked the beginning of a new era with a new calendar, and under Robespierre, even attempted to institute a cult of reason with a supreme being as its deity. Above all, however, the new political religion of the French Revolution that passed on to international political culture was the ideology of Jacobinism, so named after the radical egalitarian

---

1 See the introduction.

revolutionary Jacobin clubs in which it took shape. Through Jacobinism, revolution itself became a new political myth in modern culture, a myth or value-idea with an autonomous power akin to the millennial myth of old religions.

The modern and politically autonomous myth of revolution produced the first modern revolution in Iran in 1906. Meanwhile, the mid-nineteenth century is remarkable for giving us a spectrum of modern revolutions and millennial uprisings. The arena of the former was in Europe, of the latter exclusively in Asia. The revolutions of 1848 in Europe, in which religion played no significant role, were enactments of the myth of revolution central to modern political messianism generated by the great French Revolution. At that time, older forms of messianism, Shi'ite and Christian, were the motive force in two millennial uprisings in Asia: the Babi movement in Iran, and the Taiping movement in China. These other revolutions of 1848 offer a sharp contrast to the more familiar European revolutions. The contrast with Iran's two modern revolutions of the twentieth century is less sharp due to the persistence of the Mahdist myth in them.

1   The Other Revolutions of 1848: the Babi Uprisings in Iran in Comparison to the Taiping Revolution in China

Although several movements in medieval Europe arose at the time of the millennium—the thousand-year reign of Christ after the second coming—none of them succeeded in bringing about any revolutionary political change.[2] Similarly, a series of millennial movements that proclaimed the dawn of a new era under charismatic leaders who claimed to be the Mahdi failed in the eighth/fourteenth and ninth/fifteenth centuries in the Ottoman Empire, Iran, and Central Asia. But as we have seen,[3] one Mahdist movement succeeded in conquering Iran and establishing the Safavid Empire, and it provoked far-reaching reactions in other early modern Muslim empires. Millennialism was also a factor in the English (Puritan) revolution in two forms: in the mild form of a general expectation that a new world could be built after a thorough reformation of both the Church and the commonwealth and in the spectacular form it took among the Fifth Monarchy Men, a sect who took the execution of Charles I in 1649 as the signal of the end of the fourth empire of world domination, predicted in the Book of Daniel, and by the rise of Cromwell as the beginning of the Fifth Monarchy, meaning the thousand-year reign of Christ and the

---

2   Cohn 1957.
3   In chapters 5 and 6.

saints. Their millennial hope survived the revolution itself by a year but was extinguished with the bloody suppression in 1661.

As we move to the twentieth century, the order of causation is reversed; the primary motivating factor in these revolutions is the modern myth of revolution, not millennialism. With this reversal, the activation of millennial beliefs that rekindles Mahdism becomes the *effect* of modern revolutionary situations rather than their cause. Nevertheless, its rekindling undoubtedly reinforces the twentieth-century revolutionaries' commitment to millennial action in the here and now, albeit with millennium in effect redefined as revolution.

While the myth of revolution championed by the first generation of professional revolutionaries like Karl Marx was fueling the European revolutions of 1848, the millennial myth remained effective in propelling major uprisings in Asia, both in the Mahdist Shi'ite variant we know well and in its Christian variant, which we briefly examine to gain some comparative perspective.[4]

As noted, the messianic figure of the Mahdi, the rightly-guided leader of the End of Time is particularly prominent in Shi'ite Islam, where it fully retains the apocalyptic messianism of the Qā'im. In the fourth/tenth century, for Imami or Twelver Shi'ism it merged with the belief in the Hidden Imam, the twelfth holy Imam who was said to have gone into occultation in 260/874 and would reappear as the Mahdi at the End of Time. The Mahdist revolution of the Safavid Shah Esmā'il gave rise to counter-millennial sovereignty throughout the Persianate world. In the Safavid Empire itself, the messianic charisma of Esmā'il was routinized into the charisma of the Safavid lineage/dynasty as the house of sovereignty (*velāyat*) and the Safavid kings as lieutenants of the Hidden Imam or Mahdi in occultation.

The prolonged revolution that followed the fall of the Safavid dynasty profoundly changed the structure of domination in Iran as the main successor state of the Safavids. By the early decades of the Qājār period (1785–1925), the Shi'ite hierocracy had freed itself from the tutelage of political authority characteristic of the Safavid era and secured its autonomy. The societal structure of domination in Iran changed completely. An autonomous Shi'ite hierocracy or hierarchy arose, one whose high-ranking clerical jurists built on the medieval containment of millennialism through the doctrine of occultation. The religious jurists authorized to interpret the sacred law that prevails during the period of the so-called Greater Occultation now claimed to be the general deputies (*niyābat-e 'āmma*) of the Hidden Imam. This, however, left the temporal rule of monarchy to the shah. In this dual structure of domination, the Shi'ite

---

4 Our comparison is theoretical, as we have no evidence of any historical interplay between the two.

hierocracy exercised its religio-legal authority independently of the shah as the head of the state.[5] Under such a dual structure of authority, the claim to Mahdihood was primarily a challenge to the clerical authority of the deputies of the Mahdi as the Hidden Imam.

The Babi (*bābi*) movement was launched by a young merchant in Shi'ite Iran on the thousandth anniversary of the birth of the Hidden Imam. Its founder first claimed to be the gate (*bāb*) to the Mahdi, then, bringing a new revolution, he claimed to be the Mahdi himself. The apocalyptic use of this term can be traced back to clandestine revolutionary Isma'ili Shi'ism. The word "*bāb*" was used as a title among those high-ranking missionaries who had access to the concealed Imam. They were called gate(s) (*bāb*), and were headed by the gate of gates (*bāb al-abwāb*). The latter term was retained as the title of the head of the Isma'ili mission after the Fatimid revolution in the fourth/tenth century.[6] The armed Babi rebellions began in 1848, and the last one was suppressed in 1850. The movement thus failed as a political revolution.

Sayyed 'Ali Mohammad of Shiraz, known as the Bab for his initial, more publicized—and more modest—claim to be the *bāb* (gate) to the Hidden Imam in occultation, was a young merchant nurtured in a religious culture. This culture was permeated by Sufi mysticism and by millenarian expectations cultivated by Akhbāri (traditionalist) and Shaykhi theosophical trends of the followers of Shaykh Ahmad Ahsā'i (d. 1826). Ahmed Ahsā'i became convinced of his millennial mission at the age of twenty-five. In 1844, exactly one thousand years after the traditionally accepted date for the disappearance of the Twelfth Imam, he claimed to be the Mahdi, the Hidden Imam returning from occultation. The Shaykhi theosophical doctrines of non-material resurrection (*ma'ad*) and the inner-worldly presence of the Imam, and especially the cultivation of intense expectation of the millennium by the Shaykhi leader, Sayyed Kāzem Rashti (d. 1844), paved the way for the claimant who was indeed discovered by a party of Shaykhi seminarians traveling from the Shi'ite holy lands ('*atabāt*) to Shiraz in search of the expected Mahdi. The declaration of the manifestation (*zohur*) was planned in detail in accordance with Shi'ite traditions; the Bab was to proclaim his Mahdihood in Mecca and proceed to the holy cities of Iraq. But his emissary to the holy lands was arrested, tried by a joint gathering of Shi'ite and Sunni '*olamā*' of Iraq, and eventually sent to Istanbul where he died in a labor camp. The Bab arrived in Mecca in December 1844 after an arduous sea voyage, but his proclamation fell pathetically flat. He canceled the journey to the holy lands, and returned to Shiraz (now termed the "city of

---

5 Arjomand 1984.
6 Arjomand 2022: ch. 7.

safety") on the same boat. But things did not turn out much better in Shiraz, where, in June 1845, he was forced to recant his beliefs publicly and in writing.[7] Despite these inauspicious beginnings and serious setbacks, the Babi movement spread rapidly during the rest of the decade.

The process of radicalization in the Babi movement can be traced in some detail. These details strongly suggest that the movement stemmed not from the personal charisma of its leader but rather from the Shi'ite messianic belief in the coming of the Mahdi. Messianic expectancy was endemic to popular Shi'ism, especially among heterodox groups; a number of individuals had claimed Mahdihood in the decades preceding the Bab. On this point it is telling that Zarrin-Tāj Baraghānī, known as Qurrat al-'Ayn (lit., "delight of the eye") (d. 1852), the Babi heroine who played the most important role in the movement other than the Bab himself, never met the Bab in person. Furthermore, from the beginning, the Bab appears to have been much more cautious than his radical disciples. In 1844, while claiming to be the "great remembrance," "true guardian," and the "measure of cognition," in line with Shaykhi theosophy, the Bab recommended dissimulation (*taqiyya*) to his followers. In the following year, he recanted in public in Shiraz; and in 1847, en route to imprisonment in the fortress of Maku he rejected an offer of rescue by the Babis of Zanjan. The Bab endorsed the radical moves, both in doctrine, that is, in the escalated claim to Mahdihood and, like the Isma'ili leader of Alamut in 1166, to being the Qā'im of the Resurrection,[8] and in action, that is, in revolutionary militancy and the call to arms from Khorasan, but he did not initiate radical moves. Such moves were initiated by his followers, especially by Qurrat al-'Ayn. She acted as the spearhead of doctrinal radicalism by advocating the termination of the sharia in 1847 and forced the Bab's hand.[9] The Bab, who was in prison by that point, decided to endorse his most radical disciple "perhaps for the first time." Somewhat later, the Bab disseminated a sermon on his being the Qā'im, abrogating the law of Islam as the Qā'im. He stated in this serman that he was the Qā'im "who by God's benevolence has now manifested himself": "I am the divine fire which God kindles on the Day of Resurrection."[10] Some of the more moderate Babis who would have preferred to remain within the parameters of Shaykhi theosophy balked at the escalation of the Bab's claim and left the Babi ranks; others, who found the millenarian claim appealing, joined the movement.

---

7   Amanat 1989: 255.
8   See chapter 2.
9   Browne 1897: 775–777; Amanat 1989: 86, 307.
10   Amanat 1989: 374.

In 1847, drawing on the rich cabalistic and numerological symbolism of Shi'ite millennial sects, most notably the Isma'ilis and the Horufis, the Bab designated a group consisting of himself and eighteen of his disciples as the *horuf-e hayy* (lit., "letters of the living"), corresponding to the nineteen Arabic letters of *bismillah al-rahman al-rahim* (In the name of God, the merciful, the compassionate). They were equated with "His [God's] face" (*vajhahu*) [= 19 numerologically], and pantheistically taken to be representatives of all things (*kullu shay'*) [= 361 = 19 × 19], in reference to Q. 28:88: "All things perish except His face." These disciples were soon regarded as reincarnations of the sacred figures of the earlier prophetic cycles, such as Mohammad and 'Ali. The Bab also made references to the heavenly Father, and compared himself and his disciples to Christ and his apostles. He knew about Christianity from the missionary, Henry Martin, who was active in Iran at the time. This makes the presence of Christian missionaries in Iran a minor factor in the Bab's millennialism and it invites comparison with the uprising in China in which Christianity was a truly major factor. The Bab's contemporary, Hong Xiuquan, claimed to be the younger son of God the Father and began an armed uprising to establish the Taiping tien-kuo (Heavenly Kingdom of the Great Peace) in the first days of January 1851.[11] Unlike Hong, the Bab never converted.

All these apocalyptic beliefs came into full play during the millennial uprisings of the Babi saints in 1848. In preparation for a millennial battle in the summer of 1848, the young cleric, Molla Mohammad 'Ali Bārforushi, was recognized as the "Spirit of the Messiah" and took over the charismatic leadership of the Babis.[12] The Babis raised the black banner of millennial uprising in Khorasan and marched westward, reaching the ruins of a fort named Shaykh-e Tabarsi in Mazandaran; they made this the site of their uprising on behalf of the imprisoned Qā'im of the Resurrection.

Qurrat al-'Ayn's radicalism extended from theology into the realm of social and political action. She arrived in the holy cities of Iraq to reside in the house of her late teacher and the Shaykhi herald of the millennium, Sayyed Kāzem Rashti. By then she had acquired a following, though it was not until 1846 that there was a definitive confluence of her millenarian expectations and the Bab's ideas that resulted in her acknowledgment of the latter's claims. Qurrat al-'Ayn was surrounded by a small circle of literate women, but her audience was, as one would expect, predominantly male. At first, she spoke to large audiences from behind a curtain. In December 1845, on the Bab's birthday, she appeared unveiled at a gathering of the Babis. Her final and dramatic act of defiance

---

11   Spence 1996.
12   Amanat 1989: 187–198.

against the religious hierarchy came in the summer of 1848, when she removed her veil in the middle of a speech at the congress of 81 Babis in Badasht, and proclaimed that she was the word of the Qā'im, "the word that shall put to flight the chiefs and nobles of the earth."[13] Qurrat al-'Ayn was thus decisive in assuring the final victory of revolutionary millenarianism and the call to arms. By this point, political militancy and the use of physical violence at the grassroots level had begun, specifically with the assassination of Qurrat al-'Ayn's uncle, an influential orthodox Shi'ite cleric. It was well underway as the Babis armed themselves in Khorasan in northeastern Iran.

A series of millenarian uprisings followed Qurrat al-'Ayn's sounding of the trumpet. These began, first in Tabarsi, with the spectacular scene of millennial reenactment of sacred history; then in Nayriz; and finally in Zanjan. In this last uprising, which began in May 1850, coins were struck, bearing the inscriptions of Qā'im on one side, and *ya sāhib al-zamān* ("O Lord of Time!") on the other.[14]

As noted, Qurrat al-'Ayn never met the Bab in person and could not be considered a personal follower of his charismatic leadership. Like other Babi leaders of the uprising who had learned their millennial revolutionary faith in the madrasa seminars of Sayyed Kāzem Rashti, Qurrat al-'Ayn was inspired by the divine love of the mystic to translate her inner-worldly faith into this-worldly militant action in *kairotic* time—the millennium.[15] To show her infusion with divine love that propelled her to collective action as a millenarian in sacred time, it is sufficient to translate from one of her poems:

> I became ashamed of calling you God
> [many] gods have arisen among your worshippers (*bandagān*)
> Saying "I am God" (*ana Allāh*)[16] are your worshippers
> Makers of gods are your servants.[17]

The largest Babi uprising and the one with the largest number of casualties, in which some 2,000 Babi men and a few women and children took part, began in Zanjan in May 1850. It started somewhat haphazardly in reaction to the killing of a Babi at the instigation of the governor and a leading orthodox Shi'ite *mojtahed*, and was led by Akhund Mohammad 'Ali of Zanjan, who was

---

13   Cited in Amanat 1989: 326.
14   Browne 1897: 769.
15   See the introduction for an explanation of these terms.
16   Famous words of the great fourth-/tenth-century Sufi, Mansur Hallāj for which he was executed.
17   Browne 1918: 346. For similar poems by another Babi poet, Nabil Zarandi, some of which are also attributed to Qurrat al-'Ayn, see Browne 1918: 347–358.

a troublesome Shi'ite traditionalist (Akhbāri), who had taken off his turban on conversion and was given the title of Hojjat (lit., "the proof") by the Bab. This uprising was less focused on the millennial aspect, in fact the Bab provided no direction for it in the two months before his execution when his followers held most of the city of Zanjan. Their leader, the Hojjat, was forced to continue to maintain a holding pattern; he was wounded and died in December 1850. The number of rebels then dwindled to a couple hundred until they surrendered unconditionally in 1851 and most were executed.

The actual charismatic leaders of the Babi uprisings were Qurrat al-'Ayn (the daughter of a *mojtahed*), Bārforushi, and the Hojjat (two converted clerics), but not the Bab himself. The uprisings were put down by government troops one by one between 1848 and 1850. The Bab himself remained in prison throughout and was executed in July 1850, two months after the haphazard beginning of the uprising in Zanjan.

This very brief account of the Babi uprising aims solely to highlight its millenarian motivation. Its failure, however, must be accounted for sociologically and comparatively—that is, in terms of our Khaldunian model of revolution and in contrast to the success of the Safavid Mahdist revolution three centuries earlier. Although at least one-third of Iran's population in the mid-nineteenth century consisted of nomadic tribes; interestingly, the Bab and his disciples did not appeal to or attempt to convert them. The Babi movement was entirely urban and mainly consisted of seminarians, traders, and merchants. With the government's ill-prepared defenses, the uprisings were put down very slowly (the suppression of Tabarsi and Zanjan took about nine months each) by uninterested, unmotivated, and mostly tribal contingents of the Qājār government.[18]

The Babi movement was ferociously suppressed in the cities after a group of Babis attempted to assassinate the monarch in 1852. Mirzā Hosayn 'Ali Nuri (d. 1892), a government official who had joined the Babi movement in 1844 and was imprisoned for his role. Cleared of the charge of complicity in the plot, he was nevertheless exiled to Ottoman Baghdad in 1853. Ten years later, in a garden in Baghdad, Nuri proclaimed himself to be "he whom God shall manifest," of whom the Bab had spoken. He assumed the title of Bahā'ullāh (lit., "the glory of God") and his followers considered him the last prophet and manifestation of God. The Bahai religion was thus founded in April 1863 as a diasporic world religion. The great majority of Babis accepted Bahā'ullāh's messianic claims and became Bahais. A small minority led by his brother, Mirzā Yahyā (known as Subh-e Azal; lit., "dawn of eternity"), who remained close to the

---

18   Browne 1897: 796–800; Walbridge 1996.

initial inner-worldly apocalyptic faith of the Babis and died on 29 April 1912, after fifty years in exile in Cyprus, refused to join the Bahais. Mirzā Yaḥyā's followers continued to be called Babis.

Not long after the execution of the Bab in the fortress of Maku in Iran in 1850, the Taiping uprising began in China, and in contrast to Babism, it succeeded in creating a revolutionary state that lasted for a decade (from the capture of Nanjing in 1853 until a few months before its collapse in 1864) in a prosperous area in southern China with a population of some thirty million. The Babi movement was primarily a millennial movement in the Mahdist tradition, and only a secondary or tertiary response to Christian influence through Western missionaries. The Taiping, by contrast, was a Chinese Christian movement whose leader claimed to be the brother of Jesus and God's Chinese son; he was inspired by missionary tracts and briefly instructed by an American Baptist missionary in Canton.

In 1843, having failed the Mandarins' examination for the imperial bureaucracy for the fourth time, the founder of the Taiping movement, Hong Xiuquan, found the key to understanding the dream of a heavenly journey that had obsessed him for six years in a missionary book by a Chinese convert to Christianity. He said he came to understand that he was the younger son of God the Father whom he had visited, together with Jesus, his heavenly elder brother, who accompanied him in that heavenly ascent. God the Father had sent him back with "the killing power in heaven and earth" and the mandate to eradicate evil from the world. His visionary dream was more elaborately reconstructed after he spent a few months in 1847 with a Baptist mission in Canton and studied the Bible from a Chinese translation by a German missionary. With the breakdown of law and order and the spread of banditry and smuggling in the aftermath of the Opium War, which had ended in 1842, a number of secret societies or brotherhoods—notably the Earth and Heaven Society—were established. Recruits joined by signing blood covenants; the brotherhood was especially popular among Hong's own Hakka ethnic group that had been migrating to the area for a few generations. In 1844, Hong and a disciple wandered in the countryside in Guangxi to the northwest of Canton for months, then founded the Society of God Worshippers. Hong returned to the area in the summer of 1847 after failing to receive baptism in Canton. For the next three years he built up a community of the God Worshippers around Thistle Mountain in Guangxi. Like the Pentecostalists, the Society of God Worshippers held meetings in which they were moved by the spirit to states of ecstasy, seized by fits, and uttered words of reproof or prophecy. In 1848, when Europe was in the grips of modern revolutions, Jesus came back to earth many times, and spoke to the Society of God Worshippers through Xiao Chaogui, a peasant who became his mouthpiece. In the same year, Yang Xiuqing, a charcoal burner who had just joined the movement, began to speak with the voice of God the Father. While mass baptism of recruits was gathering momentum and units (of both men and women) of the Heavenly Army were formed in 1850, Hong made public his expectation that God was about to send down calamities and pestilence.

The armed uprising of the Society of God Worshippers began on the first days of 1851, and within a few months, Hong Xiuquan, using the terms for the Kingdom of Heaven in the Chinese translation of the New Testament, declared the existence of the Taiping tien-kuo (Heavenly Kingdom of the Great Peace). Jesus gave his blessing to the enterprise and twenty-three of its named leaders through his mouthpiece, Hong Xiuquan, thereby inaugurating the distinct divinely-inspired political ritual of the Taiping; it combined policy directives with rewards for the virtuous and punishment for backsliders.

During the fall of 1851, the Taiping established their new state in the walled city of Yongan, and marked the beginning of their era with a new calendar. Hong became the Heavenly King and the Lord of Ten Thousand Years, Yang was the East King, and Xiao was the West King, followed by two kings for the two remaining cardinal points, and a Wing King as the respective Lord of Nine to Five Thousand Years in descending order. In December 1851, the Taiping rebels defended Yongan with some 20,000 troops and made a planned exodus northward with twice as many. In June 1852 the Taiping forces suffered colossal casualties at the Suoyi ford, including many of the veterans. The losses in number were, however, made up by massive recruitment from the Heaven and Earth Society and the brotherhoods. The success of this recruitment gave the Heavenly King confidence to make numerological predictions about the fall of the Manchu dynasty in 1853. Although this prediction was not fulfilled, the Taiping forces captured the rich provincial capital of Wuchang in January 1853 and moved 600 miles further along the Yangzi River to capture Nanjing in March. Their exodus, begun two years earlier from Thistle Mountain, ended in the promised earthly paradise, and Nanjing was declared the New Jerusalem.

Religious movements often open an avenue for marginal social groups, notably women, to engage in social participation; thus recruits come from these groups disproportionately. The Taiping movement continued to recruit from underprivileged social classes. In the areas they brought under their control, the Taiping forces frequently destroyed large houses while leaving the small ones belonging to villagers intact. A remarkable feature of the Taiping revolutionary movement was its wide recruitment of women and its opening of unprecedented social and political careers to them. Women participated vigorously in the Taiping army and administration. This went hand in hand with the segregation of the sexes, and austere sexual asceticism. The kings, however, were exempted from these rigors and were allowed several wives.

The Last Judgment was virtually ignored in the Taiping doctrine, in order to focus on the yearning for the fulfillment of the Heavenly Kingdom. The Christian theodicy of suffering and redemption through Christ was also discarded. The divinity of Jesus was denied while his descent to earth was made both more frequent and less consequential, with the presence of his younger brother, the Heavenly King. Furthermore, after being severely wounded in 1851, it was Xiao Chaogui, the earthly mouthpiece of Jesus, who also assumed the function of suffering on behalf of mankind. After the disastrous losses of the early converts and veterans in 1852 and the broadening of recruitment, a strong nationalistic element was introduced into the Taiping propaganda. The demons whom the Heavenly King was to eradicate were identified with the Manchus. The emperor was the Manchu demon of barbarian origin, he was seen as a Tartar dog and the "mortal enemy of us Chinese."

Nevertheless, the motive in the Taiping revolution remained primarily religious. Like the Puritans of the seventeenth-century English revolution, the Taiping militants were instilled with anxiety about sinfulness, and practiced rituals of atonement and supplication by praying on their knees. The intense activism of the Taiping is reflected in the fact that the militants received military and religious instruction together and at the same time. The disciplinarian asceticism of the Taiping movement was, however, markedly collective. Strict collective discipline was maintained by ritual shaming, dismissal from military posts for failure to answer religious questions, severe exemplary punishment of deviants, and the execution of retrograde "demons." The Taiping authority structure was shaped according to this punative framework. Officials of all ranks held both military/political and religious authority. When the victorious new regime reorganized Nanjing as a puritanical city of virtue, the quarters of men and women were separated; adulterers, homosexuals, and opium smokers were executed; and the whole army prayed regularly before meals.

While Jesus motivated Taiping militants to revolutionary political action from the beginning of the movement to the death of his earthly mouthpiece, Xiao Chaogui, in 1853, thereafter the revolutionary power struggle was marked by the constant intervention of God the Father. The second earthly mouthpiece, Yang Xiuqing, made his bid for primacy in the Heavenly City, Nanjing. Far from countermanding the typical dynamics of this power struggle in which the revolution, like Saturn, devours his own children, God the Father let the history of revolution in the Heavenly Kingdom of Great Peace take its natural course. At the end of 1853, within a year of the conquest of Nanjing, Yang Xiuqing began to criticize the Heavenly King in the voice of God the Father, and continued to use the same divine voice as well as his own (the two were distinguished) to set state policy, at times overturning his superior's decisions. In 1854, Yang, the East King, had himself declared the Paraclete and the Wind of the Holy Spirit by the Heavenly King. But in 1856, he clearly overstepped the mark by demanding the same millennial rank as the Heavenly King, whose title was the Lord of Ten Thousand Years. This was too much for the Heavenly King and two rivals whom the East King had recently demoted from their kingly ranks. A revolutionary coup was successfully executed. The East King and his entire family were killed and thousands of his supporters in Nanjing massacred.

The Taiping Heavenly Kingdom survived for eight years after the bloody revolutionary purge of 1856, but it became increasingly corrupted by the hereditary principle that it recognized from the beginning and began to work to the benefit of the incompetent and rapacious family of the Heavenly King. The latter became increasingly withdrawn and devoted himself to the revision of the Bible and with refashioning himself for posterity as the priest-king Melkizedek, and the presentation of the Heavenly Kingdom of the Great Peace (renamed God's Heavenly Kingdom in 1861) as the fulfilled New Jerusalem of the Book of Revelation. In the last days of the siege of Nanjing by the Manchu forces in the spring of 1864, he searched his palace grounds for the manna sent by God to preserve the children of Israel (Exodus, 16:31); on his deathbed he reportedly issued a decree announcing that the time had come for him to visit heaven to request a celestial army for the defense of the capital from his Heavenly Father and Heavenly Elder Brother.[19]

2   Millennial Beliefs and Iran's Constitutional Revolution (1906–1911)

The modern myth of revolution as enacted by the Europeans in 1848 was globalized by Marxism; it then produced a cycle of revolutions in the twentieth century, one that may have come to an end in 1989.[20] These cycles included the Russian revolutions of 1905 and 1917, and Iran's two revolutions in the twentieth century (1906–11). I examine the mobilizational potential of Mahdism in Iran's two revolutions, the Constitutional Revolution of 1906 analyzed in the rest of this chapter, and the Islamic Revolution of 1979, which I address in the final chapter.

If Mahdistic millennial tenets could motivate revolutionary political action, it is also true that a revolutionary political situation could activate millennial

---

19   This account of the Taiping revolution is based on Spence 1996.
20   Arjomand 2019: epilogue.

beliefs. The Russian revolutions of 1905 and 1917 occurred in an atmosphere charged with apocalyptic yearning, and the revolutions, in turn, further activated chiliastic beliefs of Orthodox Christianity.[21] Similarly, Iran's two revolutions in the twentieth century were in turn triggered by and stimulated millennial yearnings.

The belief in the return of the Mahdi played a minor role in the constitutional revolution of 1906–11, but a more considerable one in the Islamic Revolution of 1979. In the first case, it would be accurate to say that it was the (modern) revolution that reawakened and/or transformed the belief in the Mahdi. One prominent clerical historian of the constitutional revolution, Nāzem al-Eslām Kermāni, interpreted it in terms of the "signs of manifestation" of the Mahdi or the Twelfth Imam in occultation. It is clear from his book (to be considered shortly) that millennial speculations were common among clerics and laymen alike, and that the constitutional revolution was seen as a prelude to the coming of the Mahdi.

The presence of the Babis in the Constitutional Revolution is more striking evidence. The constitutionalist leaders included a number of Babis who belonged to the minority Azali sect, for whom the belief in the modern myth of revolution functioned as a secularized transformation of the traditional apocalyptic notion of the manifestation of the Hidden Imam from occultation. The Babi Azalis were counted among the intellectual leaders of the reform movement and the call for the awakening of Iran; and they supplied a disproportionately large number of constitutionalist revolutionary leaders. This enabled the opponents of the constitutionalists to brand them, indiscriminately, as Babis. Foremost among these Azali Babis were their leader, for Iran, Mirzā Yahyā Dawlat-ābādi (named after the leader of the Azali branch of Babism, Mirzā Yahyā Sobh-e Azal), the orator Malek al-Motakallemin, and the preacher Sayyed Jamal Esfahāni. Last but not least, the journalist Mirzā Jahāngir Khan, who was nicknamed Sur-e Isrāfil after his newspaper that bore that apocalyptic title referring to trumpet of the angel Isrāfil, which will be blown to summon mankind to the great resurrection.

Jahāngir Khan was by far the most influential of the Babis, thanks to the high circulation of his newspaper. *Sur-e Isrāfil* was also the leading intellectual journal of the Constitutional Revolution between the end of May 1907 and June 1908, when its editor was killed for this reason by order of Mohammad 'Ali Shah after his successful coup and restoration of autocracy. The top of the front page of *Sur-e Isrāfil*, under this title, depicted the scene of resurrection, with an angel blowing his trumpet in a corner, with appropriate Qur'ānic verses above

---

21 Sarkisyanz 1955.

FIGURE 1

and below it. One could not ask for a more eloquent equation of eschatology and revolution.

With these cultivated Azalis, we clearly witness the substitution of the modern political myth of revolution with the Shi'ite millennial myth, as eloquently demonstrated by the header image of *Sur-e Isrāfil*. As one prominent Azali constitutionalist admitted to the Cambridge Orientalist Edward G. Browne, the ideal that a national democratic Iran could be created by that revolution "seems to have inspired in the minds of no few Azalis the same fiery enthusiasm as did the idea of the reign of the saints on earth in the case of the early Babis."[22]

The political revolution in 1906–11 kindled millennial yearnings among groups other than the Azali Babis as well. In 1911, the above-mentioned clerical constitutionalist and historian of the constitutional revolution, Nāzem al-Eslām Kermāni published a book entitled *'Alā'im al-zohur* (The signs of manifestation), in which he presented the establishment of constitutional government in Iran as an indubitable sign of the imminent manifestation of the Hidden Imam as the Mahdi: "After obtaining the constitution (*mashruti-yyat*), [the Iranians] cannot be deprived of it again until they hand it to the Lord of Command (*sāheb al-amr*; i.e., the Mahdi); and every Muslim killed in

---

22 Cited in Arjomand 1993b: 227. It is interesting to note that nearly half a century later, a prominent Egyptian socialist reported a parallel substitution of Marxist ideas for his earlier belief in the appearance of the Mahdi's army against the British.

obtaining the Constitution is a martyr."[23] Kermāni noted the significant fact that his book was published one thousand (lunar) years after the onset of the Greater Occultation. In this, he sought to establish a correspondence between recent events in Iran and those predicted in detail in the Shi'ite apocalyptic traditions, including the predicted dates of the apocalyptic manifestation of the Hidden Imam.[24] The entry of women into social life figures prominently among the signs of the end of time, among which we also find the appearance of the necktie. It is evident from Kermāni's account that millennial speculations were common among clerics and laymen, revolutionaries and reactionaries alike; there are cryptic intimations of claims to sovereignty by Sayyed Rayhānallāh, a *mojtahed* who, however, belonged to a prominent Shaykhi clerical family, and whose brother had led the Babi millenarian uprising in Nayriz (in Fars) sixty years earlier. Kermāni also reports hearing, at the house of a prominent constitutionalist *mojtahed*, that a twenty-year-old man in Syria had amassed "ten thousand horsemen and is ready for the uprising."[25]

The impact of traditional Shi'ite millennial beliefs on the process of the Constitutional Revolution need not be exaggerated. In fact, the doctrine of the Greater Occultation was largely upheld by the anti-millenarian Shi'ite hierocracy which was not only well-established, but in fact also provided the leadership of the revolution in its initial stage. By the nineteenth century, a dual societal structure of domination had become established in Iran, comprising a patrimonial state under the shah and an independent Shi'ite hierocracy. This dual structure of authority explains the prominence of the Shi'ite religious leaders in the forefront of the popular agitation in 1906. The constitutionalists of the first decade of the century succeeded in obtaining the grant of a constitution from the monarch only by enlisting the support of the Shi'ite hierocracy. Far from determining the direction of the revolution, however, the Shi'ite hierocarcy was split once the secular implications of parliamentary legislation and its threat to their judiciary authority became clear. Some constitutionalists, including a few prominent Shi'ite jurists, were unmoved by millennial expectations and helped the minister of justice, Moshir al-Dawla Pirniā, adapt Shi'ite jurisprudence to the needs of the modern constitutional state. Interestingly, Kermānī, the clerical author of the above-mentioned *'Alā'im al-zohur* (The signs of manifestation) voiced the opinion that the apocalyptic council traditionally considered one of the signs of the approaching Mahdistic age may well be the judiciary council formed in order to interfere in the

---

23 Cited in Arjomand 1993b.
24 Kermāni 1911: 76–77, 95–130.
25 Arjomand 1993b: 227.

"general matters" (*omur 'āmma*)—matters subject to the "general deputyship" of the *mojtahed*s of Shi'ite hierocracy.[26]

This last millennialist reference to parliamentary interference with the prerogatives of the *mojtahed*s by Nāzem al-Eslām Kermāni rested in a realistic apprehensiveness about its secular consequences. In fact, the subsequent modernization of the state under constitutional monarchy entailed a drastic diminution of the institutional prerogatives and social power of the hierocracy. It did not impair the legitimacy of the exclusive hierocratic authority of the *mojtahed*s, however, which assured the continued financial independence of the hierocracy. The autonomy of the Shi'ite hierocracy, institutionalized in the late eighteenth and early nineteenth centuries, thus assured its survival despite relentless pressure from the state in the twentieth century. Consequently, not only did it survive, but it also withstood the challenge posed by the modernization of the state to its virtually exclusive control over religious learning and over the authoritative interpretation of Shi'ite Islam.

---

26   Arjomand 1993b: 231; Arjomand 2013.

CHAPTER 10

The Millennial Motivation and Significance of the Islamic Revolution of 1979 in Iran

The Europeans enacted the modern myth of revolution born of the great French Revolution of 1789 that was then globalized by Marxism, producing a cycle of revolutions in the twentieth century that ended in 1989. The modern myth provided the primary motivation for the 1979 Iranian Islamic revolution, whose structural causes and consequences have been examined elsewhere.[1] Having undergone a number of very significant changes from the original idea of the revolution of the proletariat as the industrial working class to the idea that the nations of the Third World were exploited by capitalist imperialism, the very latest model of the myth of revolution entered Iran through Cuba.[2]

Most agree that the Islamic Revolution in Iran was one of the major events of the twentieth century, and that it is theoretically as significant as any of the great revolutions of modern times. But where, exactly, does its significance lie? Is it significant primarily for falsifying theories of modernization? Or for demonstrating the vitality of religion in modern politics? Or for showing that secularization could be reversed to the point that a theocracy could be established? Some of these questions have been examined elsewhere,[3] and are not directly relevant to the goal of this study, which is to understand the relation between the Shiʿite myth of the Mahdi and the modern myth of revolution. I therefore focus on the transmission of the latest variant of the modern myth of revolution and its systematic reconciliation with the Mahdist myth during the years preceding and following the Islamic Revolution in 1979. My limited goal is to show the motivation of the revolution and its charismatic leader, as derived from a combination of millennial and revolutionary myths.

As for the larger questions, I articulate my macrohistorical reflections in a section on the significance of the Islamic Revolution of 1979 with two foci: (1) the transition from the Mahdist to the modern myth of revolution, and (2) the routinization of Khomeini's revolutionary charisma in the context of the dual structure of domination in Shiʿite Iran. That structure was examined

---

1 Arjomand 1988.
2 Arjomand 2019: epilogue.
3 Arjomand 1988; Arjomand 2009.

in *The Shadow of God and the Hidden Imam*[4] where it was established as the long-term consequence of Shah Esmāʿil's first Shiʿite revolution which can be seen, from the present angle, as the routinization of Esmāʿil's Mahdist charisma in the long run with the historically contingent vicissitudes in the dynamics of ideas and interests involved in the process of routinization.[5] In that broad macrohistorical context, the routinization of Khomeini's charismatic leadership will be shown to follow a typical modern post-revolutionary path based on the way it is institutionalized in the constitution of a modern theocratic state.

1   The Modern Myth of Revolution and Its Unexpected Protagonists

The modern myth of revolution has undergone a number of remarkable changes since the beginning of the twentieth century. In fact, the version of the myth than inspired Iran's Constitutional Revolution in 1906 looked rather innocent and naïve in 1979. Lenin, Mao, and Che Guevara elaborated on this myth between 1906 and 1979. Lenin confined the proletariat to the dustbin of history by making the Communist Party the vanguard of revolution, Mao militarized the myth. Meanwhile Ho Chi Minh, Franz Fanon, and other theorists introduced the people of the Third World who were made the wretched of the earth by imperialist exploitation. Last but not least, Che Guevara replaced the Leninist party with guerrilla freedom fighters as the vanguard of the wretched of the earth. Furthermore, the revolutionary protagonists of the myth, who experienced spectacular success days after the "proletarian revolution" of Cambodia collapsed, were a new type. They were not Marxists but Islamists. As we shall see presently, the new protagonists, as exemplified by ʿAli Shariʿati and Mostafa Chamran, were modern Iranian intellectuals from religious Shiʿite families who took the latest available model of the myth of revolution and made it into the theory and praxis of Islamic revolution.

First I examine the latest model of the myth and its source. Referring to earlier upheavals in Cuban history devoid of any world-historical significance, on 3 January 1959 Fidel Castro declared his intent to enact the pure (myth of) revolution: "It will not be like 1895 … it will not be like 1933 … We will have no thievery, no treason, no intervention. This time, it is truly *the* Revolution!"[6] The main invention of Castro's Cuban revolution that was immediately

---

4 Arjomand 1984.
5 See Kahlberg 2021 for a discussion of the dynamics of the process.
6 Cited in Lawson 2019: 216, emphasis added.

internationalized was Che Guevara's *foco*, the idea that replaced the Leninist vanguard party with the guerrilla army engaged in a total war of liberation throughout the Third World. Militarized vanguardism and guerrilla warfare thus became the hallmark of the new millennial myth that was to serve as the instrument of the global export of revolution. In the 1960s, Cuba accordingly supported revolutionary guerrilla groups throughout Latin America. In the 1970s, Cuba turned to the Middle East and Africa and vigorously supported the Palestinian Liberation Organization (PLO), and sent over 60,000 Cuban soldiers to Ethiopia and Angola to fight in African wars of liberation.[7]

Like Che Guevara, Mostafa Chamran (d. 1981) was trained in medicine. Unlike Guevara, he was born and raised in a religious family from Saveh in central Iran, obtained his first degree in physics from the University of Tehran and then made his way to the United States for graduate studies. When he was just over thirty-years-old, in 1963, he graduated with a PhD in plasma physics from the University of California at Berkeley, then went to Cuba for guerrilla training and from there to Egypt, where Nasser was supporting the Shah's opponents. He organized an anti-Shah guerilla group there, then returned to the United States as a medical researcher and took a leading part in the Iranian student opposition organizations against the Shah, while forming his own radical group called "Red Shi'ism." Mehdi, his younger brother by nine years, was one of the few radical students recruited into Red Shi'ism. Mostafa Chamran left the United States for Lebanon in 1976, joined the PLO camps and is said to have helped organize a camp for the Lebanese Amal movement. He returned to Iran for the Islamic Revolution and became deputy prime minister and then, in September 1979, became defense minister in the provisional revolutionary government. He died under suspicious circumstances in June 1981 during the war with Iraq.[8] Mehdi Chamran thrived in the Islamic Republic of Iran, and as a member of the Tehran City Council after 2003 he supported the fellow hardliner, Mahmoud Ahmadinejad, to become the mayor of Tehran and then the president of the Islamic Republic of Iran. Before he died peacefully in Tehran in 2017 Mehdi Chamran even had the satisfaction of seeing the rise of the Sunni apocalyptic monster DAESH in reaction to the Islamic Revolution.

The decisive fighting in the city of Tehran in the last three days of the Shah that established the Islamic Republic was undertaken by three guerilla groups who believed they were enacting the (myth of) revolution and were assured victory: the Marxist Feda'yān-e Khalq, the Islamist Mojāhedin-e Khalq, and the Maoist Peykār, which was the smallest. As the revolutionary defense minister,

---

7 Lawson 2019: 91, 134–135.
8 Zabih 1982: 90.

Mostafa Chamran immediately invited the PLO leader, Yasser Arafat to Tehran. Arafat was given a dramatic welcome in Iran, an event that can be taken as a celebration—the (myth of) revolution by the Islamists had manifested itself. The PLO collaborated cordially with the newly formed Corps of the Guards of the Islamic Revolution and helped them organized Hizbullah in Lebanon. In Iran itself, however, the leader of the Islamic Revolution, Imam Khomeini, did not care for the latest model of the revolution, or for the models of guerilla liberation warfare promoted by Arafat and Chamran. Instead, he harked back to the Shi'ite millennial model and gave it his own new inflection.

2   Khomeini's Apocalyptic Theosophy and Post-modern Apocalypticism in the Islamic Revolution of 1979

Khomeini's political attitude must have been influenced by Shi'ite millennial dispositions. As a young man and a junior cleric in his twenties (most probably in 1924), he was moved by the coincidence of the Persian new year (which begins at the vernal equinox) and the birthday of the Hidden Imam to compose a long poem that offers a glimpse of the coming apocalyptic battlefield:

> From the shelling of [his] army blood will pour on the darkened earth
> With pierced hearts and falling upon the plain
> Two hundred million will be felled from chariots upon the darkened earth
> Caesar's gut will split; Napoleon's heart will burst
> Yet from that bombardment the world will become the eternal paradise.

In a manner somewhat reminiscent of the extremist beliefs of the early Safavid revolutionaries described in chapter 5, Khomeini and the future revolutionary Imam poetically present the Mahdi as the re-embodiment of the attributes of the Prophet and the other eleven Imams, Indeed, they present him as "a manifestation of the Lord of the Universe," whose return as the king at the End of Time is thus implored:

> O King! The predicament of Islam and of Muslims are desperate
>   On such a day of festivity when everyone should be chanting
> I see a heart-broken person weeping on every side,
>   Rise, O Chosroe, and help the faithful.[9]

---

9 Cited in Arjomand 1993b: 229.

Khomeini's interest in theosophy (*'erfān*) made him a very atypical Shi'ite jurist. Throughout his life, he was deeply influenced by the inner-worldly transposition of Mahdism in the tradition transmitted by the eighteenth-century thinker, Āqā Mohammad Bidābādi and toward the very end of his life, in 1988, his aides, whom he had appointed to revise the constitution of the Islamic Republic of Iran, appropriated the theosophical notion of the absolute mandate (*velayat-e motlaqa*) for the jurist (*faqih*) as the leader of the Islamic Republic.[10] After the revolution he supported the teaching of theosophical philosophy.[11] However, given the climate of Iranian educated opinion and the general anti-millenarian attitude of the Shi'ite hierocracy which he mobilized, it is not surprising that Khomeini did not make any explicit millenarian claims. He signed the early decrees of the Islamic Revolution as the deputy of the (Hidden) Imam as befitted a Grand Ayatollah at the apex of the Shi'ite hierocracy. Without claiming to be the returning Mahdi, however, from about 1970 onward he ingeniously exploited the Shi'ite messianic yearning by encouraging his acclamation as the Imam. Since the time the majority of them had become Shi'ite in the tenth/sixteenth century, no one had called a living person "Imam."

During the anti-Shah revolutionary mobilization, the apocalyptic mood was observable among the masses during the fateful month of Muharram 1399/ December 1978. With the fourteenth-century Islamic lunar year about to expire and a new one to begin, the quasi-millennial charisma of Khomeini, the man called Imam, was compounded for the young intelligentsia by his portrayal as the renewer (*mojadded*) of the coming century. More concretely, Khomeini's face was allegedly seen on the moon in several cities, and those who were privileged to see it sacrificed lambs to symbolize their joy. Intense discussions were reported as to whether or not Khomeini was the Imam of the Age and the Lord of time. Those who answered in the affirmative were undoubtedly among the millions who massed in the streets of Tehran to welcome him upon his return from exile in February 1979.

In the first few years of the Iran-Iraq war, revolutionary Iran was awash with rampant Mahdism, with frequent sightings of the Mahdi and public expressions of the certainty of meeting him when the Revolutionary Guards reached Jerusalem. In November 1982, *Sorush*, the intellectual journal of Islamic radicals, published an article on the "Connectedness of the two movements" (those of Khomeini and the Mahdi), in which the slogan "O God, O God, keep Khomeini until the revolution of the Mahdi" was recommended to readers as a

---

10   Arjomand 1993b: 229.
11   Mirsepassi 2019: Interview with Abdolkarim Sorush, 304–324.

constant prayer. The article referred to an earlier interview in which a wounded man reported that he met the Mahdi on the battlefront and he was told by the Mahdi that the above prayer had expedited his return by a few hundred years.[12]

Many of the millions of people who were televised globally crowding into Tehran to welcome Khomeini in January 1979 did so with some apocalyptic expectation stimulated by his assumption of the title of Imam, hitherto reserved for the Imam in occultation (*ghaybat*), who was expected to reappear as the Mahdi at the End of Time to save the world. Khomeini did not claim to be the Mahdi but the temptation to see him as the forerunner of the latter was irresistible, as in the case of Shah Esmaʻil, the leader of the Safavid revolution 475 years earlier. This Messianic disposition was captured in one of the most frequent slogans of the Islamic revolution: "O God, preserve Khomeini until the revolution of the Mahdi." It was visually displayed in the televised frenzy of the millions who amassed for his funeral procession to the burial grounds in Behesht-e Zahra in June 1989. Nearly three decades after Khomeini's death, this slogan still appears on banners hanging across the streets, even in the affluent neighborhoods of northern Tehran we find the affirmation that Imam Khomeini's revolution would continue until the revolution of the Mahdi.

Khomeini was once asked by a zealous supporter to indicate if he was indeed the Imam of the Age and the Mahdi, and in response, he observed a noble silence.[13] I have to confess that when Khomeini died in June 1989, I expected his political last will and testament (*vasiyyatnāma-ye Imām Khomeini*) to assert that he, Imam Khomeini, was indeed the expected Mahdi. But perhaps he could not bring himself to make this claim because he ultimately failed to export his Islamic revolution to Iraq, where he had spent many years in exile. Less than a year before his death he had to acknowledge this failure; he said that agreeing to a ceasefire with Saddam Hussein in July 1988 amounted to "drinking a cup of poison."

Khomeini was the most important, but by no means the only figure in the Islamic Revolution in Iran that was deeply influenced by the Shiʻite apocalyptic tradition. The conservative, anti-millennial implication of the presence of the Hidden Imam in occultation was brought out by the Hojjatiyya Society, which was founded by an old friend of Ayatollah Khomeini, Shaykh Mahmud Halabi, and then disbanded by Khomeini in the early years of the Islamic Revolution. The Society was founded to promote anti-Baha'i agitation, and took its name from the epithet of the Hidden Imam as the *hojjat* (proof) of God. Interestingly, before its dissolution, the influence of the Hojjatiyya was

---

12   Arjomand 1993b: 230–231.
13   Arjomand 1984: 269.

demonstrated by the large number of ballots cast for the Mahdi/Hidden Imam in first presidential elections of the Islamic Republic of Iran in 1980. President Ahmadinejad (2005–13) and former foreign minister Velayati are said to have begun their public careers as Hojjatiyya activists.[14]

During his two terms as the president of the Islamic Republic of Iran, Ahmadinejad systematically exploited the mobilization potential of the intensified expectation of the imminent reappearance of the Mahdi in Iran and Iraq. Ahmadinejad is reliably reported to have predicted his highly improbable election in 2005 as a favor from the Hidden Imam, whom he also believed to have supernaturally intervened to open the eyes and ears of the delegates to his message during the speech he delivered at the General Assembly of the United Nations later that year in September. In an early cabinet decision, Ahmadinejad's administration allocated the equivalent of 17 million USD to the Jamkarān pilgrimage site near Qom, approximately one hundred kilometers south of Tehran, where the Hidden Imam is believed to have disappeared down a well. Ahmadinejad ordered that a mosque be built after he dreamed about a virtuous believer. Furthermore, there are rumors that he threw the names of the cabinet ministers (before their presentation to the Majles) down the well in Jamkarān and as mayor of Tehran made plans to build a road connecting Jamkarān to the center of Tehran in expectation of the imminent appearance of the Mahdi. Ahmadinejad, however, encouraged millennial yearnings not for mobilizational purposes but rather to strengthen his own purely secular authority vis-à-vis the leader, Ayatollah Sayyed 'Ali Khāmane'i, whose office of the supreme jurist (*vali-ye faqih*) would become redundant with the return of the Hidden Imam.[15]

Over and above this largely implicit substratum of traditional Messianic beliefs, the myth of revolution as the quintessential form of modern political Messianism was also fully and explicitly operative. The Islamic ideologue, 'Ali Shari'ati, who died in 1977 shortly before the revolution, interpreted the idea of the return of the Mahdi as an allegory of revolution. Many revolutionaries, and certainly the revolutionary clerical leadership, did not accept this assimilation and subordination of traditional Shi'ite political Messianism to the modern political myth of revolution, though they did not initially challenge the idea of a revolution willed by the people as an autonomous principle but sought to use it as a pillar of their legitimacy as followers of the charismatic Imam of the people.

14   Bāqi 1984; Arjomand 1988: 157–159.
15   Arjomand 2009: 156.

During the 1960s, there were indications of increased millennial yearning among the population. The prayer of supplication for the return of the Mahdi appeared to enjoy wide popularity and special groups were formed to recite it. This practice drew criticism from Islamic modernists but was defended by traditional ayatollahs. Meanwhile, the modernization of Iran and secularization of its educational system and literate culture in the twentieth century had eroded the plausibility of the literal reappearance of the Hidden Imam as the Mahdi among educated classes. The Mahdistic tenet was in need of a modern interpretation, as the longevity of the Hidden Imam believed to be still alive after eleven hundred years of "occultation" challenged the credulity of the scientifically-minded youth. But subconsciously it must have retained some of its emotional potency—this is what 'Ali Shari'ati sought to tap into in the early 1970s. He reinterpreted the belief in the return of the Hidden Imam as an allegory of the imminent revolution of the oppressed masses of the Third World.

Shari'ati combined the modern myth of revolution and Third Worldism he had inhaled in the atmosphere of the Latin quarter in Paris, where he discovered Islam while studying Durkheim's sociology of religion. Islam had to be rediscovered, however. Only an Islamic revolution could remove the distortions and deviant encrustations of centuries and recover the potency of pristine Islam as the source of a reinvigorated collective conscience.[16] For Shari'ati, the cornerstone of Islam is *tawhid* (the unity of God). Given the Durkheimian equation of God and society, monotheism at the theological level corresponds to a "monistic" social order, which Shari'ati explicates as an egalitarian social order marked by the absence of all forms of stratification. All pluralistic worldviews are anathematized as variants of polytheism, and are said to correspond to a "polytheistic" (pluralistic, stratified) social order. Furthermore, and this is the crucial step in his politicization of Islam, the Qur'ān views God and the people as equivalent in social matters. In this variant of Islamist sociologism, the Islamic revolution would thus establish a monistic, not to say totalitarian, Islamic political order, presumably infused with the spirit of God.

As a former Marxist, Shari'ati was greatly impressed with the notion of ideology and adopted it as a weapon for revolutionary struggle against Western cultural domination. He promoted the notion of Islamic ideology in his search for a reinvigorated collective conscience through the reform of Islam and poured Islam into the ideological frame borrowed from Marxism, thereby redefining it as an ideology of the wretched of the Third World as described by Franz Fanon, whom he identified with the Qur'ānic term *mostaz'afin* (the disinherited). Shari'ati thus took "Those who are weakened [the disinherited]

---

16   Arjomand 1982: 97–101.

(*istad'afu*) on the earth, We favor by making them leaders and inheritors [of the earth]" (Q. 28:4) to be the precise equivalent of Franz Fanon's "wretched of the earth" (*les damnés de la terre*).[17]

Shari'ati died in his forties two years before Khomeini's return to Iran; but he is rightly considered the foremost ideologue of the Islamic revolution. As he began his career as a public intellectual after returning to Iran at the Hosayniyya Ershad center recently opened by Islamic modernists in Tehran, Shari'ati took it upon himself to combat the erosion of religious beliefs among the educated Muslim youth, maintaining that "Islam is the religion of life, and has not become outdated: every story in the Qur'ān and every belief found in Islam and the Shi'ite religion (*mazhab*) must play a role in today's life and our individual and collective destiny."[18]

In a lecture on 30 October 1971, subsequently published under the title *Entezār, mazhab-e e'terāz* (Expectation, the religion of protest), he accordingly dealt with the expectation of the return of the Hidden Imam from occultation as the Mahdi of the End of Time. He noted the importance of the topic, given the yearning for the return of the Hidden Imam as the Mahdi, as indicated by the popularity of gatherings to read the special prayer (*nodba*) for his return. He argued that the scientific approach to any belief had to be pragmatic in terms of its social and political effects. Thus, it was imperative to examine the implication of the belief by any "individual, group or nation in the Imam of the Age, the expectation [of his return] and the principle of the revolution of the end of time (*enqelāb-e ākher al-zamān*), and to understand our responsibility entailed by this belief during the era of occultation and act upon them."[19]

After discussing the traditions accepted by the Shi'a for acquiescing to the authority of the Shi'ite hierocracy by virtue of the "general deputyship" of the Hidden Imam during his so-called Greater Occultation, Shari'ati considered it a major source of corruption in the contemporary world and accused those claiming to be the general deputies of the Imam of the Age of perpetuating their domination of "gold and power" (*zar o zur*) and using the stupidity of the masses (*estehmār*) to perpetuate "exploitation and imperialism" (*esteshmār o este'mār*). The highest ranking clerics lacked the qualifications for this authority and were responsible for making the principle of expectation "negative," which resulted in the inaction and resignation of the believers in the face of the contemporary exploitive and oppressive regimes. Although this is not

---

17   Shari'ati 2007: 288–289 n. 1.
18   Shari'ati 2007: 259.
19   Shari'ati 2007: 250–251 n. 1, 259–260.

stated explicitly, he denies the authority of the general deputyship of the Shi'ite *mojtahed*s as the continuation of the imamate, which his clerical rival, Ayatollah Sayyed Mohammad Hosayni Beheshti, was to make the cornerstone of the 1979 constitution of the Islamic Republic of Iran.[20] For Shari'ati, science is "the continuation of the Imamate." This leaves no room for any general vice-regency or clerical authority in the global revolution, as the culmination of "the movement led in one epoch by prophecy, then by the Imamate and then during the long period of Occultation by science." In its place, he proposes his own principle of "positive" expectation as a revolutionary principle of hope. Positive expectation is "the religion of protest" as the ideology and the strongest weapon and source of energy for the revolutionary overthrowing at the End of Time (*najāt-e ākher al-zamān*).[21]

Shari'ati acknowledges that the principle of expectation when interpreted positively is indeed a type of messianism. Its Qur'ānic justification is God's promise to the weak (*mostaz'afin*) on the earth, to make them its leaders and inheritors (Q. 28:4). He identifies the term *mostaz'afin*, which gained wide currency during the Islamic revolution and was used as the name for the foundation Khomeini set up and endowed with property confiscated from the supporters of the old regime, with Fanon's "wretched of the earth" who will rise up in the revolution of the Third World. He also identified the Dajjāl (anti-Christ) of the End of Time in the Islamic tradition with the "one-dimensional man" of Herbert Marcuse. The core of his argument, however, was the identification of the apocalyptic revolution of the Mahdi with the modern myth of revolution as the inescapable end of history as elaborated in Marxism-Leninism. The belief in the expectation of the manifestation of the Imam of the Age was nothing other than belief in "historical determinism" (*jabr-e tārikhh*), which means that "justice would be victorious, class conflict would be eliminated and a classless society without exploitation, without gold and violence, [would be] realized." Here and frequently elsewhere, Marx's classless society is called the monistic (*tawhidi*) society, which Shari'ati sees as the monotheistic society required by Islam. Its realization is the foregone conclusion of historical determinism as fated by God, when He "promised that he would make the weak masses and peoples of the world leaders of mankind and give them the earth."[22]

---

20 Arjomand 2009: 26–28.
21 Shari'ati 2007: 266–268, 271, 283–286.
22 Shari'ati 2007: 277, 280–281, 287.

To demonstrate the equivalence of the modern myth of revolution and ancient political messianism, one cannot do better than to quote Shari'ati's translation of the former into the Shi'ite variant of the latter in the scientific-socialist parody of a millennial flourish with which he ended this lecture:

> So we see that the [positively] expectant believer is the prepared human being who thinks it probable that at any moment the trumpet of the final revolution shall sound, and considers himself responsible for participating in this jihad which will definitely begin by the laws of divine determinism.[23]

The positively expectant believer is described in the final phrase as "every Shi'ite who goes to be with the hope of hearing the call (*āvāz*) of the Imam [to revolution]"; and the jihad ordained by divine decree (i.e., historical determinism) is evidently none other than "the struggle for liberty and justice" that will continue till the End of Time.[24]

In his other lectures, too, Shari'ati spoke of the belief in the return of the Hidden Imam as the Mahdi as an allegory of the imminent revolution of the oppressed masses of the Third World: "The belief in the final savior of human history is the continuation and the Shi'ite Imam and the Twelfth Imam means that the world revolution and the final victory is the continuation and result of a great movement [i.e., Shi'ite Islam] for seeking justice against tyranny in the world."[25]

During the Islamic revolution after Shari'ati's death, his interpretation of the Mahdist tenet as the Shi'ite version of the modern myth of revolution was espoused by the most organized group among his followers, the Mojāhedin-e Khalq-e Mosalmān (Muslim People's Mojāhedin). In a lecture delivered at the Polytechnic University of Tehran a few months into the revolution on 10 July 1979, one of the Mojāhedin leaders, Mehdi Abrishamchi, hailed the Hidden Imam of the Age as the "great leader of the classless monistic society," the restorer of the pristine egalitarian society that was perverted by exploitation, oppression, and the monopolistic greed of the dominant classes. After following Shari'ati in stressing the importance of the correct understanding of religious beliefs in the framework of Islamic ideology, he himself accordingly interpreted the belief in resurrection (*qiyāmat*) as an "existential and ontological response" to the freedom of the human will. In the same vein, the proper

---

23   Shari'ati 2007: 283.
24   Shari'ati 2007: 279–281, 283.
25   Cited in Arjomand 1993b: 228.

ideological "understanding of the Imam of the Age within a monistic (*tawhidi*) worldview" amounted to a "philosophy of hope." The belief in the Imam of the Age thus required "combatting the great idol of our age, which is imperialism," and entailed the "belief in the hope, indeed certainty, of the victory of the masses.[26]

The Islamic modernist cleric and for a while Shari'ati's fellow speaker at the Hosayniyya Ershad, Mortaza Motahhari, who was assassinated by Islamic radicals after the revolution, felt constrained to rein in Shari'ati's radicalism. He rejected the latter's politicized interpretation of the Mahdistic tenet, but nevertheless offered an allegorical interpretation of his own. He presented the idea of the Mahdi as a restorer of justice and true religion which will be contained in the utopia of the perfect society, gradually approximated in the course of the evolution of human society, which will be realized only at the end of the process of human evolution.[27]

Shari'ati was not the only thinker to be deeply influenced by the modern myth of revolution as a result of post-graduate study in Paris in the 1960s. There he picked up his Marxist Third-Worldism in order to retool the idea of revolution for the liberation of Shi'ite Iran as the leader of the Third World in the establishment of a "divine classless society." At the other end of Western-inspired political-ideological spectrum, on the far right, his older contemporary, Ahmad Fardid (d. 1994), turned to Heidegger instead of Shari'ati's Marxian classless society in search of cultural authenticity.[28] Fardid had gone to Paris a decade or so earlier than Shari'ati; similarly he did not complete his doctoral dissertation but moved on to hang around Heidelberg, Heidegger's old university.

Unlike Shari'ati, he was a diffident, dyspeptic, unfriendly person, and a poor public speaker; he did not attract a mass audience, but cultivated a small circle of intellectuals who took his small classes at the University of Tehran.[29] He had an adjunct appointment in a number of departments until Sayyed Hossein Nasr, the bright light of Islamic modernism under the Shah, returned when he was not yet thirty with a PhD from Harvard. In the early 1960s he served as the Dean of the Faculty of Letters at the University of Tehran, where he reportedly hailed Fardid as the Plotinus of Iran and made his teaching position permanent.[30] While rejecting Shari'ati's idea of Islam as an ideology and his Marxist version

---

26 Arjomand 1993b: 228–229.
27 Motahhari 1975; Arjomand 1993b: 228.
28 Amanat 2017: 992–993.
29 Mirsepassi 2017.
30 Mirsepassi 2019.

of Islamist authenticity as an expression of a Third World inferiority complex and resentment, Fardid often presented Heidegger, whose mantle he claimed as an Islamic Heidegger, indeed a religious Messianic (*Mahdigarayane*) Heidegger (in the words of an interviewee who knew him well), but also a fierce critic of the West, like Oswald Spengler. He constantly spoke of the perils of technology that would make it impossible, in Heideggerian terms, to rescue the future of the "day after tomorrow (*pasfarda*)," without journeying through today (*emruz*) and tomorrow (*farda*). He constantly used a string of conceptual terms he had coined, such as "self-autonomous" (*khodbonyad*) and "historical destiny" (*havalat-e tarikhi*), thereby motivating students to seek out the mystique of his hidden message.

Fardid complained of Greece-toxication (*Yunānzadagi*), or alternately, Westoxication (*gharbzadegi*) as the plight of modern Iran that had been infected with it. When the writer Jalal Al-e Ahmad, one of his disciples, popularized the latter term in a bestseller, he complained bitterly so the latter's socioeconomic presentation of Westoxification as a vulgar distortion.

> According to one former student who took his class in 1960, Fardid had already spoken about the need for a philosophy for "imperial resurrection under the Shah which was changed, after the revolution of 1979, to coming of Mehdi (*qiyām-e zohur*). This Messianic aspect of his thinking was [evident in] the issue of a Messianic resurrection (*qiyām-e zohur*). By the 1970s, he was talking about the end times. He put the mold aside, tore down the curtain, pulling the end times and the Imam out from behind it! Perhaps his compass was pointing toward the Islamic Republic, and the Messiah. "I'm alone," and he would treat this as a positive aspect of his character, saying, "I can't come to terms with any systems and viewpoints but my own." I remember the word he used for this—he would say, "I'm Ahmad *Layansaref* (not conjugated)."[31] .... Like the apocalypse, which he introduced after the revolution. And this was the Coming of the Messiah (*qiyām-e zohur*), who appeared with Hitler and in Nazi thought.[32]

---

31 In Arabic conjugation—and those who understand Arabic conjugations know this—Ahmad is a word that cannot be conjugated in Arabic (that is, there is no Ahmada, Ahmadah, Ahmadu; rather it is always Ahmad). They call these types of words *layansaref Ahmad*. According to his former student, Professor Abbas Amanat, Fardid got the idea from a poem in praise of Ahmed Shah Qājār by Iraj Mirza.

32 Cited in Mirsepassi 2019: Interview with Abbas Amanat, 137–139. The last phrase referring to Hitler is taken from the transcript of the interview and was rephrased in copyediting.

The revolution gave Fardid the opportunity to express his totalitarian and Nazi sympathies, his hostility toward the intellect, especially Jewish intellectuals as exemplified by Karl Popper, and to opt for millennial violence. Fardid's attempt to participate in the Islamic Revolution of 1979 was a complete failure. He failed to gain a seat in either the Iranian parliament (Majles) or the Assembly of Constitutional Experts, as the clerical elite of the Islamic Republic of Iran could not understand his message. Nevertheless, he had a pernicious influence on lay revolutionary intellectuals in the security forces and the press, and one of his disciples remained the editor of the leading, semi-official newspaper, *Keyhān*. After his death, Fardid's disciples published a collection of his largely incomprehensible lectures under the very appropriate title *Didār-e Farrahi va fotuhāt-e akhir al-zamān* (The divine encounter and the revelations of the end of time).[33]

3   The Significance of the Islamic Revolution in Iran

The Islamic Revolution of 1979 in Iran was a critical turning point in world history for the way it replaced the Shi'ite millennial myth by the modern myth of revolution. I was a witness to this turning point, and I suspected that it would soon assume a great significance. As the Iranian revolution against the Shah was unfolding in full light of the global media, I left New York for Paris to seek an interview with the leader of the Islamic revolutionary movement, who was in temporary exile in France. While waiting to interview Ayatollah Ruhollah Khomeini in Neauphle-le-Chateau near Paris before his return to Iran,[34] I vividly recollect hearing late at night on the BBC World News on 23 December 1978 that Malcolm Caldwell, a British Marxist academic and well-wisher of the Red Khmer revolution in Cambodia, had been murdered in Phnom Penh. Years later, I read that Caldwell he had "returned delighted" from an interview with the Red Khmer leader, Pol Pot, hours before his murder. Pol Pot, whose aunt had been a dancer in the Royal Ballet and borne a child to Sihanouk's predecessor, King Monivong (r. 1927–41), then invited the former king, Norodom Sihanouk, to dinner on 5 January 1979, and apologized for failing to talk to the prince in five years. As compensation, he offered Norodom Sihanouk a delicious dinner, impeccably served. Two days later, Pol Pot fled Phnom Penh by

---

33   Fardid 2008.
34   Arjomand 1988: vii, 179. The interview was summarized and discussed in "Through Persian Eyes" BBC Radio 4 (http://www.bbc.co.uk/programmes/b01kbq9p).

helicopter and the Democratic Kampuchea collapsed on 7 January 1979. The Shah left Iran within two weeks of Pol Pot's ignominious flight.

In the same month, January 1979, a revolution collapsed, and with it died the myth of communist revolutions forged a third of a century earlier. Meanwhile, another revolution, motivated by a significantly modified version of the 200 year-old modern myth of revolution, triumphed and shortly thereafter, on 11 February 1979, it gave birth to the Islamic Republic of Iran. The Shi'ite apocalyptic myth of the Mahdi, whose transformative impact on Khomeini, Shari'ati, and Fardid we have surveyed above, also influenced the last modification the modern myth of revolution that took place in the incipient Islamic revolution in Iran. This modification was enshrined in the constitution of the Islamic Republic of Iran promulgated in December 1979. The modern communist myth of revolution was replaced by the new modern myth of the Islamic revolution. Thus, in the closing decades of the twentieth century, the myth of the Islamic revolution began a life of its own, generating a new model of apocalypse for the twenty-first century; I examine this in the excursus.

The Islamic Revolution of 1979 in Iran also had significant consequences for the sociopolitical structure of modern Iran. The creation of centralized bureaucratic states has been identified as a fundamental precondition of modern revolutions. It requires the concentration of coercive, material, and cultural resources and thus entails the dispossession of some privileged strata. Such dispossessed strata have been prominently represented among revolutionary leaders throughout history.[35] In Iran, state-building made serious headway only under the Pahlavis (1921–79) whose centralization and modernization of the state seriously undermined the foundations of religious authority and curbed its cultural influence.

The erosion of clerical control over education had begun earlier, even before the Constitutional Revolution of 1906–11. But it culminated in the 1920s and 1930s with the creation of a secular, national educational system under Reza Shah. Its control over education was the least defensible of the hierocracy's prerogatives, as it was a contingent fact, lacking any Shi'ite doctrinal basis. More defensible citadels also fell under the attack of the centralizing state. The major defeat of the hierocracy took place in the legal sphere, where clerical domination rested on a firm doctrinal basis. Under Reza Shah (1925– 41), the judiciary was secularized and centralized under a branch of the state. Finally, the Endowment Act of 1934 established centralized supervision over religious endowments throughout Iran; these had largely been under direct

---

35   Arjomand 1988: 193–194.

or delegated control of the Shi'ite clerics. Though less important in its consequences than his father's policies, Mohammad Reza Shah's Land Reform of the 1960s resulted in the redistribution of land owned by mosques, seminaries, and individual clerics. The hierocracy's remaining links to the state through the supervision of the religious endowments were virtually broken. Religious institutions became totally independent of the state; and this independence was sustained by the one last source of income, which was inevitably immune from state encroachment, namely, the voluntary payment of religious taxes to the leaders of the Shi'ite hierocracy as the vicegerents of the Hidden Imam.

These developments seriously weakened the hierocracy, but they had another important consequence: These developments completed the differentiation and separation of religious and political powers. The loss of judicial and educational functions on the one hand, and the loss of control of religious endowments and land ownership on the other, meant that the Shi'ite hierocracy was largely "disembedded" from the Pahlavi regime. This economic and political disengagement of the hierocracy was strongly complemented by their social "disembeddedness": there had always been a tendency for the upper echelons of the hierocracy to intermarry, forming a highly endogamous group. Bright young men often entered into it through marriage to daughters or close relatives of their teachers. This tendency was accentuated by the clerical elite's loss of social prestige, which greatly reduced the frequency of intermarriage between them and the increasingly secularized social and political elites.

Khomeini led the revolutionary movement to overthrow the Shah and his modernizing state in order to restore and preserve a Shi'ite tradition threatened by modernization and Westernization. However, the restoration of a tradition in practice always entails its transformation. In fact, the Islamic Revolution of 1979 brought about a revolution in Shi'ism. One of the unintended consequences of the direct takeover of the state by the clerical elite in 1980 has been the extension of the principle of bureaucratic organization from the state to the hitherto organizationally amorphous Shi'ite hierocracy itself. Khomeini's revolutionary project required the sweeping extension of hierocratic authority. The autonomy of the Shi'ite hierocracy had assured its survival despite relentless pressure by those engaged in state-building and modernization in the twentieth century. The modernization of the state entailed a drastic diminution of the institutional prerogatives and social power of the hierocracy. However, it did not impair the legitimacy of the exclusive hierocratic authority of the clerical elite, which assured the continued financial independence of the hierocracy. Consequently, it not only survived but also withstood the Pahlavi state's challenge to its virtually exclusive control over religious learning and over the authoritative interpretation of Shi'ite Islam.

The leaders of the Islamic Revolution in Iran recognized that the legal order of the modernized Pahlavi state they were taking over varied greatly from the sharia (the sacred law of Islam) even though they would rather not talk about it. In December 1984, in an outburst against the recalcitrant traditionalists who considered taxation at variance with the Shi'ite tradition, the shrewd majles speaker, Hojjat al-Islam Hashemi-Rafsanjani who became the president of the Islamic Republic of Iran after Khomeini's death in 1989, remarked:

> Is whatever occurs in the Western world contrary to the Shari'a? ... You are sitting in Parliament. Where is the precedent for parliament in Islamic history? ... [or for] a president, cabinet of ministers, prime minister and the like? ... You say that no *fatvas* [sharia injunctions] were issued [in support of] taxes. No *fatvas* were issued for a great many things. In fact, we lack *fatvas* in Islam for 80 per cent of the things on which today we base Islamic government.[36]

The legal framework of the modern nation-state is thus the framework for the routinization of the charisma of Khomeini's messianic leadership. As we would expect, therefore, his charisma was routinized and found institutional embodiment in the constitution of the Islamic Republic of Iran under the "Principle of Leadership," which embodied his novel theory of the *velāyat-e faqih* (mandate of the jurist). Imam Khomeini was called the *rahbar* (leader) of the Islamic Republic of Iran and the office of leadership (*rahbari*) was defined as the head of the state and given more extensive constitutional power than any contemporary head of the state in the world. Albeit with deep historic roots over centuries of the growth of the Shi'ite hierocracy in Iran, the principle of the mandate of the jurist to rule on behalf of the Hidden Imam was a revolutionary innovation to routinize and institutionalize the charisma of the Mahdi as the Hidden Imam. From our viewpoint it is quite telling that the idea that the mandate of the jurist (*velāyat-e faqih*) developed in Shi'ite jurisprudence after the mid-nineteenth century to buttress the clerical authority and help contain the Babi millennialism championed by Shi'ite clerical jurists. The routinization of Khomeini's Mahdistic charisma somewhat ironically resulted in the establishment of an anti-millenarian hierocratic authority under a clerical monarchy.

Elsewhere, I have examined the principle of leadership and the evolution of what I have called the clerical monarchy in the Islamic Republic of Iran.[37]

---

36   Cited in Bakhash 1986: 113.
37   Arjomand 2009.

The basic constitutional fault line of this clerical monarchy as a political regime lies between the clerical elite and the military elite, or the generals of the Revolutionary Guards who have developed a personal system of authority that is fragile because of its undue dependence on the leader. We can end with the question as to whether the institutionalization of Khomeini's charismatic leadership in this form is definitive, leaving us at a dead end for the history of Shi'ite Iran, or whether the fault line can be corrected by another revolution, perhaps a dystopian, post-1989 model of revolution.[38]

---

38   Arjomand 2019: epilogue.

EXCURSUS

A Sunni Apocalypse at Last: the Islamic State of Iraq and Syria

Mahdist messianism served as a reinforcing motive of the Islamic revolution in Iran. It was of secondary causal importance in its motivation, but nevertheless had important long-term consequences in the Muslim world beyond Iran. In this excursus, I propose a new hypothesis concerning the now defunct Islamic State of Iraq and Syria (ISIS), also known by its Arabic acronym as DAESH, by arguing that the most spectacular and surprising millennial impact of the Islamic revolution in Iran was the reactionary Sunni apocalypse we now see.

As we have seen, after 1981 the Mahdi as the Twelfth and Hidden Imam was frequently sighted on the Iraqi war front alongside the slogan that the revolution of Khomeini was to continue until the revolution of the Mahdi, I would nevertheless argue that Mahdism was a secondary feature of the Islamic Revolution of 1979 in Iran, the primary distinctive feature being Khomeini's principle of *velāyat-e faqih* (mandate of the jurist) to rule on behalf of the Hidden Imam. It was Khomeini's clericalism that stifled the millenarian features of the revolution as his charismatic leadership approached its end. Another motivating factor in the Islamic revolutionary movement in Iran that was incorporated into the preamble to the 1979 constitution of the Islamic Republic of Iran, was the *ideology* of Islam. Needless to say, neither feature can be found in DAESH, or alternatively, as the Islamic State of the Caliphate. Mahdism, by contrast, was stolen from the caliphate's Shi'ite revolutionary rivals, then fundamentally modified.

The Mahdist impulse, albeit secondary in revolutionary Iran itself, was nevertheless transmitted to neighboring Iraq immediately after the downfall of Saddam Hussein by the American invasion in 2003. It soon became embodied in Muqtadā al-Sadr's *jaysh al-mahdi* (army of the Mahdi). A novel and historically unprecedented form of Sunni revolutionary Mahdism was stimulated by Muqtadā's army of the Mahdi in Iraq.

One cannot imagine a better example of what an early sociologist of globalization, Roland Robertson, termed "glocal" than the global spread and impact of al-Qaeda and its recent offshoot in Iraq and Syria, DAESH, and the international jihadism and alternative Islamist revolutionary politics they engendered.[1] After 9/11, new forms of online recruitment into al-Qaeda emerged. It acquired greater significance but remained secondary to real-world recruitment by militant Islamist networks such as those in

---

1   Robertson 1992.

prisons and around mosques of radical imams.[2] Meanwhile, given the local conditions of state disintegration, war, and other destructive developments in the Middle East, global and increasingly online recruitment has been used by DAESH with astonishing success. The local feature I analyze against the global feature of political messianism is the involvement of tribes in these latest Islamist revolutionary movements, alongside what might be called a neo-Khaldunian pattern discussed in chapter 1. The prophets and religious reformers who fail are precisely those who do *not* recognize the significance of group solidarity. Those who succeed are the ones who do.

The disarming and settlement of Bedouin tribes since the Iraqi revolution of 1958 followed the same disintegrative pattern of forced sedentarization of tribes that took place during the course of modernization of states in the rest of the Middle East. However, during the Iran-Iraq War (1980–88), the process was arrested by Saddam Hussein and in fact he reversed it in the 1990s after the Kuwait war. This retribalization entailed considerable recruitment of tribesmen into the police force and the army. After the Kuwait war, in 1991, the tribal chiefs took oaths of allegiance to Saddam Hussein, and tribalism was made the fourth principle of his reconstituted Iraqi polity. Consequently, the majority of policemen and the military in the Missan province in the south and al-Anbar in the west belong to a very small number of tribes.[3]

Muqtadā al-Sadr recruited his Army of the Mahdi mainly in the poor neighborhoods of Baghdad known as the Sadr City. Among those recruited a significant number were immigrants belonging to the southern Shiʿite Iraqi tribes; this pattern can be described as "neo-Khaldunian" with reference to our Khaldunian Type of Integrative Revolution. The tribes of the southern region of Amara, such as Abu Mohammad, al-Sawaid, Eziraj, Bani Lam, al-Sudan, al-Budraj, and al-Fartus, migrated in the middle decades of the twentieth century in response to the harsh economic conditions in southern Iraq and were forced to settle during the course of state modernization after 1958. The tribesmen continued to live in their self-contained neighborhoods and remained segregated from the surrounding population; they were not successfully integrated into the cities surrounding the areas they had been forced to relocate to.[4]

As in Iran after the 1979 revolution, Muqtadā al-Sadr's support of the Mahdi succumbed to the weight of Shiʿite clericalism in Iraq. Just as in Iran, the need for the return of the Mahdi as the authoritative clerical leaders (*marājiʿ al-taqlid*) were the latter's revered general deputies (sing., *nāʾib al-ʿāmm*). Sadr himself was continuing the clerical leadership of his late father, Ayatollah Mohammad Sādiq al-Sadr (d. 1999), who had written a pamphlet against tribal customary law (*ʿurf*) as a Shiʿite clerical jurist;[5] and

---

2 Neumann 2008.
3 Dawood 2013: 222, 225.
4 Hasan 2018a; Baalbaky and Mhidi 2018: 15–18.
5 I am grateful to Dr. Harith Hasan for this information.

the creation of the army of the Mahdi was in fact legitimized from its beginning by a *fatwa* from Ayatollah Ha'iri.[6] Therefore, from the beginning, Sadr's millennialism was subordinate to his clericalism and was stifled by it. The millennialism of the army of the Mahdi began to wane. Indeed, when it was revived and reorganized a few years later, it changed its name to the "army of peace." Nevertheless, as it was on its last legs in 2006–07, the millennial appeal of the Mahdi's army at the End of Time was appropriated by Sadr's mortal rival, Abu Musā al-Zarqāwi (d. 2006), who had just formed al-Qaeda in Iraq, the predecessor of the Islamic State, and transformed the millennial idea into its own distinctive doomsday scenario. Quite apart from the army of the Mahdi, various Shi'ite militia groups were calling themselves Khorasan, the region where it was believed that the black banners of the returning Mahdi would be raised again, as they had been raised by Abu Moslem in the mid-second/eighth century.[7]

To frustrate the militias of Muqtadā al-Sadr and those of Khorasan and other Shi'ite militias,[8] Zarqāwi took over the apocalyptic message for the global jihad, according to William McCants, the author of one of two books on the subject with "Apocalypse" in the title.[9] Or to quote Zarqāwi himself, "the spark has been lit here in Iraq, and its heat will continue to infinity ... until it burns the crusade army in Dabiq."[10] Dabiq (in Syria) was Zarqāwi's substitution for Khorasan in northeastern Iran in Shi'ite Mahdistic topography. The spark instantly triggered an ardent search for the Signs of the Hour (*al-sa'a*) among the bloggers of the jihad movement in Iraq and Syria; their interpretation became the foremost technique for DAESH's digital mobilization. The newsletter launched for the purpose was appropriately called *Dabiq*, the location of the apocalyptic burning of the army of the infidels.

On the tribal front, Zarqāwi, who was Jordanian, was ruthlessly uncompromising on global jihadism and intolerant of any compromise with assertions of tribal identity in Iraq. In fact, he ordered the assassination of tribal leaders who refused to observe his boycott of the first Iraqi elections and/or joined forces with other militias, a policy that continued against the Sunni tribesmen who joined the so-called tribal awakening (*sahwa*) movement initiated by General David Petraeus. Petraeus arrived in Iraq in 2006 with anthropologists and other academics and launched a tribal awakening

---

6   Hasan 2018b.
7   The apocalyptic traditions on the black banners were *ex eventu* prophecies that arose out of Abu Moslem's revolution in Khorasan on behalf of the Abbasids. (Arjomand 2019: ch. 9)
8   In retrospect, Zarqāwi did a great favor for Muqtadā al-Sadr by forcing him to opt for a strategy other than a Khaldunian revolution. He successfully broadened his support bases and has flourished in Iraqi politics. In fact, his party, or rather movement, increased the number of its parliamentary seats in the elections of November 2021 to 73, or well over four times those of the next largest Iraqi party.
9   Filiu 2011; McCants 2015; Woods 2017: 252.
10 Woods 2017: 262.

(*sahwa*) policy in the Sunni triangle. It was partially successful in the Anbar region because the tribal leaders faced a dire threat from al-Qaeda of Iraq under Zarqāwi's leadership.[11] We may safely assume that Zarqāwi had not read and understood Ibn Khaldun's conclusion that the prophets and religious leaders who fail are precisely those who do *not* recognize the significance of tribal group solidarity and those who succeed are the ones who see its significance. His policy was doomed to fail according to the Khaldunian model of revolution.

Zarqāwi's policy was changed by his Iraqi successors who established DAESH, namely, Abu Omar al-Baghdadi, and Abu Bakr al-Baghdadi, the first caliph of DAESH. DAESH pursued the policy described in *Dabiq* as one of "attending tribal forums, addressing the concerns of the tribal leaders and accepting their *bayʿah* [oath of allegiance]" in order to "Unite them under one Imam, and work together toward the establishment of the Prophetic Caliphate."[12] The local political environment of DAESH in Syria, in the absence of any centralized state, also drew in the tribes along neo-Khaldunian lines. In Syria, the Nusra Front (the rival branch of al-Qaeda from which the Islamic State dissociated in April 2013) sought to make alliances with some tribes and tribal military factions in Deir ez-Zor, and recruited marginalized tribesmen to conquer regions in the surrounding areas. DAESH received defecting Nusra tribal allies, such as ʿĀmir al-Rafdān, who became a prominent commander who mobilized tribesmen who had been marginalized by the Nusra Front.[13] On the other hand, they ruthlessly punished tribes they suspected of disloyalty; mass graves are evidence of the extermination of an entire tribe.[14] All this was in accord with the Khaldunian practice of combining religious and tribal solidarity.

This neo-Khaldunian aspect is, however, a minor feature as compared to the major cataclysmic Mahdism of DAESH. The apocalyptic traditions, or hadith, drawn upon by the DAESH are not the Shiʿite traditions we know of, but those of the southern Arabian tribes that were stationed in Syria for the projected conquest of Constantinople in the seventh century. Dabiq and al-Aʿmāq (lit., "the depths") were apocalyptic sites of confrontation at the End of Time in this body of traditions and were chosen by DAESH as the names of its journal and news agency respectively. From the beginning of its publication, *Dabiq* described the final doomsday battle between the "Abode of Islam" and the "Army of Rome," which stood for the apostate state of Turkey comprising Constantinople/Istanbul and the entire infidel West that was behind it.[15] Furthermore,

---

11   Baalbaky and Mhidi 2018: 18.
12   *Dabiq*, 1, as cited in Mabon and Royle 2017: 152.
13   Baalbaky and Mhidi 2018: 29–31.
14   Here there is a striking parallel with the extermination of an entire tribe of followers suspected of disloyalty by Mahdi b. Tumart in his Khaldunian Almohad revolution, as discussed in Arjomand 2019: ch. 8.
15   Mabon and Royle 2017: 2.

I had no trouble recognizing the addition of an antiquarian observation, *dabiq* is an important sign of *al-malhama al-kubrā* ("the great slaughter"), which is indeed the *milhama* of the Qumran War Scroll and in turn, the *vozorg nakhjir* ("great hunt") of Zoroastrian apocalyptics. The *dabiq* of Sunni apocalyptic lore, which originates among the southern tribes, differs from that of the Shi'a whose apocalyptic savior is the Mahdi of the House of the Prophet, *al-qā'im bi'l-sayf* ("the one who rises with the sword").[16]

The salience of the otherwise obscure body of hadith drawn upon by radical Sunni Muslims is, however, undoubtedly related to the Islamic revolution of 1979 in Shi'ite Iran. The corpus was studied by Juhaymān al-'Utaybi who seized the Ka'ba in Mecca on 20 November 1979, some two weeks after the seizure of the American embassy by Islamic revolutionary students in Tehran. Juhaymān identified his brother-in-law as the Qahtāni Mahdi (not the Mahdi of the House of the Prophet), Mohammad b. 'Abdallāh. Various mutually inconsistent hadiths about the Mahdi of the southern Arabs existed, and Juhaymān appears to have conflated them. As we saw in chapter 3, in the oldest source, this Mahdi would be followed by the Qahtāni (also called the Yamāni), who would lead the Yemeni tribes in fierce warfare against the Quraysh and destroy the latter. Qahtāni is said to be his brother in some traditions or a figure who would conquer Constantinople; in this case, he is not the same figure as the second Mahdi who will conquer Constantinople. Be that as it may, Juhaymān's Qahtāni Mahdi was killed after four days while throwing grenades.[17]

The global jihad that changed the world on 9/11 has been aptly described as the first apocalyptic movement of the twenty-first century. Already by 9/11, it had generated a conspicuous literature that drew heavily on contemporary Protestant apocalyptic pamphlets and websites concerned with doomsday battles and dating the end of the world.[18] A monumental treatise published online in 2004 by Abu Mus'ab al-Suri (a major theorist of global jihad), presented a large number of apocalyptic hadith prefaced by a long essay on the imminent collapse of Western civilization written by his Palestinian mentor, 'Abdallāh al-'Azzām. We know that al-Suri did not get along with his superior, Usama bin Laden, and the latter, as the leader of global jihad operating in Afghanistan, showed little interest in citing traditions on the final battle of the End of Time.[19] Zarqāwi thought otherwise about the intense Shi'ite-Sunni confrontation in Iraq after the American invasion. He conceived of his dire struggle in Falluja as an apocalyptic struggle against Persians or the Shi'a, and this conception was taken over by the successor movement, DAESH.

---

16 See chapter 3.
17 Woods 2017: 267.
18 Woods 2017; Landes 2018: 22–24.
19 Cook 2018: 284–287, 290.

The DAESH leaders did not repeat Juhaymān's mistake of identifying their Mahdi. On the contrary, they had the savvy to highlight a different hadith that focuses on the doomsday aspect of the End of Time (*ākhir al-zamān*) over all others. According to them, God will not send Jesus to convert to Islam, break the crosses, and help the Mahdi until after the virtuous remnant of Muslims have lost battle after battle and are helplessly besieged in Jerusalem. This vision of doomsday acts as a safety valve against disillusionment resulting from military defeat.

The doomsday scenario is fully integrated to the Islamic State's spectacular ritualization of the cult of violence. In contrast to the Islamic Republic of Iran whose constitution of 1979 declares it to be based on the Islamic ideology that would set the stage for an Islamic world revolution (in the preamble), DAESH vehemently rejects the notion of Islam as an ideology. It maintains a strictly Salafi anti-ideological position; the caliphate has a "prophetic methodology (*minhāj*)" but no ideology. The cult of violence and its elaborate and gruesome rituals is the cornerstone and most distinctively novel feature of this purportedly prophetic methodology. Videos of beheadings, ritual murder, most notably the burning of the captured Jordanian pilot in a cage based on a *fatwā*, were broadly disseminated, and barbarous and atavistic destruction of pre-Islamic heritage of the antiquity in Petra and elsewhere was carefully staged.[20]

Its appropriation of apocalyptic Mahdism from the Shi'a notwithstanding, the violent sectarianism of DAESH is the complete opposite of the pan-Islamic pretensions of the Islamic Revolution of 1979 in Iran, and in the Muslim world, it renders the Shi'a, whom it considers apostates, the prime target of its jihad. It sets itself up as the diametrical opposite of the Islamic Republic of Iran (IRI). Its Islamic State is emphatically not a republic based on the deputyship of the Twelfth and Hidden Shi'ite Imam, but the revived caliphate of Mohammad's first successor, Abu Bakr, who they believe was reincarnated in July 2013 in the man who called himself Abu Bakr al-Baghdadi al-Qurayshi. Nevertheless, DAESH mimicked its *bête noire*, Iran's Islamic Revolution according to the dynamics of revolution and counter-revolution that are well-known from its instances in the Persianate world.

At the beginning of the Iranian revolution, when Imam Khomeini was committed to pan-Islamism and the export of the Islamic revolution, he proclaimed: "State boundaries are the product of a deficient human mind ... The Revolution does not recognize borders, it will go through them ... Until the cry 'There is no god but God' resounds over the whole world, there will be struggle!"[21] The IRI appropriated the Shah's modernized bureaucratic state apparatus and its legal order that recognizes borders and states. In sharp contrast to the IRI, DAESH characterizes the nation-state as the new idol set up by man against God, and is therefore far from adopting such a legal and political

---

20 Revkin 2016: 6; Isakhan 2018.
21 Cited in Abrahamian 1993: 49.

order. The caliphate in fact marked its establishment by the ritualized destruction of the border between the two nation-states of Iraq and Syria. And far from adopting the positive laws (*qawānin wad'iyya*) of an apostate modern state, as Khomeini and his followers did, DAESH emphasized the smashing of those laws as idols (*tawāghit*), like the modernized states that imposed them.[22]

The IRI constitution used the 1958 French Fifth Republic as its initial model, by contrast, the so called *wathiqat al-madina* (Covenant of the City), digitally issued in January 2016, cannot be considered a constitution, as it is by some people, as it is really a declaration of jihad against the secular state as a modern idol (*taghut*) based on apostasy, and this includes republics that call themselves Islamic.[23] The IRI is an apostate state twice over in the eyes of DAESH, because it is Shi'ite and accepts the legal/constitutional framework of the modern state. The only resemblance I see between the *wathiqa* of DAESH and a constitution is its substitution of citizens enjoying constitutional rights with the subjects (*ra'iyya*, lit., "flock") of the Islamic State. The subjects/flock of the Islamic State are only entitled to justice dispensed by the caliph (as their shepherd); this is institutionalized in what it calls the court of complaints against wrongdoing (*diwān al-mazālim*), first created by the Abbasid caliphs in Baghdad on the model of ancient Persian kings, and a court of Islamic city regulations (*hisba*).[24]

Competition with Shi'ism over the appropriation of messianic symbols went on side by side with the unacknowledged appropriation of Persianate political ethics. It is worth noting that the very first air raid by the United States in Syria in September 2014 was a strike against the training camp of a group called Khorasan, an offshoot of al-Qaeda declared (by the director of US national intelligence) to be a greater danger to homeland security than ISIS. In 2012, the group's leader, Muhsin al-Fadhli, was identified by the State Department as an al-Qaeda operative who had been given asylum in Tehran after the American invasion of Afghanistan; he became the director of its operations from Iran, and was then killed by a military drone.[25] Another group affiliated with the Badr Iraqi Shi'ite militia first organized in exile in Iran continued to use Khorasan as part of its designation. Khorasan, as we have seen, is a large area in northern Iran, where the black banners of revolution in the name of the House of the Prophet was unfurled in the mid-second/eighth century. But by then, the Sunni Salafism of DAESH had achieved the effective return to the original succession of the Prophet Mohammad himself, by his first rightly-guided caliph reincarnated as Abu Bakr al-Qurayshi al-Baghdadi, had frustrated all rival groups who were waging global

---

22 Revkin 2016.
23 Revkin 2016: 15.
24 Revkin 2016: 25–27.
25 *New York Times*, 21 July 2015. Iranian intelligence against the Khorasan group was very probably supplied to the American forces through General Sulaymani's Qods Force in the context of rapprochement and nuclear negotiations with the Obama administration.

jihad, leaving little or no purchase to Khorasan as a symbol of Islamic revolution for the IS caliphate.

In 2017 DAESH was pushed out of Mosul, and defeated in its capital, Raqqa, in Syria, after a siege of some three months. It kept a small territory (less than one percent of what it had seized in 2014) as its last stronghold in Syria, and the campaign to recapture it by American-supported Kurdish groups was suspended early in November 2018. The inflow of Muslim emigrants from the Western diaspora continued, though their estimated number dropped to 100 per month from a peak of 1,500 per month. In March 2019 DAESH finally lost its last Syrian territorial stronghold to US-backed forces. Five months later, its fighters were still conducting guerilla attacks across Iraq and Syria and regaining their strength by mid-August 2019 while some 10,000 fighters, including 2,000 foreigners, were being held by American-backed Kurdish forces, according to a *New York Times* report.[26] Meanwhile, DAESH was pushed back to its electronic roots, sustaining a network of clandestine cells preparing for global jihad. There is little prospect for its definitive defeat in cyberspace, as the motivating appeal of doomsday and divine violence of the End of Time has not lost its appeal, as is clear from the Easter 2019 massacres at a Catholic church in Sri Lanka. News of DAESH has since sporadically surfaced in Libya and more generally in cyberspace.

---

26   *New York Times*, 7 Nov. 2018; and *New York Times*, 19 Aug. 2019: https://www.nytimes.com/2019/08/19/us/politics/isis-iraq-syria.html?module=inline.

References

'Abdi Beg Shīrāzi, 1369/1990. *Takmilāt al-akhbār*, ed. 'A.-H. Navā'i, Tehran: Nashr-e Ney.

Abrahamian, E., 1993. *Khomeinism*, Berkeley: University of California Press.

Acton, H.B., 1955. *The Illusion of the Epoch: Marxism-Leninism as a Philosophical Creed*, Indianapolis, IN: Liberty Fund.

Adas, M., 1979. *Prophets of Rebellion: Millenarian Protest Movements against the European Colonial Order*, Chapel Hill: University of North Carolina Press.

Afzal al-Din Ahmad b. Hāmed Kermāni, 1947. *Tārīkh-e Afzal yā Badāye' al-zamān fi vaqāye'-e Kermān*, ed. M. Bayāni, Tehran: Sherkat-e Sahāmi-ye Chāp.

Afzal al-Din Ahmad b. Hāmed Kermāni, 1356 Sh./1977. *'Eqd al-'olā l'il Mawāqif al-A'lā*, ed. 'A.-M. 'Āmeri Nā'ini, Tehran: Bonyād-e Farhang-e Irān.

Ahmed, T., 1982. *Religio-Political Ferment in the N.W. Frontier During the Mughal Period: The Raushaniya Movement*, Delhi: Idarah-i Adabiyat-i Delhi.

'Ālamārā-ye Shāh Esmā'il, 1349 Sh./1970. ed. Asghar Montazer-e Sāheb, Tehran: Bonyād-e Farhang-e Irān.

Algar, H., 1985. "'Ali al-A'lā," *EIr*, 1.8: 858.

Algar, H., 2004. "Horufism," *EIr*, 12.5: 483–490.

Amanat, A., 1989. *Resurrection and Renewal: The Making of the Babi Movement in Iran, 1844–1850*, Ithaca: Cornell University Press.

Amanat, A., 2014. "Persian Muqtawis and the Shaping of the Doctrine of 'Universal Reconciliation' (*sulh-i kull*) in Mughal India," in *Unity in Diversity: Mysticism, Messianism and the Construction of Religious Authority in Islam*, Orkhan Mir-Kasimov, ed., Leiden: Brill, pp. 367–391.

Amanat, A., 2017. *Iran: A Modern History*, New Haven, CT: Yale University Press.

Amini, Ebrāhim, *Fotuhāt-e shāhi*, University of Tehran Central Library, Meshkāt Collection, no. 1103.

Anderson, P., 1974. *The Passage from Antiquity to Feudalism*, London: NLB.

Ardestāni, Pir Jamāl al-Din Mohammad (1380/2001). *Misbāh al-arwāh*, ed. S.A. Mir-'Abedini, Tehran: Anjoman-e Āthār o Mafākher-e Farhangi.

Arjomand, S.A., 1982. "A la recherche de la conscience collective: The Ideological Impact of Durkheim in Turkey and Iran," *American Sociologist* 17.2: 94–102.

Arjomand, S.A., 1984. *The Shadow of God and the Hidden Imam: Religion, Political Organization and Societal Change in Shi'ite Iran from the Beginning to 1890*, Chicago: University of Chicago Press.

Arjomand, S.A., 1988. *The Turban for the Crown: The Islamic Revolution in Iran*, New York: Oxford University Press.

Arjomand, S.A., 1993a. "Religion and Constitutionalism in Western History and in Modern Iran and Pakistan," in *The Political Dimensions of Religion*, S.A. Arjomand, ed., Albany: State University of New York Press, pp. 69–99.

Arjomand, S.A., 1993b. "Millennial Beliefs, Hierocratic Authority and Revolution in Shi'ite Iran," in *The Political Dimensions of Religion*, S.A. Arjomand, ed., Albany: State University of New York Press, pp. 219–239.

Arjomand, S.A., 1996. "The Consolation of Theology: The Shi'ite Doctrine of Occultation and the Transition from Chiliasm to Law," *Journal of Religion* 76.4: 548–571; repr. in *Sociology of Shi'ite Islam: Collected Essays*, S.A. Arjomand, ed. Leiden: Brill, 2016, pp. 96–120.

Arjomand, S.A., 1998. "Islamic Apocalypticism in the Classical Period," in *The Encyclopedia of Apocalypticism*, B. McGinn, ed., New York: Continuum, vol. 2, pp. 238–283.

Arjomand, S.A., 1999. "The Law, Agency and Policy in Medieval Islamic Society: Development of the Institutions of Learning from the Tenth to the Fifteenth Century," *CSSH* 41.2: 263–293.

Arjomand, S.A., 2000. "Ğayba," *EIr*, 10:341–344.

Arjomand, S.A., 2001. "Perso-Indian Statecraft, Greek Political Science and the Muslim Idea of Government," *International Sociology* 16.3: 455–473.

Arjomand, S.A., 2003. "Medieval Persianate Political Ethic," *Studies on Persianate Societies* 1: 3–28.

Arjomand, S.A., 2004. "Transformation of the Islamicate Civilization: A Turning Point in the Thirteenth Century?" in *Eurasian Transformations, 10th to 13th Centuries: Crystallizations, Divergences, Renaissances*, J. Arnason and B. Wittrock, eds., Leiden: Brill, pp. 213–245.

Arjomand, S.A., 2005. "Rise of Shāh Esmāʿil as a Mahdist Revolution," *Studies on Persianate Societies* 3: 44–65.

Arjomand, S.A., 2009. *After Khomeini: Iran under His Successors*, New York: Oxford University Press.

Arjomand, S.A., 2010. "Legitimacy and Political Organisation: Caliphs, Kings and Regimes," in *The New Cambridge History of Islam*, vol. 4, ch. 7, R. Irwin and M. Cook, eds., pp. 225–273.

Arjomand, S.A., 2012. "The Conception of Revolution in Persianate Political Thought," *JPS* 5.1: 1–16.

Arjomand, S.A., 2013. "The Shi'ite Jurists and Iran's Constitutional Order in the Twentieth Century," in S.A. Arjomand and N.J. Brown, eds., *The Rule of Law, Islam and Constitutional Politics in Egypt and Iran*, Albany: State University of New York Press, pp. 15–56.

Arjomand, S.A., 2014. "Crystallization of Islam and the Developmental Paths in the Islamicate Civilization," in *Social Theory and Regional Studies in the Global Age*, S.A. Arjomand, ed., Albany: State University of New York Press, pp. 203–220.

Arjomand, S.A., 2015. "The Arab Revolution of 2011 and Its Counterrevolutions in Comparative Perspective," in S.A. Arjomand, ed., *The Arab Revolution of 2011: A Comparative Perspective*, Albany: State University of New York Press, pp. 9–51.

Arjomand, S.A., 2016a. *Sociology of Shi'ite Islam: Collected Essays*, S.A. Arjomand, ed. Leiden: Brill.

Arjomand, S.A., 2016b. "State Formation in Early Modern Muslim Empires: Common Origin and Divergent Paths," *Social Imaginaries* 2.2: 35–51.

Arjomand, S.A., 2016c. "Unity of the Persianate World under Turko-Mongolian Domination and Divergent Development of Imperial Autocracies in the Sixteenth Century," *JPS* 9.1: 1–18.

Arjomand, S.A., 2019. *Revolution: Structure and Meaning in World History*, Chicago: University of Chicago Press.

Arjomand, S.A., 2020. "The Emergence and Development of Persianate Sufism: Khorasan, Ninth to Twelfth Centuries," *JPS* 13.1: 1–35.

Arjomand, S.A., 2021. "Manichaeism as a World Religion of Salvation and Its Influence on Islam," *JPS* 14.1–2: 196–219.

Arjomand, S.A., 2022. *Messianism and Sociopolitical Revolution in Medieval Islam*, University of California Press.

Arjomand, S.A., forthcoming. *Sufi World Renunciation and the Legitimacy of Kingship in the Persianate World*.

Arslan, H.O., 2022. "'Ali al-A'lā' and the Early History of Hurufism," *JPS* 15.1.

al-Ash'arī al-Qummī, Sa'd b. 'Abd Allāh, 1963. *Kitāb al-Maqālāt wa'l-firaq*, ed. M.J. Mashkur, Tehran: N.p., 1963.

Astarābādi, Mehdi Khān, 1387/2009. *Dorra-ye nāderi*, ed. S.J. Shahidi, Tehran: Entesharāt-e 'Elmi va Farhangi.

Astarābādi, Mehdi Khān, 1394/2015. *Tārikh-e jahāngoshā-ye nāderi*, Tehran: Donya-ye Ketāb.

Aubin, J., 1959a. "Le Mécénat timouride à Chiraz," *SI* 8.8: 71–88.

Aubin, J., 1959b. "Études Safavides. I. Šah Ismā'il et les notables de l'Iraq persan," *Journal of the Economic and Social History of the Orient* 2: 37–81.

Aubin, J., 1984. "Revolution chiite et conservatisme. Les Soufis de Lāhijān (Études Safavides. II)," *Moyen Orient & Océan Indien* 1: 1–40.

Aubin, J., 1988. "L'Avènement des Safavides Réconsidéré (Études Safavides. III)," *Moyen Orient & Océan Indien*, 5: 1–130.

Āzhang, Y., 1369/1990. *Horufiyya dar tārikh*, Tehran: Nashr-e Ney.

al-Azmeh, A., 2007. "God's Chronography and Dissipative Time," in *The Times of History: Universal Topics in Islamic Historiography*, Budapest: Central European University Press.

Baalbaky, R. and A. Mhidi, 2018. *Tribes and the Rule of the Islamic State: The Case of the Syrian City of Deir ez-Zor*, Beirut: American University of Beirut (Issam Fares Institute for Public Policy and International Affairs).

Babayan, K., 2002. *Mystics, Monarchs and Messiahs: Cultural Landscapes of Early Modern Iran*, Cambridge, MA: Harvard University Press.

Babinger, F., 1921. *Schejch Bedr ed-Din, der Sohn des Richters von Simäw; ein Beitrag zur Geschichte des Sektenwesens im altosmanischen Reich*, Berlin and Leipzig: W. de Gruyter & Co.

Baker, K., 2013. "Revolution 1.0," *Journal of Modern European History* 11.2: 187–219.

Bakhash, Sh., 1986. *Reign of the Ayatollahs: Iran and the Islamic Revolution*, New York: Basic Books.

Balland, D., 1987. "Ašraf Ġilzay," *EIr* 2:796–797.

Bāqi, 'A., 1363/1984. *Dar shenākht-e hezb-e qā'din-e zamān*, Tehran: Nashr-e Dānesh-e Eslāmi.

Barthold, W., [1928] 1968. *Turkestan down to the Mongol Invasion*, trans. H.A.R. Gibb; repr. London: Luzac.

Bashir, Sh., 2001. "The Risālat al-hudā of Muhammad Nurbakhsh," *Rivista degli Studi Orientali* 75.1–4: 87–138.

Bashir, Sh., 2003. *Messianic Hopes and Mystical Visions*, Columbia: University of South Carolina Press.

Bashir, Sh., 2005. *Fazlallah Astarabadi and the Hurufis*, Oxford: Oneworld, 2005.

Bashir, Sh., 2014. "The World as a Hat: Symbolism and Materiality in Safavid Iran," in *Unity in Diversity: Mysticism, Messianism and the Construction of Religious Authority in Islam*, Orkhan Mir-Kasimov, ed., Leiden: Brill, pp. 343–365.

Baumann, B., 2013. "By the Power of Eternal Heaven: The Meaning of Tenggeri to the Government of the Pre-Buddhist Mongols," *Extrême-Orient Extrême-Occident* 35: 233–284.

Bayāt, N., ed., 1383/2004. *Gozida'yi az monsha'āt-e Mirzā Mahdi Khān Astarābādi*, Tehran: Ministry of Foreign Affairs.

Bayhaqi, Abu'l-Fazl Mohammad b. Hosyan, 1376/1997. *Tārikh-e Bayhaqi*, ed. M. Dāneshpazhuh, 2 vols. Tehran: Hirmand.

Bedlisi, Edris [Bitlisi, Idris], 1974. *Qānun-e shānshāhi*, ed. Hasan Tavakkoli, "Idris Bitlisi'nin Kanun-I Şâhenşâhisi'in tenkidli neşri ve Türkçeye tercümesi," PhD diss., Istanbul University.

Binbaş, I.E., 2013. "The Anatomy of a Regicide Attempt: Shāhrukh, the Ḥurūfis, and the Timurid Intellectuals in 830/1426–27," *JRAS* 23: 391–428.

Binbaş, I.E., 2014. "Timurid Experimentation with Eschatological Absolutism: Mīrzā Iskandar, Shāh Ni'matullāh Walī, and Sayyid Sharīf Jurjānī in 815/1412," in *Unity in Diversity: Patterns of Religious Authority in Islam*, Orkhan Mir-Kasimov, ed., Leiden: Brill, pp. 277–303.

Binbaş, I.E., 2016. *Intellectual Networks in Timurid Iran: Sharaf al-Dīn 'Alī Yazdī and the Islamicate Republic of Letters*. Cambridge: Cambridge University Press.

Binbaş, I.E., 2020. "The Jalayirid Hidden King and the Unbelief of Shah Mohammad Qara Qoyunlu," *JPS* 12.2: 206–236.

Bloch, E., 1954, 1955, 1959. *Das Prinzip Hoffnung*, 3 vols., Berlin: Suhrkampf.

Brack, J., 2018. "Theologies of Auspicious Kingship: The Islamicization of Ghinggisid Sacral Kingship in the Islamic World," *CSSH* 60.4: 1143–1171.

Brack, J., 2019. "A Mongol Mahdi in Medieval Anatolia: Rebellion, Reform and Divine Right in the Post-Mongol Islamic World," *JAOS* 139.3: 611–630.

Brinton, C., 1965. *The Anatomy of Revolution*. New York: Vintage.

Browne, E.G., 1897. "Personal Reminiscences of the Babi Insurrection at Zanjan in 1850, written in Persian by Aqa 'Abdu'l-Ahad-i Zanjani," *JOAS*, 761–827.

Browne, E.G., 1902. *Literary History of Persia*, 4 vols., London: T. Fisher Unwin.

Browne, E.G., ed., 1918. *Materials for the Study of the Babi Religion*, Cambridge: Cambridge University Press.

Bukhārī (Ṣūfiyānī), Muḥammad Amīn b. Mīrzā Muḥammad Zamān, 2014. *Muḥīṭ al-Tāvarīkh (The Sea of Chronicles)*, M. Fallahzadeh and F. Hashbeiky, eds., Leiden: Brill.

Cahen, C., 1970. *Le Shi'isme imâmite. Colloque de Strasbourg (6–9 mai 1968)*, Paris: Presses Universitaires de France.

Cahen, C., 1979. "Bābā'ī," *EI*², 1:843–844.

Chann, N.S., 2009. "Lord of the Auspicious Conjunction: Origins of the *Ṣāḥib-Qirān*," *Iran and the Caucasus* 13.1: 93–110.

Chattopadhyaya, D., 1996. *History of Science and Technology in Ancient India, vol. 3. Astronomy, Science and Society*, Calcutta: N.p., 1996.

Chittick, W.C., 2013. *Divine Love: Islamic Literature and the Path to God*, New Haven, CT: Yale University Press.

Chodkiewicz, M., 1993. "The Esoteric Foundations of Political Legitimacy in Ibn 'Arabi," in *Muhyiddin Ibn 'Arabi: A Commemorative Volume*, S. Histenstein and M. Tierman, eds., Shaftesbury: Element, pp. 190–198.

Cohn, N., 1957. *The Pursuit of the Millennium: Revolutionary Messianism in Medieval and Reformation Europe and Its Bearing on Modern Totalitarian Movements*, London: Weidenfeld and Nicolson.

Cole, J.R.I., 1989. *Roots of North Indian Shī'ism in Iran and Iraq: Religion and the State in Awadh 1722–1859*, Berkeley and Los Angeles: University of California Press.

Collins, R., 1998. *Sociology of Philosophies: A Global Theory of Intellectual Change*, Cambridge, MA: Harvard University Press, 1998.

Cook, D., 2018. "Abu Mus'ab al-Suri and Abu Mus'ab al-Zarqāwi: The Apocalyptic Theorist and the Apocalyptic Practitioner," in *The Apocalyptic Complex: Perspectives, Histories, Persistence*, N. al-Baghdadi, D. Marno, and Matthias Riedl, eds., Budapest: Central University Press.

Crossman, R. and Arthur Koestler, 1949. *The God that Failed*, New York: Harper and Brothers.

Csirkés, F., 2015. "Messianic Oeuvre in Interaction: Misattributed Poems by Shah Esmā'il and Nesimi," *JPS* 8.2: 155–194.

Czeglédy, K., 1958. "Bahrām VI Čōbin and the Persian Apocalyptic Literature," *Acta Orientalia Hungarica* 8.1: 21–43.

Dale, S.F., 2006. "Ibn Khaldun: The Last Greek and the First *Annaliste* Historian," *IJMES* 38.3: 431–451.

Dale, S.F., 2010. *The Muslim Empires of the Ottomans, Safavids and Mughals*, New York: Cambridge University Press.

Darling, L., 2000. "Contested Territory: Ottoman Holy War in Comparative Context," *SI* 91: 133–163.

Darling, L., 2004. "Persianate Sources in Anatolia and the Early History of the Ottomans," *Studies on Persianate Societies* 2: 126–144.

Davvāni, Jalāl al-Din, 1393/2014. *Akhlāq-e Jalāli*, ed. 'A. Mas'udi-Ārāni, Tehran: Enteshārāt-e Ettelā'āt.

Dawood, H., 2013. "Tribus et pouvoirs en Irak: de Saddam Hussein á David Petraeus," in *La constante "tribu," vaiations arabo-musulanes*, H. Dawood, ed., Paris: Demopolice, pp. 215–242.

De Jong, F., 1993. "Problems Concerning the Origins of the Qizilbāş in Bulgaria: Remnants of the Safaviyya?" in *Convegno sul Tema La Shi'a Nell'Imperio Ottomano*, Rome: Academia Nazionale dei Lincei, pp. 203–215.

De Weese, D., 1988. "The Eclipse of the Kubraviyah in Central Asia," *Iranian Studies* 21.1–2: 45–83.

Dehkhodā, 'A.-A., 1337–1352/1959–1974. *Loghatnāma*, 15 vols., Tehran: Sāzmān-e Loghatnāma.

Eberhard, E., 1970. *Osmanische Polemik gegen die Safawiden im 16. Jahrhundert nach arabischen Handschriften*, Freiburg: N.p.

Edwards, L., 1927. *The Natural History of Revolution*, Chicago: University of Chicago Press.

Ettehadieh Nezam-Mafi, M., 1989. "The Council for the Investigation of Grievances," *Iranian Studies* 22.1: 51–61.

Fardid, A., 1387/2008. *Diāar-e farrahi va fotuhāt-e ākhir al-zamān* [The divine encounter and apocalyptic revelations], Tehran: Moasseseh-ye Farhangi va Pajuheshi-ye Chap va Nashr-e Nazar.
Filiu, J.-P., 2011. *Apocalypse in Islam*, trans. M.B. DeBevoise, Berkeley: University of California Press.
Finlay, R., 1998. "Prophecy and Politics in Istanbul: Charles V, Sultan Suleyman and the Habsburg Embassy of 1533–34," *Journal of Early Modern History* 2: 1–31.
Fleet, K., 2010. "The Rise of the Ottomans," in *The New Cambridge History of Islam*, vol. 2: *The Western Islamic World, Eleventh to Eighteenth Centuries*. Cambridge: Cambridge University Press, M. Fierro, ed., pp. 313–331.
Fleischer, C.H., 1989. "Bedlisi, Mawlānā Hakim al-Din," *EIr*, 4:75–76.
Fleischer, C.H., 1992. "The Lawgiver as Messiah: The Making of the Imperial Image in the Reign of Süleymân," in *Soliman le magnifique et son temps*, Gilles Veinstein, ed., Paris: Documentation Française, pp. 159–177.
Fleischer, C.H., 2001. "Seer to the Sultan: Haydar-i Remmal and Sultan Süleyman," in *Cultural Horizons: A Festschrift in Honor of Talat S. Halman*, Jayne L. Warner, ed., Syracuse: Syracuse University Press, pp. 290–304.
Fleischer, C.H., 2009. "Ancient Wisdom and New Sciences: Prophecies at the Ottoman Court in the Fifteenth and Early Sixteenth Centuries," in *Falnama: The Book of Omens*, Massumeh Farhad and Serpil Bağcı eds., Washington: Thames & Hudson, pp. 232–243, 329–330.
Fleischer, C.H., 2018. "A Mediterranean Apocalypse: Prophecies of Empire in the Fifteenth and Sixteenth Centuries," *JESHO* 16.1–2: 19–91.
Flemming, B., 1987. "Ṣāḥib-ḳırān und Mahdī: Turkische Endzeiterwartungen im ersten Jahrzent der Regierung Süleymans," in *Between the Danube and the Caucasus: A Collection of Papers Concerning the Oriental Sources on the History of the Peoples of Central and South-Eastern Europe*, G. Kara, ed., Budapest: Akadémiai Kiadó, pp. 43–62.
Fletcher, J., 1979–1980. "Turko-Mongolian Monarchic Tradition in the Ottoman Empire," *Harvard Ukrainian Studies* 3–4.1: 236–251.
Floor, W., 1988. *Ashraf-e Afghān bar takhtgāh-e Esfahān*, trans. A. Serri, Tehran: Tus.
Fragner, B.G., 1997. "Iran under Il-Khanid Rule in a World-Historical Perspective," in *Iran face ā la domination mongole*, D. Aigle, ed., Tehran: Bibliothque Iranienne, no. 45, pp. 123–131.
Fragner, B.G., 1999. *Die "Persophonie": Regionalität, Identität und Sprachkontakt in der Geschichte Asiens*, Berlin: N.p.
Freud, S., 1910 [1957]. "The Antithetical Sense of Primal Words," in *Collected Papers*, trans. J. Rivier, London: Hogarth Press, pp. 184–191.

Gandjeï, T., 1959. *Il Canzoniere di Šāh Ismāʻīl Hatāʼī*, Naples: Istituto Universitario Orientale.

Gardiner, Noah, 2017. "The Occultist Encyclopaedism of ʻAbd al-Rahman al-Bistami," *Mamluk Studies Review* 20: 3–38.

Genç, V., 2019. "Rethinking Idris-i Bidlisi: An Iranian Bureaucrat and Historian between the Shah and the Sultan," *Iranian Studies*, 52.3–4: 425–447.

Genç, V., 2020. "An Iranian Shāh-nāma Writer at the Court of Bāyezid II: Malekzāda Āhi," *JPS* 13: 119–145.

Gibb, H.A.R., 1962. "Lutfi Paşa on the Ottoman Caliphate," *Oriens* 15: 287–295.

Gibbon, E., 1932. *The Decline and Fall of the Roman Empire*, 2 vols., New York: Modern Library.

Gilanentz, P.S., 1344/1965. *Soqut-e Esfāhān/The Chronicle of Petros di Sarkis Gilanentz*, trans. M. Mehryār and K. Minasian, ed. M. Mehryār, Isfahan: Shahryār.

Goldstone, J.A., 1991. *Revolution and Rebellion in the Early Modern World*, Berkeley: University of California Press.

Gril, D., 2005. "Ésotérisme contre Hérésie: ʻAbd al-Rahmân al-Bistâmî, un représentant de la science des letters à Bursa dans la première moitié du XVe siècle," in *Syncrétismes et hérésies dans l'Orient seldjoukide et ottoman (XIVe–XVIIIe siècle)*, Gilles Veinstein, ed., Paris: Peeters, pp. 183–195.

Hāfez, 1980. *Diwān-e Hāfez*, ed. P. Nātel-Khānlari, 2 vols., Tehran: Sherkat-e Offset.

Hamavi, Mohammad b. Eshāq, 1363/1984. *Anis al-moʼmenin*, ed. M.H. Mohaddeth, N.p.: Bonyad-e Beʻthat.

Hammuya, Saʻd al-Din, [1362/]1983. *al-Mesbāh fiʼl-tasavvuf*, ed. N. Mayel Heravi, Tehran: Enteshārāt-e Mawlā.

Haneda, Messahi, 1987. *Le Châh et les Qizilbaş. Le système militaire safavide*, Berlin: Klaus Schwarz Verlag.

Hasan [Qarawi], H., 2018a. "al-ʻAshira waʼl-jihād waʼl-dawla fi Irāq: Ishtirātāt al-rayh wa dynāmiyāt al-tatyif," Paper presented to the conference "Tribes in Jihadi Lands," American University of Beirut (Issam Fares Institute for Public Policy and International Affairs) (12 March 2018).

Hasan [Qarawi], H., 2018b. "Religious Actors, Political (Dis)order and the Reconfiguration of Margin-Center Relations in Iraq: The Case of the Shiʻi Clerical Authority," Paper presented at the MESA convention in San Antonio, Texas (16 November 2018).

Hasan [Qarawi], H., 2021. "The Making of a New Orthodoxy: Shiʻi Religious Authority and Political (Dis-)order in Iraq," in *Striking from the Margins: State, Religion and Devolution of Authority in the Middle East*, Aziz Al-Azmeh, Nadia al-Baghdadi, Harout Akdedian, and Harith Hasan, eds., London: Saqi, pp. 119–141.

Hinz, W., 1936. *Irans Aufstieg zum Nationalstaat in funfzchenten Jahrhundert*, Berlin: Walter de Gruyter.

Hobsbaum, R., 1959. *Primitive Rebels: Studies in Archaic Forms of Social Movements in the 19th and 20th Centuries*, New York: Norton.

Hodgson, M.G.S., 1955. *The Order of Assassins: The Struggle of the Early Nizârî Ismâ'îlîs against the Islamic World*. The Hague: Mouton.

Hodgson, M.G.S., 1974. *The Venture of Islam: Conscience and History in a World Civilization*, 3 vols., Chicago: University of Chicago Press.

Hojviri, Abu'l-Hasan 'Ali b. 'Othmān, 1383/2004. *Kasfh al-mahjub*, ed. M. 'Ābedi, Tehran: Sorush. [Note that the asterisk (*) indicates 'Ābedi's footnotes to Hojviri, which in fact serve as a concordance to other eleventh-century sources.]

Huff, T.E., 1993. *The Rise of Early Modern Science: Islam, China and the West*, Cambridge, UK: Cambridge University Press.

Hunt, S., 2001. "The Revolutionary Dimension of Millenarianism: The Case of the T'aiping Rebellion," in *Christian Millenarianism: From the Early Church to Waco*, Stephen Hunt, ed., Bloomington: Indiana University Press, pp. 116–130.

Ibn Abī Tāhir Tayfur, Untitled Treatise, British Library Oriental MS. Add 7473.

Ibn Bibi, Hosayn (Yāhyā) b. Mohammad b. 'Ali al-Ja'fari al-Raghadi, 1971. *Akhbār-e Salājeqa-ye Rum*, ed. M.J. Mashkur, Tehran: N.p.

Ibn Khaldūn, 1992. *Kitāb al-'Ibar (Tārīkh Ibn Khaldūn)*. 6 vols. Beirut: Dār al-Kutub al-'Ilmiyya.

Ibn Khaldūn, 1958. *Ibn Khaldûn: The Muqaddimah: An Introduction to History*, trans. Franz Rosenthal, 3 vols., Princeton, NJ: Princeton University Press.

Imber, C., 1997. *Ebu su'ud: The Islamic Legal Tradition*, Edinburgh: Edinburgh University Press.

Inalcik, H., 1962. "The Rise of Ottoman Historiography," in *Historians of the Middle East*, B. Lewis and P.M. Holt, eds., London: Oxford University Press, pp. 152–167.

Inalcik, H., 1991. "Mehmed I," *EI*, 6:973–977.

Inalcik, H., [1973] 2000. *The Ottoman Empire: The Classical Age 1300–1600*, London: Phoenix Press.

Irwin, R., 2018. *Ibn Khaldun: An Intellectual Biography*, Princeton, NJ: Princeton University Press.

Isakhan, B., 2018. "How to Interpret ISIS's Heritage Destruction," *Current History* 117 (803): 344–350.

Ja'fariyān, R., 1379/2001. *Safaviyya dar 'arsa-ye din, farhang va siyāsat*, 3 vols., Qomm: Pajhuheh-kada-ye Hawza va Dāneshgāh.

Jahāngoshā-ye Khāqān, 1364 Sh./1985. A.D. Moztar, facs. ed., Islamabad: N.p.

Jorbāzqāni, Abu Sharaf Nāseh b. Zafar, 1996. *Tarjoma-ye Tārikh-e Yamini*, ed. Ja'far She'ār, Tehran: Bongāh-e Tarjoma va Nashr-e Ketāb.

Kahlberg, S., 2021. "Ideas and Interests: From Weber's *Protestant Ethic* to the Later Writings on the Sociology of Religion," in *From World Religions to Axial Civilizations and Beyond*, S.A. Arjomand and S. Kahlberg, eds., Albany: State University of New York Press, pp. 49–65.

Karakaya-Stump, Ayfer, 2020. *The Kizilbash/Alevis in Ottoman Anatolia: Sufism, Politics and Community*, Edinburgh: Edinburgh University Press.

Karamustafa, A.T., 1994. *God's Unruly Friends: Dervish Groups in the Islamic Middle Period 1200–1550*, Oxford, Oneworld.

Karamustafa, A.T., 2014. "Kaygysuz Abdal: A Medieval Turkish Saint and the Formation of Vernacular Islam in Anatolia," in *Unity in Diversity: Mysticism, Messianism and the Construction of Religious Authority in Islam*, O. Mir-Kasimov, ed., Leiden: Brill, pp. 329–342.

Kastritsis, D., 2012. "The Şeyh Bedreddin Uprising in the Context of the Ottoman Civil War of 1402–13," in *Political Initiatives "from the Bottom Up" in the Ottoman Empire: Halcyon Days in Crete VII, a Symposium Held in Rethymno 9–11 January 2009*, A. Anastasopoulos, ed., Rethymno: Crete University Press, pp. 221–238.

Kermāni, Nāzem al-Eslām, 1329/1911. *'Alā'im al-zohur* [Signs of manifestation], Tehran: N.p.

Khonji Esfahāni, Fazlallāh Ruzbehān, 1355/1976. *Mihmān-nāmeh-ye Bokhārā*, ed. M. Sotudeh, Tehran: Tarjomeh va Nashr-e Ketāb.

Khonji Esfahāni, Fazlallāh Ruzbehān [Khunji-Isfāhāni], 1992. *Tārikh-i 'Ālam-ārā-yi Amini*, ed. J.E. Woods, London: Royal Asiatic Society.

Khwāju Kermāni, 1387/2008. *Rawzat al-Anvār*, ed. M. 'Abedi, Tehran: Mirās-e Maktub.

Khʷānd-Amir, 1362/1984. *Habib a-siyar*, vol. 4, ed. M. Dabir-Siyāqi, Tehran: Khayyām.

Khʷānd-Amir, 1372 Sh./1993. "Qānun-e homāyuni," in *Ma'āther al-moluk*, Mir Hāshem Mohaddeth, ed., Tehran: Rasā, pp. 257–307.

Koselleck, R., 1984. "Revolution. IV. Von der Früen Neuzeit bis zur Französischen revolution," in *Geschichtliche Grundbegriffe* v, O. Brunner, W. Conze, and R. Koselleck, eds., Stuttgart: Klett, pp. 689–788.

Koselleck, R., 1985. *Futures Past: On the Semantics of Historical Time*, trans. Keith Tribe, Cambridge, MA: MIT Press.

Koselleck, R., 2002. *The Practice of Conceptual History: Timing History, Spacing Concepts*, Stanford: Stanford University Press.

Lambton, A.K.S., 1977. "The Tribal Resurgence and the Decline of the Bureaucracy in the Eighteenth Century," in *Studies in Eighteenth-Century Islamic History*, Thomas Naff and Roger Owen, eds., Carbondale, IL: Southern Illinois University Press, pp. 95–128.

Landes, R., 2011. *Heaven on Earth: The Varieties of Millennial Experience*, New York: Oxford University Press.

Landes, R., 2018. "The Varieties of Millennial Experience," in *The Apocalyptic Complex: Perspectives, Histories, Persistence*, N. al-Baghdadi, D. Marno, and Matthias Riedl, eds., Budapest: Central University Press.

Landolt, H., 1973. "Introduction," Najm al-Dīn Abū Bakr b. Mohammad Rāzi, *Marmuzāt-e asadi dar mazmurāt-e Dāwudi*, M.R. Shafi'i-Kadkani, ed., Tehran: McGill Institute of Islamic Studies.

Lane, G., 2003. *Early Mongol Rule in Thirteenth-Century Iran: A Persian Renaissance*, London: Routledge.

Lāri, Mosleh al-Din Mohammad, 1394/2014. *Mer'āt al-advār o merqāt al-akhbār*, Sayyed Jalil Sāghravāniān, ed., Tehran: Miras-e Maktub.

Lawson, G., 2019. *Anatomies of Revolution*, Cambridge: Cambridge University Press.

Leyden, J., 1812. "The Rosheniah Sect and its Founder Bayezid Ansari," *Asiatic Researches* 11: 363–428; repr. as appendix D in T. Ahmed, 1982, *Religio-Political Ferment in the N.W. Frontier during the Mughal Period*, Delhi: Idarah-i Adabiyyat-i Delhi, pp. 79–111. [Our page references are to the reprint.]

Mabon, S. and S. Royle, 2017. *The Origins of ISIS*, London: I.B. Tauris.

MacLean, D., 2000. "La sociologie de l'engagement politique: le Mahdawiya indien et l'État," *Revue du monde musulman et de la Méditerranée* 91–94: 239–256.

Madelung, W., 1978. "Ḳā'im Āl Muḥammad," EI^2, 4:456–457.

Mahabharata, 1398/2019. Persian translation by Mir Ghiyāth al-Din 'Ali Qazvini, 4 vols., S.M.R. Jalāli-Nā'ini and N.S. Shukla, eds., with a preface by S. Sharma, Tehran: Association for the Study of Persianate Societies.

Malek Shāh Hosayn, 1965. *Ehyā' al-moluk*, ed. M. Sotuda, Tehran: Enteshārāt-e 'Elmi va Farhangi.

Malik, S.J., 1993. "16th Century Mahdism: The Rawšaniya Movement among Pakhtun Tribes," in *Islam and Indian Regions*, Anna Libera Dahmen-Dallapiccola and S. Zingel-Avé Lallemant, eds., Stuttgart: Franz Steiner Verlag, pp. 31–59.

Mannheim, K., 1978. *Ideologie und Utpoie*, Frankfurt: Verlag G. Schulte-Bulmke.

Manz, B.F., 1989. *The Rise and Rule of Tamerlane*, New York: Cambridge University Press.

Manz, B.F., 2007. *Power, Politics and Religion in Timurid Iran*, Cambridge: Cambridge University Press.

Marcinkowski, M. Ismail, 2005. "Dastur al-Moluk," *EIr* Online edition (https://iranica online.org/articles/dastur-al-moluk).

Markiewicz, Ch., 2019. *The Crisis of Kingship in Late Medieval Islam: Persian Emigres and the Making of Ottoman Sovereignty*, Cambridge: Cambridge University Press.

Marquet, Y., 1972. "Les Cycles de la souveraineté selon les Épîtres des Ikhwān al-safā'," *SI* 36.

Marvi, Mohammad Kāzem, 1374/1995. *'Ālamārā-ye Nāderi*, ed. M.A. Riyāhi, Tehran: Enteshārāt-e 'Elmi.

Mashkur, M.J., 1348/1969. "Fetna-ye Horufiya dar Tabriz," *Barrasihā-ye tāriḵi*, 4.4: 133–146.
Mas'ud Sa'd Salmān, 1339/1960. *Divān*, ed. Rashid Yāsami, Tehran: Enteshārāt-e Piruz.
Ma'sum 'Ali Shāh, Nā'eb al-sadāra, 1345/1966. *Tarā'eq al-haqā'eq*, ed. M.J. Mahjub, 3 vols., Tehran: Bārāni.
Matthee, R., 1996. "Unwalled Cities and Restless Nomads: Firearms and Artillery in Safavid Iran," in *Safavid Persia*, Ch. Melveille, ed., London: I.B. Tauris, pp. 389–416.
Matthee, R., 2012. *Persia in Crisis: Safavid Decline and the Fall of Isfahan*, London: I.B. Tauris.
Mawlavi, Jalāl al-Din Mohammad, 1369/1990. *Ketāb-e fiha mā fiha*, ed. B. Foruzānfar, Tehran: Amir Kabir, 1990.
Mazzaoui, M., 1972. *The Origins of the Safawids, Šiʿism, Sufism, and the Ġulāt*, Wiesbaden: Franz Steiner Verlag.
McCants, W.F., 2015. *The ISIS Apocalypse: The History, Strategy, and Doomsday Vision of the Islamic State*, New York: St. Martin's Press.
McChesney, R.D. 2009. "The Chinggisid Restoration in Central Asia, 1500–1785," in *The Cambridge History of Inner Asia: The Chinggisid Age*, Nicola di Cosmo, Allen J. Frank, and Peter B. Golden, eds., Cambridge: Cambridge University Press, pp. 277–291.
Meisami, J.S., 1999. *Persian Historiography to the End of the Twelfth Century*, Edinburgh: Edinburgh University Press.
Meisami, J.S., 2004. "Rulers and the Writing of History," in *Writers and Rulers*, B. Gruendler and L. Marlow, eds., Wiesbaden, pp. 73–95.
Mélikoff, I., 1962. *Abū Muslim. Le "porte-hache" du Khorasan*, Paris: Mainsonneuve.
Melvin-Koushki, M., 2012. "The Quest for a Universal Science: The Occult Philosophy of Ṣā'in al-Dīn Turka Iṣfahānī (1369–1432) and Intellectual Millenarianism in Early Timurid Iran," PhD diss., Yale University.
Melvin-Koushki, M., 2018. "Early Modern Islamicate Empire: New Forms of Religio-political Legitimacy," in *The Wiley-Blackwell History of Islam*, A. Salvatore, R. Tottoli, and B. Rahimi, eds., Hoboken, pp. 353–375.
Melvin-Koushki, M., 2019. "Imperial Talismanic Love: Ibn Turka's *Debate of Feast and Fight* (1426) as Philosophical Romance and Lettrist Mirror for Timurid Princes," *Der Islam* 96.1: 42–86.
Membré, M. 1993. *Mission to the Lord Sophy of Persia (1539–42)*, trans. A.H. Morton, London: School of Oriental and African Studies.
Menhāj-e Serāj Juzjāni, 1363/1984. *Tabaqāt-e nāseri*, ed. 'A. Habibi, 2 vols., Tehran: Donyā-ye Ketāb.
Minorsky, V., 1939. "A Civil and Military Review in Fārs in 881/1476," *BSOAS* 10.1: 141–178.
Minorsky, V., 1942. "The Poetry of Shāh Ismā'il I," *BSOAS* 10.4: 1006–1029.

Minorsky, V., 1954. "Jihān-shāh Qara-Qoyunlu and His Poetry (Turkmenica 9)," *BSOAS* 16.2: 271–297.

Mir-Kasimov, O., 2008. "*Jāvdān-nāma*," *EIr*, 14.6: 603–605.

Mir-Kasimov, O., 2014. "Ummis versus Imāms in Hurufi Prophetology: An Attempt at a Sunni/Shi'i Synthesis?" In *Unity in Diversity: Patterns of Religious Authority in Islam*, Orkhan Mir-Kasimov, ed., Leiden: Brill, pp. 221–246.

Mir-Kasimov, O., 2015. *Words of Power: Hurufi Teachings between Shi'ism and Sufism in Medieval Islam*, London: I.B. Tauris.

Mirsepassi, A., 2017. *Transnationalism in Iranian Political Thought: The Life and Times of Ahmad Fardid*, Cambridge: Cambridge University Press.

Mirsepassi, A., 2019. *Iran's Troubled Modernity: Debating Ahmad Fardid's Legacy*, New York: Cambridge University Press.

Moin, A. Afzar, 2012. *The Millennial Sovereign: Sacred Kingship and Sainthood in Islam*, New York: Columbia University Press.

Mokāfāt-nāma, 2001. R. Ja'farian, *Safaviyya dar 'arsa-ye din, farhang va siyāsat*, Qomm: Pajhuheh kada-ye Hawza va Dāneshgāh, vol. 3, pp. 1231–1295.

Momen, M., 1985. *Shi'i Islam: An Introduction*, Oxford: George Ronald.

Morimoto, K., 2010. "The Earliest 'Alid Genealogy for the Safavids: New Evidence for the Pre-dynastic Claim to Sayyid Status," *Iranian Studies* 43.4: 447–469.

Morton, A.H., 1990. "The Date and Attribution of the *Ross Anonymous*. Notes on a Persian History of Shāh Ismā'il I," *Pembroke Papers 1, Persian and Islamic Studies in honour of P.W. Avery*, Cambridge: N.p., pp. 179–212.

Morton, A.H., 1993. "Introduction," Michele Membré, *Mission to the Lord Sophy of Persia (1539–42)*, pp. vii–xxviii.

Morton, A.H. 1996. "The Early Years of Shāh Ismā'il in the *Afzal al-tavārikh* and Elsewhere," in *Safavid Persia: The History and Politics of an Islamic Society*, Ch. Melville, ed., London: I.B. Tauris.

Motahhari, M., 1354/1975. *Qiyām o enqelāb-e mahdi az didgāh-e falsafa-ye tārikh*, Tehran: Entesharāt-e Vahy.

Motarjem, Mohammad, *Enqelāb al-eslām bayn al-khāss wa'l-'āmm*, National Library MS no. 1634, Tehran.

Mottahedeh, R.P., 2012. "The Idea of Iran in the Buyid Dominions," in *Early Islamic Iran*, vol. 5: *The Idea of Iran*, E. Herzig and S. Stewart, eds., London: I.B. Tauris, pp. 153–160.

Naji, K., 2008. *Ahmadinejad: The Secret History of Iran's Radical Leader*, New York: I.B. Tauris.

Nasavi, Shehāb al-Din Mohammad Khorandazi, 1343/1964. *Nafaqat al-masdur*, ed. A.-H. Yazdgerdi, Tehran: Virāstār.

Navā'i, 'A.-H., 1347/1969. *Shāh Esmā'il Safavi: Asnād va mokātebāt-e tārikhi*, Tehran: Bonyād-e Farhang-e Irān.

Necipoğlu, G., 1985. "The Süleymaniye Complex in Istanbul: An Interpretation," *Muqarnas* 3: 92–117.

Neumann, P.R., 2008. *Joining al-Qaeda: Jihadist Recruitment in Europe* (Adelphi Paper 399), London: International Institute for Strategic Studies.

Nişanci, Celalzade, *Ma'āthir-i Selim Khān*, British Library, Add. MS 7848.

Nurbaskhsh, Mohammad, 1351/1971. *The Writings of Sayyed Mohammad Nurbakhsh*, in J. Sadaqiyānlu, *Tahqiq dar ahvāl va āthār-e Sayyed Mohammad Nurbakhsh Ovaysi Qohestāni*, Tehran: Tābesh.

Ocak, A.Y., 1989. *La Révolte de Baba Resul ou la formation de l'hétérodoxie musulmane en Anatolie au XIIIᵉ siècle*, Ankara: N.p.

Ocak, A.Y., 1992. "Idéologie officielle et reaction populaire: un aperçu general sur les mouvements et les courants socio-religieux a l'époque de Soliman le Magnifique," in *Soliman le Magnifique et son temps*, Gilles Veinstein, ed., Paris: Documentation Française, pp. 185–194.

Pārsādust, M., 1381/2002. *Shāh Esmā'il avval*, Tehran: Sherkat-e Enteshār.

Pfeiffer, J., 2014. "Confessional Ambiguity vs. Confessional Polarization: Politics and the Negotiation of Religious Boundaries in the Il-Khanatee," in *Politics, Patronage and the Transmission of Knowledge in 13–15th Century Tabriz*, Leiden: Brill, pp. 129–168.

Pizzorno, A., 1994. *Le Radici della Politica Assoluta e altri Saggi*, Milan: Feltrinelli.

de Planhol, X., 1988. "Bandar-e 'Abbas, i. The City," *EIr*, 3:685–668.

Qāyeni, 'Ubaydollāh, *Nasāyeh-e Shahrokhi*, Vienna: Österreiche Nazionalbibliothek, MS # ONVA10559.

Qazvini, M., 1906. "Introduction," Mohammad 'Awfi, *Lobāb al-albāb* I, ed. E.G. Browne and Mohammad Qazvini, London: N.p.

Qomi, Qazi Ahmad, 1359/1980. *Kholāsat al-Tavārikh*, ed. E. Eshrāqi, 2 vols., Tehran: Tehran University Publications.

Quinn, Sh. A., 2015. "A Historian on the Move: An Early Modern Persian Chronicler under the Safavids and Mughals," in *Mapping Safavid Iran*, N. Kondo, ed., Tokyo: Research Institute for Language and Cultures of Asia and Africa, pp. 171–188.

de Rachewiltz, I., 2007. "Heaven, Earth and the Mongols in the Time of Činggis Qan and His Immediate Successors (ca. 1160–1260)—a Preliminary Investigation," in *Lifelong Dedication to the China Mission: Essays Presented in Honor of Father Jeroom Heyndrickx, CICM, on the Occasion of His 75th Birthday and the 25th Anniversary of the F. Verbiest Institute K.U. Leuven*, Noël Golvers and Sara Lievens, eds., Leuven: Fedinand Verbiest Institute, pp. 107–144.

Ragin, C.C., 1987. *The Comparative Method: Moving Beyond Qualitative and Quantitative Strategies*, Berkeley: University of California Press.

Rashid al-Din Fazlallāh Hamadāni, 1994. *Jāme' al-Tavārikh*, ed. M. Rawshan and M. Musavi, 4 vols., Tehran: Nashr-e Alborz.

Rāzī, Najm al-Din Abu Bakr b. Mohammad, 1352/1973a. *Mersād al-'ebād*, ed. M.A. Riyāhi, Tehran Enteshārāt-e 'Elmi va Farhangi.
Rāzi, Najm al-Dīn Abū Bakr b. Mohammad, 1973b. *Marmuzāt-e asadi dar mazmurāt-e Dāwudi*, ed. M.R. Shafi'i-Kadkani, Tehran: McGill University Institute of Islamic Studies.
Rāzi, Najm al-Dīn Abū Bakr b. Mohammad, 1982. Trans. Hamid Algar, *The Path of God's Bondsmen from Origin to Return*, New York: Persian Heritage Series, 1982.
Reeves, M., 1976. *Joachim of Fiore and the Prophetic Future*, New York: Harper Torchbooks.
Revkin, M., 2016. *The Legal Foundations of the Islamic State*, Washington, DC: Brookings Center for Middle East Policy.
Richards, J.F., 1993. *The Mughal Empire*, Cambridge: Cambridge University Press.
Richards, J.F., 1998. "The Formation of Imperial Authority under Akbar and Jahangir," in *The Mughal State 1526–1750*, Muzaffar Alam and Sanjay Subrahmanyam, eds., Delhi: Oxford University Press.
Rizvi, S.A.A., 1965–66. "Rawshaniyya Movement I," *Abr-Nahrain* 6:63–91.
Rizvi, S.A.A., 1967–68. "Rawshaniyya Movement II–IV," *Abr-Nahrain* 7:62–98.
Robertson, R., 1992. *Globalization: Social Theory and Global Culture*, London and Newbury Park: Sage.
Roemer, H.R., 1986. "The Successors of Timur," in *The Cambridge History of Iran*, vol. 6, P. Jackson and L. Lockhart, eds., Cambridge: Cambridge University Press, pp. 98–145.
Rumlu, H., 1931. *The Chronicle of the Early Safawis, Being the Ahsanu't-Tawārikh*, C.N. Seddon, ed., Baroda: Oriental Institute.
Sa'di, Mosleh al-Din, 1345/1966. *Golestān*, ed. Sa'id Nafisi, Tehran: Forughi.
Sa'di, Mosleh al-Din, 1363/1984. *Bustān*, Tehran: Amir Kabir.
Sa'di, Mosleh al-Din, 1383/2004. *Kolliyāt*, H. Anvari, ed., Tehran: Qatra.
Şahin, K., 2010. "Constantinople and the End Time: The Ottoman Conquest as a Portent of the Last Hour," *Journal of Early Modern History* 14: 317–354.
Sanudo, M., 1979. *Šāh Ismā'il I nei "Diarii" di Marin Sanudo*, ed. B. Scarcia Amoretti, Rome: Istituto per l'Oriente.
Sarkisyanz, M., 1955. *Russland und der Messianismus des Orients*, Tübingen: Mohr.
Sawyer, C., 1996. "Sword of Conquest, Dove of the Soul: Political and Spiritual Values in Ahmadi's *Iskandarnāma*," in *The Problematics of Power: Eastern and Western Representations of Alexander the Great*, M. Bridges and J.C. Bürgel, eds., Bern: Peter Lang.
Şen, A.T., 2017. "Bayezid II (r. 1481–1512) and His Celestial Interests," *Arabica* 64: 557–608.
Shahbazi, A. Sh., O. Klíma, and William Hanaway, 2020. "Bahrām vii Bahrām VI Čōbin," *EIr* online edition (http://dx.doi.org/10.1163/2330-4804_EIRO_COM_6433).
Shaked, Sh., 1972. "Qumran and Iran: Further Considerations," *Israel Oriental Studies* 2: 433–446.

Shari'ati, 'A., 1386/2007. "Entezār, mazhab-e entezār," in *Hosayn vāreth-e Ādam (Majmu'a-ye āthār 19)*, Tehran: Qalam, pp. 239–290.

Shervāni, Hosayn b. 'Abdallāh, 1379/2001. "Ahkām diniyya fi takfir Qezelbāsh," in *Safaviyya dar 'arsa-ye din, farhang va siyāsat* 1, Rasul Ja'fariyān, ed., Qomm: N.p., pp. 89–107.

Shirāzi, Ebn 'Abdol-Karim, A.R., 1986. *Tārikh-e Zandiyya (Jāneshinān-e Karim Khān Zand)*, ed. Gh. Varahrām, Tehran: Nashr-e Gostarda. (The text is a reprint of *Das Tārikh-i Zendije*, ed. Ernst Beer, Leiden: Brill, 1888.)

Skocpol, T., 1979. *States and Social Revolutions: A Comparative Analysis of France, Russia and China*, Cambridge: Cambridge University Press.

Sohravardi, Shehāb al-Din Yahyā, 1993. *Majmu'a-ye mosannafāt- Shaykh-e Eshrāq*, ed. H. Corbin, 3 vols., Tehran: Pazhuhashgāh-e 'Olum-e Ensani va Motāle'āt-e Farhangi.

Sohrweide, H., 1965. "Der Sieg der Safaviden in Persien und seine Rückwirkungen auf die Schiiten Anatoliens im 16. Jahrdundert," *Der Islam* 40: 95–223.

Spence, J.D., 1996. *God's Chinese Son: The Taiping Heavenly Kingdom of Hong Xiuquan*, New York: W.W. Norton & Company.

Spooner, B. and W.J. Hanaway, eds., 2012. *Literacy in the Persianate World: Writing and the Social Order*, Philadelphia: University of Pennsylvania Museum of Archaeology and Anthropology.

Subrahmaniyam, S., 2003. "Turning the Stones Over: Sixteenth-Century Millenarianism from the Tagus to the Ganges," *Indian Economic and Social History Review* 40.2: 129–161.

Sümer, F., 1992. *Safevî devletinin kurulu, su ve geli, smesinde Anadolu Türklerinin rolü*, Ankara: N.p.; trans. Ehsān Eshrāqi and M.T. Emāmi, 1371/1992. *Naqsh-e torkān-e Ānātoli dar tashkil va tawse'a-ye dawlat-e Safavi*, Tehran: N.p.

al-Ṭabarī, Muḥammad b. Jarīr, 1879–1901. *Ta'rikh al-rusul wa-l-mulūk*, ed. M.J. de Goeje, 15 vols., Leiden: E.J. Brill.

Tārikh-e Qezelbāshān, 1361/1982. ed. M.H. Mohaddeth, Tehran: Behnām.

Tatawi, Qāzi Ahmad Āsef Khān Qazvini et al., 2003. *Tārikh-e alfi*, ed. Gh.-R. Tabātabā'i-Majd, 8 vols., Tehran: Enteshārāt-e Kolba.

Thapar, R., 2003. *The Penguin History of Early India from the Origins to 1300*, New Delhi: Penguin Books India.

Tiryakian, E.A., 1995. "Collective Effervescence, Social Change and Charisma: Durkheim, Weber and 1989," *International Sociology* 10.3: 269–281.

de Tocqueville, A., 1955. *The Old Régime and the French Revolution*, trans. S. Gilbert, New York: Doubleday.

Togan, Zeki Velidi, 1959. "Sur l'origine des Safavides," in *Mélanges Massignon III*, Damascus, N.p., pp. 345–357.

Torka Eshahāni, Sā'en al-Din 'Ali b. Mohammad, 1351/1972. *Chahārdah resāla-ye fārsi*, ed. S.A. Musavi-Behbahāni and S.E. Dibāji, Tehran: Chāpkhāna-ye Ferdawsi.

Toynbee, A., 1935. *A Study of History*, vol. 5, Oxford: Oxford University Press.
Truschke, A., 2016. "Translating the Solar Cosmology of Sacred Kingship," *Medieval History Journal* 19: 136–141.
Tucker, E., 1994. "Nadir Shah and the Ja'fari Madhhab Reconsidered," *IS* 27.1–4: 163–179.
Tucker, W.F., 2014. "The Kufan Ghulāt and the Millenarian (Mahdist) in the Mongol-Türkmen Iran," in *Unity in Diversity: Patterns of Religious Authority in Islam*, Orkhan Mir-Kasimov, ed., Leiden: Brill, pp. 177–196.
Tūsi, Abu 'Alī Hasan, 1978. *The book of government, or, Rules for Kings: The Siyar al-muluk or Siyasat-nama of Nizam al-Mulk*, ed. and trans. H. Darke, London: Routledge and Kegan Paul.
Uğur, A., 1985. *The Reign of Sultan Selim I in the Light of the Selim-nāme Literature*, Berlin: Kluas Schwarz Verlag.
Vāsefi, Zayn al-Din Mahmud, 1970. *Badāye' al-vaqāye'*, ed. A.N. Boldyrev, 2 vols., Tehran: Bonyād-e Farhang-e Irān.
Walbridge, J., 1996. "The Babi Uprising in Zanjan: Causes and Issues," *Iranian Studies* 29.3–4: 339–362.
Weber, M., 1978. *Economy and Society*, ed. and trans. G. Roth and C. Wittich, 2 vols., Berkeley: University of California Press.
Woods, G., 2017. *The Way of the Strangers: Encounters with the Islamic State*, New York: Random House.
Woods, J.E., 1976. *The Aqquyunlu: Clan, Confederation, Empire*, Minneapolis and Chicago: Bibliotheca Islamica.
Woods, J.E., 1992. "Introduction," *Tārikh-i 'Ālam-ārā-yi Amini*, ed. J.E. Woods, London: Royal Asiatic Society.
Yamamoto, K. and Ch. Burnett, ed. and trans., 2000. *Abu Ma'šar on Historical Astrology: The Book of Religions and Dynasties (on the Great Conjunctions)*, 2 vols., Leiden: Brill.
Yazdi, Tāj al-Din Hasan b. Shehāb, 1987. *Jāme' al-tavārikh-e hasani*, ed. H. Modarresi Tabātabā'i and I. Afshār, Karachi: University of Karachi.
Yazdi, Sharaf al-Don 'Ali. 1388/2009. *Monsha'āt*, I. Afshar and M.-R. Abu'i-Mahrizi, eds., Tehran: Farhang-e Irānzamin.
Yildirim, R., 2008. "Turkomans between Two Empires: The Origins of the Qizilbash Identity in Anatolia (1447–1514)," PhD diss., Bilkent University, Ankara.
Yildirim, R., 2013. "Shi'itization of the *Futuwwa* Tradition in the Fifteenth Century," *British Journal of Middle Eastern Studies* 40.1: 53–70.
Yildirim, R., 2015. "In the Name of Hosayn's Blood: The Memory of Karbala as Ideological Stimulus to the Safavid Revolution," *JPS* 8.2: 127–154.
Yildiz, S.N., 2004. "Persian in the Service of the Sultan: Historical Writing in Persian under the Ottomans during the 15th and 16th Centuries," *Studies on Persianate Societies* 2.

Yilmaz, H., 2018. *The Caliphate Redefined: The Mystical Turn in Ottoman Political Thought*. Princeton, NJ: Princeton University Press.

Zabih, S., 1982. "Aspects of Terrorism in Iran," *Annals of the American Academy of Political and Social Science*, 463: 84–94.

Zarrinkub, 'A.-H., 1357/1978. *Jostoju dar tasavvof-e irān*, Tehran: Amir Kabir.

Zarrinkub, 'A.-H., 1362/1983. *Donbāla-ye Jostoju dar tasavvof-e irān*, Tehran: Amir Kabir.

Index

Abāqā, Il-Khan 48
'Abbas I, Shah 109, 145–146
'Abbās III, late Safavid 160, 162
Abbasid (Hashemite) Revolution 12, 18, 24, 27–28
'Abd al-Karim Sam'āni 30
'Abdallāh al-'Azzām 205
'Abdallāh Ansāri, Khwāja 30, 130
'Abdallāh b. Mas'ud 2
'Abdi Beg 93–94, 97, 107
Abrishamchi, Mehdi 193–194
Abu 'Abdallāh al-Shi'i 98
Abu Bakr al-Baghdadi al-Qurayshi 204, 206–208
Abu Bakr b. Mirānshāh 22
Abu Bakr b. Sa'd b. Zangi, *atabeg* 40–41
Abu'l-Fayz Khan 160
Abu'l-Fazl Bayhaqi 12–13
Abu'l-Hasan Kharaqāni 30
Abu'l-Khayr/Shaybāni dynasty 115
Abu'l-Sharaf Jorbāzqāni 19
Abu'l-So'ud (Ebu's-su'ud) al-'Emādi 120, 122–125
Abu Mansur Tusi 26
Abu Mash'ar 17
Abu Moslem Khorāsāni 28, 100–101, 203
Abu Moslem Nāma 91
Abu Mus'ab al-Suri 205
Abu Rayhān Biruni 26
Abu Sa'id, Il-Khan 50
advice to kings 12, 37–41, 51
al-'Adliyya al-sulaymāniyya 124
Afghan interregnum (1722–1729) 140, 144–158
Afghans 142
    Abdāli 147, 152–5, 159
    Ghelzai 146–48, 152–4, 159
Afghanistan 127–138, 148–159, 205
    Conversion to Islam 127
Āfrids 133, 135
Afshār dynasty 162
Afzal al-Din Kermāni 18–19, 142
Afshār dynasty 162
Ahad-dād Rawshani 136
Ahmad b. Fahd al-Hilli 67
Ahmad Ahsā'i, Shaykh 170

Ahmad Jāmi, Shaykh 130
Ahmad Khan/Shah Abdāli (Dorrāni) 162
Ahmad Lor 58–60
Ahmadinejad, Mahmud 185, 189
Ahmed, Ottoman prince 98, 103, 105, 119
Akbar, Mughal 112, 135–136
Akhi Ahmed Shah 49
akhi brotherhoods 42, 52. *See also fotowwat*
Akhi Evrān 52
Akhi Mohammad Divāna 49
Akhi Mu'azzam Sharaf al-Din 52
Akhi Ya'qub 52
Akhlāq-e 'Alā'i 119
Akhlāq-e Jalāli 83–85
Akhlāti, Sayyed Hosayn 58–59, 62, 72, 76
'Alā' al-Dawla Zu'l-Qadr 102
'Alā' al-Din Kayqobād 36, 49
'Alā'im al-zohur (The signs of manifestation) 180–181
Al-e Ahmad, Jalal 195
Aleppo 64–65
'Ali Shir Navā'i 99
'Ali al-A'lā, Horufi leader 54–58, 60, 65
    as God's deputy 57
'Ali al-Karaki, Shaykh 101, 120
'Ali Pasha 105
'Ali-Qoli Khan Shāmlu 155
Almohad revolution 10*n*24, 29, 137, 204*n*14
Alvand Mirzā, Āq Qoyunlu 99
Amānallāh Khan Afghan 150–512
Amasya 96, 98
Amir al-mu'minin 121, 125
Amir 'Ali Dāmghāni 53
Amir Mo'ayyad 52
Amir Nurallāh 58
Anatolia 36, 39–40, 42, 46–52, 86–89, 95–105
    conversion to Islam 42, 47, 148
Ankara, *akhi* "republic" of 44, 52
    Battle of 61
Antalya 98
Apocalyptic traditions
    revival of the southern Arabian 204–06
    Zoroastrian 205

Apocalypticism 1–2, 5
  and occult sciences 61–66
  and politics 4, 81, 188–196
  and transfer of sovereignty 12
  realized apocalypticism 33
  of DAESH 203–208. *See also*, Mahdism, messianism, millennialism
Āq Qoyunlu 45, 82–84
Āqā Mohammad Khan Qājār 140, 163–164
Āqsarā'i 49–50
Arab revolutions of 2011 10, 98
Arafat, Yasser 186
Ardabil 88–96, 153
Arghun, Il-Khan 21, 49
Armenians 149–151, in Jolf
Asrār al-khilāfa (Secrets of the caliphate) 122
'asabiyya (group solidarity) 6, 137, 202, 204
atabegs 18–19
'Attār, Farid al-Din 33, 39, 130
Aubin, Jean 86, 106–107
awliyā' Allāh (friends of God) 31, 39, 58, 69–71, 77, 124, 131
'ayyārān 30, 41–44
'Ayn al-Qozāt Hamadāni 30, 130
Azali Babis 179–180
Azerbaijan 59–60, 82, 99–100, 105, 116, 128
'Aziz b. Ardashir Astarābādi Baghdādi 20

bāb (gate) 170
Bābā Eshāq, called Bābā Rasul Allāh 48
Bābā Qodrati, Hajj Mohammad 155–156
Bābā Shāhqoli (Şahkulu) 103–106, 108
Bābā'i rebellion 48, 51, 88
Babi movement 171–175
  its urban social base 174
  its uprisings in Badasht 173
  Nayriz 173, 181
  Zanjan 173–174
Bābor, Zahir al-Din Mohammad, Mughal 111–113, 127
Badāye' al-waqāye' (Marvelous events) 113
Badr militia, Iraqi Shi'ite 207
Baghdad 40, 82, 100, 107, 174, 202, 207
Bahādur khan 115
Bahādur Shah 128
Bahā'ullāh, Mirzā Hosayn 'Ali Nuri 174
Bahai religion 174

bakht (fortune) 16, 21–22
Bakhtiyāris 146
Balkh 29, 39, 99
Baluchis 144, 147–148, 154, 159
Banu al-Asfar (the Blond People) 81, 87
Barquq, Mamluk Sultan 59, 72
Bāyandor. *See* Āq Qoyunlu
Bāyazid Ansāri/Rawshani 127–134, 159
  his Mahdihood 132, 134
Bāyazid Bastāmi 29–30, 131
Baybars, Malek al-Zaher (Mamluk Sultan) 17, 48
Bāyezid I, Yıldırım, Ottoman Sultan 44
Bāyezid II, Ottoman Sultan 23, 86, 98, 102, 108, 116–117, 119–121
Baysonghor Mirzā 76–78
Bedreddin Mahmud, Kadi[oğlu] of Samawna 53, 59, 61–66, 79–81, 86–87
  his millennial uprising 64–66
  its connection with the Horufi movement 65–66, 68
  its social basis 64, 66
Beheshti, Sayyed Mohammad Hosayni 192
Berbers 98, 133, 137
Bestāmi, 'Abd al-Rahmān 62–63, 79–81, 131
Bidābādi, Āqā Mohammad 187
Brack, Jonathan 48
Brethren of Purity (*ekhwān al-safā'*), Cairene 58–59, 63
British East India Company 154–155
Browne, Edward G. 180
Bukhara 115–116, 160
Bürkülje Mustafā 66
Bursa 52, 79–80, 104
Bustān 40

Cairo 58–59, 62–63, 65
Caldwell, Malcolm 196
Caliphate 119
  Abbasid 119, 123
  of God (*khelāfat Allāh*) 82–85
  of the Prophet 121–123
  the ruler as God's Deputy 37, 74, 83, 93, 117
  as the Deputy of the Merciful (*khalifat al-Rahmān*) 83–85, 113–122
Cambodian (Red Khmer) Revolution 184, 196
Castro, Fidel 185

INDEX

Chaldiran, Battle of 105, 109
Charisma of the Mahdi 9, 105
  its routinization 9–10, 105–109, 183–184, 199–200
Chinggisid restoration in the Uzbek empire 115–116
Chinggis Khan 12, 20–22, 33–34, 44–45, 159–161
  his imperial principle 61, 115–116
  the Yasa of 4, 78, 161
Chiliasm. *See* millennialism
Chishti Sufi order 127, 130
Chobān, Amir 49
Chamran, Mustafa 184–186
Chamran, Mehdi 185
Cohn, Norman 6
clerical monarchy 199–201
Collapse of the Safavid empire, a revolution in world history 140, 165–166
  as proto-modern Persianate *revolutio regni* 140–144
  as Tocquevillian 165
  and the Khaldunian model 159, 165–166
  and foreign armed intervention 151–153, 161–162
  its causes 140–148
  its process 140
  power struggle, in Isfahan 149–155
  in Kerman 148–149, 154, 157–158
  in Mashhad 141, 147, 154–156
  in Qazvin 150–151
  in Sistan 154–158
  in Yazd 154, 157–158
  on the Persian Gulf littoral 156–158
Condorcet 141
confessional ambiguity, age of 34–42, 53
  disestablishment of Islam 34–36
  rivalry between the Sufi shaykhs and the 'olamā' 35–36
Constantinople (Byzantium), conquest of 45, 63, 80–81, 87, 205
constitutional politics. *See* revolution, process of
Constitutional Revolution of 1906–1911, 178–182, 197
  as prelude to the advent of the Mahdi 179–181

Corps of the Guards of the Islamic Revolution 186, 200
counter-elite (dispossessed notables) as revolutionary leaders 62, 64, 67, 104–05, 120–21, 187, 199
counter-revolution 8
  Sunni 111–126
  exiles of Safavid revolution as its proponents 112–125
  as preemptive reaction to apocalyptic Mahdism 8–10, 71–85, 117
  and *fatwā*s against the Qezelbāsh 114, 119–120
  and orthodox (Sunni) reform 82–85
counter-millennial sovereignty 10
The Cry of the Owl (*sayhat al-bum*) *on the Events of Rum* 63
Cuban Revolution 184–185

DAESH 185, 201–208
  comparison with the IRI 206–207
  its anathemization of the nation-state 206–207
  its counter-Shi'ite doomsday apocalypticism 206, 208
  Neo-Khaldunian pattern 202–204
  online recruitment 201–202, 208
  rejection of Islamic ideology for prophetic methodology 206
Dabiq 203–204
Dastur al-moluk 153
Dawr tribe 133
Dawlat (turn in power) 6, 11–24, 41, 142
  as the state 6, 17, 153–154, 160–161
Dajjāl (Antichrist) 57, 192
Daniel, Book of 11, 14, 81, 168
Dāneshmand-nāma 47
Davvāni, Jalāl al-Din Mohammad 82–85, 119
darvish 30, 41, 43
  dervishes as political leaders 52–53. *See also* Sufism, antinomian
Deccan, the 31, 45, 102, 111, 129
Dede 'Omar Rawshani 131
Delhi 160, 162
Delhi Sultanate 17, 19, 31, 127
Didār-e Farrahi va fotuhāt-e akhir al-zamān (The divine encounter and the revelations of the end of time) 196

Diyarbekir (Diyār Bakr) 96, 99–100, 102
Dorr-e maknun 80
Dutch East India Company (VOC) 154–157

Ebrāhim-e Adham 29–30
Ebrāhim-Soltān, Timurid 74
Edris Bedlisi 23, 83–84, 105, 116–122
Empires, Turko-Mongolian-Persianate 10, 44–45, 61
   Āq Qoyunlu 23, 82–84, 89–90, 98–102
   Il-Khanid 20–21, 47–52
   its disintegration 47, 52–53
   Mongol 20, 33–34
   Mughal (Timurids of India) 111–112
   of Nāder Shah 139, 158–166
   Ottoman 61–66
   Safavid 89, 106–109
End of Time (*ākhir al-zamān*) ix, 1–2, 63, 67–71, 74, 81, 94, 132, 181, 186, 193, 196, 203–208
   the Mahdi of 51, 73, 121, 128, 169, 186, 191
   malāhem (tribulations) of 63
   the revolution (*enqelāb*) of 191–192
English (Puritan) Revolution 168–169
enqelāb (revolution) 11–24, 141, 144, 158, 163, 191
Entezār, mazhab-e e'terāz (Expectation, the religion of protest) 191
Epic of Kings (*Shāhnāma*) 26, 43
Erāqi, Fakhr al-Din 40
Erzinjān 92, 96–99
Esmā'il the Safavid, Shah 10, 23, 90–109, 159
   his divinity 90–92
   his poetry as Khatā'i 91–92
   his policy of "Shi'ism in one country," 108–109
Eskandar Mirzā b. 'Omar Shaykh 58, 61, 72–77
   adherence to Horufis 72–73
Eskandarnāma 51
Estevā-nāma 60
European revolutions of 1848 3, 10, 98, 168–169, 175

fanāi' fil-shaykh (self-annihilation in the master) 132
Fanon, Franz 184, 191

Fardid, Ahmad 194–196
farr (royal charisma) 41
Fatimid Revolution 9–10n24, 29, 170
Fath-'Ali Khan Dāghestāni 144, 148, 151, 155
Fath-'Ali Khan Qājār 163–164
Fath-'Ali Shah (Bābā Khan) 164–165
fatrat 13, 21, 144
Fazlallāh Astarābādi (Horufi) 53–61
Fazlallāh Ruzbehān Khonji Esfahāni 84, 114–115
Fletcher, Joseph 45
fotowwat (chivalry, youth organizations) 30, 35, 41–44, 52–53
French Revolution of 1789 2–3, 7, 24, 141, 165, 167, 183
Freud, Sigmund 11

Gelunābād, Battle of 141, 149
Georgian troops, Safavid 146, 148–149
Germiyān 49–51
Geykhātu, Il-Khan 49–50
ghaybat (occultation of the Hidden Imam) 8–9, 28, 95, 188–191
ghazā (holy raid) 42, 47, 127
Ghazāli, Shaykh Ahmad 30
Ghāzān Khan 20–21, 42
ghāzi (holy warrior) 52, 65, 88
Ghaznin 135–136
Ghiyās al-Din Jamshid Kāshi 73
Ghiyās al-Din Mohammad 58–60
Ghojdovān, Battle of 1512 107–109, 114–115
*gholām*s (Safavid royal slaves) 145, 147, 150
gholoww (Shi'ite extremism) 86–89
Gilanentz, Petros 141
Gog and Magog 63, 81, 119
Golestān 40–41
Gombroon (Bandar 'Abbās) 154, 156–158
Gorgin Khan (Shahnavāz) Khan 147
Guerrilla armed struggle (*foco*) 185–186
   Iranian guerrilla organizations
      Fedā'yān-e Khalq (Marxist) 185
      Mojāhedin-e Khalq-e Mosalmān (Islamist) 185, 193
      Peykār (Maoist) 185
      Red Shi'ism 185
Guevara, Che 184–185
Gujarat 128–129

Habib al-siyar 94
hādi (righteous guide) 131, 134
Hadiqat al-Haqiqa wa shari'at al-tariqa 31
Hāfez of Shiraz 16
Hājji Bayrām Vali 52
Hājji Bektāsh 52
Hājji Bektāsh Ilbeg 64
Hājji Sorkha, Horufi leader 59, 61
Halabi, Shaykh Mahmud 188
Hamdallāh Mostawfi 12
Hamza Bāli Effendi's uprising 131–132
Hasan II b. Mohammad b. Bozorg-Omid 32
Hasan Khalifa Tekelu 103
Hasan Pahlavān 54
Hasan Sabbāh 29, 32
Hashemi-Rafsanjani, Hojjat al-Islam, later President 199
Hasht Behesht 117
Haydar, Safavid Shaykh 88–90, 127
Haydari crown (*tāj*) 89–90, 95
Hazāra 134–136
Heidegger, Martin 194–195
hejrat 132
Herat 30, 68, 100–101, 111, 113–115, 147–148, 155, 161
Hizbullah in Lebanon 186
Ho Chi Minh 184
Hodgson, Marshall 26–27, 30–31
Hojjatiyya Society 188–189
Homāyun, Mughal 111–112, 127–129
Hong Xiuquan 172, 175–78
  as brother of Jesus and Heavenly King 176–79
Horufi movement 53–61, 72, 86
  doctrine 54–57, 60
  persecution of 57–59
  uprisings 59–61, 66
  urban social background of members 60–61
Horufiyya 80. *See also* Horufi movement
Hosām al-Din Bedlisi 83
Hosayn. *See* Shi'ite theodicy of martyrdom
Hosayniyya Ershad 191–192
Hülegü, the first Il-Khan 34

Ibn Abi Tāher Tayfur 18, 142
Ibn al-'Arabi, Shaykh Muhyi al-Din 40, 65, 83

Ibn Bibi 13
Ibn Khaldun, 'Abd al-Rahmān xxx, 6
Ibrāhim Pasha 122, 124
Ilāh-dād Rawshani 136
Isfahan 54, 58–61, 75, 107, 145, 148–158, 165
  Afghan siege of 140–141, 149–150
Imam of the Age. *See* Lord of Time
Imamate 28–29, 42
  Shi'ite theory of 204
  its revolutionary modification into "continuous Imamate" 192
  Sunni polemics against it 125
Integrative Revolution 13–14, 18, 74
  Aristotelian-Paretan 14*n*26, 24–26
  Khaldunian 14, 28–30, 174, 202–208
Irakli (Hercules), king of Georgia 162
Iran, emergence as a nation-state 142, 144, 161–165
  its incorporation into the Westphalian international system 152, 162–165
Iran-Iraq War 185, 187–189, 202
Irān-zamin (the land of Iran) 34, 142, 144, 161
Iraq 67, 82, 99–100, 170, 172, 188–189, 201–208
Islām Shah Sur 129, 136
Islamicate civilization 2–5, 27, 29, 31
  its dual tribal/urban social structure 6, 165
Islamic Republic of Iran (IRI) 185–189, 192, 195–199, 201, 206
  as clerical monarchy 189, 199–201
Islamic Revolution of 1979 in Iran 6–7, 178, 183–200
  as a revolution in Shi'ism 198–199
  its export 188
Islamic State of the Caliphate/Iraq and Syria. *See* DAESH

Jacobinism 4, 6, 167–168
Ja'far, Safavid Shaykh 87–88
Ja'far b. Abi Tālib 79
Ja'far b. Muhammad al-Sādiq 190–191, 212
jafr (science of divination) 12, 63, 77
Jahāngir Khan Sur-e Isrāfil 179–180
Jahān Pahlavān, *atabeg* 19
Jahānshāh Qara Qoyunlu 59, 82, 87
Jalāl al-Din Mohammad Kh^wārazmshāh 13

Jalāl al-Din Rawshani (Jalāla)   133–137
Jalāl al-Din Rumi, Mawlānā   39–40, 48
Jāmeʿ al-tavārikh   21
Jāmeʿ-e soltāni   73
Jamkarān   189
Jamāl al-Din Ay Aba   19
Javānmard-e Qassāb, Abu'l-ʿAbbās Ahmad   43
Javānmardi. See fotowwat
Jāvdān-nāma   54, 56
jihād   128, 133–136, 193
    global jihad   201–208
Jonayd, Safavid Shaykh   65, 86–90, 103, 127
Juri, Shaykh Hasan   53
Juriyya dervish order   53

Kabul, Timurid kingdom of   127, 133–137
Kadizāda Musā Čelebi (Rumi)   62, 65
Kāmrān Mirzā   127
kairotic time   3–4
Kalimat al-ʿOlyā', daughter of Fazallāh Horufi   59
Kanz al-Jawāher   121
Karbala   55, 97
Kalāt   161–162
Karim Khan Zand, *vakil al-raʿāyā* (representative of the subjects)   162–63
Kaysāniyya   89
Kāzem Rashti, Sayyed   170, 172–173
Kemāl Pāshāzāda (Ibn Kamal)   119–124
Keyhān   196
Khādem Beg Khalifa   107
Khalil tribe   133, 135
khāneqāh (Sufi convent)   42, 52, 62, 64, 67, 73, 87, 104, 128
Khārijites (secessionists)   120
    of Oman   142, 144
Khalwati Sufi order   130–132
Khāmaneʾi, Sayyed ʿAli   188
Khomeini, Ayatollah Ruhollāh   186–189, 196–200, 206
    as the forerunner of the revolution of the Mahdi   187–188
    his acclamation as the Imam   187
    routinization of his charisma   199–200
Khorasan   12, 18, 24, 127–132, 140–141, 147–148, 154–157, 161–162, 172–173, 203, 207–208
    and the emergence of Persianate Sufism   28–33

Buddhism in   29
    its Mazdaean-Manichaean heritage   29–30, 130–131
    its conversion to Islam   28
khoruj (uprising)   75, 93, 97
Khʷāja/Soltān ʿAli Siāhpush   87
Khʷāja Azod al-Din   58
Khwāja Eshāq b. Ārāmshāh Khottalāni   66–67
Khʷāju of Kerman   15–17, 142
Khʷānd-Amir   94, 100, 110–111
Khʷarazm   48, 53, 160–161
Kingship, Persianate   22, 27, 34, 50, 105, 108, 143, 153
    as caliphate   37, 74
    legitimacy of   14
    justice as first principle   13, 31, 40–41
    and religion   18–19, 74
    and Sufism   32, 36–39, 78–80, 118
    "unification of dervishhood and kingship"   89, 101, 117
    its institutionalization in the Safavid revolution   109–110
    Greek input   83
    king of Islam (*pādshāh-e eslām*)   36, 42, 45, 50, 78–79, 117
    prophets and kings   80
    recast as caliphate   117–122
kitāb-e qawānin-e ʿorfiyya-ye ʿothmāniyya   98
Kobravi, Sufi order   36, 39, 67–70
Kojaji, Amir Shams al-Din Zakariyā   100, 106
Konya   48–51
Khʷāndiyya Sufi order   101–102
Kurds   146, 149, 159

Lāhijān   95–96, 106
    the Sufis of   106–107
Lenin, V.I.   184
Lezghis   141, 144, 151, 153
Lord of the Conjunction (*sāheb-qerān*)   17, 20–21, 51, 54, 74–75, 81, 91, 121
    coupled with the Mahdi   20
Lord of Time (*sāhib al-zamān*)   39, 54, 68, 83, 91, 96, 115, 173, 187
Lors   146
Lotf-ʿAli Khan Dāghestāni   144
Lotf-ʿAli Khan Zand   163–164
Lutfi Pasha   124–125

Mahdaviyya (Mahdavi movement) 128–129, 136
Mahdi, the (rightly-guided) 1–2, 50–51, 53, 64, 66–67, 104, 188
　the mystical 69–71
　as Muhammad redivivus 2, 70
　as Adam and the Word of God 56
　as the myth of revolution xxx
　as the Perfect Guide 69–71
　Mahdi's army 52, 94–95, 180n22, 201–203
　Mahdi's deputy 94
　his general deputies 169–170
Mahdi Ibn Tumart 9–10n24, 98, 133, 137
Mahdism 1
　apocalyptic 1–2
　as charismatic messianic leadership 9, 183–184. See also Shi'ite millennial beliefs, Qa'im-Mahdi
Mahdist Sufi movements 5, 10–11, 127–138
　their Shi'ite millennial inflection 53, 55
Mahmud, Ghelzai Afghan 142, 147–148
　as governor of Qandahar 148–149
　his rule in Isfahan 149–152, 158
Mahram-nāma 57, 59
Malek Mahmud Sistāni 154–156
Malekshāh (Seljuq king) 14
Man Singh 135
Mannheim, Karl 3
Mao 184
Marino Sanudo 92
Martin, Henry 172
Marmuzāt 39
Martha (Halima Begum) 88–89
Ma'ruf-e Khattāt 58
Marv, Battle of 108, 113
Marx, Karl 2–3, 167, 169, 192
Marxism-Leninism ix, 2–3, 183, 192
Mas'ud Sa'd Salmān 17
Māshā'allāh 17
Mashkur, Mohammad Javad 59
Mazdaean religion 11, 24, 76–77, 97
Mazdakites 77–78, 84
McCants, William 203
Mecca 53, 87–88, 116, 121, 170
　seizure of the Ka'ba in 1979 205–206
Medina 88, 93, 121
Mehmān-nāma-ye Bokhārā 114

Mehmed I, Ottoman Sultan 61, 64, 66, 79–80
Mehmed II, the Conqueror 42, 45, 80–81, 98
Meisami, Julie 13
Menhāj-e Serāj Juzjāni 19
Mer'āt al-jamāl (Mirror of beauty) 118
Mersād al-'ebād men al-mabda' ela'l-ma'ād 36, 39
al-Mesbāh fi'l-tasavvuf 39
messianism 1–2, 89
　apocalyptic 1–2, 9, 63, 68, 76–78, 80, 169–174, 201
　Horufi 57–59
　occultist 72–77, 80–81
　Shi'ite 44, 45
　as charismatic leadership 11, 86, 88–94, 100–101, 106–119, 248
　and the Islamic Revolution in Iran 189–200
　and modern myth of revolution 2
　"realized" 2, 4, 9, 12, 81, 194
　Marxism-Leninism as 2–3, 183, 192. See also Mahdism
Michele Membré 94
millennialism 1–2, 8–9, 93, 168–169
　its containment 8–10, 105–109, 201–203
　Buddhist 3–4
　in early modern Germany 3
　medieval Christian 4, 81n32
　of the Fifth Monarchy Men 168
　Russian Orthodox 3–4, 179
　Sufi in the Indian subcontinent 127–129
　See also Shi'ite millennial beliefs
Mir Sayyed Sharif Jorjāni 73
Mir Wais b. Shah 'Alam 147
Mirānshāh b. Timur 55, 57
mirrors for princes. See advice to kings
Mirzā Mehdi Khan Astarābādi 160–161
Mirzā Mohammad Hakim 127, 133–136
Mirzā Rafi'ā Ansāri 153
Mo'ezz al-Din Ghuri 31
Moghan assembly 160
Mohammad 'Ali Bārforushi, Molla 172
Mohammad 'Ali Zanjāni, Akhund 173–174
Mohammad Hasan Khān E'temād al-Saltana 24
Mohammad Khan Baluch 154, 156

Mohammad Mohsen Mostawfi 141, 144, 149
Mohammad Reza Shah 198
Mohammad Sādiq al-Sadr, Ayatollah 202
Mohammad-Amin Āqā Mashhadi 155
Mohammad-Taqi Āqā Mashhadi 155
Mohammadzai 133–135
Mohmand 133, 135
Moin, Afzar 111
Moʻin al-Din Parvāna 39, 48
mojadded (Sunni renewer) 78, 82, 114
mojtahed 164, 181–182
Mokāfāt-nāma 141–144
Mokhtār's uprising in Kufa 2, 28n9
Mollābāshi (royal chaplain) 148, 159–160
Monāzara-ye bazm o razm 76–77
Möngke Qāʾān 20, 34
Mongol revolution 33–34
morshed-e kāmel (the Perfect Guide) 68, 71, 110, 112
monshi (chancery secretary) 83, 85, 116, 119
Montehā 81
Moshir al-Dawla Pirniā 181
mostazʻafin (the disinherited) as the wretched of the earth 190–92
Motahhari, Mortaza 194
motivation of revolutionary action 1–2, 11
  by millennial beliefs 1–2, 86–98, 105, 169–182
  by the modern myth of revolution 1–3, 167–169, 178
  substitution of the former by the latter 169, 178–180, 196
  combination of the two in the myth of the Islamic Revolution 183–186, 192–194
Muhsin al-Fadli 207
multiple sovereignty 148–158
Muqtadā al-Sadr 201–203
Murād I, Ottoman Sultan 52
Murād II, Ottoman Sultan 62, 79–81
Musā al-Kāzem 67
Musā Čelebi (Ottoman) 63–65, 72
Mustafā, "the false" 62, 65
Muzaffar II of Gujarat 128
myth of revolution 1
  millennial 1–4, 167–169, 179–181
  modern 2–4, 167–169, 178, 183
  as the new Islam 3
  as *the* Revolution 184
  as the Third World revolution 184–186, 191
  myth of the Islamic Revolution 184, 191–194, 197

Nafasat al-masdur 78
Najaf 159
Najm al-Din Kobrā, Shaykh 36
Najm al-Din Tashi 50
Najm al-Din Rāzi 36–39, 48, 51
Najm al-Din Zargar Rashti 107
Nanjing 175–178
Nasavi, Shehāb al-Din Mohammad 13
Nāder Shah Afshār 139, 154–166
Napoleon 164–165, 186
Nasāyeh-e Shāhrokhi 78–79
Nāser al-Din Shah 24
al-Nāser li-Din Allāh, Abbasid caliph 35
Nasr, Sayyed Hossein 194
Nāzem al-Eslām Kermāni 179–182
Nazm al-soluk fi mosammarāt al-moluk 80
Nesimi, ʻEmād al-Din 55, 66, 91
Nezām al-Molk Tusi 14–15
Nezāri Ismaʻilism 32–33
  its transformation into a Sufi order 33, 46, 101–102
nodba prayer 191
Nur-ʻAli Khalifa Rumlu 23
nur-e Mohammadi (the light of Mohammad) 130–131
Nurbakhsh, Sayyed Mohammad 67–71, 83, 86, 131
  his final conception of Mahdihood 69–71
  social background of his followers 67–68

ʻObayd Allāh Ahrār, Khʷāja 115
ʻObayd Allāh Khan, Uzbek 111, 113–115
occult sciences 72–73, 76–78, 80
occultation. *See ghaybat*
Ögödei Qāʾān 20
Olugh Beg, Timurid 58, 73
Orkhān 52
Ovays, Jalayerid Soltān 22, 54–55

Pahlavi dynasty 197–198
Pakhtun region 129

INDEX   235

Palestinian Liberation Organization (PLO)   185–186
Pashtu   133–134
Pashtun tribes   129, 133–137
patrimonialism, nomadic   44, 112, 122, 162
    patrimonial monarchy   9, 162, 165, 181
Persianate Islam   27, 29–31
    formation of   28–42, 46
Persianate polity   29, 31
Perso-Russian wars   164
Peter the Great   151
Petraeus, General David   203–204
Pir Jamāl Ardestāni   131
Pir-e rawshan. See Bāyazid Ansāri
political ethic, Persianate   40–41, 49–50, 80, 83–85
    and Aristotelian political science   6, 40, 83
    theory of imperial autocracy   75, 78–79, 117–119. See also advice to kings
Persianate world, the   10–11, 26–27
    its intellectual elite   58–59, 63–64
    the Persian language in the emergence of   27–42
Pol Pot   196–197
political astrology   15, 17–18
Pollock, Sheldon   27
Popper, Karl   196
Prophecy   8–10
    and the End of Time   9, 72, 88–89, 95–96
    ex eventu   225, 253, 267
    Muhammad's   101–105
prophets   9, 34, 74, 90–93, 110
    the gentile prophet (al-nabiyy al-ummi)   74, 90, 100. See also
political religion   3–6
power structure. See structure of domination

al-Qaeda in Iraq   203
Qahtāni Mahdi   205
Qā'im, the (riser, redresser)   2, 169, 171–174, 205
Qa'im of the Resurrection   32, 171–173
Qa'im-Mahdi   2, 9, 28, 32
Qājār, tribe   90, 98, 159, 163
    dynasty   159, 169, 174–175
    patrimonial state   164–165
Qandahar   129, 147–150
Qanun-e Homāyuni   111

Qānun-e shāhanshāhi   117–118
qānun-nāma   82
Qarāmān (Karaman)   48–49, 79, 96
Qahtāni   205
Qalandar Esmā'il   153
Qara Qoyunlu   45, 53, 55, 57, 59, 66, 82, 87
Qara Yusof   55
Qaragöz Pasha   102, 104
Qāyeni, Shāhrokh's Shaykh al-Islam   78
Qāzi 'Isā Sāvaji   84
Qāzizāda-ye Rumi   58, 73
Qazvin   68, 101, 140, 147, 150–151, 158
Qazvini, Mohammad   24
Qelich Arslān   17
Qezelbāsh/Kizilbash (red heads)   48, 89, 106
    confederation of Turkmen tribes   97–98, 100
    clans of
        Afshār   96, 154
        Ayqutoghlu   90, 96
        Bāybortly   98
        Khenselu   98
        Ostājlu   96, 98, 106–107
        Qājār   90, 98
        Qāramānlu   90, 98, 100
        Qarajadāghlu   96, 98
        Rumlu   96
        Shāmlu   90, 96, 98, 106–107
        Tekelu   96–98
        Varsaq   96
        and Zu'l-Qadr   96, 100
    Qezelbāsh cavalry   145–146, 150, 152
Qiyāmat-nāma   57
Qohestān   67
Qollar-āqāsi   145, 150
Qorqud, Ottoman prince   98, 102–103
qotb (axis mundi)   131
Qotb al-Din Aybek   17
Qubilai Qā'ān   34
Qumran War Scroll   205
Qurchi-bāshi   145, 150, 156

Rashid al-Din Fazlallāh   20–21
Rashid al-Din Maybodi   30
Rashid Khan Rawshani   136
Rasht   107, 119, 153, 163, 182, 184
Rationalization. See Charisma of the Mahdi, its routinization

Rawshani movement 129–138
Rayy 68
Raziya, Delhi Sultan 19
Reaction. *See* counter-revolution
Resālat al-Hodā 69–70
Resurrection (*qiyāmat*) 32–33, 57, 91, 170, 179–180, 193, 195
revolutio regni xx, 19, 23–24
revolution 1–10
   apocalyptic motivation of 1–4
   causes of 5, 7, 13–14, 99–100, 106–107, 143–144
   reversal of the causal order 169, 178–180
   conceptions of, Marxist-Leninist 2–3
     Persianate conception of 11–25, 28, 139–144
   consequences of 5, 7–8, 86, 109–110, 139
   export of 102–107, 139–140, 159
   Mahdist 86–109, 127–133-38
   periodization of 86, 106–109
   process of revolution
     as constitutional politics 9, 106–09
     revolutionary power struggle 9, 86, 98–107
     its opportunity structure revolution and counter-revolution 5, 9–10, 64
     revolution and liminality 2–4
   structural models of 5, 7, 13
     Aristotelian-Paretan (counter-elites') Integrative Revolution 5–6
     Constitutive Revolution 5
     Khaldunian (from peripheries of empires) 5–7, 86, 95–98, 127, 133–38, 159, 165–66, 174
     Tocquevillian (centralization of power) 7, 109, 139–40, 165
     modified 5–7, 197
   teleology of
     institutionalization of value-ideas 7
   Third World revolution 190–192. *See also* Abbasid (Hashemite) Revolution; Arab revolutions; Cambodian Revolution; Cuban Revolution; Constitutional Revolution; English (Puritan) Revolution; European revolutions of 1848; Islamic Revolution; Mahdist movements; Mongol revolution; Safavid revolution, Sasanian Revolution
Revolutionism. *See* modern myth of revolution
Reza Shah 197–198
Rostam Beg, Āq Qoyunlu 89
Robertson, Roland 201
Rum. *See* Anatolia
Rumelia 53, 61–66, 72, 86
Rumlu, Hasan 23, 99
Russian revolutions of 1905 and 1917 179

al-sā'a (the Hour of Apocalypse) 12, 63, 71, 76, 80, 203
Sabzavar 52–53, 156
Sa'd b. Abu Bakr, *atabeg* 40
Sa'd al-Din Hammuya 39, 65
Sa'dallāh Khan Abdāli 147
Saddam Hussein 201–202
Sa'di of Shiraz, Shaykh Mosleh al-Din 15–16, 40–41, 142
Sadr al-Din Musā Safavi 87
Sadr al-Din Qonavi 40
Sadr City 202
Sā'en al-Din Torka 58, 72–78
Safvat al-safā 95
Safi al-Din Ardabili 87, 95
Safi Mirzā, Safavid 156–157
Safavid revolution 11, 86–109, 137–138
Safavid Sufi order 87–95
   in Anatolia 65, 98, 103–05, 120–21
   its *kalifas* (representatives) 88–92, 97, 103–107
Sāheb Fakhr al-Din 49
sahwa (tribal awakening) 203–204
Saints, Sufi. *See awliyā' Allāh*
Samak-e 'ayyār 43–44
Samarqand 47, 58, 62, 73, 113, 127, 129
Samanids 27, 29, 31
Sanā'i, Majdud b. Ādam 30–32
Sarbedār movement ("republic") 52–53
Sarkisyanz, Manuel 3–4
Sasanian Revolution 112
Sayyed Ahmad Khan, Safavid 154, 157–158
Sayyed 'Ali Mohammad, the *bāb* 170–175
   as the Mahdi and the Qa'im of the Resurrection 171–173
   Christian and Horufi influences 172

Sayyed Amir Eshāq 59
Sayyed Mohammad b. Fallāh, the "Radiant" (*Mosha'sha'*) 131
Sayyed Mohammad Gisu-darāz 130
Sayyed Mohammad Jaunpuri 127–128
  his Mahdihood 128
Sayyed Khundmir, Mahdavi leader 128
Science of letters (*'ilm al-horuf*) 54, 65, 72, 79–80
science of the saints 80. *See also* occult sciences
Seal of the Saints (*khātam al-awliyā'*) 39, 69, 78, 129
Seal of the Prophets (*khātam al-nabiyyin*) 69
Second Coming of Jesus 55, 57
Selim I, Ottoman Sultan 45, 103, 105, 119–121
Selim-nāma 121
Seljuqs xxx, 14
  of Kerman 18–19
  of Rum xxx, 13, 17, 36–40
Seljuqshāh Begum 83–84
The Shadow of God and the Hidden Imam 184
Shāh Ne'matollāh Vali 73
Shāh Qāsem Nurbakhsh 71
Shāh Qāsem Tabrizi 121
Shāh Shojā', Mozaffarid 55
Shah Shojā' of Kerman 43
shāhanshāh (king of kings) 43, 91, 101, 142, 160–161
Shāhrokh, Timurid 44, 57–59, 67–68, 74–79, 84
Shams al-Din Lāhiji 107
Shaqq al-qamar 77
Sharaf al-Din Mahmud Daylami 84, 106
Sharaf al-Din 'Ali Yazdi 58, 72–75
Shari'ati, 'Ali 189–194
Shaybāni Khan Uzbek, Mohammad 108, 113–114
Shaykh 'Omar Rawshani 133–136
Shehanshāh, Ottoman prince 104
Sher Shah Sur 127–129
Shervān 88, 96
Shervānshāh 55, 99
Sihanouk, Norodom 198
Shi'a: Extremist (*ghulāt*) 86–88
  Imami (Twelver) 8–9, 28, 46, 93, 125, 169
  in India 111–112
  in Iraq 202, 205–206
  Akhbāri 170, 174
  Shaykhi 170
  Ismā'ili 28–29, 32, 61, 67, 101–102, 132, 170. *See also* Nezāri Isma'ilism
Shi'ism
  establishment by Esmā'il the Safavid 100–101
  as the Ja'fari rite (*madhhab*) under Nāder 159–160
Shi'ite hierocracy 164, 169–170, 187
  as "general deputies" of the Hidden Imam 169–170, 191–192, 199
  its anti-millennial clericalism 181–182, 201–203
  challenges to its authority, by the Babis 171–175, 178–181
  by the constitutionalists 181–182
  by the modernizing state 181–182, 197–198
  its independence from the state 198–199
Shi'ite millennial beliefs 1–2, 82
  and mobilization for *ghazā* 47–49
  and oppositional mobilization against Turko-Mongolian domination 53–71
  and preemptive royal appropriation 50–51, 64, 71, 81n32, 113–115, 120, 125. *See also* counter-revolution
  and Sufism 47–48, 66–70
  in the Islamic Revolution of 1979 in Iran 183, 186–191, 196
  their Sunni appropriation by DAESH 201, 203–205
Shi'ite theodicy of martyrdom 48, 55, 57–60, 97, 144
Shi'itization 28, 35
  of Sufi Mahdist movements 47–48, 52, 55, 66–70
  and the veneration of 'Ali 47, 52
*sipāhi*s 64, 102–104
Siyāsat-nāma 14
social stratification into estates 10, 42–46
  their segregation 44
  Turkish military ruling (*'askeri*) 10, 44–45
  nomadic tribesmen 47–51, 84–85
  Persian/Tajik civilian urban notables 52, 60–61
  clerical (*'olamā'*) 7, 18, 57, 132, 170

Persian/Tajik civilian (*cont.*)
  Sufi shaykhs   30, 35
  craftsmen   155. *See also fotowwat*
  subjects (*ra'iyyat*)   10, 40–44, 161, 207
Society of God Worshippers in Guangxi   175–176
Sohravardi, Shaykh Abu Hasf 'Omar   35–36, 42
Sohravardi, Shehāb al-Din Yahyā   30
Soltān Ahmed, Āq Qoyunlu   84–85
Soltān-'Ali Safavi   90
Soltān-Ashraf Afghan   150–151
  as Ashraf Shah   152–55
Soltān-Ebrāhim Safavi   90, 96
Soltān-Ebrāhim, the Shaykh-Shah   87
Soltān-Hosayn Bayqarā   99
Soltān-Hosayn, Safavid Shah   140–152
  as Mollā Hosayn   146
Soltān-Khalil, Āq Qoyunlu   83–84
Soltān-Mohammad, Safavid   156–157
Soltān-Mohammad b. Baysonghor   75
Soltān-Morād, Āq Qoyunlu   99–102
Soltān-Murād, Ottoman prince   119
Soltān-e jemri (the "beggar Sultan")   49
Soleymān, Safavid Shah   145, 157
soluk (spiritual wayfaring)   33, 38, 51, 79–80
Soluk al-moluk   114–115
Sorush   187
sovereignty (*saltanat*)   163–164
  counter-millennial   10
  Āq Quyunlu   82–85
  Mughal   111–112
  Ottoman   10, 79–82, 116–122
  Timurid   72–79
  Safavid   109–110, 169
  Uzbek   10, 112–116
  Qur'anic verses on transfer of   12, 18, 37–38, 76, 109, 164. *See also* Lord of the Conjunction
soyurghāl   84
Spengler, Oswald   195
state, the. *See* structure of domination
structure of domination   74–75, 169–170
  breakdown of (state-breakdown)   7, 139–148, 165
  fragility of   142–143
  Mahdistic   5
  state-hierocracy duality in Qājār Iran   181–184

Sufism, Persianate   5, 28–30, 89
  antinomian (dervishes)   52
  Abdāl of Rum   43, 88
  Haydaris   43
  Malāmatis (Melamis)   43, 131–32, 136
  Qalandars   43, 53, 89
  ascetic   39, 41
  formation of   29–42
  as inner-worldly mysticism   37, 39–40, 46
  the Janus face of   71
  suppression of   101–102, 144
  synergy with Shi'ism   35, 39, 66–70, 110, 114. *See also* Mahdist Sufi movements
Sufi shaykhs   30, 35–39
Suleymān the Lawgiver, Ottoman Sultan   10, 45, 119–126
  as champion of Sunni orthodoxy   122–123
  as the Mahdi   121
  as Roman Caesar   122
sultanate (*saltanat*)   83
  soltān (ruler) as the shadow of God   83
Sunni Islam   42, 78, 82, 101, 113–114, 119, 122
Sur-e Isrāfil   179–180
Syria   17, 55, 60, 96–97, 103, 117, 121, 203–208

*tabarrā'i*s   100–101
Tabriz   54–55, 59, 65–66, 84–85, 88–89, 96–100, 105, 111, 113, 116–117, 150–153
Tadhkerat al-moluk   145
Tahmāsb, Shah   94, 101, 109, 122, 124
Tahmāsp II (Tahmāsb Mirzā)   150–151, 154–158, 160, 163
Tahmāsb-qoli (Nāder)   154–156, 158, 161
Taiping Revolution   172, 175–178
  Taiping tien-kuo (Heavenly Kingdom of the Great Peace)   172, 176
  as realized messianism   178
  its asceticism   177
  women in its social background   176–177
Tāj al-Din Yazdi   22–23
Tālesh   90, 95–96, 151
Tamhidāt   130
Tārikh-e Afzal   18
Tegüder (Ahmad), Il-Khan   21
Tehran   147–148, 154–155, 186, 207
  the University of   194

INDEX

Tekke-eli 65, 97, 103
The History of the Late Revolutions of Persia 139
theocracy. *See* clerical monarchy
timār 64, 96, 102–104
Timur (Tamerlane) 21, 44–45, 61, 74–75, 160
Timurtāsh 50–51, 62
Tirāh 133–135
Tocqueville, Alexis de 3, 7, 167
Togrel II, Seljuq Sultan 19
Toynbee, Arnold 26–27
Treaties, of Constantinople in 1723, 152
  of Finkenstein in 1807
  Golestan in 1812 and Turkamanchai in 1828 164
Transoxiana 28, 31, 33, 37, 48, 113–114
Turkmen, of Anatolia 48–51, 64, 88, 96
  of Iran 84–85, 89
  under Nāder 154, 159, 165
Turko-Mongolian domination 44–45
  millennial popular challenges to 52–61, 68, 86
Turluk Hu Kemāl 66

uj (Byzantine frontier) 47–49, 88–89
  frontier millennialism 48–52
Üljeitü (Mohammad Khodā-banda) 21, 42
Ulus Chaghatay 44
Ulus Hülegü 34
Ulus Jochi (the Golden Horde) 34
Usama bin Laden 205
Uzbeks 147, 159
Uzun Hasan Āq Qoyunlu 82–84, 88–90, 99

Vāez Kāshefi, Molla Hosayn 113
Vāsefi, Mawlānā Zaynal-Din Mahmud 113–115
velāyat (friendship of God) 69, 110
  as Sufi sainthood 69, 131
  the age of 54, 69
  its Shi'ite conception 109–110
velāyat-e faqih (mandate of the jurist) 187, 189, 199
  its institutionalization as Leadership (*rahbari*) of the IRI 198–99
Voegelin, Eric 3

Waziristan 129, 134–137
Westoxification (*gharbzadegi*) 195
world renunciation (*tark-e donyā*) 29, 37, 39, 112, 127, 132

Xiao Chaogui 175–177

Yahyā Dawlat-ābādi 179
Yahyā Subh-e Azal, Mirzā 174–175, 179
Yang Xiuqing 176–178
Ya'qub, Āq Qoyunlu 23, 84–85, 99, 116
Yār Ahmad Khuzāni 107
Yazicizāda Ahmed Bijān 12, 79–81, 89
Yusof 'Ādelshāh of Bijāpur 111
Yusufzais 133–135

Zafarnāma (Book of Victory) 74–75
Zahir al-Din Bābor, Timurid prince 23
Zarqāwi, Abu Musā 203, 205
Zarrinkub, 'Abdol-Hosayn 54, 69
Zarrin-Tāj Baraghāni, the Qurratal-'Ayn 171–174
zohur (manifestation) 50, 56–57, 93, 96, 170, 174, 179–181, 186, 192
Zoroastrians 148–150

www.ingramcontent.com/pod-product-compliance
Lightning Source LLC
Chambersburg PA
CBHW021942290426
44108CB00012B/929